CONTESTED CITIZENSHIP

Social Movements, Protest, and Contention

Series Editor: Bert Klandermans, Free University, Amsterdam

Associate Editors: Ron R. Aminzade, University of Minnesota
David S. Meyer, University of California, Irvine
Verta A. Taylor, University of California, Santa Barbara

For more books in the series, see page 314.

CONTESTED CITIZENSHIP

Immigration and Cultural Diversity in Europe

Ruud Koopmans, Paul Statham, Marco Giugni, and Florence Passy

Social Movements, Protest, and Contention
Volume 25

University of Minnesota Press
Minneapolis • London

Published by the University of Minnesota Press
111 Third Avenue South, Suite 290
Minneapolis, MN 55401-2520
http://www.upress.umn.edu

Library of Congress Cataloging-in-Publication Data

Contested citizenship : immigration and cultural diversity in Europe / Ruud
Koopmans . . . [et al.].
    p.   cm. — (Social movements, protest, and contention ; v. 25)
Includes bibliographical references and index.
ISBN 978-0-8166-4662-3 (hc : alk. paper) — ISBN 978-0-8166-4663-0 (pb : alk. paper)
    1. Europe—Emigration and immigration. 2. Citizenship—Europe.
3. Europe—Ethnic relations. 4. Multiculturalism—Europe. I. Koopmans,
Ruud. II. Series.
JV7590.C666 2005
325.4—dc22

                                     2005017425

15 14 13 12 11 10 09 08   10 9 8 7 6 5 4 3 2

Contents

Preface

This book is based on the Mobilization on Ethnic Relations, Immigration, and Citizenship project (MERCI, http://ics.leeds.ac.uk/eurpolcom/research _projects_merci.cfm). The origins of this project go back to 1994, when Ruud Koopmans started a project on extreme right violence in Germany at the Political Communication and Mobilization Department at the Wissenschaftszentrum Berlin (WZB). Paul Statham joined the department in 1996, bringing with him a new project funded by the British Economic and Social Research Council (R000236558—1996-9) and hosted at the Institute of Communication Studies, University of Leeds. Subsequently, the idea arose to link the two projects and to set up a systematic comparison of public mobilization and discourse on immigration and ethnic relations in Germany and Britain. Stimulated by the striking contrasts between the two countries that our first results indicated, we set out to look for partners in additional countries. Marco Giugni and Florence Passy, with whom one of us had already fruitfully collaborated in an earlier comparative project, joined the project in 1997, and they developed the French and Swiss country studies with assistance from the Swiss National Science Foundation (project no. 4039-44908). In addition, Rinus Penninx and Meindert Fennema of the Institute for Migration and Ethnic Studies of the University of Amsterdam generously provided funding for the appointment of a PhD student, Thom Duyvené de Wit, who was cofinanced by the Amsterdam School of Communications Research. We thank the Wissenschaftszentrum Berlin, the Economic and Social Research Council, the Swiss National Fund for Research, and the Institute for Migration and Ethnic Studies for their confidence in our project and for making our large primary data gathering efforts possible.

Among the people to whom we would like to say "merci," Thom Duyvené de Wit is first in line. He did much of the Dutch data gathering for the citizenship indicators reported in chapter 1, and organized and supervised the content coding in the Netherlands. In addition, he was the source of many valuable comments and ideas during the various project meetings that we had over the years. Thom is presently concluding his dissertation, which will analyze the Dutch case in more depth than is possible within our comparative framework. In Berlin, Christian Galonska provided valuable research assistance and gathered much of the German information for the citizenship indicators. Janice Cornwall at the WZB and Fidessa Voormolen at the Vrije Universiteit Amsterdam skillfully helped with some of the editing and formatting of the manuscript at various stages. Paul Statham would like especially to thank David Morrison at the Institute of Communications Studies, Leeds, for his institutional support, intellectual thoughts, and good humor over the full decade. In addition, the team at the Centre for European Political Communications (EurPolCom) at Leeds, Julie Firmstone, Emily Gray, and Manlio Cinalli, have continued to assist and work on the further development of this project, which has been made possible by the receipt of another ESRC grant (R000239221—2001-4) that is also gratefully acknowledged.

Colleagues who commented on intermediary papers and articles in the project are too numerous to mention individually, but they often forced us to refine and reconsider our arguments. Special thanks, however, go to Gianni D'Amato, Thomas Faist, Virginie Guiraudon, Betty de Hart, and Jonathan Laurence, who provided extremely useful comments on a draft of chapter 1 (and in Jonathan's case also on chapter 4 and many other aspects of our research). We also thank the University of Minnesota Press reviewer Nella Van Dyke for her kind words and very helpful comments on the draft manuscript. We extend a special thanks to Emily Gray for compiling our index.

Last but not least, for their dedication, precision, and especially their perseverance, we extend thanks to our coders: Anja Baukloh, Uwe Breitenborn, Angelica Costa, Britta Gerike, Windsor Holden, Vibha Mehta, Dirk Meurer, Inken Schröder, Daniella Simon, Annett Wahnschaffe, and Bernd Wölki. We ask them to forgive us for the years it may take before they can again leisurely read a newspaper without thinking in codes.

Introduction

The Contentious Politics of Immigration and Ethnic Relations

In the early days of labor and postcolonial migration, few observers foresaw the profound long-term consequences for Western European democracies. What were meant to be temporary labor hands, economically active but otherwise invisible, turned out to be permanent immigrants, whose activities, needs, demands, and social impacts extended far beyond the economic sphere. Unlike the proactive, self-identifying immigration countries of the New World, the nations of Western Europe have become immigration countries largely unintentionally and reactively, and often against the explicit will of sizable parts of both the political elite and the native population (Hollifield 1992). This explains, for instance, why as late as 1998 it was still the official position of the German government that "Germany is not a country of immigration" in spite of the fact that, de facto, Germany had in the 1990s become the world's most important destination for migrants, putting even classical immigration countries such as the United States and Australia in the shade.

Germany's counterfactual insistence on not being a country of immigration may stand as a symbolic marker for the difficulties that all Western European societies are experiencing in coming to terms with the challenges associated with the arrival and settlement of millions of culturally, religiously, and racially different immigrants. Much previous work on immigration and ethnic relations in the European context has approached this problematic from the socioeconomic side, but we maintain in this book that the challenges of immigration are perhaps more fundamentally related to the political culture and institutions of the receiving countries and to

1

national identity, sovereignty, and citizenship in particular. Europe is not unique in this respect, as similar challenges confront other immigration countries. However, because of Europe's comparatively "thicker," more ethnoculturally based traditions of nationhood, conflicts around immigration and cultural diversity have often emerged in more pronounced, more sharply defined forms than in the classical immigration countries of the New World.

In recent years, immigration and ethnic relations have become heavily politicized issues worldwide, and in Europe in particular. To begin with, migrants themselves have become active participants in the political process. This includes many forms of mobilization that can easily be integrated into existing political processes and policies. However, migrant activism also includes—and some say increasingly so—controversial demands for special cultural rights and privileges, such as the wearing of the Islamic headscarf in public institutions or the right to education in minority languages and religions. Perhaps the most notorious case in point has been the campaign by Muslim groups in several countries to ban Salman Rushdie's book *The Satanic Verses* on the grounds of blasphemy. Some Muslim groups went further and openly supported the Iranian fatwa against Rushdie, as did a speaker at a meeting of the Muslim Youth Movement in Bradford, England, in March 1990: "Salman Rushdie knows exactly what he has done. Let us take him to Medina and let us stone him to death. Every Muslim should be prepared to cast the first stone." Another aspect of migrant activism that is frequently regarded as problematic is the continued involvement of migrants with political conflicts in their countries of origin. Such activism, too, may take relatively harmless forms, but it also includes violent conflicts among different immigrant groups, as well as attacks on institutions within the receiving societies. For instance, in February 1999, three demonstrators were shot to death and sixteen were wounded when a crowd of Kurdish immigrants protesting the arrest of their leader Abdullah Öcalan by the Turkish secret service—allegedly with the help of Israeli intelligence—stormed the Israeli embassy in Berlin. Needless to say, such an import of violent conflicts from the region of origin into the countries of immigration has been propelled to the center of critical attention by the events of September 11, 2001. Most of the perpetrators of 9/11 had lived as legal immigrants in various European countries before moving to the United States to carry out the attacks.

The political challenges related to immigration and ethnic relations are, however, by no means limited to migrant activism. Real problems related to the failed integration of some migrants as well as racist sentiments among parts of the majority population have spurred the rise of radical right-wing, xenophobic political parties since the mid-1980s. The most enduring and successful figurehead of this new European radical right is Jean-Marie Le Pen, who in the first round of the 2002 French presidential elections managed to beat the Socialist ruling prime minister Jospin. Meanwhile, xenophobic parties of the radical right wing have participated in several European governments, including Umberto Bossi's Lega Nord in Italy, Jörg Haider's Freedom Party in Austria, and the party of Pim Fortuyn—who was assassinated shortly before the 2002 elections—in the Netherlands. Besides the electoral challenge of radical-right parties, there has also been a strong increase in the number of violent attacks—mostly by youth linked to the right-wing skinhead subculture—against ethnic minorities and immigrants. Germany has been severely affected by this form of xenophobic activism, which claimed more than one hundred deaths over the course of the 1990s. In May 1993, for instance, a Turkish woman and four of her children died in an arson attack on their family home in Solingen. Four skinheads were found guilty of the attack and were sentenced to prison terms of up to fifteen years.

The rise of the radical right in its various guises signals the opposition of parts of the receiving societies against what is perceived as too much immigration and a threat to the national cultural integrity. However, at least as noteworthy is the massive mobilization of European citizens in support of migrants and their rights and against right-wing parties and violence. On November 8, 1992, for instance, more than 300,000 people, almost exclusively native Germans, gathered in Berlin to protest against xenophobic violence. Even more impressive perhaps was a series of antiracist demonstrations in the German state of Baden-Württemberg in January 1993, which mobilized over one million people, about one-tenth of the state's population.

Combined, these three types of political mobilization around issues of immigration and ethnic relations—*by* migrants, *against* migrants, and *on behalf of* migrants—constitute since the early 1990s the most prominent and controversial fields of political contention in West European polities. Data gathered by Dieter Rucht and Friedhelm Neidhardt for Germany indicate that about one-third of all protests in the first half of the 1990s were related to the immigration issue, making it by far the most important field of contention, far ahead of unemployment and labor issues, war and peace, democracy, or the environment (Neidhardt and Rucht 2001, 39).

Why have immigration and ethnic relations become such contentious issues in Europe? The explanation partly lies in the increased numbers of immigrants and in the fact that compared to earlier waves of immigration to Western Europe—e.g., immigration from Eastern Europe between the two World Wars—present-day migrants tend to be more clearly distinct from the native population in terms of their skin color, cultural markers, or religion. However, we argue in this book that the deeper reasons why increased numbers and diversity have sparked such high levels of political conflict are related to the impacts of migration and ethnocultural diversity on three core elements underpinning the nation-state: the sovereign control over external borders, the regulation of access to citizenship, and a nation's cultural self-understanding, i.e., its national identity. In our age of economic globalization and worldwide pressures toward cultural blending and homogenization, all three core principles have come under pressure. As a result, many people experience a loss of identity and of control over their destinies. At the same time, there so far is nothing beyond the nation-state that can serve as a new anchor for collective identities and can renew the sense of control. Our age of globalization is therefore also a time of nationalism, of ethnic mobilization, of the rise of xenophobic movements and of a proliferation of new nation-states with newly invented national histories, anthems, flags, and languages. As the single force giving at least some counterplay against the impersonal forces of globalization, many turn to the nation-state and the national community as havens in a heartless world.

Immigration and minority integration politics are particularly well suited to such attempts to reinvigorate the nation-state. Precisely because it seems futile (and in many respects clearly disadvantageous) to try to stem the tide of economic globalization, those policy fields where the nation-state can still display its capacity to act become the focus of such reinvigoration attempts: "The control of entry becomes one of the few domains in which states can still be strong—'renationalizing' immigration policies as an antidote to the 'denationalizing' logic of globalization" (Joppke 1998, 3). The same applies to the cultural realm of minority integration politics. As a macro force, cultural globalization seems unstoppable and because of its many advantages irresistible as well—after all, who wants to miss Hollywood, ethnic restaurants, and holidays in the sun? However, its manifestations in everyday life in Western cities in the form of mosques, women wearing headscarves, black people, or "strange" cooking smells seem within people's and nation-states' reach of control, and have for many people become the focus for everything they dislike about our global age.

Against theories that argue that the nation-state is no longer the most relevant unit of analysis for studying the politics of immigration and cultural diversity—which we will discuss in detail in chapter 2—we will show that there are important differences in the patterns of political contention over these issues among European countries. While some of them, such as the Netherlands, are confronted with a relatively high level of migrant claims for special cultural rights, in other countries, such as Germany, such demands hardly play a role. Similar differences can be found regarding homeland-related mobilization, which is widespread in Switzerland but very limited in France. The strength of the extreme right likewise varies strongly. While the British extreme right is quite irrelevant, its French counterpart has been a serious challenger to the political establishment for almost two decades. While in countries such as France we find strong extreme-right parties but little xenophobic violence, in others such as Germany we find the reverse pattern. Levels of antiracist and pro-minority mobilization, finally, also differ strongly, and these differences do not necessarily correspond to the strength of the extreme right—for instance in Britain, where a relatively weak extreme right combines with high levels of antiracist claims making.

Our central aim in this book is to explain these striking cross-national differences in contention over immigration and cultural diversity. To this end, we will analyze data on political claims making in five European countries: Germany, France, Britain, the Netherlands, and Switzerland, in the period 1992–98. These are the five most important immigration countries in Europe, in which about four-fifths of Western Europe's immigrant population lives.[1] Migrants and their second-generation descendants make up a roughly comparable percentage of the population in these countries, from almost 8 percent in Britain to about 20 percent in Switzerland. However, there are important differences in the types and countries of origin of immigrants. Our five countries cover the two most important historical sources of migration to Western Europe: a predominance of postcolonial migration in Britain and France, immigration flows that can be traced back to the guest worker programs of the first postwar decades in Germany and Switzerland, and a mix between the two in the Netherlands. Regarding the regions of origin from which immigrants have been drawn, we can distinguish nation-specific predominant areas of recruitment: the Maghreb countries by France; Turkey by Germany; the Caribbean and the Indian subcontinent by Great Britain; Italy and other Southern European countries by Switzerland; and Indonesia, the Caribbean, Morocco, and Turkey by the Netherlands (see also Castles and Miller 1993). In relation to controversies over cultural rights and diversity, which have mainly centered around the position of Muslims, it is important to note that all five countries have sizable populations of Muslims which make up between 1 percent (Switzerland) and 6 percent (the Netherlands) of the overall population.

Differences in the composition of the immigrant population may help explain some of the cross-national variation in contention over immigration and ethnic relations. However, we will show that cross-national variation depends primarily on the different conceptions of national identity and their crystallization in nation-specific integration and citizenship policies. These national self-understandings and policies act as institutional and discursive opportunities and constraints. On the institutional side, they determine the rights and duties offered to immigrants, and the resources and institutional channels available to them—but also to their opponents and supporters among the majority population for making claims on the state and on other societal actors. On the discursive side, cultural notions of citizenship and national identity determine which points of view on the relation between immigrants and the majority society are considered sensible, which constructions of reality are considered realistic, and which claims and collective actors are held as legitimate within the polity. Together, these institutional and discursive opportunities facilitate the mobilization of some collective actors with certain types of collective identity and specific types of demands while constraining the mobilization of other actors and the expression of other identities and demands.

However, the relation between citizenship and national identity, and political contention over immigration, is not a one-way street. Existing notions of citizenship and national identity are challenged and sometimes changed by the experience of immigration and the resulting ethnic, racial, cultural, and religious diversification of the population. Because the immigrant "other" often functions as the mirror in which we can observe and by which we can redefine ourselves, immigration tends to create pressures and opportunities for a redefinition and reinvention of the conceptions of citizenship and national identity of the receiving nation-states. As we will show in chapter 1, the degree to which immigration has led to such changes varies among countries. The most spectacular case of change among the five countries we analyze here is Germany, which changed its citizenship legislation in important ways over the course of the 1990s. In 2000, it introduced a form of jus soli acquisition of the German nationality for children of migrants born in the country and thereby departed radically from the ethnic conception of German nation prevailing until then. Important changes have also occurred in the Netherlands and to a lesser degree in the other three countries. To understand how and why immigration leads to changes in national identity and citizenship, and thus to a redefinition of the very basis of nation-states, is another important aim of this book.

In this introduction, we will establish the theoretical framework for our analysis of political contention over immigration and cultural diversity, and we will explain our methodological approach. We begin with a discussion of national models of citizenship, which will be at the center of our analysis. Then we show how we integrate citizenship in a broader theoretical framework, as a central element of the institutional and discursive opportunity structures that shape patterns of contention over immigration and cultural diversity. We thereby consciously deviate from much of the recent literature on immigration, which no longer views the nation-state as the most relevant context for analyzing the politics of immigration and cultural diversity. We continue by presenting our methodology, which is based on content-analytic data from print media sources, on public claims making related to immigration. We conclude with an overview of the chapters to follow.

Citizenship and Conceptions of Nationhood

Citizenship—the set of rights, duties, and identities linking citizens to the nation-state—has recently emerged as a central analytic category in studies of immigration and ethnic relations. This interest in citizenship is rooted in the reinvigoration of this concept in wider political-philosophical debates on civil society, social cohesion, and communitarianism (e.g., Walzer 1983; Schlesinger 1998; Steenbergen 1994; Young 1998). Particularly in the United States, there has been a strong preoccupation in these debates with the position of ethnic minorities and the beneficial or harmful effects of "multiculturalism," the extension of cultural group recognition and rights to ethnic minorities (e.g., Taylor 1994; Kymlicka 1995a; Shapiro and Kymlicka 1997; Glazer 1997). While these philosophical debates have remained largely normative and prescriptive, they have inspired a number of studies with a more empirical focus in Europe (e.g., Ålund and Schierup 1991; Rex 1996; Modood and Werbner 1997; Martiniello 1998; Parekh 1998). At the same time, interest in citizenship has been revived in a somewhat different way through the rise of nationalist and xenophobic movements throughout the world and the subsequent boom in academic studies addressing these phenomena (e.g., Hobsbawm 1990; Greenfeld 1992; Canovan 1996; Jenkins and Sofos 1996; Calhoun 1997).

Taking up the distinction between "ethnic" and "civic" forms of nationalism that is common in the literature on nationalism, Rogers Brubaker's (1992) comparative historical work on citizenship and traditions of nationhood in France and Germany provided an important catalyst for an increase in comparative work on ethnic relations in the 1990s. Brubaker explains the divergent ways in which France and Germany have dealt with postwar migrants by the different cultural idioms of citizenship—based on ethnocultural belonging in Germany and on civic culture and political institutions in France—that have historically guided institutional practices and legal traditions in the two countries. Thus, Brubaker explains the persistently higher naturalization rates in France compared to Germany by contrasting the jus soli acquisition of nationality (by birth in the national territory), dominant in the French tradition of nationhood, to the jus sanguinis basis of nationality (acquisition by descent), the dominant tradition in Germany. Brubaker's distinction between ethnic and civic forms of citizenship, though, largely ignores the cultural rights dimension that has been central to the multiculturalism debate. This causes him to overstate the "openness" of the French citizenship regime, which may provide for easy formal access to citizenship yet couples this with the expectation that new citizens of migrant origin will assimilate to a unitary, national political culture.

Therefore, it seems to be valuable to combine the cultural group rights dimension of the multiculturalism debate with the formal criteria for individual access to citizenship central in Brubaker's analysis. This is what many scholars in the migration and ethnic relations field have done in distinguishing different citizenship models or regimes (e.g., Castles and Miller 1993; D. Smith and Blanc 1996; Kleger and D'Amato 1995; Safran 1997). Generally, these authors have come up with three types of citizenship regimes, each defining a specific institutional and discursive setting for political contention over migration and ethnic relations. The first regime, labeled "ethnic" or "exclusive," denies migrants and their descendants access to the political community or at least makes such access very difficult by way of high (institutional and cultural) barriers to naturalization. Germany is usually the typical example for this model; other examples that are mentioned in the literature include Austria, Switzerland, and Israel. The second type of regime, labeled "assimilationist" or "republican," and exemplified by France or the old "melting pot" approach in the United States, provides for easy access to citizenship, among other things through jus soli acquisition at birth, but requires from migrants a high degree of assimilation in the public sphere and gives little or no recognition to their cultural differences. Third, "multicultural" or "pluralist" regimes, usually including the present-day United States, Canada, and Australia and in Europe, Britain, Sweden, and the Netherlands, provide for both easy formal access to citizenship and recognition of the right of ethnic minority groups to maintain their cultural differences.

This three-fold typology has two drawbacks. First, it does not exhaust the logical possibilities. If indeed there are two dimensions to citizenship, one (ethnic versus civic) defining the formal criteria of individual access, and another (multicultural versus assimilationist) defining the cultural obligations and rights that such citizenship entails for minority groups, we end up with four, not three models (see Koopmans and Kriesi 1997; Koopmans and Statham 1999b). In addition, this typology approach to citizenship has rightly been criticized for its tendency to obscure both the dynamic aspects of the process of migrant integration and the important differences within states, both among the integration approaches advocated by different political actors and among those applied to different categories of migrants (Joppke 1996; Entzinger 2000). We propose to address these two problems by conceiving of citizenship not in the static categories of typological "models" or "regimes" but as a conceptual (and political) space in which different actors (which include nation-states, but also subnational actors such as political parties or civil society actors) and policies can be situated and developments can be traced over time. The contours of this conceptual space, which is visualized in Figure 1, are defined by the equality of individual access to citizenship on the one hand, and the amount of cultural difference and group rights that citizenship allows on the other. Thus conceptualized, the stability of citizenship regimes and the uniformity with which they cover different political actors, policies, and immigrant groups become issues for empirical investigation, not implicit assumptions tied to the rigidity of a conceptual typology.

On the vertical axis, the continuum runs from conceptions of citizenship that favor ethnic bonds as the basis for the constitution of the political community to those that emphasize equal civic rights and attribute citizenship on the basis of the territorial principle. It is easily argued that these extremes hardly ever occur in reality. Few nation-states completely exclude the possibility of naturalization for those who do not belong to their own ethnocultural group,[2] and every civic nation attributes citizenship on the basis of descent in addition to the territorial principle. It has even become somewhat fashionable in the migration and ethnic relations literature to give up the distinction between ethnic and civic nationhood altogether.[3] However, in view of the important cross-national differences that can be found along this dimension, which we will discuss in detail in chapter 1, we must consider this rejection as an overreaction to the rigidity of some of the earlier formulations of this distinction, including Brubaker's.

On the horizontal axis, the continuum runs from conceptions of citizenship that insist on conformity to a single cultural model that is to be shared by all citizens, to culturally pluralist conceptions that seek to retain,

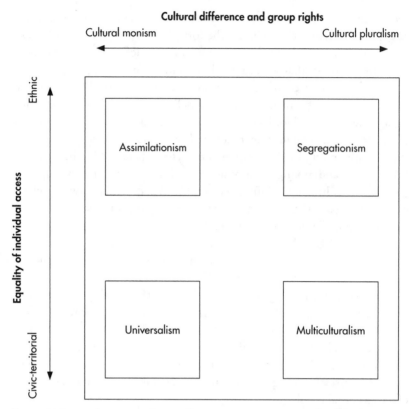

Figure 1. A two-dimensional space for situating conceptions of citizenship.

or even stimulate, diversity and allow their subjects to follow a variety of cultural patterns. Again, it hardly needs to be pointed out that these ideal types do not empirically occur in their purest form. In liberal democracies, assimilation mainly concerns cultural conformity outside the private sphere, e.g., in the sphere of law, the education system, or the media. There are also clear boundaries to cultural pluralism, which in Western societies are usually related to the respect of individual human rights and notions of equality. For instance, no Western democracy has legalized female circumcision, although some advocates of multiculturalism have gone as far as proposing to tolerate it in a "limited" form so as to respect cultural pluralism. Nevertheless, as we show in chapter 1, differences among countries remain large enough to make the distinction between cultural monism and pluralism a fruitful one for analytical purposes.

In Figure 1, we have put small boxes in the corners of the conceptual space; these boxes indicate the four ideal-typical configurations of citizenship and migrant incorporation that arise from the combination of the vertical and horizontal axes. We are well aware that most countries, actors, or policies will be situated between—or on the move somewhere in the space between—these boxes. Nevertheless, we think they are usually closer to some ideal-types than to others, and even if they are in the process of moving from one point to another, we need a conceptual system of coordinates in order to tell where they are going and where they are coming from.

The logical starting point for a discussion of these ideal-typical models of citizenship is segregationism, because this is often the point of departure in the process from migration to settlement. Segregationism is defined by exclusion from the political community of migrant newcomers who do not share the ethnocultural background of the majority society. At the same time, migrants are not being forced to give up their own cultures, and the state may even actively promote such cultures and discourage assimilation to the majority culture.[4] This comes close to the typical "guest worker" approach, which did not give migrant workers any political rights or much prospect to attain these through naturalization, yet did not make any cultural demands on them either. On the contrary, countries with guest worker programs often put quite some effort and financial resources into stimulating migrants to retain their cultural heritage and ties to their homelands, which were seen as facilitating their eventual repatriation. Even today, several countries still offer "education in own language and culture" to children of migrants. Nowadays, such educational programs are often legitimized with reference to "multiculturalism" instead of as a means to facilitate migrants' eventual return. This serves to demonstrate that in spite of the ideological rifts that separate the two, it is in actual practice not always such a long way from the segregationist guest worker philosophy to the multicultural approach. This is because—as Figure 1 illustrates—both share the idea of retaining cultural boundaries between ethnic groups and of preventing assimilation. Consequently, the educational approach in conservative Bavaria has a surprisingly cultural-pluralist touch. Bavaria is one of very few German states to have instituted Islamic education for pupils from Turkey in public schools: in separate classes, in Turkish, and given by religious teachers appointed by the Turkish Ministry of Religious Affairs.

Segregationist approaches have not disappeared with the formal end of the guest worker programs. In almost all European countries, similar policies are now applied with regard to asylum seekers and refugees, who are usually physically separated from the rest of society, have no right or a very restricted right to work, and are generally not stimulated in any other way to assimilate since that would only make it more difficult to send them back if their asylum requests are denied. In addition, segregationism is the leading ideology of the so-called New Right *(nouvelle droite, neue Rechte)*, whose ideologues, such as Alain de Benoist, advocate the notion of ethno-pluralism (Gessenharter and Fröchling 1998). This notion entails the claim that all cultures are equal but should be kept separate and "intact" in order to prevent a loss of identity and social cohesion that would benefit neither the majority society nor minority cultures. This makes it understandable why extreme-right parties such as the Front National or the Vlaams Blok sometimes have warm relations with right-wing organizations from migrant homelands, such as the Turkish Grey Wolves or the Maghrebian Amicales, which share the same objective.

The latter examples indicate that segregationism even has its advocates among minority representatives. First and foremost, this includes those organizations closely linked to homeland governments, which often have little interest in too much integration of migrants into the host society. For instance, when migrants were first allowed to vote in the Dutch local elections of 1986, the Moroccan authorities prohibited Moroccan nationals in the Netherlands to use their right to vote. Nongovernmental organizations based in migrant homelands may also have reasons to promote ethnic segregationism. This includes movements for regional independence such as the Kurdish PKK, which has little to gain from Kurdish ethnics in Germany obtaining the German nationality or assimilating to German culture.

Although segregationism still has its defenders, most of the guest worker countries have moved away from it. In view of the fact that former guest workers have become permanent settlers, this seems to be an inevitable development. No democratic state can uphold a situation for very long in which a significant percentage of the permanently resident population is excluded from political rights. From the figure it becomes clear that two basic options present themselves. One option is to retain the idea of distinct and separate cultures but to give up ethnicity as the formal basis of citizenship, which can then be extended through easier naturalization and the introduction of jus soli elements to include migrants from different ethnic and cultural backgrounds. This constitutes a move in the direction of the multicultural model. In this case, allowing dual nationality may offer itself as an additional instrument to include migrants as citizens, for in the multicultural view the fact that retaining the nationality of the homeland might constitute a barrier to adaptation to the majority culture is seen not as a problem but as a fundamental right or even a virtue.

The other option, which is philosophically close to the communitarian position (J. Cohen 1999), is to retain the formal ethnocultural basis of citizenship in its essence, but to make it easier for migrants to obtain citizenship through naturalization on the condition that they fulfill certain criteria of assimilation to the culture of the dominant ethnic group. In this case, conditional naturalization remains the single option for becoming a member of the community, and unconditional attribution of citizenship through jus soli is not considered. Dual citizenship is problematic from this perspective, since it would mean extending citizenship without demanding that the candidate give up her original ties to the homeland culture. In other words, it would imply a move toward multiculturalism, which in the eyes of ethnic assimilationists can lead to nothing but "balkanization" and dangerous "parallel societies."

While the story so far captures the experience of countries such as Germany or Switzerland, it does not describe the typical pattern for countries that already had some civic-territorial notion of citizenship in place when postwar immigrants began to arrive on a massive scale. This applies to countries that used to be colonial powers and have in the postwar period become the target of large flows of postcolonial migration, such as Britain, France, and the Netherlands. In an effort to continue their domination over their colonies, these countries transformed the relation with the colonies from one of pure domination and patronage to an at least formally more equal partnership (e.g., the British idea of the "Commonwealth") between the "mother country" and the "overseas territories." This implied certain rights to settlement and citizenship in the mother country for the inhabitants of the colonies (Miles and Thränhardt 1995). For instance, according to the new statute for the Kingdom of the Netherlands of 1954, the inhabitants of Surinam and the Dutch Antilles obtained full citizenship rights and unlimited rights of settlement in the European part of the kingdom. Conceptions of nationhood based on a notion of ethnic purity became untenable as a result of the colonial experience. Thus, after Indonesian independence, more than 300,000 people who could claim Dutch citizenship came to the Netherlands, many of mixed Dutch-Indonesian descent or ethnic Indonesians who had cooperated with the colonial regime.

The problems the former colonial powers have had in the field of migration and ethnic relations derive from the fact that what worked well as a recipe for colonial rule has not always been the optimal solution toward the integration of postwar migrants. France's main problem has been that while in the colonial situation conformism to the French republican political culture could simply be imposed, postwar migrants, particularly those of Muslim belief, have not been so easily assimilated and have sometimes demanded a *droit à la différence,* a right to be different. Furthermore, the

French approach has difficulty in dealing with the fact that cultural group differences, which are denied as legitimate policy categories, do form the basis of discrimination and racism from the side of the majority population, most clearly voiced by the Front National's polemic against "inassimilable" immigrants. Insisting on the equal treatment of all and loathing group-specific approaches, France to some extent ties its own hands when it comes to combating forms of social exclusion that are rooted in ethnic and cultural differences.

As a result, France has been confronted with two countervailing pressures for change (Favell 1998). The Socialists, supported by some migrant organizations, in the 1980s tried to steer France in the direction of a more culturally pluralist approach, offering limited recognition to the right to be different. One important policy change in this context was the Socialist-led government's 1981 liberalization of association law, which for the first time allowed migrant organization based on nationality or ethnicity. However, the cautious moves in this direction seem to have come to a complete halt afterward, especially after the notorious headscarf affair, which demonstrated the strong resistance among important sections of the French political and intellectual elites against making even the slightest concession away from unitary citizenship. The French approach is also vulnerable to a challenge from the right, which proposes to resolve the dilemma by moving in another direction, toward an assimilationist model in the thicker, ethno-cultural sense.[5] Thus, one of the most important and successful demands—partly implemented in the so-called Pasqua Law and later withdrawn by the Socialists—of the Front National has been the abolition of the jus soli attribution of citizenship and making naturalization dependent on assimilation to French culture. In the eyes of the extreme right (and many French voters), easy access to French citizenship has created increasing numbers of *faux français* (false Frenchmen), who are French by nationality but not by culture—culture understood, of course, not in the "thin" sense of adherence to universal republican values such as democracy, liberty, and equality, but in the "thick" sense of folk traditions, Catholicism, and sometimes plainly race.

Great Britain's and the Netherlands' multicultural approaches to migrant incorporation have had their own problems. Here the difficulty has been not a lack of policy instruments to tackle disadvantage based on ethnic, cultural, or racial difference, but rather that these instruments have sometimes reinforced and solidified the very disadvantages they were meant to combat. Taking ethnic and racial criteria as a basis for policies to combat disadvantage and discrimination on the basis of ethnicity and race has often been much like trying to drive the Devil out with Beelzebub. As Miles (1982) has argued for Britain and Rath (1991) for the Netherlands, the labeling of migrant groups as disadvantaged minorities has led to a process of racialization or minoritization that has tended to reproduce race and ethnicity as bases for social disadvantage and discrimination.

This problem seems to have been aggravated by the particular mixture of paternalism and guilt that describes these countries' postcolonial hangovers. On the one hand, there has often been a tendency on the side of the authorities to see migrants as incapable of ameliorating their own position and thus in need of benevolent assistance. This tendency has been reinforced by a sense of postcolonial guilt and the ever-present fear among authorities of being accused of racism, which have led to a rather "soft" handling of problems that disproportionately affect minorities, such as social welfare dependence and crime, and a great wariness in using the state's sanctioning powers in order to push migrants themselves into making a contribution to alleviating their disadvantage (e.g., to learn the language of the host country in order to improve employment opportunities). Particularly in the Netherlands, the combination of these factors has led to a vicious circle in which state policies have reinforced the image of migrants as a problematic, disadvantaged category in need of constant state assistance. To the majority population, migrants thus appear as a group deserving help, respect, tolerance, and solidarity, but not the kind of people that anyone would want to employ or would want one's child to be in school with. As a result, in spite of the liberal rhetoric, the much better legal position, and the much higher level of tolerance for cultural diversity in the public sphere and in political debate, levels of ethnic residential segregation, segregation in the school system, as well as levels of unemployment and social security dependence (relative to the majority population) are higher in the Netherlands than in Germany (Thränhardt 2000; Koopmans 2003a, 2003b).

More recently, this tendency of multiculturalism in a postcolonial context to slide into a form of segregationism has inspired a reappreciation of the universalist model, especially in the Netherlands. Instead of policies geared to specific ethnic groups, the authorities now prefer general policies for socioeconomically disadvantaged groups, including not only minorities but also the "native" underclass. Policies have also become more demanding with regard to migrants. For instance, newly arriving migrants are now obliged to follow a course program to facilitate their integration (*inburgering,* literally, "to become a citizen") into Dutch society, which encompasses Dutch language instruction and basic information about Dutch politics and culture.

This discussion shows that, unlike the more rigid typologies, our model of a two-dimensional conceptual space assumes neither fixed nor uniform national coordinates. Each of the countries discussed has been shifting its position over the course of the last few decades. This reflects that everywhere the incorporation of large numbers of culturally different migrants—a hitherto unknown challenge—was much of a trial and error process. However, the elements these countries used, combined, and varied during this learning process were drawn from preexisting institutional and cultural repertoires of citizenship and nationhood.

The Theoretical Framework: Institutional and Discursive Opportunity Structures

To understand how conceptions of citizenship and nationhood affect political contention, we propose a theoretical approach that builds on theories of so-called political opportunity structures in the study of social movements and collective action (McAdam 1982; Tarrow 1994; Kriesi et al. 1995). The basic idea is that collective action does not directly reflect underlying social structures or the extent and nature of social problems and circumstances. Instead, each form of collective action is understood as part of a larger political process and as being shaped by the opportunities and constraints offered by its political environment. The impact of social structures, problems, and circumstances—e.g., migration processes and cultural diversification—is, in this view, indirect and conditional to the extent that they lead to a reconfiguration of the political context of mobilization and thereby alter the balance of opportunities and constraints for particular collective actors and demands. In following this theoretical approach, we deviate from much of the literature in the field of migration and ethnic relations where political mobilization and conflicts are explained in terms of migration patterns and flows, the socioeconomic situation in the country of immigration, and the cultural characteristics and national background of specific migrant groups. We do not deny that such variables play a role, and we will consider them as alternative or additional explanations in the chapters to follow. We contend, however, that their explanatory power is limited compared to the impact of the political context on patterns of collective action.

Some examples drawn from subsequent chapters can serve as illustrations of how this approach differs from other accounts of migration and ethnic relations politics. The mobilization of migrants is often explained in terms of their cultural characteristics and national background. We show in chapter 3 that homeland cultural and political influences play a significant role in some of our countries but not in others—depending on the degree to which national citizenship and integration regimes offer migrants incentives and opportunities to orient themselves politically toward the country of immigration. As a result, the patterns of mobilization of different ethnic groups in the same receiving country resemble each other, while the same ethnic group may behave very differently in a dissimilar political context of another country of immigration. Current explanations for extreme-right and xenophobic mobilization emphasize processes of ethnic competition between immigrants and the native population resulting from a combination of high immigration levels and socioeconomic crisis. In chapter 5, we find no systematic connection between immigration levels or socioeconomic variables and the extent of extreme-right and xenophobic mobilization. Instead, we argue that xenophobic mobilization thrives better where its claims resonate with dominant notions of citizenship and national identity and where established political parties do not already occupy its niche in the political space. In chapter 6, we show that, in a similar vein, the strength of antiracist mobilization is not a simple function of the strength of xenophobic and extreme-right groups. Antiracism is also a form of affirmation of a specific notion of national identity and therefore tends to have a more universalist flavor in France, a multicultural touch in Britain and the Netherlands, and is strongly affected by the historical legacy of Nazism and the Holocaust in Germany.

The applications of the opportunity model of social movements and collective action have, however, also revealed a number of omissions and weaknesses. We identify three major shortcomings of the opportunity model, which we seek to redress in the theoretical model displayed in Figure 2, which will serve as a point of reference throughout the book.

The first shortcoming of political opportunity approaches has been their one-sided emphasis on institutional opportunities in the form of the chances of access and influence of citizens in the decision-making process (institutional openness versus closure) and the material reactions of authorities to challengers (repression or facilitation of mobilization). Political opportunity theorists have focused on explaining the extent and forms of mobilization of collective actors, whose identity and aims, however, were largely treated as pregiven. In other words, the opportunity model—like the related resource mobilization approach, e.g., McCarthy and Zald 1977—has focused on the *how* of mobilization and neglected the important question of *why* social movements constitute themselves around particular collective identities and aims (Melucci 1990).

The question of the constitution of identities and aims of collective actors appears in an especially pregnant way in the field of migration and

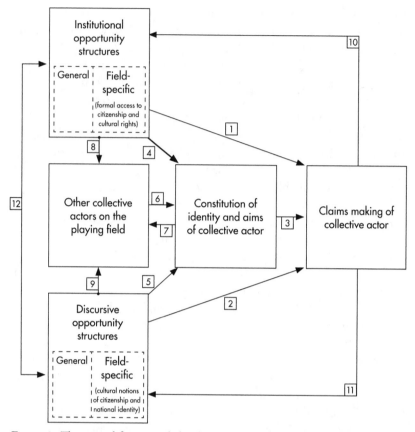

Figure 2. Theoretical framework for the analysis of political contention in the migration and ethnic relations field.

ethnic relations. What is at issue in this field to an important extent re-volves around questions of identity, the national identity of the receiving nation-state and its relation to the group identities of migrants as well as to tendencies toward ethnonationalist closure from the side of the majority population. The prominent role of identity issues in this field practically forbids one to treat the identities of collective actors as pregiven. For in-stance, the labels that are used in different national contexts to denote mi-grants are not coincidental or inconsequential. The dominant vocabulary of *immigrés* (immigrants) in France, *Ausländer* (foreigners) in Germany and Switzerland, *etnische minderheden* (ethnic minorities) in the Netherlands, and racial groups in the United Kingdom indicates widely diverging discur-sive contexts, characterized by specific constructions of the relation between immigrants and the receiving nation-state. These discursive constructions have important consequences, as we will see, both for the self-definition of migrants and for the identities and aims of other collective actors who mobilize against or in support of them.

In addition to institutional variables, we must therefore take discursive opportunities and constraints into account. Institutional opportunities determine a collective actor's chances of gaining recognized access and new advantages (Gamson 1975) in its interactions with decision makers, as well as the likelihood of repression and facilitation from the side of power holders (Tilly 1978; Koopmans 1999). Discursive opportunities determine which collective identities and substantive demands have a high likelihood to gain *visibility* in the mass media, to *resonate* with the claims of other collective actors, and to achieve *legitimacy* in the public discourse (Koopmans and Statham 1999b; Koopmans 2004b; Koopmans and Olzak 2004). As a result of cross-nationally diverging discursive opportunity structures linked to models of citizenship and notions of national identity, the same type of claim—say, a demand for recognition of cultural difference by a group that defines itself in racial terms—may have widely different chances of gaining media attention (visibility), provoking reactions by other actors (resonance), and gaining public legitimacy. By integrating these discursive variables into the wider theoretical framework of the political opportunity model, we aim to build a bridge to the framing approach of David Snow and his colleagues (Snow et al. 1986; Snow and Benford 1992), who have also emphasized the constructed nature of collective identities and aims but have had difficulty explaining why some framing attempts are successful and others are not.

There is also a tendency to specify political opportunity structures at a level that is too general, as if they could be defined irrespective of the characteristics of particular issue fields and collective actors. The field of migration and ethnic relations illustrates that such a one-size-fits-all approach to political opportunity structures is untenable. Perhaps the most central element of this field is the question of the conditions of access of migrants to membership in the political community. From the point of view of migrants who are barred access to citizenship, it does not matter much if a polity, such as the Swiss, offers its citizens many points of access in the form of decentralized state structures and direct-democratic instruments, which migrants as noncitizens are unable to utilize. Although the exclusion of migrants from political rights is an extreme case, it exemplifies the more general rule that opportunity structures can vary enormously from one issue field to another and may differ importantly between collective actors. The lesson we draw is that we put a strong emphasis on opportunity structures that are specific to the field of migration and ethnic relations in the form of the citizenship and migrant integration regimes that we have discussed in the preceding section and will elaborate in chapter 1.

While we emphasize field-specific opportunities, we do not want to throw away the baby with the bath water and deny any relevance to more general features of the political context of a particular country. While Switzerland's open institutional structure and France's high degree of centralization of power are relativized or to some extent even counteracted by the more specific opportunity structures of the migration and ethnic relations field, we may still expect them to exert an influence on the claims making of actors in this field. For instance, even without citizenship rights, migrants in Switzerland will be affected by the tradition of accommodation and consensus seeking that pervades Swiss political life. And even with easy access to citizenship, their French counterparts face a state that is relatively shielded from the citizenry, and they will quickly learn the lesson that their compatriots have internalized over the generations, that extraparliamentary pressure on the state is often necessary in order to be heard. Therefore, we have indicated in Figure 2 that institutional as well as discursive opportunity structures have both general and issue-specific dimensions that need to be considered.

According to our model, there are two basic ways in which opportunity structures may affect the claims making of collective actors. The first, indicated by arrows 1 and 2, is direct and indicates that even if we assume the identities and aims of collective actors to be pregiven and identical across political contexts, we may expect the same actor to mobilize differently and with diverging success according to the opportunities and constraints offered by its political environment. For example, on the institutional side (arrow 1) we may expect the accessibility of citizenship to be positively related to the participation of immigrants in public debates on immigration and ethnic relations. Immigrants are more likely to find a positive hearing for their demands with policy makers if they are potential voters than if they are foreigners without institutional leverage. On the discursive side (arrow 2), we may expect that beyond formal rights, open citizenship also increases the legitimacy of immigrant demands. For example, it is easier for the state to deny non-Christian religions equal treatment as long as most of the adherents of these religions are foreign citizens and the issue is defined in terms of tolerance for the cultural differences of guests—as is the case in Germany and Switzerland. Claims for religious equality are likely to be much more resonant and legitimate if they can be made in the name of equal treatment among citizens.

Arrows 1 and 2 capture the strategic relation between opportunity structures and patterns of claims making. Depending on the institutional and discursive political context, certain types of claims making are more likely to be stimulated by positive responses, whereas other types of claims making are made less attractive because they meet with negative reactions or none at all. However, as arrow 3 indicates, the impact of opportunity structures may also be indirect, via their effect on the identities and aims of collective actors. This is a much more subtle process in which opportunity structures affect how people define themselves and their aims, as well as their relation to the wider society, in ways that go beyond mere strategic adaptation to given opportunities and constraints. Take, for instance, the position of immigrants in Switzerland as an example of the indirect effect of institutional opportunities (arrow 4). Faced with a political context that provides them with very few channels of access to the policy process and that puts up high barriers to their acquisition of the Swiss nationality, immigrants in Switzerland are not likely to develop an interest in Swiss politics or to see themselves as members of the Swiss polity. As a result, we find in chapter 3 a very strong orientation of Swiss immigrants toward the politics of their countries of origin and very few claims that relate to their situation in Switzerland. Similarly, discursive opportunity structures influence how people see themselves in relation to others, as well as the kind of collective aims they pursue (arrow 5). Examples are the dominant discursive categories for immigrants that follow from national citizenship and integration regimes. The British regime, for instance, is built around the category of race, and the racial vocabulary is highly visible, resonant, and legitimate in the public discourse in this country. As a result of the discursive omnipresence of race, British immigrants are much more likely to see themselves as "black" and to make concomitant claims for racial equality and against racial discrimination than in countries like France, where racial categories are virtually absent—yes, almost taboo—within the public discourse.

The third and final shortcoming of the "traditional" political opportunity model that we seek to redress is its insufficient appreciation of the fact that contentious politics is fundamentally interactive and dynamic. Political opportunity explanations have offered relatively static explanations of the mobilization of particular actors as a function of structural characteristics of their political environment. However, collective actors never mobilize in a vacuum. They are always confronted with established actors who already occupy certain positions in the "playing field" with whom they enter into relations of competition, alliance, or opposition. The entry of new collective actors on the scene often draws other actors into contention, for instance, in the form of countermovements. In a coevolutionary process, the reactions of established actors as well as new rivals and supporters may in turn alter the identities, aims, and strategies of the original contender (Koopmans 2004c).

Although the emphasis in this book is not on explaining developments over time but rather on cross-national comparison, we believe that it is nonetheless necessary to take these interactive dimensions into account. In Figure 2, the mutual influences among actors on the playing field of contentious politics are indicated by arrows 6 and 7. An example of what we mean here is the relation between extreme-right and antiracist movements. Although, as we will see in chapter 6, it is too simple to see the antiracist movement as a mere reaction to extreme-right mobilization, it is nevertheless clear that the mobilization of antiracist groups is not independent from the presence, nature, and strength of the extreme right in a particular context. Another example is our explanation in chapter 5 for the strength of extreme-right parties in different countries. One reason for the differential success of extreme-right parties, we argue, is the differential degree to which established political parties have occupied anti-immigrant positions within the public discourse. Where this is not the case, extreme-right parties have better chances to be electorally successful (arrow 6). Strong extreme-right parties, in turn, influence the mobilization repertoire of the extreme right as a whole, leading to a moderation and conventionalization of its repertoire of claims making (arrow 3). Of course, the identities, aims, and strategies of other collective actors on the playing field depend on political opportunity structures—institutional and discursive, field-specific and general—in much the same way as those of the actor whose mobilization is at the center of analysis. Arrows 8 and 9 in the figure indicate this.

Finally, arrows 10 and 11 indicate that political opportunity structures can naturally be changed as a result of political contention, and double arrow 12 indicates that institutional changes may have consequences for the structure of public discourse and vice versa. Much political action is about changing or preventing changes in the fundamental features of political life; in the absence of real possibilities for such changes, collective action would not make much sense. However, to talk about political opportunity *structures* does not make any sense if we assume that such fundamental changes are easily achieved. The distinction between more stable political opportunity structures (top and bottom of the figure) and the volatile interactive processes among collective actors in the middle of the figure is therefore relative rather than absolute. As we have already indicated, the clearest case where important structural change has occurred in our period of study is Germany, where after the reunification of the country the ethnic conception of citizenship came under increasing pressure, leading ultimately to the partial introduction of the jus soli and easier naturalization in 2000. If our arguments in this book are correct, a repetition of this study five or ten years ahead should display clear changes in the German pattern of contention over migration and ethnic relations, bringing it closer to countries such as Britain or France.

Method: Political Claims Analysis

With the exception of chapter 1, where we develop indicators based on secondary sources to empirically measure our main independent variable, models of citizenship, the empirical core of our study is data on political claims making in the public sphere, measured by way of a content analysis of daily newspapers in the five countries. Political claims analysis builds on protest event analyses as developed in the field of social movements and collective action, but extends the method to include speech acts and public discourse variables. Protest event analysis records instances of collective protest, usually from newspaper sources, sometimes also from police records (for an overview, see Rucht, Koopmans, and Neidhardt 1999). Political discourse analysis is associated with the constructivist framing perspective and is perhaps best represented by the work of William Gamson and his collaborators (Gamson 1988, 1992; Gamson and Modigliani 1989; see also Gitlin 1980; Donati 1992). Whereas protest event analysis takes protest as an indicator of the level of challenges to the political system, political discourse analysis takes the emergence and public visibility of movement frames as an indicator for the "meaning giving" side of challenges to dominant political and cultural norms, values, and problem definitions. The two approaches focus on different dimensions of collective challenges to political power: the first relating an action type variable—protests—to institutional political opportunities; and the second relating an interpretative scheme variable—frames—to the dominant sets of cultural and political norms, i.e., in our terminology, to discursive opportunity structures.

We integrate these two approaches by combining the quantitative rigor of protest event analysis with the sensitivity to discursive content of political discourse approaches. This is achieved first by moving beyond protest and analyzing *all* forms of public claims making, including purely discursive forms such as public statements, press releases and conferences, publications, and interviews, alongside conventional forms of political action such as litigation or petitioning, as well as classical protest forms such as demonstrations and political violence. Thus, we take up one of the main criticisms against protest event analysis from the political discourse camp: that protest event analysis has a deficient appreciation of public discourse as a medium of social conflict and symbolic struggles. Second, we extend the range of actors to include not just the forms of collective action we are primarily interested in explaining—migrants, the extreme right, and pro-migrant and antiracist mobilization—but simply *any* act of claims making in our fields of interest, regardless of the actor who made the claim, including the usual suspects of protest event analysis (social movement groups, NGOs, and so on), as well as interest groups (e.g., employers associations or churches), but also political party, parliamentary, governmental, and other state actors.

We define an instance of claims making (shorthand: a claim) as a unit of strategic action in the public sphere that consists of *the purposive and public articulation of political demands, calls to action, proposals, criticisms, or physical attacks, which actually or potentially affect the interests or integrity of the claimants and/or other collective actors.*[6] Political decisions and policy implementation are included and seen as special forms of claims making, ones that have direct and binding effects on the objects of the claim. We also include violence between contending groups, even if no explicit verbal claim is made or reported, e.g., mutual attacks between radical-right, immigrant, and antiracist groups or between different ethnic or religious groups. This redefinition of contentious politics shifts the focus of inquiry away from the single-movement perspective and toward processes of interaction between actors and the coalitions, alliances and networks, and conflict lines that connect and relate different types of collective actors in a multiorganizational field (see also McAdam, Tarrow, and Tilly 2001).

Our core data on political claims were retrieved from one national newspaper for each country. The selected newspapers are the *Frankfurter Rundschau* for Germany, *Le Monde* for France, the *Guardian* for Britain, *NRC Handelsblad* for the Netherlands, and the *Neue Zürcher Zeitung* for Switzerland. These are all independent newspapers of public record with a nationwide scope of coverage and readership. All of them are broadsheet newspapers with a reputation for consistent and detailed coverage of the field of migration and ethnic relations. From these newspapers, the main news sections of every Monday, Wednesday, and Friday issue were sampled and coded for all political claims relating to immigration, migrant integration, and racism and xenophobia. For two collective actors of special interest to us—migrants and extreme-right organizations and groups—we also coded claims that were not related to immigration issues, e.g., homeland political issues in the case of immigrants, and claims on the Nazi regime or the Holocaust in the case of the extreme right.

We are fully aware that newspaper coverage is not undistorted nor is it a complete mirror of reality. From the multitude of claims that are made on a daily basis by a variety of groups in liberal democracies, only a small part is actually reported in the media. However, it is precisely this publicly visible part of claims making that we are interested in; this is the part that can have an impact on the perceptions of the public or on policy making. Discursive forms of claims making such as press releases or public statements that do not make it into the media may be considered not to have occurred at all, for their brief existence and subsequent failure are known only to the would-be claimant himself. To a large extent this also holds for physical forms of claims making such as demonstrations or violence. Even a violent attack by skinheads on a group of immigrants becomes meaningful as an act of claims making only when it is reported to a wider audience. Without such coverage, it remains a largely private event known only to the attackers and their victims, and perhaps a few occasional bystanders or the police officers who investigate the case.

Our theoretical argument actually presupposes that there are strong selection mechanisms in the public sphere that determine the chances of access of specific types of claims making. We find in chapter 3, for instance, that there are almost no claims by immigrants using a racial identity in Germany, and explain this with reference to the delegitimacy of race as a policy and discursive category as a result of the Nazis' misuse of this terminology. It may well be that there are some migrant groups in Germany who do try to make claims in the name of racial identities. These groups will, however, have much greater difficulty in penetrating the German media than other migrant groups with different identities that better fit Germany's discursive opportunity structures. The fact that our data in such cases are partly the result of media selection processes is not a problem for our approach; instead, our data capture precisely what we want to measure. A data set including all attempts at claims making, including the large numbers of failures, would be interesting for investigating selection processes, but such an effort could only feasibly be undertaken for a very delimited set of actors, times, and places. However, as a measurement of politically relevant claims making, such data would be far inferior to data based on media-reported claims. It would be invalid because our aim is not to provide a full picture of all the attempts at claims making that occur, but to explain the pattern of those claims that are actually able to penetrate the mass media and thereby may become part of the processes of policy making and public debate and deliberation. Moreover, on theoretical grounds, we believe that the difference between failed and (in terms of media coverage) successful attempts at claims making should not be overstated. As a tendency, attempted claims making will mirror successful claims making because collective actors are likely either to disband or to change strategy if their attempts structurally fail to reach a wider audience. They learn to employ strategies that fit the selection criteria of what is considered relevant and legitimate in the public discourse of a particular setting, either the hard way through differential survival or by way of strategic adaptation and anticipation (see Koopmans 2004b, 2004c).[7]

Another objection to the use of data drawn from mass media to measure claims making is that some forms of claims making are successful in spite of, or sometimes even because of, not being reported in the media. Some collective actors, especially more powerful ones, do not need the mass media or may even prefer to operate away from the public eye because they can exert pressure on decision makers more effectively by using direct access to and influence on them. The most important form of such nonpublic claims making is lobbying. Some groups may be successful in the lobbying circuit without having to demonstrate broad public resonance and support. For example, a multinational corporation may be effective simply by threatening decision makers with disinvestments or capital flight. However, for most groups, and particularly for those in the immigration field, successful lobbying must be backed by public visibility, resonance, and legitimacy. Therefore, we are confident that a survey of the nonpublic claims making of lobby groups in the immigration and ethnic relations field would not show patterns very different from the ones we present, apart from the fact that the distribution of actors in such lobbying data would be skewed toward the more institutionalized and resourceful ones. It should be made clear, however, that with the data we use we cannot, in a strict sense, generalize beyond public forms of claims making.[8]

Even if we have compelling reasons to draw on mass media sources, it remains an important question whether our primary sources are representative for the wider media landscape. We have tried to minimize the problem of description bias (McCarthy, McPhail, and Smith 1996) by coding only the factual coverage of statements and events that appear in the newspapers and excluding any comments and evaluations by editors or reporters. Even when disregarding the explicit opinions of journalists and editors, it could be that the picture we obtain of claims making in a particular country depends strongly on the newspaper chosen. To check for such biases in Germany and the United Kingdom, where we first started the data gathering for this study, we drew additional samples from other newspaper sources. The comparisons of these alternative sources to our main sources (as shown in the appendix) reveal important differences in the *rate* of coverage of relevant claims, especially between national quality papers and the much more limited and concise coverage in tabloid and regional papers. However, such differences in coverage *rates* coincide with strikingly similar *distributions* of acts on important variables. These intermedia comparisons therefore suggest that by using national-quality newspapers as our source we obtain a valid picture of the patterns of claims making in our field of interest.

Important variables that were coded refer to the identity of the actors making the claim, including full organizational names, action forms, and (where present) the size, target, and intensity of protest. Regarding the contents of the claims, for each act we coded up to three aims or demands, up to two frames, and the actors on whom demands are made (addressee) or who are objects of criticism. Further methodological details can be found in the appendix. As the subsequent chapters will show, the resulting data set is suitable for macrolevel comparative analyses of broad issue fields but at the same time can zoom in on qualitative aspects of particular actors and claims.

Plan of the Book

Although models of citizenship and national identity play an important role in the recent literature on migration and ethnic relations, the evidence presented for classifying countries as belonging to one model or another is usually impressionistic. This has justifiably provoked the criticism that such categorization may simply reproduce national clichés that have little to do with reality. For all the talk about citizenship, we lack a systematically comparative empirical assessment of where countries stand. In chapter 1, we move beyond this empirical indeterminacy and develop a set of empirical indicators for the two dimensions of citizenship—individual equality and cultural difference—that we have introduced. Drawing on secondary data from a variety of sources, we are able to place our five countries relative to each other in the two-dimensional space of Figure 2 and to show what important shifts in position have occurred over the last two decades. This chapter allows us a more precise assessment of citizenship as a factor shaping political contention in the migration and ethnic relations field than has been possible so far.

Having thus laid an empirical basis for our main independent variable, the subsequent chapters deal with the analysis of different types of political contention over migration and ethnic relations. In each of these chapters, we analyze patterns of claims making along the lines indicated in Figure 2. However, these chapters offer more than an application of our own theoretical approach to different types of contention. Each chapter also has a specific focus on an alternative theoretical perspective that is of particular relevance to the particular form of contention at issue. We develop our argument in constant dialogue with other perspectives, which sometimes offer competing and mutually exclusive predictions and assessments but that are sometimes also complementary to our own approach.

In chapter 2, we start with an overview of claims making on migration and ethnic relations in our five countries across all actors and issues. We present data on the actors involved in claims making as well as the substantive topics they address. The main theoretical issue in this chapter is to what extent national politics still matters in explaining political contention. To this end, we put the claims of theories of postnational citizenship—which assert that the nation-state has lost much of its relevance and sovereignty in the immigration and ethnic relations field—to a systematic test. We look at the level at which actors in the field organize and whether they remain within the context of the receiving nation-state or extend to the transnational or supranational levels. We do the same for the way in which actors' claims are framed: are issues in the field defined and debated entirely within the national context, or is reference made to authorities in other countries or to European or supranational institutions, conventions, legal frameworks, and norms? Finally, to the extent that the scope of claims extends beyond the nation-state, we look at the actors and the content of such claims. We address whether the political space beyond the nation-state indeed has the empowering effects for migrants and their rights that the postnational perspective asserts. Or do supranational developments benefit those actors most who were already in a privileged position at the national level?

In chapter 3, we focus attention on the category of actors that is at the core of contention in this field, immigrants and ethnic minorities of migrant origin. The theoretical discussion in this chapter is between our political perspective and the emphasis on migrants' cultural and national background in theories of transnational communities or diasporas. We distinguish different types of collective identities—formal policy status, race, religion, and ethnicity or nationality—that migrants may embrace, and we ask whether the collective identities around which immigrants mobilize are determined more by their links to particular countries and cultures of origin or by the opportunity structures offered by the receiving nation-states. In this light, we also ask to what extent migrant claims making refers to the context of the immigration country, to the politics of the country of origin, or to some combination of the two, and whether there are important differences between countries and ethnic groups in this regard. In addition, we seek to explain cross-national differences in the action forms used by migrants to make their claims, as well as in the substantive content of claims by migrants on the receiving society.

The issue of the substance of migrant claims on the host society is taken up in greater detail in chapter 4, which zooms in on claims for cultural and religious rights, specifically by migrants of Muslim belief. The position of Muslims is at the center of controversies over multicultural citizenship, opposing those who argue for a differentiation of citizenship in order to accommodate group cultures to those who fear that this will lead to a decline in social cohesion. This theoretical debate is the central theme of this chapter, and we begin by asking how important demands for cultural and religious rights are among the claims of migrants, and which migrant groups are most likely to make such claims. We then focus on Muslims and take a detailed look at the kind of cultural claims they make. Are these of the incommensurate type that conflicts with the standards of liberal democracy, or are they mostly benign? And to what extent do Muslims make claims for special rights and exemption from duties, or are they primarily demanding parity with native (i.e., Christian) religious groups? Last but not least, to what extent are there cross-national differences in the type of claims made by Muslims, and to what extent can they be explained with reference to national models of citizenship and opportunity structures?

In chapter 5, we move on to migrants' clearest opponents within the field of contention, the organizations, groups, and political parties that make up the extreme right. We contrast our approach to perspectives that explain the extreme right as directly related to socioeconomic conditions such as high immigration levels and economic decline and unemployment, which heighten competition between native groups and immigrants. We call attention to another type of competition, electoral competition between extreme right and established political parties and the political space this creates—or closes off—for the extreme right. Also, we pay attention to the type of actors involved in extreme-right claims making and offer an explanation for the puzzling finding that xenophobic violence by neo-Nazi and skinhead groups tends to be less widespread where extreme-right parties are strong.

Chapter 6 completes our picture of contention in the field by analyzing the mobilization of constituencies from within the majority population on behalf of migrants and their interests and against the extreme right and xenophobia. This type of solidarity mobilization by groups on behalf of the interests of others is generally considered a theoretical puzzle, certainly from the point of view of theories of rational choice. The sometimes proposed way out of this dilemma is to see such mobilization as being genuinely altruistic.

This would lead us to expect solidarity mobilization to be strongest where the legal position of immigrants is weakest and the threat of the extreme right strongest. We investigate to what extent this is indeed the case and propose an alternative explanation that sees pro-migrant and antiracist mobilization as part of a larger contest about redefinitions of conceptions of citizenship and nationhood. Seen from this perspective, solidarity mobilization with migrants is misconceived as a form of altruism and is better explained as the assertion and defense of a particular conception of the nation, and in that sense it has objectives that reach far beyond the improvement of the position of migrants.

The concluding chapter summarizes the most important results of our study, integrates the main theoretical conclusions, and identifies questions for further research. Looking at the overall picture of the different countries, we try to answer the difficult but politically important question: which approach to citizenship, nationhood, and migrant integration seems to work best in integrating migrants in constructive ways in the liberal-democratic political process while preventing the rise of xenophobic counterreactions? Needless to say, none of our five countries has fully achieved this ideal, and all have at least partly failed in meeting their own set objectives. Nonetheless, we believe that besides a contribution to the academic debate, this study also offers important political lessons, and we therefore conclude this book with some policy-relevant suggestions for how nation-states—but also emergent polities such as the European Union—might adapt their citizenship and integration regimes in ways that can help to prevent or mend the counterproductive, unintended consequences that policies in this field have often had in the past.

1

Configurations of Citizenship in Five European Countries

Citizenship has become a central category in the debate on immigration and ethnic relations. Following in the footsteps of Brubaker (1992), many studies have focused on the rules for nationality acquisition (e.g., Cinar 1994; Kleger and D'Amato 1995; Safran 1997), often contrasting jus soli and jus sanguinis regimes of citizenship attribution. Nationality acquisition is a crucial determinant of migrants' access to citizenship rights, since it entails that migrants become fully equal before the law. However, access to citizenship rights neither starts nor ends with the acquisition of nationality. Even immigration countries with a relatively easily accessible nationality harbor large numbers of immigrants who have remained foreign nationals, either because they do not (yet) fulfill the nationality acquisition criteria or because they do not want to become nationals of their new countries of residence.

If we consider T. H. Marshall's (1950) three categories of rights—civic-legal, political, and social—Western countries have extended most civil rights to all the people living on their territory, including recent immigrants. Fundamental human rights historically inscribed in Western constitutions, such as the right to a fair trial, the right of association and demonstration, and freedom of speech, in most cases do not discriminate according to whether someone is a national or not. The same is true for many social rights (see, e.g., Bauböck 1995; Guiraudon 1998, 2000). Dependent to some extent on the type of residence permit they hold, legal immigrants in all the important European immigration countries have access to most welfare state and social security provisions, with the qualification that social

31

welfare benefits (public assistance not based on social security contributions) are as a rule only available for permanent residents, and may be an expulsion ground for those with a less secure status. The right to family unification is also quite firmly established in all Western European countries, although there may be restrictions related to economic independence and the type of residence permit held by the requesting party. The political rights to vote and to stand for election have, by contrast, generally not been granted to nonnationals (Layton-Henry 1990). In spite of these broad cross-national similarities, there are some significant differences in the rights of nonnationals between countries that we will address.

Of course, for migrants who naturalize, differences in the rights of foreign residents become irrelevant. At the same time, however, holding the nationality of the country of residence is not always a guarantee for migrants' actual access to the fully equal treatment it formally promises. Racism and discrimination, both within state institutions (e.g., the police) and from societal actors such as employers or landlords, can be important barriers to the actual realization of equal rights. Therefore, it becomes important what provisions immigration countries have set up to protect citizens with different ethnic or cultural backgrounds from discriminatory exclusion by the majority society.

Together, rules governing nationality acquisition, the extension of rights to foreign residents, and antidiscrimination provisions govern the degree to which migrants as individuals have access to equal citizenship rights. However, as we have argued in the introduction, there is a second important dimension to citizenship rights. These cultural group rights have been at the center of philosophical discussions and political controversies on multiculturalism and assimilation (e.g., Kymlicka 1995a; Parekh 2002; Bauböck 1996; Joppke and Lukes 1999). While the relevance of cultural factors for migrant integration is widely acknowledged, this discussion has been strongly dominated by normative considerations. To date few attempts have been made to empirically systematize cross-national differences regarding the regulation of cultural differences (partial exceptions are Vermeulen 1997 and Rath et al. 1999). Given the lack of comparative knowledge, the classification of countries in one or another type of "citizenship regime" that is widespread in the literature does not always rest on firm empirical grounds and has therefore been open to the criticism that it merely reproduces existing national clichés. Moreover, there has sometimes been a tendency to view citizenship in an overly static way. While Brubaker's point about the deep historical roots of traditions of citizenship and related conceptions of national identity is valid and important, this does not imply that they are immutable, especially not when states are confronted with a qualitatively and quantitatively novel challenge such as the massive influx of culturally and racially different migrants in the postwar period.

In this chapter, we want to remedy these conceptual and empirical shortcomings of the work on citizenship rights for migrants by developing a set of empirical indicators for the two dimensions of citizenship that we presented in Figure 1 in the introduction. For the individual equality dimension of citizenship in our five countries, we have been able to draw to an important extent on the available academic literature. We have also gathered systematically comparable information for the cultural difference and group rights dimension from a variety of sources (legal texts, academic literature, media sources, Internet Web sites).[1] The cultural dimension of citizenship is not so strongly inscribed in formal legislation as the individual equality dimension, which can be measured relatively adequately by looking at aliens' and nationality legislation. This lower degree of formalization of the cultural dimension may explain why the legal scholars who have been most prominent in comparative studies of migrant rights have so far largely ignored this aspect of citizenship.

The indicators we will discuss have been chosen in such a way that they allow us to find meaningful variation among our countries of study. This implies, first, that we ignore rights and regulations that do not differentiate. For instance, whether or not female circumcision is allowed is not included among our cultural rights indicators because none of our countries—nor any other Western European country—tolerates this practice. Second, we have not included indicators that are not relevant in one or more countries. An example is provision of halal food in school canteens, which in some countries such as the United Kingdom has been an issue, but in others such as the Netherlands it has not, for the simple reason that the phenomenon of school canteens does not exist in the Netherlands. Finally, we have ignored indicators that are too difficult to compare because of the complexity of the regulations. An example is the cost of naturalization. There are differences in this regard, but in each country, reduced fees apply for lower-income applicants, with minimum fees that are very similar. Therefore, it is very difficult to judge comparatively whether there are significant differences in the degree to which the costs are a barrier to naturalization. We have gathered information for three points in time: 2002, 1990, and 1980. For obvious reasons, it proved much easier to find complete information for the most recent year, whereas especially for 1980 we had to base our judgments on a much thinner body of information. The main reason for presenting figures for 1980 and 1990 is therefore not to give exact data on the situation in our five countries at those points in time, but to give a rough indication of the magnitude and direction of temporal trends (compared to the base year 2002).

A final note to make at the outset is that we will not judge the regulations in place in our five countries in relation to some abstract theoretical or normative standard, which would be difficult to develop and must be necessarily arbitrary. Instead, we use the actual range of variation among our five countries as the standard of comparison. This implies that if we conclude, for instance, that Switzerland is situated near the ethnic pole of the continuum on a particular indicator, we mean this in a relative sense, compared to the other countries in our study. Were we to use another standard of comparison, e.g., countries with very strong ethnic conceptions of citizenship such as Israel or Japan, Switzerland's relative position would shift in the direction of the civic-territorial pole.

The First Dimension of Citizenship: Individual Equality

On the first dimension of citizenship, the question is to what extent access to citizenship rights is color-blind in the sense that every legal resident in the state's territory has access to equal citizenship rights, regardless of his or her race, ethnicity, or cultural background. Referring back to Figure 1, we label the extreme positions on this dimension as "ethnic" and "civic-territorial" conceptions of citizenship. A pronouncedly ethnic conception of citizenship implies that there are high barriers to nationality acquisition by immigrants, thus strongly privileging the attribution of nationality by way of descent (jus sanguinis). In addition, such a citizenship conception implies a comparatively strong differentiation of rights according to nationality, with significant restrictions to the civic, social, and political rights of nonnationals. Since ethnicity and nationality are used by the state itself as differentiating markers for access to citizenship rights, it follows that ethnic conceptions of citizenship will also have weakly developed sanctions to combat discrimination. Conversely, a pronounced version of a civic-territorial conception of citizenship would be characterized by easy access to the nationality, including automatic and unconditional attribution to children born on the territory (jus soli). In addition, there should be relatively little differentiation of access to rights according to nationality, and strong and enforceable sanctions against discrimination based on ethnicity or race.

Nationality Acquisition

Regarding nationality acquisition, we consider the following indicators:

1. Number of years of residence before naturalization can be requested
2. Welfare and social security dependence as an obstacle to naturalization
3. Automatic attribution or facilitated naturalization for the second generation
4. Allowance of double nationality
5. Privileged access to nationality for co-ethnics
6. Actual naturalization rates

Switzerland is the extreme case when it comes to the number of years an immigrant has to wait before naturalization can be requested.[2] Federal law requires a residence period of at least twelve years, but since naturalization is a conjoint prerogative of the cantons and local government, they can stipulate additional waiting times. In liberal cantons such as Zurich and Geneva, the local residence time required is two years, but in many cantons, it is considerably more. The extreme cases are the cantons of Uri and Nidwalden, which require fifteen and twelve years respectively of local residence. Particularly if a migrant has moved between communes and/or cantons during his stay in Switzerland, the total waiting time required for naturalization may therefore be considerably more than the minimum of twelve years required by federal law. France, the United Kingdom, and the Netherlands stand at the other extreme and require a residence period of only five years. Germany is in an intermediary position. Since the liberalization of the Nationality Law in 2000, a minimum of eight years of residence is required, as against ten years before that date.[3]

Besides residence times, the granting of nationality depends on the fulfillment by the applicant of a number of additional criteria. We will address cultural requirements as part of the cultural rights dimension of citizenship later. Here we are concerned with an applicant's social and economic situation as a possible barrier to naturalization. Particularly, dependence on social security or welfare benefits may in some countries be a reason to refuse naturalization. This is generally the case in Switzerland, as well as in Germany. In the latter country, however, there has been a liberalization with the new Nationality Law of 2000, which stipulates that dependence on welfare or unemployment benefits is not a hindrance for naturalization if the applicant "cannot be held personally responsible" for this situation. In France, Britain, and the Netherlands, no such restrictions apply at all.[4]

In all five countries, there are special, less restrictive provisions for the acquisition of nationality by the second generation of immigrants. The relatively limited variant in Switzerland (in force since 1952) stipulates that, in calculating the twelve years of minimum residence, years spent in Switzerland between the ages of ten and twenty count double. Along similar lines, the modified German Foreigners Law of 1991 reduced the residence requirements for second-generation immigrants born or educated in Germany to eight years. The 2000 revision of the Nationality Law brought a radical change in the form of the automatic acquisition of German citizenship for children born in Germany to foreign parents if one of the latter has lived at least eight years in Germany or has held a permanent residence permit for at least three years. However, this attribution of nationality according to the territorial principle is conditional in the sense that if the child also obtains the parents' nationality, he or she must give it up before reaching the age of twenty-three or the German nationality will automatically be withdrawn. In the Netherlands, since 1984, foreign children born in the country have an "option right," which makes it possible for them to obtain Dutch citizenship between the ages of eighteen and twenty-five by "unilateral declaration" with no further conditions attached. In addition, the Dutch nationality can be automatically acquired at birth by way of the so-called double jus soli, which applies to children born in the Netherlands to at least one parent who is also born in the Netherlands. The French system is again different. Next to a double jus soli as in the Netherlands, children born to foreign parents in France automatically become French nationals at majority, unless they explicitly inform the authorities that they do not want to.[5] Britain, finally, has for a long time had a full form of jus soli, by which nationality is automatically and unconditionally—apart from the fact that at least one parent is a legal resident—attributed at birth to children born on British soil.

The requirement to give up one's old nationality can be an important material—e.g., because of the loss of inheritance or land ownership rights in the country of origin—as well as psychological barrier on the side of potential applicants for naturalization. In Germany and the Netherlands, this requirement has been significantly relaxed since the early 1990s. Exceptions are made on a relatively massive scale if significant material disadvantages would arise for the applicant.[6] Switzerland has gone further and has passed a law formally allowing double nationality in 1992. In France and the United Kingdom, naturalization has not been subject to the requirement to give up one's original nationality at any time during our period of reference. This would have been difficult to legitimate in these countries, which by way of their automatic attribution of citizenship to children born in the country inevitably create many dual nationals (presuming that most of these children also obtain their parents' nationality by descent).

Ethnic conceptions of citizenship are not only characterized by high barriers to naturalization, but may also include special regulations for foreign nationals who are seen as co-ethnics. In Germany, ethnic Germans—many of whom have never been German citizens and whose ancestors had left the territory of what is now Germany as much as eight hundred years ago—from Eastern Europe, the Balkans, and Central Asia are defined constitutionally as part of the German people *(deutsche Volkszugehörige)*. Until 1993, they had an unrestricted right to the German nationality, which was automatically attributed to them upon arrival in Germany.[7] This right was so unconditional that German authorities were not even allowed to refuse naturalization to German ethnics who had committed serious crimes or could be considered a threat to national security (Hailbronner and Renner 1998). According to the constitution, "members of the German people are those who have committed themselves to German culture *(Deutschtum)* in their homelands, insofar as this commitment is confirmed by certain facts such as descent, language, upbringing or culture." De facto, until 1993 descent was a necessary and sufficient condition, resulting in the influx of many of these so-called resettlers *(Aussiedler)* who spoke no German at all and were culturally Russians, Poles, or Romanians rather than Germans. Since 1993, the rights to residence and citizenship of these ethnic Germans have been significantly reduced. By administrative decree the right applies now—with very few exceptions—only to ethnic Germans from the former Soviet Union. Moreover, the right no longer applies to children born to German ethnics after 1993, which implies that this way of obtaining German citizenship will ultimately disappear since it can no longer be inherited.

To understand why Germany stuck to such an extreme form of ethnically privileged access to citizenship, one must refer to the special conditions of post–World War II territory losses, actual persecution and expulsions of ethnic Germans in Eastern Europe until deep into the 1950s, as well as the division of the country into two competing states, which all stood in the way of a civic-territorial conception of the nation. The disappearance of these reasons—plus the never-intended large numbers of ethnic Germans who after the fall of the Iron Curtain actually made use of their rights—explains why ethnically privileged immigration was soon curtailed after unification (see further, Joppke 1999; Koopmans 1999). In this reduced form of a temporally limited solution to a specific historical problem, *Aussiedler* access to German citizenship resembles the patriality clause that was introduced in the British Immigration Act of 1971. This clause regulates residence rights—and by way of the British Nationality Act of 1981 also access to citizenship—for residents of the Overseas Territories and former colonies. It grants the rights to abode and full British citizenship only to (former) colonial subjects who have at least one grandparent born in the United Kingdom. The other three countries have no special provisions for the naturalization of co-ethnics. This absence, it should be noted, is not self-evident, since apart from Germany and Britain, many other countries have such special provisions. The most famous example is perhaps Israel's "law of return," which gives Jews all over the world the right to Israeli citizenship. Other examples are Greece, which has legislation similar to Germany for the Greek diaspora (e.g., in the former Soviet Union), or Spain, which grants easier access to citizenship for immigrants from the former Latin American colonies.[8]

Finally, we need to look at the actual naturalization rates. Thus far, we have discussed formal rules and requirements, but there are many informal factors that may affect access of migrants to the nationality of the host country. For instance, the naturalization procedures in Germany have a notorious reputation for their bureaucratic complexity and long duration. Contrary to such uninviting informal procedures, other countries such as the Netherlands have followed a very proactive approach toward naturalization, among other things by actively inviting immigrants by way of various sorts of publicity campaigns to make use of their right to be naturalized. Such informal factors are difficult to pinpoint, but they may have an important impact on the actual use that is made of formally available rights. If this is true, such impacts should be visible in the naturalization rates, which are shown in Table 1.[9]

A first thing to note in the table is the rise in the naturalization rate over the course of time—particularly since 1990—in all five countries. This is only partly a result of the liberalizations in naturalization laws, as suggested by the fact that Britain and France, whose nationality legislations have not changed significantly, also show important increases over time. More important, the rise reflects the fact that a growing number of immigrants have been in the country for an extended period or belong to the second or even third generations. As a result, increasing numbers of immigrants not only fulfill the formal naturalization criteria but also regard themselves as permanent residents.

Beyond these similar trends, there are consistent differences in the levels of naturalization between the countries. Germany and Switzerland stand out as the countries with the lowest naturalization rates. Especially for Germany, these figures testify to the importance of informal barriers to

Table 1. Naturalization rates (naturalizations as a percentage of the foreign population)

Country	1980 (%)	1990 (%)	2000 (%)
Germany	0.3	0.4	2.5
France	1.2	1.5	4.6
Britain	2.1	3.3	3.6
Netherlands	3.5	1.8	7.1
Switzerland	1.0	0.8	2.0

Note: The German figures exclude naturalizations of ethnic Germans; the figures for Britain and France exclude acquisition by way of the jus soli (likewise the Dutch figures are exclusive of acquisitions by way of the double jus soli, but these numbers are very small). The 1980 and 1990 figures were computed on the basis of Lederer (1997, 76–77, 36–37). The 2000 figures have been taken directly from the various national statistics offices.

naturalization in the form of uninvitingly long and complex procedures. For 2000, the automatic acquisition of German nationality at birth are included in the figure, and additionally there was the temporary possibility to include children less than ten years of age under this rule. Nonetheless, the naturalization rate in 2000 is still very modest (and has decreased considerably in subsequent years). The Netherlands stand at the other extreme, with very high naturalization rates, particularly in the 1990s. The 2000 figure, which is very high compared to the other countries, actually represents a significant decline in the rate, which peaked in 1996, when in one year over 11 percent of all foreign residents were naturalized.[10]

We can now bring the results for nationality acquisition together. Here, as well as in the rest of this chapter, we summarize each indicator in a relatively simple and standardized way. The country (or countries) that is closest to the ethnic pole receives a score of –1.00 for that indicator; the country (or countries) closest to the civic-territorial pole receives a score of 1.00. A country that is situated in between these extremes scores 0. While for some indicators this is a relatively crude procedure that cannot reflect all the detail of cross-national differences, it allows us to measure our indicators in a similar way and thus to derive from the ensemble of the individual indicators a general measurement of migrants' access to citizenship rights.[11] Table 2 presents the scores given to each country for the three reference years for each of the six indicators of nationality acquisition, as well as the average of these scores. The table shows that Switzerland has been relatively stably positioned close to the ethnic pole of the continuum, with a slight move into the direction of a more civic-territorial conception as a result of

Table 2. Summary scores for indicators of nationality acquisition

Indicators	Netherlands			Britain			France			Germany			Switzerland		
	1980	1990	2002	1980	1990	2002	1980	1990	2002	1980	1990	2002	1980	1990	2002
Years of residence	1	1	1	1	1	1	1	1	1	0	0	0	-1	-1	-1
Welfare dependence	1	1	1	1	1	1	1	1	1	-1	-1	0	-1	-1	-1
Facilitated access for second generation[a]	-1	0	0	1	1	1	1	1	1	-1	-1	1	-1	-1	-1
Double nationality	-1	-1	0	1	1	1	1	1	1	-1	-1	0	-1	-1	1
(Absence of) Special rights for co-ethnics	1	1	1	0	0	0	1	1	1	-1	-1	0	1	1	1
Naturalization rate[b]	1	1	1	0	0	0	0	0	0	-1	-1	-1	-1	-1	-1
Average score	0.33	0.50	0.67	0.67	0.67	0.67	0.84	0.84	0.84	-0.84	-0.84	0.00	-0.84	-0.84	-0.66

[a] A score of +1.00 was given to all countries that attribute citizenship automatically to children born in the country, either at birth or at majority. The Dutch option rule is taken as the intermediary case and scores 0, while all other regimes, which remain limited to reduced waiting times for naturalization of the second generation, receive a score of -1.00. Obviously, this way of scoring does not allow the expression of the fine differences between the French, German, and British systems of jus soli.

[b] We have not differentiated the naturalization rate scores by year because the temporal trend is similar in all countries and only partly a result of changes in naturalization rules and procedures. The scores are therefore based on the differences in levels between the countries across all three points in time.

the acceptance of double nationality since 1992. Germany, originally in the same position as Switzerland, has recently made a much more radical move into that direction as a result of the overhaul of the Nationality Law in 2000. As a result, Germany now finds itself right at the center of the continuum, halfway between an ethnic and a civic-territorial regime of nationality acquisition. The Netherlands have also seen relatively important changes over time. The introduction of the optional right by declaration for children of foreign parents born in the Netherlands, the high level of toleration in practice for double nationality, and the very high naturalization rates have brought the Netherlands close to France and Britain. In the latter two countries, no significant changes have occurred during our period of reference—they have stayed close to the civic-territorial pole.[12]

Citizenship Rights for Foreign Nationals

A few efforts to map cross-national differences in access to rights for foreign residents have already been made (e.g., Cinar, Hofinger, and Waldrauch 1995; Groenendijk, Guild, and Barzilay 2000; Waldrauch and Hofinger 1997; Guiraudon 2000; Davy 2001). These studies show that there are many similarities in foreigners' access to different types of civic and social rights (Groenendijk and Guild 2001; Mahning and Wimmer 2000). The differences that exist tend to be highly complex because of the relation of rights to residence duration, variation across different categories of immigrants, and a wide variety of different types of residence permit. It is therefore very difficult to determine whether a country gives easier access to a particular right than other countries.[13] We will therefore here consider only two relatively clear-cut cases in which there are substantial differences among our five countries:

1. The conditions for expulsion of foreign residents
2. Voting rights for foreign residents

One of the few areas where a large difference in civic rights between nationals and nonnationals remains is that nationals cannot be expelled under any circumstance. The residence permits of foreign nationals can, however, under certain circumstances be terminated (or not renewed), which may in turn lead to the foreigner's expulsion.[14] This may hold even for those who hold a so-called permanent residence permit, as well as for those born or raised in the host country if they have not automatically become nationals at birth.[15] Expulsion regulations are interesting not only because they radically touch on (the termination of) migrants' citizenship rights, but also because the grounds for expulsion specify limits to the access to other kinds of civic and social rights. For instance, even if social welfare benefits are in principle available to nationals and nonnationals alike—as is the case for most migrants in most countries—this can hardly be called a right if at the same time dependence on social welfare is a potential ground for expulsion. The same is true for the freedom to associate or to demonstrate if participation in certain kinds of political activity may entail the risk of expulsion.

In Switzerland, foreigners, including those with a permanent resident status, may be expelled under a wide range of conditions, including being a threat to public order and national security, prolonged dependence on social welfare benefits, "serious offenses against the public mores," any conviction for criminal offenses, and "living in indecency or idleness." Additionally— and relevant for the cultural dimension of citizenship that we will discuss later—the Foreigners' Law (ANAG) specifies unwillingness to adapt to the Swiss ways as a possible ground for expulsion of a foreigner "if his entire behavior and his acts permit the conclusion that he does not want to adapt to the established order of the country that offers him hospitality" (Slominski 2001, 727, 774–75).

Germany's expulsion rules are less severe. Temporary residence permits can be terminated or not renewed if the foreigner has insufficient independent means of subsistence or has committed offenses that need not necessarily be punishable by criminal law. Included are, for instance, prostitution and prolonged homelessness. With a permanent residence permit—available after five years of residence if none of the above reasons for refusing apply and if the applicant has a basic knowledge of German—the foreigner is better protected against expulsion. Foreigners belonging to this category can only be expelled for criminal sentences of more than two years in prison or—irrespective of the severity of the sentence—for drug trafficking or politically motivated public violence. The latter condition was added after a series of violent demonstrations by Kurdish PKK adherents in the mid-1990s. Being arrested at a banned demonstration that has turned violent may under these stipulations be a sufficient reason for expulsion. Expulsion orders may be issued to minors of fifteen years and older, as became clear in the notorious Mehmet affair in which a minor, German-born serial offender was expelled to Turkey.

A wide range of discretion for the authorities characterizes the British expulsion regime, like the system of permits to which it is linked. To begin with, foreigners who come to Britain and do not fall into a privileged category, such as recognized asylum seekers or children and spouses of permanent residents, have no entitlement to obtain the British equivalent of a permanent residence permit, the Indefinite Leave to Remain (ILR). This is at the discretion of the authorities, although as a rule the ILR is granted after ten years of legal residence or fourteen years of residence of any legality—unless the applicant has a criminal record. ILR, however, does not offer complete protection against expulsion, which may be ordered by the courts in case of criminal activity or by the secretary of state if deportation is deemed in the public interest. Dependence on public benefits may also be a reason for expulsion, regardless of the type of residence permit (Cinar, Hofinger, and Waldrauch 1995, 35).

According to the new Dutch Aliens Act of 2000, a resident foreigner may be expelled because of a threat to national security, at the minister's discretion if it is necessary for the public interest, and in case of insufficient independent means of subsistence (i.e., dependence on social welfare benefits). The latter condition, however, no longer applies to foreigners who have lived at least ten years in the Netherlands. A further reason for expulsion may be conviction for a crime that has a maximum punishment of more than two years (even if the actual sentence was lower). However, with a longer period of residence the barriers for expulsion because of a criminal conviction become progressively higher. With ten years of residence, foreigners can be expelled only for crimes punishable with at least five years in prison; with fifteen years of residence, eight years in prison. Second-generation foreigners who reside in the country for at least fifteen years cannot be expelled at all. Other foreigners reach the same full protection against expulsion after twenty years of residence.

A somewhat comparable regime applies in France, although dependence on public assistance cannot be a reason for expulsion here. However, convictions punishable with at least one year in prison may lead to expulsion, as may certain crimes such as drug trafficking or breaches of the Labor Code regardless of the level of punishment. Several categories of foreigners, however, enjoy better protection against expulsion. Foreigners who have legally lived in France for ten years, parents of children who have acquired the French nationality, and those married to a French citizen can be expelled only for crimes punishable by at least five years in prison. Persons who have lived in France since they were ten years old can be expelled only if they constitute a serious threat to national security. Minors below the age of eighteen cannot be expelled under any circumstance. A detail, which is interesting in the light of our discussion later about the cultural dimension of citizenship, is that polygamy may in France be a reason for the nonrenewal or termination of a residence permit.

All in all, France and the Netherlands offer the widest protection of resident foreigners against expulsion, especially by increasing the barriers for expulsion with the length of stay and offering long-term residents and second-generation foreigners complete or virtually complete protection against expulsion. Switzerland is situated at the other extreme. It stipulates a long list of conditions that may lead to expulsion and offers no improved protection for long-term residents or the second generation. Germany and the United Kingdom are situated in between. Germany differs from Switzerland especially in offering a higher level of protection for long-term residents. In the United Kingdom, the security of residence of foreigners is negatively affected by the fact that there are few enforceable entitlements and much is at the discretion of the authorities.

The second indicator of citizenship rights for foreigners is more easily dealt with. No European country has extended the right to vote on the national level to all foreign residents.[16] However, in the United Kingdom this right is available to resident citizens of countries with which Britain has a historical (colonial) relationship, i.e., the Commonwealth countries, as well as Ireland (Davy and Cinar 2001, 852–53). Since this includes many countries that are important sources of migration to Britain (India, Bangladesh, Pakistan, many Caribbean and African countries), this regulation extends the right to vote on the national level to about 50 percent of the foreigners living in the United Kingdom. The Netherlands have also made advances toward extending voting rights to foreign citizens. Since 1985, all foreigners who have lived at least five years in the Netherlands have voting rights on the municipal level, both active and passive. In three of the twenty-four Swiss cantons—Neuchâtel (since 1848), Jura (since 1979), and Appenzell Ausserrhoden (since 1995)—voting rights have been extended to foreigners on the local level. However, only a very small percentage of the Swiss foreign population lives in these three cantons.

At the end of the 1980s, three northern German federal states tried to introduce local voting rights for foreigners along the lines of the Dutch model. However, the Federal Constitutional Court ruled that such a regulation would be unconstitutional. The passage in the constitution where it says that "all power derives from the people" *(Alle Macht geht vom Volk aus)* was interpreted by the Court in a restrictive way in the sense that only German nationals could be considered as part of "the people." Strangely enough, only a few years later the Court did endorse the extension of local voting rights to citizens from other EU member states in the context of the implementation of the Maastricht Treaty of 1992, which also led to the extension of local (and European-level) voting rights to EU citizens in France, the United Kingdom, and the Netherlands. Even though some countries, such as France, have implemented EU voting rights quite reluctantly, they do benefit a significant share of the immigrant population and relativize to some extent the coupling of political rights to national citizenship.

Table 3 summarizes the results for the extension of citizenship rights to foreign nationals. The cross-national differences displayed in the table are very similar to those we found earlier for nationality acquisition. Generally speaking, countries that are reluctant to make immigrants into nationals are also those that differentiate most between the rights of foreigners and of nationals. The only difference between the country rank orders in Tables 2 and 3 is that the Netherlands surpass Britain and France when it comes to rights for foreigners.

Antidiscrimination Rights

All five countries subscribe to the basic principle of equal treatment regardless of race, ethnicity, or national origin. With the exception of the United Kingdom, which does not have a basic law, this principle forms part of the constitution. However, the practical value of such constitutional articles is limited. They are declarations of intent rather than providing concrete legal opportunities for those who feel racially harassed or discriminated against. Insofar as they have binding power, they apply only to the relation between the state and the citizenry and not to racial abuse or defamation by non-state actors. The latter type of offenses are covered by the 1965 International Convention on the Elimination of All Forms of Racial Discrimination (ICERD). All five countries are signatories to this treaty—four of them did so at an early stage, between 1969 and 1971, and Switzerland finally followed suit in 1994. Like constitutional statements on equal treatment, this convention has little practical impact as long as its provisions have not been integrated into national penal law. We therefore start our investigation of antidiscrimination rights with the implementation of the minimum ICERD provisions against incitement to racial hatred and racial abuse in national law, and consider three additional indicators:

1. Implementation of basic ICERD provisions in national criminal law
2. Inclusion of discrimination next to explicit racism in such laws
3. Existence of specific antidiscrimination legislation in civil law
4. Establishment by the state of antidiscrimination bodies with investigative and/or decision-making powers

In all five countries, provisions against incitement to racial hatred (or *Volksverhetzung* as it is called in Germany), defamation, and racial abuse were implemented in national criminal law soon after the ratification of the convention. Such laws can be effective instruments against explicitly racist

Table 3. Summary scores for indicators of citizenship rights for foreign nationals

Indicators	Netherlands			Britain			France			Germany			Switzerland		
	1980	1990	2002	1980	1990	2002	1980	1990	2002	1980	1990	2002	1980	1990	2002
Protection against expulsion[a]	1	1	1	0	0	0	1	1	1	0	0	0	−1	−1	−1
Voting rights[b]	−1	1	1	1	1	1	−1	−1	0	−1	−1	0	−1	−1	−1
Average score	0.00	1.00	1.00	0.50	0.50	0.50	0.00	0.00	0.50	−0.50	−0.50	0.00	−1.00	−1.00	−1.00

[a]For protection against expulsion, we were not able to find reliable and comparable information for the situations in 1980 and 1990. We have therefore given the same (2002) score to all three measurement years.

[b]Since twenty-one out of twenty-four Swiss cantons do not give foreigners local voting rights, and the three where they have such rights do not include the cantons where many foreigners live (e.g., Zurich, Geneva, Bern, Basel), we have given Switzerland a score of −1. The extension of voting rights to EU citizens in the other four countries affects a much larger part of the immigrant population and is not limited to a few localities. On this basis, France and Germany receive a score of 0 for 2002.

or anti-Semitic statements and acts and have, particularly in Germany, frequently been used against radical-right spokespersons, parties, and organizations (Fennema 2000). However, they do not cover discrimination when it is not accompanied by explicit statements of racist intent. Discrimination may seriously affect immigrants' access to employment, housing, or leisure activities (e.g., bars and clubs). Only Germany has not included such forms of discrimination in its penal code. By contrast, in the Swiss article 261-bis, introduced in 1995, any "refusal of a service meant for public usage to a person or group of persons on the basis of their racial, ethnic, or religious appearance" is made unlawful. This is similar to article 225 of the French penal code, which in addition refers to discrimination related to employment and economic activities. In the light of the cultural difference dimension of citizenship, it is noteworthy that the subsequent article 226 bans the registration of people's racial, ethnic, or religious background.

While antidiscrimination provisions in criminal law are important, they tend to be effective only against blatant forms of racism and discrimination. Moreover, the interest of victims of discrimination is often not so much to get the perpetrator convicted, but to get access to the positions, goods, or services that were denied on discriminatory grounds or to receive compensation for such denial. Therefore, additional antidiscrimination provisions in civil law provide a more effective protection against discrimination. Encompassing antidiscrimination legislation in civil law exists only in Britain and the Netherlands. In Britain, the first such legislation was already implemented in 1965 with the Race Relations Act (RRA), which has been revised and extended several times since then. Drawing partially on the British example, the Netherlands introduced a Law on Equal Treatment (Algemene wet gelijke behandeling, AWGB) in 1994. Both the RRA and the AWGB contain detailed stipulations against discrimination in a wide range of social spheres. An important distinction between the two is that the British RRA covers discrimination only on the basis of race or ethnicity, whereas the AWGB extends to discrimination on the basis of religion also (as well as a range of other bases such as gender and sexual preference that need not concern us here).

In France, the Labor Code offers additional protection against discrimination in the field of employment, especially since November 2001 when the antidiscrimination provisions in article 122 were extended and enforcement provisions improved. Thus, France responded to the EU directive against discrimination of June 2001, which requires the member states to implement civil law provisions against discrimination on a range of grounds including race and ethnicity. Compared to the civil antidiscrimination legislation in Britain and the Netherlands, the French revision of the Labor Code remains limited in scope because it covers only employment, professional training, and related labor issues, and not areas such as education, housing, and leisure activities.[17] The EU antidiscrimination directive is also relevant for Germany as it required member states to implement it by December 2003. Although the German government has been considering an anti-discrimination law, there is as yet no concrete proposal.

Our final indicator is whether the state has set up special offices to deal with discrimination complaints and/or to undertake investigations into dis-criminatory practices. Because the victims of discrimination tend to have few resources, such offices, which exist in Britain and the Netherlands, can contribute significantly to the effectiveness of antidiscrimination legislation. The British Commission for Racial Equality (CRE) has statutory powers to investigate possible discriminatory practices in private and public institu-tions. It can require the production of documents and oral evidence and can issue a notice to organizations found guilty of unlawful discrimina-tions. To enforce these notices—which are not legally binding—the CRE may put the case before a civil court (Niessen and Chopin 2002, report on the United Kingdom, 28). The Dutch Commission for Equal Treatment (Commissie gelijke behandeling, CGB) does not have such investigative powers, but unlike the CRE it is authorized to decide on discrimination complaints. While its decisions do not have binding power, they carry great weight and are usually followed by the parties involved. If this is not the case, both the plaintiff and the CGB can pass the case on to the civil courts, which will only in exceptional cases deviate from the CGB's recommendations.

In 1999 France set up Commissions for Access to Citizenship (Com-missions d'accès à la citoyenneté, CODAC) in the various *départements,* which have very similar aims to those of the CRE and the CGB. However, the powers of these commissions are much more limited than those of their British and Dutch counterparts. They are authorized to receive complaints about discrimination and to pass these on to the legal authorities for in-vestigation or prosecution (Niessen and Chopin 2002, report on France, 37). Switzerland has recently set up a Federal Commission against Racism (Eidgenössiche Kommission gegen Rassismus) and a Service to Combat Rac-ism (Fachstelle für Rassismusbekämpfung). However, these organizations' tasks are limited to engaging in the public debate, advising the government, and funding antiracist initiatives. They have no formal powers to deal with antidiscrimination complaints or to undertake investigations. In Germany, there are no state-sponsored offices dealing with discrimination issues at all.

Table 4 brings together the four indicators of antidiscrimination rights. The table shows that such rights are most developed in Britain and recently also in the Netherlands. Signing up to the ICERD only in 1994, Switzerland used to have no specific legislation against racism and discrimination, but has recently made important advances and now surpasses Germany, whose legislation still covers only the most extreme and explicit forms of racism and fails to comply with the EU antidiscrimination directive. France is situated in between. The antidiscrimination provisions in the Penal Code and the Labor Code are quite strong, and progress toward an effective implementation has been made, but France still lacks encompassing antidiscrimination provisions in civil law.

Summary Results for the Individual Equality Dimension of Citizenship

We can now bring together the results for the three aspects of the individual equality dimension of citizenship that we distinguished: nationality acquisition, rights for resident foreigners, and antidiscrimination rights. Table 5 reproduces the average scores from Tables 2, 3, and 4, and in addition shows the resulting overall score for the individual equality dimension. Because of its important impacts on the two other aspects, we have given nationality acquisition a double weight in computing the overall average. First, the importance of rights for resident foreigners depends considerably on the accessibility of the nationality. In Switzerland and Germany, most immigrants, even if they are long-time residents or born in the country, fall under the restrictive regime of aliens legislation because, as a result of the difficult access to the nationality, they have remained foreign citizens. In the other three countries, only about half of the population of immigrant origin fall under this restrictive regime, and very few long-term residents, and in France and Britain none of those born in the country do so. Second, nationality acquisition does away with an important source of discrimination that is not covered by antidiscrimination legislation. Even in countries such as the Netherlands and Britain, access to certain positions, particularly public offices and professions such as the police or the judiciary, is barred to nonnationals.

The results show significant and consistent cross-national differences, as well as important changes over the course of the period 1980–2002. These temporal changes all go in one direction—in spite of some ultimately unsuccessful attempts to reverse the trend, e.g., in France—away from an ethnic conception of citizenship and toward the extension of citizenship rights on a more civic-territorial basis. The only country where there have been no significant changes over time is the United Kingdom, which has occupied a position close to the civic-territorial pole from the beginning. France is similar to Britain in many ways but has weaker antidiscrimination legislation.

Table 4. Summary Scores for indicators of antidiscrimination rights

Indicators	Netherlands			Britain			France			Germany			Switzerland		
	1980	1990	2002	1980	1990	2002	1980	1990	2002	1980	1990	2002	1980	1990	2002
Provisions against racial hatred in penal code	1	1	1	1	1	1	1	1	1	1	1	1	-1	-1	1
Provisions against discrimination in penal code	1	1	1	1	1	1	1	1	1	-1	-1	-1	-1	-1	1
Special antidiscrimination law in civil code	-1	-1	1	1	1	1	-1	-1	0	-1	-1	-1	-1	-1	-1
State offices dealing with discrimination complaints	-1	-1	1	1	1	1	-1	-1	0	-1	-1	-1	-1	-1	-1
Average score	0.00	0.00	1.00	1.00	1.00	1.00	0.00	0.00	0.50	-0.75	-0.75	-0.75	-1.00	-1.00	0.00

Table 5. Overall summary scores for the individual equality dimension of citizenship

Aspects	Netherlands			Britain			France			Germany			Switzerland		
	1980	1990	2002	1980	1990	2002	1980	1990	2002	1980	1990	2002	1980	1990	2002
Nationality acquisition	0.33	0.50	0.67	0.67	0.67	0.67	0.84	0.84	0.84	-0.84	-0.84	0.00	-0.84	-0.84	-0.66
Rights for foreign residents	0.00	1.00	1.00	0.50	0.50	0.50	0.00	0.00	0.50	-0.50	-0.50	0.00	-1.00	-1.00	-1.00
Antidiscrimination rights	0.00	0.00	1.00	1.00	1.00	1.00	0.00	0.00	0.50	-0.75	-0.75	-0.75	-1.00	-1.00	0.00
Average score	0.17	0.50	0.83	0.71	0.71	0.71	0.42	0.42	0.67	-0.73	-0.73	-0.19	-0.92	-0.92	-0.58

The Netherlands originally occupied an ambiguous position, combining ethnic and civic-territorial elements. However, by liberalizing nationality law and introducing local voting rights for foreign residents and strong antidiscrimination legislation, the Netherlands have surpassed Great Britain and are presently situated firmly at the civic-territorial end. Until the early 1990s, Germany and Switzerland were typical representatives of an ethnic conception of citizenship. Even with some recent changes, Switzerland is still clearly situated at the ethnic end of the continuum. After the recent liberalization of its nationality law, Germany now occupies a more ambiguous position.

The Second Dimension of Citizenship: Cultural Difference

While the first dimension of citizenship refers to the equal treatment of the residents on the territory of a state *regardless* of their race, ethnicity, religion, nationality, or cultural background, the second concerns *differential* rights based on group membership. Two positions regarding differential rights can be distinguished. First, the majority society may require assimilation to dominant cultural standards. The second, multicultural position is that such a privileging of the majority culture cannot be normatively justified, and therefore measures are necessary to help minority groups to preserve their language, culture, and religion and to combat disadvantages they suffer on the basis of their cultural or religious identity.

The first aspect of this dimension that we will investigate is requirements of cultural assimilation as a precondition for naturalization. We will then consider two aspects of "poly-ethnic rights," which are, according to Kymlicka, "intended to help ethnic groups and religious minorities express their cultural particularity and pride without it hampering their success in the economic and political institutions of the dominant society" (1995a, 31). We find it important to distinguish two types of such rights because they relate differently to the assimilationist and universalist varieties of cultural monism that we identified in the introduction (see Figure 1). Assimilationists will be against any kind of poly-ethnic rights, and multiculturalists will generally be in favor of them. In the universalist philosophy, the state must stick to a position of strict neutrality in relation to the cultural and religious practices of its citizens, neither privileging the culture of the dominant ethnic or religious group nor extending rights or exemptions from duties to minority groups. The universalist position should therefore distinguish between cultural and religious practices outside of public institutions—which the state should tolerate if it is to remain culturally neutral—and the accommodation of cultural differences within public institutions, which it should reject for the same reasons of neutrality. Following this distinction, the second aspect of cultural citizenship that we investigate refers to allowances for religious practices of Muslims outside public institutions. Under the third aspect, we discuss indicators for the degree to which special rights or exemptions are granted to cultural minorities in public institutions such as the education system and public broadcasting. Again, we will refer primarily to the example of Muslims, because this religious minority is relevant in all five countries (unlike, e.g., Hindus or Sikhs), and because most of the recent public controversies over cultural differences in Europe referred to Muslims. Fourth, we look at another type of rights mentioned by Kymlicka (1995b, 31–33), special political representation rights. Here we look at the existence of state-sponsored bodies for the representation of migrant interests on the basis of race, ethnicity, or religion. Fifth and finally, we look at affirmative action programs in the labor market.

Cultural Requirements for Naturalization

A minimum requirement for naturalization in the cultural domain in all five countries is a basic knowledge of the national language (or in the Swiss case, the language of the canton where the applicant lives). We will therefore only look at requirements that go beyond basic language knowledge. Our discussion of cultural naturalization requirements in Britain can then be brief because they are limited to basic knowledge of the English language. The same was true until recently in the Netherlands, where the ability to conduct a simple conversation in Dutch was sufficient. The new Law on Dutch Citizenship, which went into force in 2003, introduces stricter criteria. It includes a formal naturalization test in which the applicant has to demonstrate oral and written knowledge of the Dutch language, as well as of Dutch politics and society. These new naturalization requirements parallel the so-called citizenship courses *(inburgeringscursussen)* that were introduced in 1998 and that newcomers are under certain conditions obliged to follow (although enforcement tends to be lax).

Language proficiency also plays an important role in France. The French civil code specifies that foreigners can only be naturalized if they are "assimilated to French society" (assimilation à la communauté française), especially in the form of sufficient knowledge of the French language. Two further reasons qualify as signs of a "lack of assimilation" (défauts d'assimilation): if the applicant "lives at the margins of the receiving society" or if he practices polygamy. The assimilation requirement is not merely symbolic but constitutes the most frequent ground for the rejection of naturalization applications. The vagueness and suggestiveness of terms such as "assimilation" and "living at the margins of society" leave much room for interpretation by the authorities. The Web page where the Ministry of Justice addresses prospective applicants makes explicit reference to the need to be "well assimilated to the French customs and manners," which is evaluated in a personal interview with the authorities and also takes into account the applicant's conduct and loyalty.[18]

This resembles the cultural requirement in Swiss federal law that stipulates that the applicant must be "familiar with the Swiss ways of life, customs, and manners" (mit den Schweizerischen Lebensgewohnheiten, Sitten und Gebräuchen vertraut). In addition, the applicant must "enjoy a good reputation." As part of the naturalization procedure, the local authorities will conduct an investigation that includes gathering information on the applicant from his employer, neighbors, and other relevant persons in the community. In many towns, the naturalization must be approved at the end of the procedure by a popular vote at a community assembly or a popular referendum. Until the recent liberalization of the Nationality Law, Germany similarly required that applicants demonstrate an "identification with German culture" (Bekenntnis zum deutschen Kulturkreis), a condition that could not be fulfilled, as the naturalization guidelines added, if the applicant was active in an ethnic association. Since 2000, this requirement has been dropped, but at the same time more precise and extensive language criteria were added. The applicant must now have completed at least four years of schooling in Germany or have a certificate from a German language school. Otherwise, the applicant must demonstrate equivalent proficiency during an interview with the naturalization authority. In most federal states, it is sufficient if the applicant is able to converse in German, but in Bavaria a formal written language test must be passed. Besides the language requirement, the new legislation requires, like the new Dutch naturalization rules, knowledge of the political system. Further, the applicant must sign a loyalty statement to the constitution.

We summarize the indicators for the cultural difference dimension similar to those for the individual equality dimension. A score of −1 is given to countries that are closest to the monist-assimilationist pole, a score of +1 to those that are closest to the pluralist-multicultural pole, and a score of 0 for those situated in between. On this basis we arrive at the scores for cultural requirements attached to naturalization as shown in Table 6. A score of 1 was given where there are no cultural requirements beyond basic language knowledge, 0 refers to cases where more extensive language proficiency as well as knowledge of the political system are required, and finally cases that refer to assimilation to or identification with the dominant culture in the sense of ways of life, manners, and customs were scored −1.

Table 6. Summary scores for cultural requirements for naturalization

	Netherlands			Britain			France			Germany			Switzerland		
	1980	1990	2002	1980	1990	2002	1980	1990	2002	1980	1990	2002	1980	1990	2002
Cultural requirements for naturalization	1.00	1.00	0.00	1.00	1.00	1.00	−1.00	−1.00	−1.00	−1.00	−1.00	0.00	−1.00	−1.00	−1.00

Allowances for (Islamic) Religious Practices outside of Public Institutions

Under this aspect, we look at the following three indicators:

1. Allowance of ritual slaughtering of animals according to the Islamic rite
2. Allowance of the Islamic call to prayer in public
3. Provisions for Muslim burials

Regarding the slaughtering of animals according to the Islamic rite, there has been no controversy in any of the five countries about the requirement of cutting the animal's throat and letting it bleed to death. However, most Muslims see it as a religious requirement that the animal may not be stunned before the cut, and this demand has in some countries come into conflict with animal protection laws. In Switzerland, Islamic (and Jewish) slaughtering without stunning the animal is not allowed for this reason. The same was true until recently in Germany for Muslims, although the similar Jewish slaughtering rite was allowed. After a long series of judicial battles, the Federal Constitutional Court finally seemed to have settled the issue in 2002 with its ruling that Muslims also have the right to slaughter animals according to their rite. However, a few months later—partly in reaction to the court ruling—the Bundestag decided to include animal protection in the constitution, thereby creating a new legal situation. At the end of 2002, North-Rhine-Westphalia was the first federal state to restrict Muslims' rights again, allowing Islamic slaughtering only on exceptional grounds, if the requesting party can demonstrate an absolute religious necessity to refrain from stunning the animal. In the Netherlands, slaughtering without stunning has, under certain conditions that would ensure the welfare of the animal (the presence of at least two certified slaughterers and the immobilization of the animal in a special apparatus), been allowed since 1977. In France and Britain, slaughtering without stunning is allowed provided that it takes place in licensed abattoirs.

The Islamic call to prayer *(azan)* has been a subject of controversy everywhere, especially if the call is amplified by a loudspeaker. The first city in Western Europe to allow the (amplified) *azan* every Friday before the main prayer was Leiden in the Netherlands in 1986. Birmingham (1986), Amsterdam (1987), and Düren in Germany (1987) soon followed. In all three countries, the decision is in the hands of the local authorities, and practices may therefore vary greatly from place to place. In Germany, the demands of local mosques have usually been denied (e.g., in Berlin, the city with the largest Muslim community in Germany), although there are quite a few cities, especially in the Ruhr area, that have been more forthcoming to Muslims' demands. The situation in Britain is similar in that, apart from relatively few exceptions, most mosques do not have (or more often do not insist on demanding) the right to publicly call to prayer. In the Netherlands, the practice is more widespread, but—as in most British and German cities where the *azan* is allowed—usually only once a week on Fridays and up to a specified duration and volume. In France and Switzerland, the *azan* is not practiced. Interestingly, there has been comparatively little controversy over the issue, probably because Muslims have refrained from bringing it up given the widespread hostility in these countries against public displays of the Muslim faith.

In French political culture, the principle of *laïcité* plays an important role. It is an outcome of the nineteenth-century struggle between (Catholic) church and state, which resulted in much stronger limitations on the sphere of influence of the churches than in most other countries, coupled with a strict commitment of the state to ensure religious neutrality in the public domain. Less outspokenly, *laïcité* also plays a role in Switzerland, with important variations among the cantons.[19] In both countries, the influence of *laïcité* is visible in the issue of Islamic burials. The Muslim faith requires that Muslims be buried with their faces in the direction of Mecca and in Islamic cemeteries or in clearly separated parts of larger cemeteries. In addition, many Muslims feel that the corpse should be buried in a shroud and without coffin. In France and Switzerland, the demand for separate Muslim graveyards has been the subject of fierce controversy. In the context of the establishment of *laïcité* in the late nineteenth and early twentieth centuries, church cemeteries were taken over by the state in both countries (though in both cases Jews were exempted). The fact that church graveyards were not open to everybody—excluding atheists, other faiths including rival Christian denominations, as well as deviants, such as people who had committed suicide—was seen by the state as unjustified discrimination and against the universalist principle of equality. Muslims' insistence not to be buried among "nonbelievers" is now often seen in the same light, as a sign of intolerance and hostility to the principle of equality. As a result, there are generally no separate sections for Muslims in French and Swiss graveyards, just as there are no separate Protestant or Catholic sections.[20] However, things have been changing recently, and there are now a few cemeteries with separate Muslim grave fields *(carrés musulmans)* in both countries. Because the controversy in France and Switzerland has focused on the right to separate burial, the issue of burial without coffin has hardly been raised yet, and Muslim demands in this regard have thus far not been met. By contrast, in many cities and towns in Germany, the United Kingdom, and the Netherlands, sections of cemeteries have been reserved for Muslims. In Germany and the United Kingdom, most local authorities have not allowed burial without coffin on the grounds of hygiene, although there are important exceptions such as Hamburg and Bradford. In the Netherlands, burial in a shroud has generally been allowed by national law since 1991.

Table 7 summarizes the results for the three indicators of poly-ethnic rights for Muslims outside of public institutions. Switzerland comes out clearly on the assimilationist side, while the Netherlands have moved far toward the multicultural end of the spectrum, meeting most Muslim demands. The other countries are situated in between, but for different reasons. At the outset, Germany was much like Switzerland, but it has granted increasing rights to Muslims in the cultural sphere, although these remain sometimes half-hearted (e.g., in the case of ritual slaughtering) or subject to important local variation (e.g., the call to prayer). The position of France is ambiguous. On the one hand, it fully recognizes ritual slaughtering; on the other, it is reluctant to make concessions regarding the call to prayer and burials. This ambiguity can be understood as a result of the narrow definition the French tend to give to the private sphere, where the expression of cultural difference is allowed. Food requirements are regarded as private affairs, but the call to prayer and Muslims' insistence on separation after death are seen as infringements on the principles of equality and religious neutrality in the public sphere. Local variation is the main reason for the intermediary position of Britain. Some cities with large Muslim populations such as Bradford have implemented multicultural policies much like the Netherlands, but elsewhere the authorities may be much more restrictive in granting rights and exemptions to Muslims.

Cultural Rights and Provisions in Public Institutions

Regarding cultural rights within public institutions, we look at five indicators:[21]

1. State recognition and funding of Islamic schools
2. Islamic religious classes in state schools
3. The right of female teachers to wear the Islamic headscarf *(hijab)*
4. Programs in immigrant languages in public broadcasting
5. Islamic religious programs in public broadcasting

The first three refer to cultural differences in the education system. This is arguably the most important public institution for migrant integration, since education is both crucial to social mobility and the main public instrument of cultural socialization. In view of the influence of *laïcité,* it

Table 7. Summary scores for religious rights outside of public institutions

Indicators	Netherlands			Britain			France			Germany			Switzerland		
	1980	1990	2002	1980	1990	2002	1980	1990	2002	1980	1990	2002	1980	1990	2002
Ritual slaughtering	1	1	1	1	1	1	1	1	1	-1	-1	0	-1	-1	-1
Call to prayer	-1	1	1	-1	0	0	-1	-1	-1	-1	0	0	-1	-1	-1
Burial	0	0	1	0	0	0	-1	-1	0	0	0	0	-1	-1	0
Average score	0.00	0.66	1.00	0.00	0.33	0.33	-0.33	-0.33	0.00	-0.66	-0.33	0.00	-1.00	-1.00	0.66

is no surprise that there are no Islamic primary or secondary schools in France and Switzerland. In Germany, two Islamic primary schools have been recognized by the state, one in Munich (since 1982), and one in Berlin (since 1995). The schools receive some state funding, but not on a par with state schools. Together, they have only a few hundred pupils. In Britain, there are now about a hundred Islamic schools—some of them for boys or girls only—with altogether some ten thousand pupils, but most of these schools are privately funded. Since 1998, four Islamic schools have received so-called grant-maintained status, which entails that the local authorities cover the costs. The Netherlands is the only country where the number of confessional schools is larger than that of state schools. This is a result of the outcome of state-church conflicts in the Netherlands in the early twentieth century, which was the exact opposite of that in France. In the Netherlands, Catholics and Protestants (and by extension all other religious groups) obtained the right to found denominational schools, which are financed by the state on a fully equal basis with state schools. Recently, Muslims have started to make use of these rights, too. In 1989, the first Islamic school was founded, and by 2002 there were thirty-seven (thirty-five primary and two secondary), altogether with more than seven thousand pupils.

Even in Britain and the Netherlands, though, only a small minority of children from Muslim families go to Islamic schools, and the large majority of them are educated in state schools. This leads us to the question of whether Islamic religious classes are offered within the curriculum of state schools. This is not the case in France, since there is no religious education in state schools whatsoever. Religious classes do exist in many cantons in Switzerland. However, in only two towns in the canton of Luzern has this right been extended to Muslims. The situation in Germany is similar in that the various denominations have in principle the right to organize religious classes in state schools, but this right has thus far been granted to Muslims only in Berlin—after a court order and against the local authorities' fierce resistance.[22]

In Britain, we encounter yet another form of church-state relations. This is the only one of our five countries that has an official state church, the Anglican Church of England. As a consequence, the Education Reform Act (1988) states that religious education in British state schools should "reflect the fact that the religious traditions in Great Britain are in the main Christian . . . whilst taking into account the principles and practices of the other principal religions represented in Great Britain." The law also prescribes daily (Anglican Christian) collective worship, from which, however, Muslim children can be exempted. If the majority of children in a school are

Muslim, parents may demand of the local Council on Religious Education (which always includes a representative of the Church of England, but must also include representatives of other locally relevant faiths) to instead hold an Islamic collective worship and install Islamic religious classes. If the council agrees—as they have in cities such as Bradford and Birmingham—the local Education Authority carries the costs. Where Muslim pupils are in a minority, the local authorities can also grant permission to organize Islamic religious education, but the parents or the Muslim community will have to pay for the costs. In the Netherlands, religious education in state schools exists and is used widely by Christian denominations; however, it is up to the local authorities to decide on subsidization of these classes. Only a small minority of state schools have in recent years begun to offer Islamic religious education. In practice, then, the situation in the Netherlands is quite similar to that in Britain.

The right of Muslim women to wear the headscarf, or *hijab,* in public institutions has been a very controversial issue, particularly in France. The well-known *foulard* affair erupted in 1989, when three schoolgirls appeared at a school in Creil insisting on wearing their headscarves. After a long debate and several legal battles, the French parliament in 2004 almost unanimously passed a law banning the wearing of the Islamic headscarf (as well as other "ostentatious" religious symbols) in state schools. Contrary to other countries, there has not been any controversy on the right of female teachers to wear the headscarf, probably because it is regarded as self-evident that a display of religious belonging by a representative of the state in a public institution is unthinkable. In Switzerland, there have been a few controversial cases, particularly one concerning a Muslim primary schoolteacher in Geneva, which went all the way up to the European Court of Human Rights. In 2001 the European Court ruled in favor of the Swiss authorities, who had denied the teacher the right to wear the headscarf on the basis of the principle of religious neutrality. In Germany, the situation is not entirely settled yet. There are about a dozen schools in several states where teachers have been allowed to wear the headscarf. In other cases, however, women wearing headscarves have been refused jobs as teachers. One case went all the way up to the Federal Constitutional Court, which ruled in 2003 that on the basis of existing legislation the wearing of a headscarf is not a legitimate reason to refuse teaching job applicants. However, it also stipulated that the states—who are primarily responsible for education—may introduce new legislation to that effect. About half of the states have decided to introduce such legislation or have already done so. In June 2004, the Federal Administrative Court endorsed a new Baden-Württemberg law, which bans the headscarf (and other ostentatious religious symbols) for teachers but at the same time declares nuns' habits to be "professional dress" that is exempt from the ban. In the Netherlands, there is some ambiguity, too. There are quite a few state schools that refuse teachers who insist on wearing the headscarf—sometimes, it should be noted, on the request of Turkish parents, who see the headscarf as a symbol of a conservative inter-pretation of Islam (in Turkey the headscarf is, as in France, not allowed in schools, either for teachers or for pupils). However, in cases that have come before the courts, the decision has in recent years always been in favor of the headscarf, provided that the woman in question is not religiously biased in her teaching. The Commission for Equal Treatment has consistently ruled that not allowing women to wear headscarves in public institutions consti-tutes a form of unlawful religious discrimination. Even more extreme forms of religious attire have received the commission's backing. In 2000, it ruled in favor of a pupil of a vocational training school who came to classes com-pletely covered in a *chador,* leaving only the eyes visible. In Britain, the *hijab* is generally allowed for teachers and pupils alike and has thus far not been the subject of much controversy.

We now turn to special provisions and rights for ethnic and religious minorities in the public (i.e., state-funded) broadcasting media. We are in-terested here in programs that are clearly differentiated from the normal programming and directed only to specific minority audiences. This can be in the form of programs in immigrant languages, religious programs, or even independent broadcasting organizations or radio and television stations catering to minority groups. While there are many private radio stations in France catering to immigrants, there are no programs in immigrant lan-guages in public radio and television. However, given the context of *laïcité,* it is remarkable that on Sunday mornings, France 2 television and France Culture radio broadcast a half-hour Islamic religious program as part of a series of religious programs that includes Protestant, Orthodox, and Jewish programs and a live broadcast Catholic mass. The Islamic program was in-troduced in 1983 by the Mitterrand government. In Switzerland, there are no Islamic religious programs in public broadcasting, but once a week there is a half-hour program in Turkish and another half hour in ex-Yugoslav lan-guages on public radio DRS 2.

In Germany, a much broader spectrum of radio programs in differ-ent immigrant languages has been offered since the 1960s. These programs make up about 2.4 percent of all airtime on German public radio. In Berlin, an entire public radio station, Radio Multikulti, is devoted to programs for immigrants, many of which are in minority languages. On television, the program *Babylon* was started in 1965 on ARD, the main German public TV channel. Originally, it was broadcast five days a week in Italian, Greek, Spanish, and Turkish. The airtime has been reduced to one hour a week, which a variety of different nationalities and languages have to share. It is important to note that these programs were originally not set up as a form of granting multicultural rights to ethnic minorities but were part of the guest worker philosophy and meant to help foreign workers to retain ties with their homelands, to which they were supposed to eventually return. When it became clear that this was not happening, the foreign-language programs were continued nonetheless, now legitimated with reference to multiculturalism and the right of minorities to retain their cultural identities. The ease with which the legitimation of such programs could shift indicates the affinities between multiculturalism and the segregationist guest worker approach. Both are based on a differentiation of rights and facilities on the basis of cultural background.

In British public radio there is also a range of programs available that cater specifically to minorities. A special version of the BBC World Service for listeners in the United Kingdom broadcasts twenty-four hours a day in Arabic, Persian, and the most important South Asian languages. Immigrants from South Asia are additionally serviced by a special BBC radio station, the Asian Network, which broadcasts in Hindi, Urdu, and four other South Asian languages. The station can be received via digital radio and in the Midlands also via regular AM. On public television, however, there are no programs in minority languages. As in Germany, there are no religious programs catering to Muslims, either on radio or on television. In line with the British race relations' framework's classification of immigrants from the Indian subcontinent, the Asian Network caters to a generic Asian audience that is differentiated by language in some of the programming but not by religion. Regular BBC radio and television do offer religious programs for (Anglican) Christians (e.g., Sunday services), but not for Muslims or any other religious group.

The Netherlands offer by far the widest range of programs catering to minorities, both on radio and on television. The Dutch public media landscape is differently structured than in other countries because concessions for broadcasting are distributed over a wide range of independent broadcasting organizations for different social and religious groups. This is a heritage of the age of pillarization, which was characterized by a segmentation of Dutch society along confessional lines, each group having its own (publicly funded) schools, media, hospitals, welfare organizations, and a wide range of other institutions. Since the mid-1980s, immigrants have made use of this opportunity, too, and there are now independent Muslim and Hindu broadcasting organizations that broadcast a few hours weekly of religious programming on public radio and television. By law, the regular state broadcasting organization NPS is required to devote 20 percent of its television time and 25 percent of radio time to minority target groups. Especially in radio, many of these programs are in immigrant languages. For instance, there is a daily news bulletin on public radio in Turkish, Arabic, and Chinese. On public television, the NPS ran a multilingual children's program in the 2002–3 season that could be watched in Turkish, Arabic, Berber, and Dutch. As in Germany, the origins of these programs in immigrant languages lie in the guest worker period, but they were later continued as part of multicultural programming. On the local level, too, there is a wide range of publicly funded broadcasts for minorities, e.g., the programs made by Multicultural Television Netherlands (MTNL), which produces weekly news programs on local public TV in the large cities in Turkish, Arabic for Moroccans, and Dutch for Surinamese and Antilleans.

After this discussion of the public media, we can summarize the results regarding cultural rights and provisions in public institutions (Table 8). In all five countries, we see a trend—weak in some countries such as Switzerland and France, strong in others such as the Netherlands—toward allowing more space for the expression of cultural differences. However, the rank order among the countries is notably stable over time. Switzerland and France emerge as the countries that allow the least space for the expression of immigrants' cultural difference in public institutions. Germany again shows an important shift over time, moving from a position close to Switzerland to a central position halfway between a monist and a pluralist position. An example of this ambiguity is the place of Islam in the education system, where the situation varies significantly from one federal state to another. Britain again emerges as a moderate variant of multiculturalism, which has been more fully embraced in the Netherlands.

Political Representation Rights

All five countries have advisory bodies or councils sponsored by the state that deal with immigration and integration issues. However, the degree to which these councils qualify as a form of special representation of cultural minorities varies greatly across countries. The Swiss Eidgenössische Ausländerkommission (EKA) certainly does not qualify as such, because most of its members are representatives of Swiss organizations, such as politicians, employers, the police, churches, and labor unions. In 2002, eight of twenty-eight commission members had an ethnic minority background.

Table 8. Summary scores for cultural rights within public institutions

Cultural provisions	Netherlands			Britain			France			Germany			Switzerland		
	1980	1990	2002	1980	1990	2002	1980	1990	2002	1980	1990	2002	1980	1990	2002
Islamic schools	-1	0	1	-1	-1	0	-1	-1	-1	-1	-1	0	-1	-1	-1
Islamic religious education	-1	1	1	-1	1	1	-1	-1	-1	-1	-1	0	-1	-1	0
Headscarf for teachers	0	0	0	1	1	1	-1	-1	-1	-1	-1	0	-1	-1	-1
Public media programs in immigrant languages[a]	1	1	1	0	0	0	-1	-1	-1	1	1	1	0	0	0
Islamic programs in public media	-1	1	1	-1	-1	-1	-1	1	1	-1	-1	-1	-1	-1	-1
Average score	-0.40	0.60	0.80	-0.40	0.00	0.20	-1.00	-0.60	-0.60	-0.60	-0.60	0.00	-0.80	-0.80	-0.60

[a] A score of 1 is obtained when programs in immigrant languages exist on both radio and television, a score of 0 when only on radio.

The same is true for local consultative councils such as those in Geneva and Lausanne. These commissions and councils are more arenas for discussion *about* foreigners than representative bodies *of* foreigners. The same can be said about two important national advisory councils in France, the Fonds d'action pour l'integration et la lutte contre la discrimination (FASILD), and the Haut conseil à l'integration. Both are composed mainly of representatives of general French organizations dealing with immigrants and integration issues, and only a few members represent organizations of immigrants. However, on the local level, for instance in Paris, Grenoble, and Strasbourg, more representative consultative councils have been set up in the last few years. They have emerged as a compensation for non-EU immigrants, who have not profited from the extension of local voting rights to EU citizens. Their members, who are all foreigners or representatives of immigrant associations, are not elected but appointed by the local authorities. A further step toward political representation was taken in 2002 when a national representative council for Muslims, the Conseil français du culte musulman, was set up. The council is modeled on the already existing representative organizations for Christian denominations and the Jewish religion. It consists of representatives of Muslim organizations and important mosques (see Laurence 2003).

The most important advisory bodies in Britain are the Commission for Racial Equality along with its local equivalents, the Racial Equality Councils, as well as the Race Relations Forum that was set up by the national government in 1998. The principle of these advisory bodies is similar to those in Switzerland: they are not representative bodies of immigrants but include a wide spectrum of institutional actors who deal with integration and issues of race relations. However, in contrast to Switzerland, minority groups are more strongly represented so that in practice these bodies function as a lobby for minority interests. In 2002, more than half of the members of the Race Relations Forum and ten out of twelve CRE commissioners (including the chair) had an immigrant background. The members of both bodies are appointed by the government. Germany has a full-blown system of special representation of foreigners on the local level. In about four hundred communities with a sufficiently large number of foreign residents, elections are held parallel to the regular local elections for Foreigners' Advisory Councils (Ausländerbeiräte). These quasi parliaments for foreigners have limited powers, often merely advisory, sometimes with additional rights to be informed and consulted before decisions are made that concern foreigners. In the Netherlands, there is an extensive system of representation of immigrant interests as well, on both the local and national levels. These representative bodies are neither elected, as in Germany, nor appointed by the government, as in Britain, but consist of delegates of ethnic organizations. If we take the national level as an example (representation on the local level tends to be organized along similar lines), there are separate councils for Turks, Moroccans, Surinamese, Antilleans, Moluccans, and "South Europeans." According to the Law on the Consultation of Minorities, there must be a consultative meeting between these bodies and the responsible minister for integration policy at least three times a year. In addition, the minister is obliged to consult them on matters that might concern the group in question. There are similar advisory councils for religious minorities, the Dutch Muslim Council and the Hindu Council of the Netherlands.

We thus arrive at the following scores in Table 9 for this indicator. The Netherlands receive a score of +1 because they have an extensive system of representation both locally and nationally and for both national groups and religious minorities. Germany receives a score of 0 because its representation system for foreigners extends only to the local level. Britain also receives a score of 0 because the two main advisory councils are not nominally representative organizations even though their members are predominantly from an ethnic minority background. In addition, their members are appointed not by ethnic minorities themselves, but by the responsible minister or local authority. Finally, Britain lacks a recognized representative body for Muslims and other religious minorities. Because France now has a representative council for Muslims and local councils for foreigners in some cities, it also receives a score of 0 for the year 2002. Switzerland receives a score of –1 because the advisory councils in this country are largely dominated by representatives of the majority society.

Affirmative Action in the Labor Market

In all five countries, national and local governments have expressed concern about the fact that immigrants and their descendants tend to be concentrated at the bottom of the labor market and have developed policies to improve their labor market opportunities, e.g., by offering language courses and additional schooling. Each of our countries also has policies to combat socioeconomic disadvantages in urban areas where many immigrants live. Such policies, however, create no differential rights on the basis of belonging to an ethnic or racial group. They are geared—like antidiscrimination policies—to create equal opportunities, but do not make group belonging a criterion for access to positions. This is the case, however, with affirmative or positive action schemes. Affirmative action consists of the setting of targets or quotas for the representation of specified ethnic or racial groups in the

Table 9. Summary scores for political representation rights

	Netherlands			Britain			France			Germany			Switzerland		
	1980	1990	2002	1980	1990	2002	1980	1990	2002	1980	1990	2002	1980	1990	2002
Political representation rights	1.00	1.00	1.00	0.00	0.00	0.00	−1.00	−1.00	0.00	0.00	0.00	0.00	−1.00	−1.00	−1.00

workforce of institutions and firms. In the case of the preceding indicators for the cultural dimension of citizenship, the expression and protection of immigrant cultures, religions, and identities were at stake in a very direct way. This is not the case for affirmative action programs. The primary intention of such programs is to promote equal socioeconomic participation. For three reasons we nonetheless consider them as part of the cultural group rights rather than the individual equality dimension of citizenship. First and most important, affirmative action amounts to giving special treatment to persons on the basis of their belonging to a particular racial or ethnic group. In that sense, affirmative action is very different from antidiscrimination legislation, which *sanctions* the making of distinctions on the basis of racial or ethnic criteria. Second, the implementation and evaluation of affirmative action programs requires the classification and registration of individuals as members of particular ethnic and racial groups. Third, the aims of affirmative action programs usually go beyond creating equal opportunities and include the representation of cultural diversity in the workforce of institutions as an aim in itself.

We look separately at affirmative action programs in the public and the private sectors. There is quite a difference between the government as an employer setting itself targets related to the representation of ethnic minorities among its workforce, and the government obliging private firms and organizations to set and meet targets. For France, Switzerland, and Germany, the distinction is irrelevant because these countries do not have any form of affirmative action for immigrant groups, in either the private or the public sector. In France, this is related to the reluctance and—as we saw in the section on antidiscrimination legislation—legal prohibition to register people's ethnic background. From the universalist perspective, such registration runs against the principle that the state is not allowed to make any distinction among its citizens on the basis of ethnicity or religion. Registration is, however, a necessity for affirmative action programs: ethnicity or race must be acknowledged both in the job application process and for the evaluation of targets. In Britain and the Netherlands, there are extensive affirmative action programs in the public sector. In Britain, they have been introduced relatively recently on the national level, but locally they have been prominent since the 1980s. In the Netherlands, the program Ethnic Minorities in the Public Service (Etnische minderheden bij de overheid, EMO) was set up in 1987 and consisted of a set of targets for different parts of the public service. Contrary to Britain, targets refer not to minorities in general but are specified for each ethnic group.

Regarding affirmative action in the private sector, Britain and the

Netherlands diverge more. There are two forms to consider. The first is the so-called contract compliance *(sociaal bestek)*, in which public authorities specify certain social criteria that a contractor who wants to obtain government contracts must meet. Such criteria may include a provision about the percentage of minorities among the contractor's workforce. In the Netherlands, contract compliance has been widely practiced since the mid-1990s, especially in the larger cities. In Britain, the measure was formally outlawed by the Thatcher government's Local Government Act of 1988 and has not been reintroduced since then. However, many local governments unofficially offer preferential treatment to firms who represent cultural diversity and adhere to norms defined by the CRE, but there is no legal basis for this. The second form of affirmative action in the private sector is when the government obliges private organizations to set and meet targets regarding the percentage of minorities in their workforce. There is no legal basis for such programs in Britain, although the threat of scrutinizing by the CRE creates pressures in this direction. In the Netherlands, the Law on the Stimulation of Labor Market Participation of Minorities applied since 1994 (Wet Samen, formerly Wbeaa). This law, which was abolished in 2004, obliged firms with more than thirty-five employees to register and publicize the ethnic background of their employees, to set targets, and to produce a yearly public report to the government on the efforts undertaken to meet them. The law met with resistance among many employers, as well as among some employees who did not want to have their ethnic background registered. Table 10 gives the scores for affirmative action in the public and private sectors, as well as the resulting average scores.

Summary Results for the Cultural Difference Dimension of Citizenship

Table 11 summarizes the results for the cultural difference dimension of citizenship and presents average scores across all indicators. The results show that in Switzerland there have been no great changes along the cultural rights dimension—it has remained close to the assimilationist end of the spectrum. In comparison, assimilation pressures in France are somewhat more moderate, and there is a trend toward limited recognition of cultural difference. The French ideology of republican universalism would lead one to expect toleration of cultural differences outside public institutions and a strict insistence on state neutrality in the public sphere. However, the overt references to customs, manners, and assimilation in the naturalization rules, as well as the refusal to grant Muslims provisions for Islamic burials and the right to publicly call to prayer, show that the public domain is interpreted so widely that basic requirements of Muslims' religious life

Table 10. Summary scores for affirmative action in the labor market

Sectors	Netherlands			Britain			France			Germany			Switzerland		
	1980	1990	2002	1980	1990	2002	1980	1990	2002	1980	1990	2002	1980	1990	2002
Public sector	–1	1	1	1	1	1	–1	–1	–1	–1	–1	–1	–1	–1	–1
Private sector	–1	–1	1	–1	–1	–1	–1	–1	–1	–1	–1	–1	–1	–1	–1
Average score	–1.00	0.00	1.00	–1.00	0.00	0.00	–1.00	–1.00	–1.00	–1.00	–1.00	–1.00	–1.00	–1.00	1.00

Table 11. Overall summary scores for the cultural difference dimension of citizenship

Indicators	Netherlands			Britain			France			Germany			Switzerland		
	1980	1990	2002	1980	1990	2002	1980	1990	2002	1980	1990	2002	1980	1990	2002
Cultural requirements for naturalization	1.00	1.00	1.00	1.00	1.00	1.00	–1.00	–1.00	–1.00	–1.00	–1.00	0.00	–1.00	–1.00	0.00
Religious rights outside public institutions	0.00	0.66	1.00	0.00	0.33	0.33	–0.33	–0.33	0.00	–0.66	–0.33	0.00	–1.00	–1.00	–0.66
Cultural rights in public institutions	–0.40	0.60	0.80	–0.40	0.00	0.20	–1.00	–0.60	–0.60	–0.60	–0.60	0.00	–0.80	–0.80	–0.60
Political representation rights	1.00	1.00	1.00	0.00	0.00	0.00	–1.00	–1.00	0.00	0.00	0.00	0.00	–1.00	–1.00	–1.00
Affirmative action	–1.00	0.00	1.00	–1.00	0.00	0.00	–1.00	–1.00	–1.00	–1.00	–1.00	–1.00	–1.00	–1.00	–1.00
Average score	0.12	0.65	0.76	–0.08	0.27	0.31	–0.87	–0.79	–0.52	–0.65	–0.59	–0.20	–0.96	–0.96	–0.85

are affected. Germany shows important changes over time, from a position close to Switzerland and France at the beginning of the 1980s to a more ambiguous position, with some multicultural and some assimilationist elements, by 2002. As a result of the liberalizations of nationality acquisition, the number of immigrants holding a German passport will substantially increase in the future. This will certainly place the issue of cultural difference higher on the agenda in the future.

Great Britain has also made steps in the direction of a more culturally pluralist conception of citizenship but remains a moderate variant of such a model. Generally, equal opportunity and antidiscrimination policies have stopped short of affirmative action, and the official position of the Church of England as the state church has sometimes stood in the way of extending religious rights to Muslims and other non-Christian faiths. However, there is important local variation in Britain, and certain cities, especially those with large concentrations of Muslims (with Bradford as the most prominent example), have gone much further in granting cultural rights. On the local level, the British situation therefore sometimes resembles that in the Netherlands, which among our five countries has made the strongest advances toward a multicultural conception of citizenship. To an important extent, the extension of multicultural rights to minorities in the Netherlands is based on the heritage of pillarization, which was a form of multiculturalism *avant la lettre,* and was meant to accommodate cultural conflicts between native religious groups. Muslims and other minorities have made use of this available institutional framework to claim their own schools, broadcasting rights, and other cultural provisions. Moreover, the government has taken the conflict resolution tradition from the pillarization era as a blueprint for the integration of immigrants, e.g., through the creation of an ethnic elite of subsidized organizations along ethnic and religious lines with access to the state by way of a corporatist system of advisory councils. More recently, after the electoral landslide victory of the List Pim Fortuyn in 2002, the Netherlands have dismantled some multicultural policies, such as minority language programs and affirmative action in the private sector.

The Two Dimensions Combined

We are now finally able to place our five countries in the conceptual space delineated by the combination of the individual equality and cultural difference dimensions of citizenship. Figure 3 shows the resulting positions for each country at the three points in time, 1980, 1990, and 2002, and allows us to relate them to the ideal-typical models of citizenship distinguished in

Figure 1 in the introduction. We have found no representative among our countries of a segregationist citizenship regime, which is characterized by unequal individual citizenship rights on the basis of ethnicity, race, or religion. Switzerland across the whole period and Germany until the mid-1990s represent the assimilationist conception of citizenship. In such a regime, it is possible for immigrants to become part of the national community and obtain full rights as individuals but only under a strict set of conditions, one of which is the willingness to give up one's original ethnocultural allegiance. The French universalist regime is different in that individual citizenship rights are granted much more easily and unconditionally to the second generation. Britain and the Netherlands are representative of a multicultural conception of citizenship. However, the Dutch version of multiculturalism—especially because it builds on the long tradition of pillarization—is more pronounced and far-reaching than the British variant. This is true not only for the range of rights but also for the basis on which they are granted. In Britain, multicultural rights are linked to the relatively broad and culturally "thin" category of race, whereas in the Netherlands cultural rights can be claimed by a wide variety of ethnic, national, and religious groups.

It is sometimes posited that there is a general trend in Europe—or even worldwide—toward a convergence of conceptions of citizenship (e.g., Groenendijk and Guild 2001). Evaluating our results, one way to approach the question of convergence or divergence is to look at the directions in which countries are moving. In this regard, there is convergence in the sense that all five countries have—to smaller or greater extents—moved in the same direction. All countries—with the exception of the United Kingdom, which was already close to the civic pole—have shifted toward a more civic-territorial conception of citizenship, although the changes have been quite marginal in the case of Switzerland. Similarly, all countries have moved away from the assimilationist pole toward a stronger recognition of cultural rights and differences. Again, the strength of this trend varies greatly among the countries; it is weak in France, and even more so in Switzerland.

The other way to approach the issue is by looking at the range of variation among the countries. In this sense, there are no signs of significant convergence. Along the individual rights dimension the distance in the conceptual space depicted in the figure between the country closest to the ethnic pole (Switzerland) and the country closest to the civic-territorial pole (Britain until 1990 and the Netherlands in 2002) has declined only slightly since 1980. On the cultural dimension, there are by contrast signs of increasing *divergence*. While Britain, and especially the Netherlands, have embarked on the path of multiculturalism (with Germany trailing behind

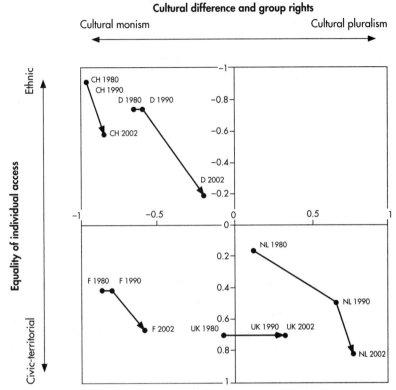

Figure 3. Configurations of citizenship in Switzerland (CH), Germany (D), France (F), the Netherlands (NL), and Britain (UK) in 1980, 1990, and 2002.

them), Switzerland and France have made only very modest concessions to immigrants in the cultural sphere. As a result, the distinction between culturally pluralist and monist approaches to migrant integration was by 2002 much more pronounced than it was in the early 1980s. However, since the events of September 11, 2001, the trend toward differential citizenship seems to have reversed, not only in countries that formerly advocated multiculturalism such as the Netherlands and Britain but also in France.

2

Beyond the Nation-State?
National and Postnational Claims Making

So far we have presented a set of conceptual tools for the cross-national comparative analysis of political contention over migration and ethnic relations. Recently, a growing number of authors have argued that such nation-state-centered approaches are obsolete. Associated with the buzzword "globalization," these critiques claim that we have entered, or are about to enter, a new postnational or transnational era characterized by complex and qualitatively new patterns of multilevel governance in which the nation-state still plays a role, though a drastically reduced one (e.g., Held 1996; Basch, Schiller, and Blanc 1994; Sassen 1998; J. Cohen 1999). This decline of the nation-state's sovereignty is accompanied by a growing importance of supranational and transnational actors, institutions, legal norms, and discourses on the one hand, and increased local autonomy from national constraints on the other.

Given the inherently transnational nature of migration, it is not surprising that this critique of national approaches has been particularly prominent in this field of study. A number of authors have seen a new form of postnational citizenship developing, superimposed on national citizenship and rendering it increasingly irrelevant (Soysal 1994; Jacobson 1996). The primary empirical example on which this conclusion is based is the presence of former guest workers in several Western European countries. Although originally invited on a temporary basis, many of them stayed after the end of the recruitment programs in the wake of the 1973 oil crisis. By way of family reunification and formation, immigration from the sending countries has continued, albeit on a lower level. The receiving countries

74

have extended many civil and social rights and even some limited political rights to these immigrants, even though many of them have not naturalized and are thus not formally citizens of the countries in which they reside.[1] Postnationalists argue that such extensions of rights to immigrants have been imposed on nation-states by their commitments to international law and conventions, pressure from homeland governments, and the growing normative force of international human rights discourses. As a result, "the (territorial) state, if present trends continue, is in the process of becoming a territorial administrative unit of a supranational legal and political order based on human rights" (Jacobson 1996, 133). More specifically for the European context, the process of European integration is often seen as another challenge to the nation-state's sovereignty generally, and in the migration and ethnic relations field in particular (e.g., Meehan 1993; Rosas and Antola 1995; Wiener 1997). The emergence of European-level human rights codes, the enhanced role of the European Court of Justice, and the embryonic European citizenship that has been introduced with the Maastricht Treaty are seen as guaranteeing basic migrant rights and thereby limiting the scope of autonomous action of the member states.

Though resonating with the present popularity of globalization and Europeanization in the scientific community and in public discourse, these perspectives have not gone unchallenged. Criticism has focused both on the extent of the alleged decline in the nation-state's sovereignty and on the degree to which such a shift to a transnational or supranational order has the beneficial effects for migrants and ethnic minorities that postnationalists emphasize. To begin with the latter point, it is striking that, parallel to the literature emphasizing the empowering effects of postnational and European citizenship, there is an equally resonant literature that comes to the opposite conclusion and sees European integration leading to a "Fortress Europe" (e.g., Roche and van Berkel 1997; Miles and Thränhardt 1995; Overbeek 1995). Pointing to agreements such as those of Schengen on border controls and of Dublin on asylum rights, the European project is seen here as curtailing migrant and minority rights by strengthening external border controls, promoting internal security cooperation, and devaluating migrant rights to the level of the lowest common denominator of the participating member states. Similar developments can be observed in other contexts of intergovernmental cooperation on migration issues, such as in the case of NAFTA. The high hopes for improving migrant rights that some people place in European citizenship presently seem to lack any foundation. According to the provisions of the Maastricht Treaty, European citizenship is fully derivative of national citizenship in one of the member states.

Similarly, the abolition of most barriers in the way of freedom of movement, settlement, and seeking employment within the European Union applies only to nationals of member states (Hailbronner 1995, 194–98). Thus, European citizenship and the rights it entails have so far not improved the rights of migrants from non-EU countries. On the contrary, while in many national contexts the rights status of permanent residents approximated that of citizens, non-EU nationals now find themselves in a second-class position on the European level (Faist 1995, 192).

It is debatable whether the improvements in migrant rights that have taken place in the last few decades are due to the rise of a new, postnational form of citizenship based in international human rights codes, emphasizing personhood instead of citizenship as the basis of rights. First, this perspective cannot explain why such extensions of rights to migrants can only be observed in Western democracies, whereas other countries, such as the Persian Gulf states, extend very few rights to their labor migrants (Joppke 1997). Moreover, more recent labor migration schemes in Western European countries (e.g., Germany's import of East European laborers) seem to indicate that if they so wish, Western nation-states, too, are well able to restrict the rights of labor migrants to a minimum: "The rights of these, mostly temporary, workers tend to be inferior to those of the former guest workers in Germany, for example, the rotational principle is strictly enforced. Thus, not only have immigration policies become more restrictive but the social rights status of labor migrants has also become more precarious" (Faist 1997, 213). What these examples suggest is that the factors that have led to the extension of rights to immigrants have been domestic rather than postnational in any meaningful sense (Joppke 1999). First, a commitment to human rights has been a founding principle of Western liberal nation-states, not something imposed on them in the postwar period by supranational institutions, conventions, or discourses (recall that the French revolutionary constitution begins by stating not just the Rights of the Citizen, but the Rights of Man and the Citizen—in that order). While the commitment to such values and rights may partly explain why Western states have not treated their labor migrants as, for example, Saudi Arabia or Nigeria has done, there were also less noble, domestic interests behind the giving up of the rotation model for Western European guest workers, e.g., the pressure on governments by employers interested in a stable, cheap, and committed workforce (Freeman 1995; Lakeman 1999).

Against the evidence brought forward for the continuing relevance of the nation-state as a frame of reference, postnationalists point to cases where collective actors frame their claims in terms of universal human rights and successfully appeal to supranational courts to prevent or overturn national incursions on their rights (see Soysal 1994, 1997, for examples). Yet such evidence remains unsystematic and does not go beyond the discussion of a few, supposedly representative examples. The extent to which the nation-state is still the most relevant context for understanding the politics of migration and ethnic relations, or whether it has been superseded by postnational and transnational contexts, is therefore still very much open to debate. In this chapter, we want to make an empirical contribution to resolving this question. We will do so by confronting the expectations on patterns of claims making that can be derived from the postnational perspective with those that follow from a perspective that emphasizes national citizenship and integration policies.

Next to this theoretical aim, this chapter fulfills the more descriptive function of giving an overview of the broad dimensions of the contentious field of immigration and ethnic relations politics, as it becomes manifest through political claims making in the five countries. The aim here is to set the scene for the detailed discussions in subsequent chapters on specific issues and collective actors by outlining some general differences between our country cases and across the three different subfields of immigration politics, integration politics, and the politics of racism and xenophobia. We will first examine the collective actors who appear as claim makers. Then we will look at variables relating to the issues around which contention takes place and how demands are discursively framed by naming responsible addressees and referring to relevant legal and normative frameworks. Finally, we will combine the different aspects of claims and look at the multilevel structure of claims across national, international, and supranational contexts, and ask which issue positions and collective actors appear to profit most from the opening of political spaces beyond the nation-state.

Collective Actors in the Public Sphere

We first look at the collective actors that appear as the carriers of claims in our media sources. The columns in Table 12 show the percentage shares of different actors in claims making on immigration and ethnic relations politics in the five countries. Actor types are grouped regardless of their scope—whether they were supranational, national, regional, or local—because in the first step we want to focus on the different opportunities that are available for specific types of actors to gain visibility and public resonance as claim makers. This means, for example, that the category "governments" includes not only national and local governments, but also supranational executive bodies such as the European Commission. We shall highlight several findings that demonstrate the relevance of national political opportunity structures.

Regarding actors with a more general range of interests, who do not specialize in immigration and ethnic relations issues, there are more similarities than differences between the countries. The overall share of state and party actors is very similar, ranging from 51 percent in France to 64 percent in Switzerland.[2] The same is true for socioeconomic interest groups such as labor unions, employers associations, and professional organizations (around 7 percent in all countries), as well as for other civil society groups such as churches, welfare organizations, and human rights groups, whose aims are broader than immigration and ethnic relations issues (between 6 percent in the Netherlands and 11 percent in Germany and France).

The political opportunity structure perspective leads us, on the contrary, to expect important cross-national differences regarding the shares of actors whose opportunities and resources depend strongly on the way in which the field of immigration and ethnic relations is structured. Indeed, the relative shares of claims made by the field-specific actors—migrants and minorities, the extreme right and racists, and antiracist and pro-minority groups—are strikingly different across the five countries. A straightforward expectation that can be drawn from the differences in national integration regimes that we have explored in the previous chapter would be that the more an inclusive definition of national citizenship and identity prevails and the more rights are granted to immigrants, the better the chances for immigrants and their pro-minority and antiracist supporters to intervene in public debates and the worse will be the opportunities for extreme-right and xenophobic groups who want to exclude immigrants from the national community. To some extent, this is indeed what we find. Regarding migrants and minorities, the shares found fit the expectation in four out of five countries. Migrants are least present in the public discourse in Switzerland (5 percent), which as we saw previously is the most explicit case of an ethnic conception of citizenship and makes few concessions to migrants' cultural differences. As a more moderate variant of the same pattern, Germany has the second-lowest share of migrants in the public discourse (7 percent). In contrast to these two countries, France does offer immigrants far-reaching individual equality, but not much in terms of cultural group rights. This results in a higher share for immigrants (10 percent) than in Switzerland and Germany, but a clearly lower share than in Britain (18 percent), where immigrants can also reckon with public legitimacy and institutional access for (moderate) demands for cultural rights. The deviant case is the Netherlands, where immigrants—according to a linear hypothesis of the link between

Table 12. Actors in immigration and ethnic relations politics

Collective actors	Netherlands	Britain	France	Germany	Switzerland
State and party actors					
Governments (%)	29.3	16.1	17.4	22.3	17.4
Legislatives and political parties (%)	24.0	14.7	24.7	22.4	33.2
Judiciary (%)	2.8	9.2	3.7	5.4	2.9
State executive agencies (%)	6.9	13.5	4.7	7.3	10.7
Total state and party actors (%)	62.9	53.6	50.6	57.3	64.1
Civil society actors					
Socioeconomic interest groups (%)	7.9	6.9	6.7	6.5	7.1
Migrants and minorities (%)	8.8	18.1	10.2	6.5	5.3
Extreme-right and racist actors (%)	6.9	2.7	10.2	10.4	7.0
Antiracist and pro-minority groups (%)	7.3	8.9	11.3	8.3	5.9
Other civil society groups (%)	6.2	9.9	11.0	11.0	10.7
Total civil society actors (%)	37.1	46.4	49.4	42.7	35.9
Total (%)	100.0	100.0	100.0	100.0	100.0
N	2,286	1,313	2,388	6,432	1,365

citizenship rights and participation in public contestation—should be even more strongly present as claim makers than in Britain. In fact, the share of immigrants in Dutch public discourse (9 percent) is lower than it is in France and not much higher than in Germany.

The explanation for this finding, which we develop further in the following chapter, is that the two dimensions of citizenship may have different effects on patterns of mobilization. At least for the range of variation we are dealing with here, extensions of individual rights to immigrants indeed seem to have a positive and linear effect on the presence of immigrants in the public debate. On the group rights dimension, however, we seem to be dealing with a curvilinear effect, in which up to a certain level the acceptance of cultural difference and the granting of group rights strengthens the involvement of immigrants in the political process of their countries of residence. When cultural differences are emphasized too strongly—and the evidence we present in the next chapter suggests that this may be the case in the Netherlands—the effect is that migrant communities turn inward and that their identities and activities are channeled away from the common public sphere.

These tendencies toward segregation along ethnic and cultural lines may not only hurt the involvement of immigrants with the political life of the majority society, but may also work against a strong involvement of the majority group with the situation of immigrants. This, too, seems to be the case in the Netherlands, where the share of pro-minority and antiracist groups (7 percent) is the second lowest after Switzerland. That these groups have a particularly difficult time mobilizing in Switzerland of course perfectly fits a linear opportunity structure hypothesis. On the other hand, as we will argue in detail in chapter 6, it is impossible to understand the level of antiracist and pro-minority activity without referring to the level of threat to immigrant interests posed by the mobilization of extreme-right and xenophobic groups. This explains why in France and Germany we find higher levels of such mobilization than we might otherwise have expected. The British case shows, however, that in the context of a conducive citizenship and integration regime even a very low level of extreme-right mobilization can provoke a fairly strong counterreaction (9 percent, the second-highest level after France).

Regarding the strength of extreme-right and xenophobic actors, the picture is again only partly in accordance with a linear opportunity hypothesis. That such mobilization remains limited in Britain, and is quite widespread in Germany, is easily understandable, but why would the extreme right be about as strong in France as in Germany? Why is the level of mobilization almost the same in the Netherlands and Switzerland, although these are the most strongly contrasting cases regarding citizenship rights for immigrants? In chapter 5, we will argue that in order to understand these results, we must take into account the political space that is available for extreme-right parties in electoral politics. Unlike antiracist or immigrant organizations, the extreme right, at least in its important party-political form, is in direct competition with traditional political parties. Therefore, it makes an important difference whether established parties occupy part of the extreme right's ideological space or leave a wide discursive field open for the mobilization of extreme-right groups. We will have separate chapters dealing with each of these three types of mobilization, and will there elaborate our arguments and evidence regarding them in much more detail and contextual nuance. The point to make here is that there are significant differences between the relative importance of these field-specific civil society actors across our five countries. These differences seem to be related to citizenship and integration regimes, although it is also clear that a linear and one-dimensional version of such an explanation is too simplistic to account for all the variation we find.

The relevance of opportunity structures for explaining which actors gain access to the public sphere receives further support from Table 13, where we focus not on cross-national differences, but on differences between the three main subfields we distinguish. Immigration politics here includes all issues pertaining to the regulation of the entry of migrants (including attempts to prevent immigration), their residence rights, and their voluntary or involuntary return. In addition to issues concerning the crossing of state borders, such as immigration and expulsion, this includes access to work and welfare for groups who do not have full residence rights, including nonrecognized asylum seekers and refugees, illegal aliens, and temporary labor migrants. By integration politics, we refer to all issues pertaining to the regulation of the integration of resident migrants relating to their social, political, and cultural rights, as well as claims about discrimination. The third subfield concerns the politics of racism and xenophobia, which covers claims relating to real and perceived acts of overt racist abuse or violence in the public domain, including both such acts themselves and the antiracist claims against them.[3] Instead of five separate tables for each country, we have here taken the countries together because the differences between the three subfields were highly consistent across them. In order not to give countries (especially Germany) with high numbers of cases a greater impact on the overall result, we have weighted the data in such a way that each country contributes equally to the total.

Table 13. Actors in immigration and ethnic relations politics

Collective actors	Immigration	Integration	Racism, xenophobia, and interethnic conflicts
State and party actors			
Governments (%)	28.0	17.5	12.8
Legislatives and political parties (%)	28.5	18.7	21.0
Judiciary (%)	5.0	5.5	4.0
State executive agencies (%)	8.9	11.7	6.3
Total state and party actors (%)	70.3	53.3	44.1
Civil society actors			
Socioeconomic interest groups (%)	5.1	11.0	6.9
Migrants and minorities (%)	5.8	19.1	9.0
Extreme-right and racist actors (%)	2.0	3.4	17.0
Antiracist and pro-minority groups (%)	8.5	3.1	11.4
Other civil society groups (%)	8.4	10.0	11.6
Total civil society actors (%)	29.7	46.7	55.9
Total (%)	100.0	100.0	100.0
N (weighted)	6,093	2,985	4,706

The notion of field-specific opportunities introduced in the introduction leads us to hypothesize about the overall level of participation of civil society actors relative to state actors in the different subfields. Immigration issues such as the regulation of entry to, and exit from, the national territory and control of external borders are among the core tasks of the national state and as such are relatively shielded from citizens' influence (see Kriesi et al. 1995, ch. 4). This is also a relatively centralized policy field, where regional, local, and nonstate authorities have little institutionalized influence. In contrast, the integration of minorities is a field where state bodies on various levels of the polity interact with resident migrants and minorities as well as with private bodies such as churches, unions, or welfare organizations. Consequently, one would expect a higher level of civil society engagement in the field of minority integration politics. For the third subfield of racism and xenophobia, one would expect the highest level of civil society activism since this is a field that is defined directly by the relationship of the host society to its migrant and minority populations as it becomes manifest through direct interaction in the public domain. Clearly, the state plays a role here, too, but it is a more reactive one in response to public acts of racism and xenophobia.

The findings in Table 13 underline these issue-specific opportunity structures. In the closed and centralized field of immigration politics, 70 percent of claims are made by state and party actors. In contrast, in the field of integration politics, state and party actors accounted for only somewhat more than half of the claims (53 percent) and less than half of the claims on racism and xenophobia (44 percent). Government actors in particular are much less important as claim makers on issues of racism (13 percent) and integration (18 percent) than they are in the field of immigration politics (28 percent). As in Table 12, we find important differences regarding the three field-specific actor types within civil society. Minorities and migrants find sufficient support and legitimacy to make almost a fifth (19 percent) of all claims in the field of integration politics, more even than government and legislative and party actors. Within the context of integration politics, where the legitimate and durable presence of immigrants is assumed rather than contested, this group enjoys a much stronger public legitimacy and can profit from stronger institutional facilitation than in the field of immigration politics, where the very legitimacy of migrants' residence and entry rights is at stake. Moreover, the immigrant groups who are concerned, such as asylum seekers or undocumented migrants, usually lack the material resources and access to organizational networks that are necessary to mount an effective challenge. Relatively often, pro-migrant groups from within the majority society take up the cause of these immigrant groups, as is evidenced by the much higher involvement of such organizations in immigration politics (9 percent) than in the field of integration (3 percent), where organizations of migrants themselves occupy a relatively strong position and advocacy mobilization is less urgent.

We also find a high level of advocacy mobilization, this time mainly in the form of antiracist organizations, in the field of racism and xenophobia. This is obviously related to the high level of extreme-right and xenophobic claims making in this field (17 percent). Regarding the extreme right, it is striking to see how limited its role is in the two substantive policy fields of immigration (2 percent) and integration (3 percent). Much of extreme-right and xenophobic claims making consists of violent acts against immigrants or verbal rejections of their integrity and legitimacy (e.g., slogans such as "White Power" or "Foreigners Out"). The extreme right only rarely makes concrete policy proposals or criticizes specific legislation. In the immigration field, the strong anti-immigration stances of the state and established parties appear to make it difficult for the extreme right to own this issue and to make any headway in the public domain other than by outright rejection of any kind of immigration. The difficulty for the extreme right lies in the fact that policy making in the integration field departs from the assumption that migrants have a legitimate right to reside in the country of settlement, so the extreme right will generally have little interest in making claims within this policy field. We will see in chapter 5 that France is a partial exception in that we find there a sizable number of extreme-right claims on integration issues. This is related to the fact that within the context of the French conception of citizenship, the extreme right finds public resonance for claims related to issues of cultural assimilation.

The results on claim makers presented so far suggest that national contexts have a significant impact on patterns of claims making, particularly regarding the three actor types that specifically mobilize in the field of immigration and ethnic relations politics. While such cross-national differences are hard to explain within a postnational theoretical framework, we have not yet presented any direct evidence that claim makers primarily mobilize and organize at the national level. Postnational theories emphasize the transnational nature of ethnic communities, linkages between policies and authorities in the countries of origin and settlement, as well as the growing role of supranational actors, such as the United Nations High Commissioner for Refugees (UNHCR), the European Commission, or the European Court of Human Rights. When looking at the territorial scope of actors operating in the immigration and ethnic relations field, the postnationalist position would therefore predict a significant involvement of actors that transcend the national context. By contrast, if national citizenship and political opportunities remain key to immigration and ethnic relations politics, one would expect to see a much more limited role for supranational, transnational, or foreign national actors.

For those acts of claims making for which an organization was explicitly mentioned, Table 14 shows the frequency of various possibilities for organization beyond the nation-state: Europe-wide, such as the European Parliament, the European Refugee Council, or the European Network Against Racism; on the supranational level beyond Europe, such as Amnesty International, UNESCO, the World Islamic Mission, or the International League for Human Rights; foreign-based, such as the American Nation of Islam, the Israeli government, the Turkish Islamic organization Milli Görüş, or government representatives and embassies of migrant homelands such as Bosnia, Surinam, or Turkey; and finally, bilateral organizations such as the German-Polish Friendship Society. In cases where an organization extended across several territorial or polity levels, as is the case for many international NGOs with national branches (e.g., Amnesty International or Pax Christi), we always coded the highest territorial level, i.e., in the "other supranational" cases. Similarly, Milli Görüş Germany is coded as a foreign, Turkish organization, even though the national branches of this organization tend to operate quite independently. Through this coding procedure, we ensured that any bias that might exist regarding ambivalent cases would be in favor of the postnational hypothesis rather than working against it.

The findings in the table are striking and clear-cut. Contrary to the expectations of postnational theory, the territorial scope of the vast majority of organizations that appear as claim makers in the public sphere of all

Table 14. Territorial scope of actors in immigration and ethnic relations politics

Organizations	Nether-lands	Britain	France	Germany	Switzer-land
European (%)	0.4	0.9	0.6	0.4	0.6
Other supranational (%)	1.3	1.3	4.2	3.1	4.0
Foreign-based/bilateral (%)	1.6	0.6	0.2	2.1	1.6
National or subnational (%)	96.8	97.2	94.8	94.8	94.5
Total (%)	100.0	100.0	100.0	100.0	100.0
N	1,999	1,117	2,033	5,098	1,255

five countries (between 95 and 97 percent) does not extend beyond the receiving nation-state. There is very little evidence of supranational or transnational organizations, either state or civil society actors, intervening to a significant extent in public controversies over immigration and ethnic relations, either from above in the form of supranational organizations or horizontally by way of interventions by organizations or authorities from other countries. In light of the fact that the academic literatures on postnationalism and multilevel governance usually point to the process of European integration as an exemplary case in point, it is perhaps most surprising that claim makers who organize on the European level are virtually absent (less than 1 percent in all countries). Other forms of supranational organization play a somewhat more important role, up to a level of 4 percent of all claim makers in France and Switzerland. The most important organizations of this type were the UNHCR and a number of supranational NGOs, with Amnesty International as the most frequently occurring example. Organizations from countries other than the country of settlement do not occur frequently either, especially in France and the United Kingdom where they are even more marginal than organizations with a European scope. In Germany, Switzerland, and the Netherlands, foreign organizations appear somewhat more frequently as claim makers (about 2 percent of all claims). These are most often governmental authorities or other organizations from migrants' countries of origin intervening on behalf of emigrant populations in Western Europe.

While our data thus contain cases that fit the type of claims making that is emphasized in theories of postnational citizenship, these remain quite marginal compared to the overwhelming majority of cases where claim makers are firmly situated within the national context of the country of settlement. On the other hand, are we not guilty of what is sometimes called methodological nationalism in drawing such conclusions about the marginality of nonnational actors based on national newspaper sources? This argument would be convincing if there really was an alternative for focusing on national public spheres as the arenas in which immigration and ethnic relations—or most other political issues, for that matter—are publicly debated and contested. In the absence in Europe of supranational media that reach transnational audiences, the only channels through which collective actors can mobilize public support and diffuse their messages to wider audiences are the national (and subnational) media. There are only a few transnational media in Europe that aim at general audiences, such as the television channel EuroNews, which in spite of strong financial support from the European Commission has remained very marginal. As for newspapers, there has been a significant attempt to establish a European-wide medium in the form of the *European,* but tellingly this newspaper no longer exists because it was not commercially viable.[4]

In another sense, we must admit to a certain degree of methodological nationalism because in our main sample we included claims that were made outside our countries of study only if they directly addressed, or referred to, actors or policies in these five countries. As a result, we may have missed some relevant claims on the supranational level. An example would be decisions or directives of European Union institutions that affect member states in a generic manner or statements by homeland governments on the situation of their emigrants in general without addressing a specific actor in one of our countries. Fortunately, we did include such claims for Britain, for the whole period, and Germany from 1997 onward. Including these claims that are indirectly relevant for public controversies in our countries of study indeed increases the relative share of nonnational actors, but not to a very great extent. Even with this expanded definition of the relevant universe of claims, national claim makers make up 91 percent of all claims in Germany and 96 percent in Britain. European claims profit most from this more inclusive definition, but they still do not rise above 2 percent of all claims in either of the two countries. Of course, the territorial level at which claim makers organize alone cannot seal the verdict on the relevance of the post-national thesis, as its advocates have often pointed out that supranational norms and legal frameworks in many cases are still channeled through national organizations and implemented by national authorities. We therefore turn to the substantive content of claims.

Issues and Their Spatial Framing

We now return to the three broad topical fields: immigration and aliens politics, integration politics, and racism and xenophobia. We expect that the relative weights of these issue fields as topics of public controversy will differ according to the institutional framework and discursive opportunities available for claims making. Within the immigration, asylum, and aliens politics field, issues of entry (e.g., border control and visas) and exit (e.g., expulsions and repatriation), as well as the granting and termination of residence and work permits, are at stake. All five countries experienced large increases in numbers of immigrants during the 1990s. The most important immigrant categories were asylum seekers, refugees (especially from the former Yugoslavia), and (particularly in France) undocumented migrants. Switzerland and Germany had the largest inflows of immigrants during the 1990s, France and Britain received significantly lower numbers, and the Netherlands occupied a position in between. Even though immigration issues were highly salient everywhere, Table 15 shows that this was significantly less the case in France and Britain (37 percent), especially compared to Switzerland (58 percent). The salience of immigration issues in the Netherlands is somewhat higher (49 percent) and that in Germany somewhat lower (40 percent) than one could expect based on immigrant numbers.

While the actual pressures arising from immigration flows play an important role in explaining the salience of immigration issues, this does not seem to be the whole story, especially if we compare the salience of immigration to that of integration issues. If we would apply the same logic of numbers to the integration field, we should again expect the largest number of claims in this field in Switzerland, which has the largest population of immigrant origin of our five countries, and the smallest number of integration claims in Britain, which has the smallest immigrant population. In fact, what we find is that Britain has by far the most claims in the integration field, and Switzerland comes second to last after Germany.

Another way to look at the same figures is by taking the proportion between the number of claims in the immigration field and in the integration field. This is an indicator of the degree to which public debate on immigrants focuses on their temporal and insecure status as aliens or foreigners, or on their status as permanent residents and members of the national community. In Britain, immigration and integration issues are about equally important; in the Netherlands and France we find roughly twice as many immigration as integration claims (1.8 times in the Netherlands and 2.0 times in France), whereas in Germany and Switzerland immigration claims are more than three times more frequent (3.7 times in Germany and 3.4 times in Switzerland). Thus, the order in which the countries appear fits the differences we found in chapter 1 regarding citizenship rights quite well. Moving toward countries with a more ethnic and monocultural conception of citizenship, we find a growing preoccupation in the public debate with immigrants as a marginal group whose entry and exit from the national territory and residence rights are at the center of the debate. In line with the results presented in Table 12 showing a relatively small role for migrants in the public debate, the Netherlands deviate somewhat from this pattern and are again situated quite close to France, in spite of the fact that in extending cultural group rights to immigrants the Dutch have gone quite a bit further than Britain. Again, we seek the explanation in the segregating effects of too strong an emphasis on cultural differences, which may be similar to the effects of a strong emphasis on assimilation. In both cases, immigrants appear as a group outside of the dominant culture. Despite the good intentions of

Table 15. Issues of claims in immigration and ethnic relations politics

Issues	Netherlands	Britain	France	Germany	Switzerland
Immigration, asylum, aliens politics (%)	49.2	37.0	36.9	40.2	57.7
Residence rights and recognition (%)	9.8	12.9	12.3	14.1	5.9
Entry and exit (%)	17.8	12.2	19.4	15.2	32.7
Institutional framework and costs (%)	15.3	7.8	0.5	3.9	5.9
Other (%)	6.3	4.1	4.7	7.0	12.2
Minority integration politics (%)	27.1	35.1	18.2	11.0	16.9
Citizenship and political rights (%)	3.1	2.3	2.9	4.0	5.6
Social rights (%)	8.0	7.5	2.0	0.9	3.3
Religious and cultural rights (%)	5.5	7.7	6.6	1.2	1.2
Discrimination and unequal treatment (%)	3.4	13.7	1.7	0.7	0.5
Minority social problems (%)	4.5	2.0	0.9	2.3	1.5
Other/general integration issues (%)	2.6	2.9	4.1	1.9	4.8
Antiracism, xenophobia, and interethnic conflicts (%)	23.7	27.9	44.9	48.8	25.4
Institutional racism (%)	3.5	7.1	2.3	3.3	1.2
Noninstitutional racism and xenophobia (%)	19.7	20.4	41.3	45.5	24.0
Interethnic conflicts (%)	0.5	1.4	1.3	0.0	0.2
Total (%)	100.0	100.0	100.0	100.0	100.0
N	2,286	1,313	2,388	6,432	1,365

advocates of multicultural rights, the ultimate outcome may be that the sense of mutual identification and belonging between immigrants and the majority group are undermined.

Focusing more closely on the field of integration politics, we should begin by noting that in countries that lean toward an ethnic conception of citizenship, i.e., Switzerland and Germany, migrants remain formally foreigners and therefore lack the political leverage derived from voting rights. Thus, immigrants remain subject to the separate body of aliens' legislation and have neither the legal basis nor the discursive legitimacy to make claims for fully equal rights and treatment. To the contrary, as we saw in chapter 1, the threat of suspension of residence rights remains in these countries, even for long-term resident aliens as well as for their children born in the country of settlement. This explains why integration politics has remained a relatively underdeveloped policy field in these countries. Germany and Switzerland largely lack a legal framework on integration issues to which claims in this field might (proactively or critically) refer. In addition, they lack specialized institutional authorities to whom such demands and criticisms could be addressed. The clearest contrast is provided by the Netherlands and Britain, which have very extensive legal frameworks and institutions in place for promoting equal opportunities and combating discrimination. France is an intermediary case, because it does extend rights to migrants as individuals, but it is reluctant to recognize migrants' collective identities and cultural differences and to grant them rights on this basis. Compared to the Dutch and British situation, this limits the institutional opportunities and discursive legitimacy of claims focusing on integration issues as a separate policy field. The French context exerts strong pressures on claim makers to formulate demands not in terms of specific rights and policy solutions for immigrants, but as part of broader policies of social equality that are directed at all citizens regardless of their immigrant origin or cultural background. Such claims disappear from our view, as they are no longer claims in the field of immigration and ethnic relations, even though immigrant groups may implicitly often be important targets of such policies.

Table 15 shows that indeed integration issues are least prominent in Germany (11 percent of all claims) and Switzerland (17 percent). Notably, the only type of claims within this subfield that are more frequent in Germany (4 percent) and Switzerland (6 percent) than in the other three countries are claims for citizenship and political rights. The fact that in these two classical guest worker countries these issues are relatively prominent is suggestive evidence against the postnational citizenship thesis. In this view, the nationality of the country of residence is seen as a relatively unimportant source of immigrant rights. While it is true that obtaining the formal nationality does not directly confer many rights, our data strongly suggest that the symbolic inclusion of immigrants through conferring citizenship creates important opportunities for claims making. In Germany and Switzerland, we find very few claims on social and cultural rights or on discrimination. This is not because migrants have less to complain about and are better protected against discrimination than in the other countries. To the contrary, it is extremely difficult for migrants to put these issues on the political agenda in Germany and Switzerland and to find public resonance and legitimacy for them because they lack formal and symbolic inclusion as equal members of the national community.

In the Netherlands and Britain, we see relatively high percentages of claims for social (8 percent in both countries) and religious and cultural rights (6 percent in the Netherlands and 8 percent in Britain). Britain, however, is clearly differentiated from the Netherlands when it comes to claims on issues of discrimination and unequal treatment, which make up no less than 14 percent of all claims in Britain, but only somewhat more than 3 percent in the Netherlands. British equal opportunity and antidiscrimination institutions and legislations thus have a much larger public impact than their Dutch counterparts do. This probably has less to do with the nature of these institutions and legislation—which, as we have seen in chapter 1, are broadly similar—than with the fact that effective antidiscrimination and equal opportunity policies were only introduced in the Netherlands over the course of the 1990s, whereas in Britain they go all the way back to the Race Relations Act of 1965. Assuming that it takes some time for new legal frameworks and institutional channels to reshape the mobilization strategies of collective actors, we may expect that claims on discrimination and unequal treatment issues will become more numerous in the Netherlands in the future. Even in the short run these policies have not been completely inconsequential, as shown by the fact that antidiscrimination claims are still twice as numerous in the Netherlands as in France (less than 2 percent) and are almost completely absent from the public agenda in Germany and Switzerland (less than 1 percent). In line with this, we also find many fewer claims on immigrants' social rights in France (2 percent), Germany (1 percent), and Switzerland (3 percent) than in Britain and the Netherlands.

It is less self-evident that we find almost as many claims on issues of cultural and religious rights in France as in Britain and even somewhat more than in the Netherlands. As we shall see in chapter 4, which deals at length with the issue of cultural pluralism, the high level of claims made in France in the field of cultural and religious rights is a consequence of the strong ambivalence of the French conception of citizenship, which is strongly open toward migrants as individuals but hostile to public assertions of group identities. As a consequence, debates about cultural rights have become a focus for a reassertion of republican secular nationalism against multiculturalism, as well as for mobilization by migrants themselves who react against the stigmatization of their cultural heritage and claim what they see as their rights to full equality as citizens. The important point here is that on issues of religious and cultural rights the state and its discourses for national identity come into institutional conflict with minorities, both in those countries that advocate cultural pluralism (Netherlands and Britain) and those that actively deny it (France). States that give rights to migrants react strongly and defensively to what they perceive as attempts to push the normative limits of these concessions further, often backed up by an indignant and vocal host civil society. In Britain and the Netherlands, such challenges occur to a significant extent within institutional arenas, since there is already a framework in place for minority politics, whereas in France, in the absence of institutionalized minority politics, these challenges and conflicts resonate more in the public sphere. By contrast, in Germany and Switzerland the religious and cultural rights of minorities are pretty much a nonissue (1 percent in both countries). In countries that institutionalize the ethnic exclusion of migrants, there is relatively little political space for them to make demands for cultural rights, and concomitantly little need for host civil society actors to defend the national cultural identity from erosion because of a proliferation of such demands.

Finally, we turn to claims within the field of (anti)racism and xenophobia. The salience of claims making in this field strongly reflects the strength of the challenge by the extreme right, which provokes countermobilization from immigrants and sections of the majority society. This type of claims is reflected in the subcategory labeled "noninstitutional racism and xenophobia." The relative share of claims in this category quite closely reflects the strength of the extreme right as an actor in the field as presented in Table 12. The only major deviation is the British case, which shows a higher level of claims making on this topic than would be expected on the basis of the low level of mobilization of the extreme right. We will not dwell on these issues any further here, because the reasons behind the strong mobilization of the extreme right in France and Germany, and the determinants of countermobilization against it, will be discussed at length in chapters 5 and 6. We will not discuss the small category of interethnic conflicts here, either. These are conflicts between different migrant groups that do not directly involve the majority society. We will deal with these conflicts in the next chapter.

What we still want to note here are the differences regarding the topic of institutional racism. The issue here is not the racist and xenophobic activity of anti-immigrant groups within civil society, but racism within established institutions, such as allegations of racial abuse and violence by the police or the use of racist language by politicians. As with discrimination claims, the issue of institutional racism is most salient in the British context (7 percent), followed at a distance by the Netherlands (3.5 percent) and then the other three countries, with Switzerland closing the ranks (1 percent). Thus, we find that the legal rights and symbolic inclusion of immigrants are inversely related to the prominence of discrimination and institutional racism in the public debate. It is highly unlikely that the differences in the salience of claims on discrimination and institutional racism result from variations in the actual proliferation of these phenomena. If this were the case, we would have to assume that discrimination and institutional racism are much more widespread in Britain than in Switzerland, which is implausible given the much greater inclusiveness of the British citizenship regime compared to the Swiss. More likely, these differences reflect the availability of an institutional framework and discursive legitimacy for putting institutional discrimination and racism on the public agenda in countries such as Britain, and their absence in countries such as Switzerland. The salience of institutional racism and discrimination as a publicly recognized problem may well be inversely related to the objective extent of the problem.

While these cross-national differences in the salience of different issues within the field point toward the importance of national citizenship and integration regimes, we additionally need to assess the validity of the postnational relativization of the nation-state more directly. We do this by looking at the substantive scope of claims. At the one extreme, we find claims that remain completely within the realm of national politics and refer only to national actors, institutions, and legal norms. An example is the accusations of the German Social Democrats during the early 1990s that the government legitimized violence against asylum seekers with its demand to abolish the constitutional right to asylum. Within that same asylum debate, there were also cases of claims where reference was made to actors, legal frameworks, or norms outside Germany. For instance, the government would point out that a reform of asylum law was necessary to harmonize Germany's legislation with that in other EU member states, opponents would say that such a reform would run against the Geneva Convention on refugees or violate the UN Children's Convention, or German authorities would call on other EU member states to do more to secure the European Union's external borders. Claims might also refer to other nation-states, e.g., when Dutch churches protested against the conclusion of a treaty between the Netherlands and Vietnam on the repatriation of refugees in return for financial aid, or when antiracist protesters gathered at Heathrow airport to protest a visit of the Italian neofascist leader Gianfranco Fini to the United Kingdom.

In Table 16, we show the distribution of the substantive scope of claims in the overall immigration and ethnic relations field. The categories "European," "other supranational," and "national or subnational" are identical to those used in Table 14 for the territorial scope of actors. The category "international relations" is used for claims referring to other countries, as in the two last-mentioned examples. As we did for the territorial scope of actors, we have always coded the widest scope of substantive reference. That is, if a claim referred mainly to national institutions, legislation, and norms, and only secondarily referred to the need for a common European solution, the substantive scope of the claim was coded as "European" and not as "national." Again, we built in a bias to the advantage of theories of postnational citizenship. A final preliminary note is that the substantive scope of a claim was defined independent of the scope of the actor who made the claim. Thus, many of the claims with a European scope were made by national actors. The reverse also happened regularly. For instance, in many cases the interventions by national branches of transnational NGOs such as Amnesty International, Pax Christi, or Medico International remained entirely within a national frame of reference.

Compared to the territorial scope of actors that we presented in Table 14, we find in Table 16 a larger number of claims with a substantive scope of reference that extends beyond the national context of the country of settlement.[5] The more important form of transnational claims making is clearly that in which national actors refer to transnational or supranational contexts, rather than collective actors organizing transnationally (for a similar conclusion regarding protest mobilization, see Imig and Tarrow 2001). Nonetheless, the extent to which the frame of reference of claims extends beyond the national context remains unimpressive. In the Netherlands, Germany, and France, between 94 and 95 percent of all claims make no references beyond the country of settlement. Surprisingly, Switzerland (which is not an EU member and only recently joined the UN) and Britain (the homeland of Euroskepticism) are the two countries with the lowest proportions of claims with a national frame of reference (89 percent in both countries). Claims with a European scope, in particular, are relatively frequent in these two countries (4.6 percent in Switzerland and 4.3 percent in Britain). This may be because the issue of European integration is more

Table 16. Substantive scope of claims in immigration and ethnic relations politics

Claims	Nether-lands	Britain	France	Germany	Switzer-land
European (%)	1.3	4.3	2.9	1.0	4.6
Other supranational (%)	1.3	2.4	1.7	1.2	3.5
International relations (%)	3.4	4.5	0.8	2.9	3.3
National or subnational (%)	94.1	88.8	94.6	94.9	88.6
Total (%)	100.0	100.0	100.0	100.0	100.0
N	2,215	1,307	2,317	5,838	1,324

controversial than in the other three countries—in Britain due to strong opposition against the political and monetary integration of Europe, and in Switzerland due to controversies over whether or not Switzerland should join the European Union. References to the European level (and to a lesser extent to other supranational levels) were as a consequence often negative, either with regard to extensions of supranational prerogatives or with regard to migrant rights. The Tories, for instance, criticized Labor on several occasions for their call for common European rules in dealing with asylum requests, stating that this would undermine immigration control and threaten peaceful race relations in Britain.

Again, we are able to take into account the possibility of a methodological bias in favor of claims with a national scope, using the wider definition of the relevant universe of claims for Britain and Germany that we already have referred to in our discussion of actor scopes. Including claims made abroad that do not directly address actors or policies in our countries of study leads to a very modest decrease in the predominance of claims with a purely national scope of reference, to 87 percent in Britain and to 92 percent in Germany.

Multilevel Patterns of Claims Making

So far, our analysis has not reached the core of what characterizes politics beyond the nation-state according to the predominant view in the literature (e.g., Held et al. 1999; Zürn 1998). These new forms of politics are not envisaged as a zero-sum game in which supranational and transnational forms of political action gain prominence at the cost of national political involvement. Rather, the growing relevance of supranational and transnational

institutions and norms leads to forms of multilevel politics, which may simultaneously involve several political levels. For instance, national actors in
conflict with other national actors may invoke arguments drawn from international treaties or norms, or they may address supranational third parties,
demanding that they exert pressure on their adversaries in the national political arena. Viewed in their entirety, such claims are neither exclusively
national nor supranational, but a hybrid combination of the two. In order
to capture such forms of multilevel claims making, we will now look at the
structure of claims in their entirety. To this end, we combine and extend the
information on actor scopes and substantive frames of reference. Tables 14
and 16 were based only on the primary actor and the primary issue and addressee of claims. To capture as much as possible of the potential for linkages
between polity levels, we will now also include information on secondary
and tertiary actors, addressees, and issues. Because claimants sometimes act
in coalitions, we allowed for the coding of up to three different subject actors per claim. Moreover, each act of claims making may refer to several
separate detailed issues, which we capture by coding not only the primary
but also, if relevant, the secondary and tertiary issues. Finally, we coded up
to three actors who in relation to these issues were mentioned as addressees
or objects of criticism. For each of these nine variables, we coded a scope
variable similar to the ones we already discussed in relation to Tables 14 and
16. Thus, we have the potential to capture very complex forms of multilevel claims making and have a very sensitive instrument that captures even
slight references to contexts other than the nation-state. For instance, we
might classify a claim as involving the European level based on its tertiary
addressee, even if all eight other variables had a national scope.

The results of this analysis are shown in Table 17. As a contrast, we
also present the percentage of purely national claims, i.e., those that made
no reference to a polity level other than the national or subnational levels.[6]
Note that in all five countries virtually all claims involved the national polity level in one way or another, whether because claimants were organized at
the national level, because the addressees were national institutions, or because issues were framed in a national context. This result remains virtually
unchanged (a decline of only 0.3 percent in the category of claims with a
national or subnational dimension in both countries) if we take the broader
definition of relevant claims for Britain and Germany (which includes
claims made abroad that may be supranational or transnational in all dimensions). Moreover, almost all claims that were coded as having no national dimension in fact did have one. This is a result of our rule to code
the highest scope level if an actor or issue extends across more than one

Table 17. Overall scopes of claims in immigration and ethnic relations politics and extent of multilevel claims making

Claims	Nether-lands	Britain	France	Germany	Switzer-land
European (%)	2.2	5.2	3.8	2.4	8.9
Other supranational (%)	2.9	5.6	8.0	6.1	10.1
International relations (%)	5.3	5.9	1.8	7.0	6.1
National or subnational (%)	99.2	98.9	99.7	99.6	99.6
Total (%)	109.6	115.6	113.3	115.1	124.7
Purely national claims (%)	90.5	85.3	86.7	86.0	76.3
N	2,231	1,307	2,323	5,859	1,324

Note: Figures add up to more than 100 percent because of claims encompassing multiple political levels. The difference between the sum total percentage per column and 100 percent indicates the percentage of multilevel claims. The figures in the bottom row for claims with a purely national scope show the percentage of claims that contained no reference whatsoever to political levels above or beyond the national level of the country in question.

polity level. For example, the claim where Pax Christi Germany called for a common European asylum policy was coded as having a European (the issue) and another supranational dimension (the actor), but the German dimension of the claimant was not captured in this case. This near universality of claims that have a national dimension implies that most of the multilevel claims are of the type involving the national level and one of the other levels. Claims involving more than two levels were relatively rare. An example was the criticism uttered by the Dutch Institute for Multicultural Development Forum that Turkish organizations in Europe were influenced too strongly by the Turkish government, a claim coded as having national Dutch (the claimant), European (the issue), and international relations dimensions (the Turkish government as the object of criticism).

Looking at claims with a European dimension, we see that, surprisingly, such claims occurred most frequently in non–EU member Switzerland (9 percent), followed at some distance by Euroskeptic Britain (5 percent). To understand this finding, we need to take a closer look at the substantive content of the different types of multilevel claims making. Table 18 shows the distribution of claims with different scopes for immigration politics, integration politics, and the subfield of (anti)racism and xenophobia separately. Again, we have taken all five countries together because the differences among the three issue fields were highly consistent across countries, and we have weighted the data in such a way that the five countries contribute equally to the overall result. Table 19 shows us additionally the average valence of claims of different scopes in these three issue fields, measured on a scale from –1.00 if all claims in a category implied a deterioration (or were against improvements) in immigrants' situations and rights, and +1.00 if all claims in a category implied improvements for immigrants (or were against deterioration). Claims received a score of 0 if they were ambivalent or neutral regarding immigrants' situations and rights. The scores in the table are averages computed across all claims in a certain category.

Combining the results in Tables 17 through 19 reveals that claims with a European dimension were strongly concentrated in the immigration field (where they make up 8 percent of all claims, see Table 18) and were more likely than the average claim to imply restrictions in the rights of immigrants and to emphasize strict entry criteria and border controls (see the average valence of 0.03 for European claims in Table 19 compared to the 0.17 overall average for immigration claims). Sometimes such claims were made in line with existing European policies to control immigration (e.g., Schengen), but in Britain and to a greater extent still in Switzerland, the European dimension of claims often consisted of a negative reference toward both the European Union and immigrants. In Switzerland, such claims were typically inserted in the conflictive debates that raged throughout the 1990s about whether or not the country should join the European Union, conclude treaties with it, or adapt its legislation to EU legislation. One prominent argument of EU opponents in this debate was that adaptation to, or membership in, the European Union would lead to increased and uncontrolled immigration to Switzerland. This would, for instance, give North African immigrants holding the French nationality unrestrained entry to Switzerland, as the radical right leader Christoph Blocher argued. Similar arguments about the linkage between EU integration and fears of losing control over immigration flows were made by the British Conservatives.

Contrary to European claims, other supranational claims were more evenly spread across the three issue fields and were—with the exception of integration issues—more often than average in favor of immigrants and the protection and improvement of their rights (see Tables 18 and 19). Switzerland also has the highest proportion of other supranational claims (10 percent) among our countries. Immigrants and their supporters in Switzerland frequently draw on supranational sources of legitimacy to criticize Swiss immigration and ethnic relations policies. Switzerland is both the seat of many supranational NGOs and institutions—e.g., the Geneva-based UNHCR—and a country that has been very reluctant to become a member of supranational institutions and subscribe to international

Table 18. Overall scopes of claims in immigration and ethnic relations politics and extent of multilevel claims making

Claims	Immigration	Integration	Racism and xenophobia
European (%)	7.9	1.9	1.6
Other supranational (%)	6.6	4.3	7.9
International relations (%)	8.1	3.6	2.1
National or subnational (%)	99.4	99.6	99.4
Total (%)	122.0	109.4	111.0
Purely national claims (%)	79.4	91.1	88.7
N (weighted)	6,090	2,973	4,239

Table 19. Average discursive position on issues in immigration and ethnic relation's politics

Claims	Immigration	Integration	Racism and xenophobia	Overall average
European	.03	.48	.54	.13
Other supranational	.47	.39	.79	.58
International relations	−.03	.20	.83	.12
All claims with non-national references	.13	.36	.76	.31
Purely national claims	.18	.41	.65	.39
Overall average	.17	.40	.66	.38
N (weighted)	6,090	2,973	4,239	13,302

Note: Discursive positions may range from −1.00 if all claims in a category were anti-immigrant to +1.00 if all claims in a category were pro-immigrant.

conventions. Like the question of EU membership, Swiss membership in other supranational bodies and conventions is highly contested. While a majority of the population—at least in the dominating German-speaking cantons—remains hostile to the European Union, Switzerland after a long and controversial debate finally joined the UN in 2002 and recently became a signatory to several international treaties relevant to immigration issues, most importantly the Convention on the Elimination of all Forms of Racial Discrimination (ICERD), which Switzerland joined in 1994. In line with the postnational thesis, these new supranational commitments of Switzerland have been welcome argumentative tools for pro-immigrant groups to demand adaptation of Swiss policies to international standards.

Claims with an international relations dimension are more similar to European than to other supranational claims. They are heavily concentrated in the field of immigration politics, where they make up 8 percent of all claims (Table 18), and they more frequently imply restrictions in immigrant rights than purely national claims. Claims involving the country of settlement and another nation-state are frequently about stricter border regimes or the repatriation of immigrants. For instance, in 1997 Gerhard Schröder (then still prime minister of Lower Saxony) proposed to make developmental aid to countries dependent on their cooperation in the repatriation of refugees. Further examples are the repatriation treaties that were concluded with countries of origin of immigrants such as Bosnia, Croatia, China, and Vietnam, or the 1994 decision of the Netherlands, Germany, and Belgium to more intensively cooperate in controlling their common borders in order to implement stricter asylum regimes. Only in the field of racism and xenophobia is there a tendency for international relations claims to be more pro-immigrant than national claims. These claims are primarily interventions by homeland organizations against discrimination and racist violence in the countries of origin. Germany, for instance, was on several occasions criticized by the Turkish government and by Turkish media for not doing enough to protect Turkish immigrants from racist violence. For similar reasons, Germany was under the scrutiny of foreign Jewish organizations, such as the American Jewish Committee, and of the Israeli government, who criticized anti-Semitic tendencies and expressed concern about the safety of Soviet Jewish immigrants to Germany.

Postnational theorists paint a picture in which restrictive nation-states are compelled by supranational norms and transnational interdependencies to relax immigration controls and grant rights to immigrants. This, our data show, is a very rosy and one-sided picture of the political space beyond the nation-state. As Table 19 shows, claims with aspects that reach beyond the country of settlement are on average *less* rather than more in favor of immigration and immigrant rights (compare the valences of claims with any nonnational reference to those of purely national claims). This is true for immigration politics as well as integration politics (but not for antiracism), and holds in four of our five countries (only in France is there no difference; not shown in the table). Behind this result lie, of course, important differences between European and international claims on the one hand, and other supranational claims on the other. The former two tend to be focused on interstate cooperation or supranational coordination of border controls, and recognition regimes, as well as the control of international crime and terrorism (e.g., several claims on Turkish-German cooperation to fight Kurdish separatism among immigrants living in Germany). Other supranational claims, by contrast, conformed more to the postnational thesis and tended to be in defense of immigrant rights, referring to international commitments and norms, as well as to treaties such as the Geneva Convention on refugees or the ICERD convention on racism.

These variations receive further profile from the results in Table 20, which shows the distribution of actors for claims with different scopes. This enables us to see which actors are able to profit from the normative and institutional spaces beyond the nation-state. We use the notion of a political space here in a nonterritorial sense, for example, a claim forms part of the European space if it refers in one or more aspects to the European level, irrespective of where the claim is made or whether it simultaneously refers to other political spaces. Against the optimism about the European Union empowering immigrants and sustaining their rights against restrictive member states that often prevails in the literature, the European Union arena turns out to be a relatively nonconducive environment for civil society actors in general, and immigrants in particular. Much more than on the national level, state and party actors—and governmental actors in particular—are the dominant actors in claims making relating to the European Union (76 percent for European claims compared to 61 percent for purely national claims). Civil society groups are correspondingly less prominent in the European political space. The most striking finding, however, is that immigrants are virtually absent from European claims making, and are five times less prominent (2 against 10 percent) than within the purely national context.

Claims with international relations dimensions resemble European claims to some extent. State and party actors (63 percent) are less prominent than among European claims, but still more than on the national level. Government actors (38 percent) are particularly prominent in claims making involving actors or policies in other states, most frequently immigrants' countries of origin. Contrary to the EU space, this international political space offers better opportunities for immigrants, who are more prominent here than in exclusively national claims making (14 percent against 10 percent). This result holds in all five countries (not shown in the table). The supranational arena beyond the European Union again deviates strongly. Here, civil society actors (66 percent) are much more prominent than in either of the other political spaces. Immigrants, with a share of 12 percent, profit somewhat from the normative and institutional opportunities of

Table 20. Distribution of actors by overall claim scope

Actors	European	Other supranational	International relations	Purely national claims
State and party actors (%)	76.3	34.0	63.4	60.6
Governments (%)	31.1	12.1	38.2	20.6
Legislatives and political parties (%)	33.2	9.6	16.0	25.6
Judiciary (%)	2.6	1.8	2.6	5.4
State executive agencies (%)	9.4	10.5	6.5	9.0
Civil society actors (%)	23.7	66.0	36.6	39.4
Socioeconomic interest groups (%)	5.5	5.9	5.2	7.5
Migrants and minorities (%)	2.3	12.4	13.6	9.9
Extreme-right and racist actors (%)	3.1	3.9	1.8	5.5
Antiracist and pro-minority groups (%)	8.0	18.5	7.0	7.6
Other civil society groups (%)	4.9	25.2	9.1	8.9
Total (%)	100.0	100.0	100.0	100.0
N (weighted)	601	868	691	11,301

these supranational spaces, which are often linked to institutions and conventions in the context of the United Nations. The most important beneficiaries, though, are advocacy NGOs that support immigrants or fight racism (19 percent against 8 percent on the purely national level), as well as the category of "other civil society groups" (25 percent against 9 percent on the purely national level), the most important component parts of which are welfare organizations, churches, and human rights and developmental NGOs, such as Amnesty International or Terre des Hommes.

With these qualifications about the ambivalent nature of nonnational political spaces in mind, we now assess the magnitude of tendencies of denationalization and multileveling. If we return to the results displayed in Table 17, we see that altogether between 10 percent (the Netherlands) and 25 percent (Switzerland) of all claims referred to political spaces beyond the country of settlement. In Table 18, we have seen that there are important differences among the three subfields in the extent of multilevel claims making, which is clearly more relevant in the immigration field (22 percent) than in the fields of integration (9 percent) and racism and xenophobia (11 percent), which have remained more strongly topics that are debated in a purely national context. It is somewhat arbitrary judging whether one sees these levels of multilevel claims making as being great or small. Compared to the almost 100 percent of claims that are embedded in the national political context in one way or another, and the 76 to 91 percent that remain fully within the national context (see Table 17), the magnitude of multilevel claims making does not seem impressive, especially if one considers the built-in bias in favor of nonnational spaces in our categorization of claims. All aspects of a claim must be national in order to classify it as a purely national claim, whereas it is sufficient for a claim to be classified as European if only a secondary or tertiary aspect refers to the European level.

One might arrive at a different assessment of these 10 to 25 percent multilevel claims if one considers them as the vanguard of a trend toward an ever-greater erosion of the exclusive relevance of national sovereignty and citizenship. The question then becomes whether references to political spaces beyond the nation-state are indeed becoming increasingly frequent over time. Our data cover a period of only eight years (1992–98), which we can extend to ten years (1990–99) for some countries. This is a rather short time period, which does not allow us to settle the issue conclusively, but if postnational citizenship and multilevel claims making are strongly emergent phenomena, we should be able to trace their rise even across a relatively short period. Figure 4 shows the development of the shares of European, other supranational, international, and purely national claims for the period

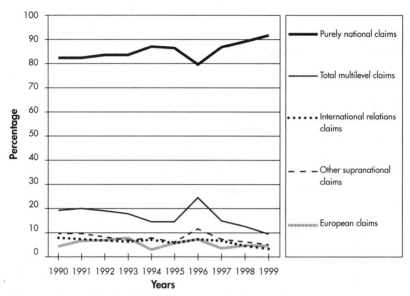

Figure 4. Development of the percentage of claims with different scopes across the five countries, 1990–99.

of 1990–99. F or 1990 and 1991, the data exclude the Netherlands, for 1999 they exclude France and Switzerland.

The figure does not reveal any trend toward a growing importance of nonnational political spaces for the field of immigration and ethnic relations. This is again perhaps most revealing and unexpected for claims with a European dimension. Since the beginning of the 1990s, the European integration process has undoubtedly accelerated, by way of milestones such as the Maastricht and Amsterdam Treaties, the introduction of a common currency and the admission of new members. These developments do not seem to have affected claims making on immigration and ethnic relations to an important extent. The institutions of the European Union do not have any competencies in integration politics (except relating to immigrants from other member states, who are not a publicly contested category of immigrants), and have only developed some symbolic policies in the field of antiracism (e.g., the 1997 European Year Against Racism). In the immigration field, there is some coordination in the context of the second Justice and Internal Affairs pillar, but decision making here is of the intergovernmental type and can only take place by unanimity among all fifteen member states. This has often stood in the way of the development of effective common policies, for instance, policies regarding asylum procedures. It is possible that changes will occur in the near future, as there are plans to move immigration issues to the first pillar where supranational EU bodies, such as the Commission and the European Parliament, will have a greater say and where single member states can no longer block policies with their veto. For the time being, however, immigration and ethnic relations is not a strongly Europeanized policy field, and neither do other supranational and transnational political spaces seem to be in the process of mounting a strong challenge against the nation-state's predominance in the field. Figure 4 shows that, with the exception of the year 1996, there even seems to be a weak trend toward a renationalization of claims making in the field. At the end of the 1990s, the share of purely national claims was almost ten percentage points higher (91 percent) than at the beginning of the decade (82 percent).

Conclusion

What conclusion on the relevance of the postnational thesis can we draw from this chapter? We have seen important cross-national differences in patterns of claims making, relating both to the prominence of different types of actors and to the issues on which public controversies focused. Such differences are hard to explain within a postnational framework, which assumes that nation-states are subjected to similar supranational and transnational constraints, obligations, and normative frameworks, which would lead us to expect cross-national similarities rather than differences. We have begun to indicate how these differences might be fruitfully explained in the context of national citizenship and integration regimes. Yet the main task of explaining these differences still lies before us. In the next four chapters, we focus in much greater detail on cross-national differences for particular categories of actors.

Regarding the more direct evidence on the relevance of the postnational thesis, a more realistic view on political spaces beyond the nation-state is clearly in order. Such a view should recognize that denationalization as such does not necessarily provide better opportunities for pro-immigrant claims making than the national political arena. State actors have powerful influence in the international and supranational arenas, and much of their efforts there are geared toward interstate cooperation with the aim of strengthening immigration controls, emphasizing a framing of immigration in the context of crime prevention and security. Against these tendencies, some supranational arenas, particularly those linked to the United Nations, provide better opportunities for pro-immigrant NGOs, and transnational linkages to migrants' homelands provide some leverage for immigrant mobilization. On balance, however, it is questionable whether the latter forms of claims making that fit the postnational view can provide an effective counterbalance against the restrictive actions of state actors in the supranational and international arenas. Our data indicate that within the context of the European Union, in particular, the balance of forces is such that, until now, denationalization tendencies have been harmful rather than beneficial for immigrants and their rights.

Finally, whether one judges the quantitative level of multilevel claims making revealed by our data to be great or small is perhaps a matter of taste. At any rate, there is no indication of a strong and rising challenge to the relevance of national sovereignty and citizenship in the immigration and ethnic relations field. We have presented some indications that perhaps we are even witnessing a renationalization rather than a further denationalization of public contestation in this field.

3

Migrants between Transnationalism and National Citizenship

While some of the political activities of migrants can easily be integrated into existing political institutions and legal frameworks, other types of migrant mobilization may pose serious challenges. Some political activities of migrants refer not to their integration into the receiving society but to the political and social issues of their countries of origin. Such transnational involvement links the hearts and minds of migrants to their homelands and may be detrimental to migrants' integration into their countries of settlement. Some fear it may even lead to a self-reinforcing process of segregation into "parallel societies" along ethnic lines, thus undermining the solidarity and social cohesion without which liberal democracies cannot function. Such interpretations are reinforced by the fact that migrants' involvement with homeland politics often involves violent conflicts among ethnic groups, attacks on representatives of the homeland regime, and sometimes even attacks on the institutions or population of the country of immigration. The terrorist attacks against the United States in September 2001 have made this dark side of migrant activism clear to even the most naive adherents of a romanticized image of transnational communities.

Migrant claims making that refers to the situation in the country of residence may also pose important challenges. These often result from the fact that receiving states have been reluctant to extend equal social, political, and cultural rights to migrants. Countries with an ethnic tradition of national identity have put up high barriers for immigrants to get access to citizenship rights, and in other cases strong assimilationist pressures prevent migrant cultures from achieving the same rights and privileges as native cultures. The realization of migrant demands for equal rights may require a difficult process of redefining the national identity of the host society. Nevertheless, by aiming at increasing the inclusiveness of democratic rights and eradicating ethnoculturally based particularisms, such forms of migrant claims making may ultimately enrich and strengthen rather than weaken democracy. This is less evident for migrant demands for special rights and exemptions from duties because of their racial, cultural, or religious difference. Such demands for multicultural rights have often been the subject of fierce controversy. Examples are demands for the right to wear the Islamic headscarf or the Sikh turban in public institutions, to allow ritual slaughtering of animals, to introduce bilingual education for migrant children, or to establish quotas in public institutions and on the labor market based on racial or ethnic criteria.

Because of their controversial nature, homeland-directed activism and claims for multicultural rights tend to draw much attention, but it is far from clear how representative they are for the wider repertoire of migrant claims making. Moreover, we know very little about possible differences in the extent of different types of claims making between countries and among migrant groups and the reasons behind such variations. This and the next chapter will be devoted to an analysis of migrant claims making in our five countries that aims to answer these questions. In this chapter, we approach the topic by comparatively analyzing claims making of a wide variety of migrant groups. In the next chapter, we will take an in-depth and more qualitative look at claims making by Muslim migrants, whose political and cultural integration poses, in the eyes of many, the greatest challenge to Western liberal democracies.

In analyzing migrant claims making, we contrast two theoretical perspectives. The first, popular in many ethnographic studies of migrant groups and in recent work on transnationalism and diasporas, emphasizes the cultural, ethnic, and political characteristics that migrants bring from their places of origin. This perspective draws attention to differences between migrant groups, for instance, between those with a stronger or weaker internal cohesion and identity, stronger or weaker ties to the homeland, and a greater or smaller cultural difference from the host society. Such cultural group characteristics are seen as resistant to host society attempts at assimilation. In the political arena, this culturalist view is shared by many assimilationists as well as multiculturalists, who obviously draw different conclusions from it. For the assimilationist, the implication is to make the cultural difference a selection criterion for immigration, such as to privilege culturally similar co-ethnics or EU immigrants over, for example,

Muslims. Cultural assimilation in this view is also a condition for granting citizenship rights. Multiculturalists likewise tend to see migrant cultures as relatively fixed and stable, but draw the opposite conclusion that the receiving society should accept and facilitate migrants' cultural differences and should refrain from attempts at assimilation. We contrast these cultural explanations with the institutional and discursive opportunities provided by national citizenship and integration politics, which we have discussed in the preceding chapters. Migrant identities and patterns of organization and participation in this view are not predetermined by migrants' cultural background, but are shaped by the receiving society's discourse and policies with regard to migrants. We begin by discussing the burgeoning literature on transnational communities and diasporas. Then we develop an integrated theoretical framework that allows us to assess the combined impacts of political and cultural factors and to gauge their relative importance. This framework is subsequently applied to the analysis of migrant claims making in our five countries.

Transnational Communities and Diasporas

In the previous chapter, we gave evidence against the postnational perspective on citizenship. With regard to the political behavior of migrants, there is a second popular theoretical perspective that challenges the national embeddedness of claims making and points at the material and symbolic links between ethnic communities across national borders. Increasingly globalized capital accumulation and transfer, the growing speed of communications technologies, and the affordability of long-distance travel are identified as structural developments that favor the emergence of transnational communities and diasporas. Transnational migrants, according to this view, are able to use these facilities to a greater degree than ever before to establish ties that transcend national boundaries, and by crossing and recrossing them physically, electronically, and financially, they increasingly produce a transnational social, cultural, political, and economic world. Transnational migrants do not leave their origins and pasts behind; they take them with them; and by maintaining their networks, they begin to act as conduits between the two or more nations where they have connections. Ethnographic and anthropological studies of migrant behavior have often observed the increasing stakes that these groups have in several places across the globe and the hybrid forms of identity that they use in relation to their homelands, countries of settlement, and scattered kith and kin (Basch, Schiller, and Szanton Blanc 1994; Portes 1997; Portes, Guarnizo, and Landolt 1999). In this view, then, it is not so much the transformation of the basis of citizenship that is eroding the capacity of nation-states to shape migrants in their national image, but the de facto behavior of migrants.

The concept of transnationalism is sometimes used so broadly as to encompass migration and immigrants per se. In a more meaningful and widely accepted definition, transnationalism consists of "the processes by which immigrants forge and sustain multi-stranded social relations that link together their societies of origin and settlement" (Basch, Schiller, and Szanton Blanc 1994, 6). This includes phenomena as diverse as import/export immigrant businesses, investments by migrants in the country of origin, sustained links among family members and co-villagers in the countries of origin and settlement, homeland-based cultural and religious organizations that set up branches in the country of settlement, as well as the mobilization of migrants by homeland political parties and social movements or the diffusion of homeland-based conflicts to the migrant community abroad. The notion of diaspora is also often used in an excessively loose way, as in Marienstras's definition as "any community that has emigrated whose numbers make it visible in the host community" (1989, 125). More precisely, "diaspora" denotes a particular kind of transnational community that originates in massive emigration and dispersal—forced or at least propelled by considerable distress—of a group from a homeland to two or more other countries (Van Hear 1998). Compared to other types of transnational community, diasporas are characterized by a strong orientation toward the homeland, coupled with a longing to return once the homeland has achieved or been restored to independence or its present regime has been overthrown. Beyond the classical template of the Jewish Diaspora, examples include the Armenians, Palestinians, Tibetans, Kurds, Tamils, and Moluccans, as well as regime opponents from Iran, Afghanistan, and Cuba.[1]

Some approaches to transnationalism acknowledge the persistence of an international world order run by nation-states (e.g., Rex 1996; Castles 2000). Transnationalism may even become a way for nation-states to extend their international influence. Receiving states may come to see resident migrants as important opportunities and conduits for establishing links with the sending country and seek to further secure their allegiance by reducing the criteria for naturalization. Conversely, sending states may loosen their direct claims of allegiance on emigrants—for example, by accepting dual citizenship—as a way of establishing a bulkhead in a wealthier receiving state, with the aim of stimulating a continued flow of economic resources and political connections from the center to the periphery (Freeman and Oegelman 1998). Another set of authors condemns the institutional framework of the nation-state to the dustbin of history. They define the particularist group identity claims of minorities and migrants as the important driving force in the creation of a new world order populated by unlimited numbers of diasporas—in the loosest sense of the word—who celebrate their ethnicity at the gates of postmodernity (e.g., Tölöyan 1996). In a less cultural studies vein, others have made similar claims about diasporas challenging the nation-state (e.g., R. Cohen 1997, Vertovec 2000). Against the globalization trends propelled "from above" by transnational capitalism and nation-states' efforts at supranational (de)regulation, several authors see migrant communities as a counterforce of "transnationalism from below" (e.g., Portes 1997; Basch, Schiller, and Szanton Blanc 1994; P. Smith 2001).

A Theoretical Framework for Understanding Migrant Claims Making

We take an intermediate position that sees transnationalism neither as a mere auxiliary to nor as a grave digger of the nation-state world order. We endorse Guarnizo and Smith's criticism of the idea of transmigrants as unbounded actors: "we wish to underline the actual mooring, and, thus, boundedness of transnationalism by the opportunities and constraints found in particular locations where transnational practices occur. . . . the fit between specific kinds of migrants and specific local and national contexts abroad shapes not only the likelihood of generating, maintaining or forsaking transnational ties, but also the very nature of the ties that migrants can forge with their place of origin" (1998, 12–13). In contrast to the polemical opposition of national citizenship on the one hand, and an unbounded transnationalism on the other, our perspective focuses attention on the *interaction* between the two.

The basic features of our theoretical model are shown in Figure 5. We see migrant claims making as determined by the interplay of three factors. First, we expect the opportunities and constraints set by national citizenship regimes and integration models to influence the type of migrant claims making (arrow 1). We expect migrants to be more inclined to make claims regarding their situation in the country of settlement where the state provides opportunities for them and their organizations to do so. Perhaps the most important factor here is whether migrants have the right to vote (which largely depends on them holding citizenship), but in addition such factors as the existence of equal opportunity and antidiscrimination legislation, state subvention and consultation of migrant organizations, or the availability of cultural group rights in domains such as education and the media will play a role.

The second determinant of migrant claims making we have broadly

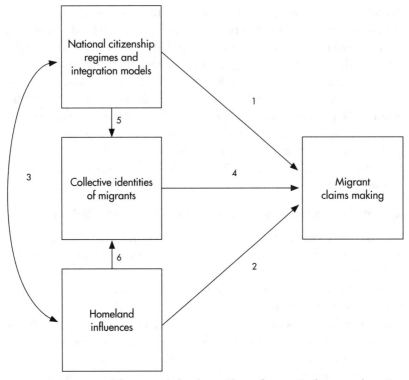

Figure 5. Theoretical framework for the analysis of migrant claims making.

labeled as "homeland influences" (arrow 2). As a corollary to citizenship and integration regimes on the country of settlement side, this includes the sending country's policies with regard to its emigrants. While some sending countries stimulate their (former) subjects to assimilate to the host society, most have an interest in retaining their emigrants' allegiance, if only in order not to lose the yearly inflow of remittances on which many sending countries' economies heavily depend. One instrument is not allowing the loss of the sending countries' citizenship or making such loss costly to migrants (e.g., when they lose inheritance or land ownership rights); another is the direct control over emigrants by way of sending-state-sponsored organizations in the country of settlement, such as the branches of the Turkish Ministry of Religious Affairs or the Maghrebian Amicales in many West European countries. Further, homeland influences include the political situation in the country of origin. Independence struggles of ethnic groups (e.g., the Kurds and Tamils), intra-ethnic conflicts (e.g., among Muslims, Hindus, and Sikhs in India), foreign occupation (e.g., Palestine, Tibet), civil war (e.g., Algeria, Bosnia), and oppressive dictatorships in the country of origin (e.g., China, Iran, Pakistan) provide fuel for homeland-directed claims making among diaspora communities of migrants from these countries. Besides the direct "pull" such homeland conflicts exert on migrants, these conflicts have often also been the "push" factor behind the flight or exile of politically active migrants. Thus, migrant communities from countries with a high level of internal political strife or oppression often harbor a disproportionate number of ideologically, ethnically, or religiously conscious members who hold a diasporic identity and wish to remain involved in the homeland struggle from a distance.

If sending and receiving countries both share an interest in retaining migrants' ties to their homelands, they may institutionally sponsor the activities of sending-country organizations in the country of settlement. Thus, the Bavarian and Turkish governments have together set up Turkish-Islamic classes in Bavarian public schools. This is one example of the ways in which the relation between the country of settlement and the sending country may influence both sides' policies with regard to immigrants (arrow 3 in Figure 5). The Bavarian example illustrates the guest worker type of relationship. A second important type of relationship is that between former imperial powers and their former or remaining colonies. Migrants from former colonies often enjoy—at least for a transitional period after independence—a right to citizenship in the "mother country" or can obtain citizenship more easily. In addition, there are preexisting cultural linkages, most importantly, the fact that many colonial migrants already know the language, which may make it easier for them to integrate. The other side of the coin is that the legacy of colonialism may also include deep-seated racism and paternalism with regard to former colonial subjects, which may counteract the integrative effects of cultural linkages. A third type of sending-receiving country relationship in the European context is the case of intra-EU migration. Migrants from other EU countries nowadays hold largely similar rights (e.g., freedom of movement and access to the labor market) as native citizens of a member state and are in many respects—not least of all in public discourse—privileged vis-à-vis less well-seen "third-country nationals" or "extracommunitari."

The third and final component of the triad of determinants of migrant claims making are the collective identities of migrant groups (arrow 4 in Figure 5). This includes migrants' belonging to a specific ethnic group, their religious affiliation, their identification in terms of a particular "race" (e.g., black), and, of course, their degree of attachment to their country of origin. In some of the literature on transnational communities, and particularly in work on diasporas, we find an almost primordial conception that such collective identities are stable attributes that migrants take with them and insert into the country of settlement. We believe that such identities are to a considerable extent influenced by other explanatory variables in our model—the receiving state's integration and citizenship regime (arrow 5) on the one hand, and homeland influences (arrow 6) on the other. Receiving states may influence migrant identities directly by offering and sponsoring new categories of identification that were unknown in the country of origin, e.g., immigrant, foreigner, ethnic minority, or asylum seeker. At least as important is the possibility that the receiving state's policies alter the balance among diverse identifications that migrants bring along. Most migrants do not arrive with just one identity but with several overlapping, cross-cutting, and competing ones. Immigrants from Surinam, for instance, may see themselves as Surinamese but also as Dutch, Hindu, Muslim, Indian, Javanese, Chinese, Christian, Jewish, Creole, or black, depending on which ethnic, religious, or racial group in Surinam they belong to, or which of their multiple identities they hold as the most important.[2] By sponsoring and rewarding some of these migrant identities and discouraging others, receiving states may alter the balance among such multiple identities and switch migrants' primary allegiance from, say, Christian into black, Javanese into Muslim, Creole into Surinamese, and so on. With this conceptual model in mind, we now turn to the empirical analysis.

Collective Identities

The first aspect of migrant claims making that we investigate concerns their collective identities as expressed in the public sphere. We distinguish four main types (Koopmans and Statham 1999a). First, migrants may identify along the status categories offered by the receiving state's policies, e.g., as foreigners, minorities, immigrants, or asylum seekers. The favored policy categories in our countries of study differ considerably. Swiss and German policies are centered around the category of foreigners, whereas in Britain the minorities category predominates. Given its partial guest worker legacy and its relatively recent turn toward a civic conception of citizenship, Dutch policy categories are to some extent a combination of the foreigners *(buitenlanders, vreemdelingen)* and minorities *(minderheden)* idioms. In France, the predominant policy category is that of *immigrés*.

Second, migrants may identify with a "racial" group, such as blacks or Asians. This type of collective identity is officially sponsored only in Great Britain, where racial categorizations form the cornerstone of race relations and equal opportunities policies. Therefore, the political perspective leads us to expect such identities to be more prominent in Britain than in the other countries. In a culturalist perspective, racial identities such as black are seen as prior to and independent from the respective groups' insertion into the receiving society. In this view, cherished by radical black activists, there exists a transnational "black nation" that connects people of color around the world through bonds of shared destiny and identity. If this view holds true, we should find a considerable amount of racial claims making in the Netherlands and France, which both have large populations of African descent, either from Africa itself or from the Caribbean.

Third, migrants may identify with their religion, e.g., Muslim or Hindu. This type of collective identity is facilitated by the state in the Netherlands, where migrant religious communities can refer to the institutional framework of pillarization to claim rights and privileges. In Germany, Switzerland, and France, by contrast, the state has offered little recognition and few concessions to minority religious communities. The United Kingdom is situated in between. On the one hand, religious identities can claim some legitimacy under Britain's policies of multiculturalism; on the other hand, religious equality and discrimination are not covered by existing race relations legislation (see further, chapter 4). Therefore, the political perspective suggests that religious identities will be more prominent in Britain, and especially in the Netherlands, than in the other three countries. The culturalist perspective makes a different prediction: that religious identifications are transnational phenomena independent from, and prior to, migrants' integration into the host society. If this is the case, we should find migrants identifying along religious lines largely independent from the context of the country of immigration.

Fourth, migrants may identify with their ethnicity or the nationality of their places of origin, for example, as Turks, Pakistani, Surinamese, Arabs, or Algerians. The culturalist perspective sees the prevalence and endurance of such collective identities as an important characteristic of the modern migrant experience. A focus on the opportunity structures set by national citizenship and integration regimes, however, predicts important differences among our countries. Identifications along national and ethnic lines should be most prominent in Germany and Switzerland, where high hurdles to obtaining citizenship have prevented migrants from joining the national community, and migrants are still primarily seen as citizens of their countries of origin. Britain and France, with their strong civic traditions of citizenship, provide the clearest contrast, while the Netherlands come in between.

Although the Dutch system offers minorities at least as much recognition and policy access as in Britain, it does so by classifying minorities and allocating resources to minorities on the basis of national origin.

As a fifth type, we include a hybrid identity category in our analysis for ethnoreligious groups such as Jews and Sikhs, for whom religion and ethnicity are indistinguishable. Sikhs are a relevant group only in Britain, so there is little to compare. We can expect the Jews to deviate from other groups, particularly in Germany. As a result of policies of reconciliation and compensation for the crimes of the Nazi regime, Jews are highly privileged in Germany compared to other migrant groups regarding immigration rights, access to citizenship, and special cultural rights and sponsorship (see Laurence 2001). To some extent, this also holds for Roma and Sinti, whom we include among the ethnic groups and who were also victims of the Nazi regime.

Finally, each of these five identity types can be combined with an identification with the country of residence. Such "hyphened" identities are well known from the U.S. context, where labels such as African-American, Asian-American, or Mexican-American are widely used. In the European context, with its ethnoculturally "thicker" traditions of nationhood, such identifications are less prevalent. Following the political perspective, we may expect them to be most frequent in the two countries with long-standing civic traditions of nationhood, France and Britain, and least prevalent in the two countries with the strongest ethnic traditions of citizenship, Germany and Switzerland.

We measure collective identities by the way in which migrant actors are described in our newspaper sources. In more than half of the cases, these characterizations are based on the full name of the organization that made the claim. Names of organizations are important vehicles for the self-presentation of groups and therefore may be considered good indicators of the group's collective identity. In somewhat less than half of the cases, the newspaper only gave a vague identification of the claim makers (e.g., "Turkish organizations" demonstrating against racism), which leaves room for the ascription of identities by journalists. Such ascriptions may be interesting in their own right because they tell us something about how the majority society sees migrants, which may well diverge from the ways in which migrants identify themselves by way of their organizational names. However, apart from one significant exception, which we will discuss later, a separate inspection of the subsample of self-described collective identities does not lead to substantively different results (see also Koopmans and Statham 1999a, 675–79).

We allow for the possibility of composite and hybrid identities by providing for multiple responses. For example, the Bund türkischer Einwanderer gets two identity codes, Turkish and immigrant; the Turks-Islamitische Culturele Federatie is coded Turkish as well as Muslim. As an indicator of hyphened identities between a minority identity and the national identification of the country of residence, we considered only such cases where the one was a direct adjective to the other, as in British Muslim Action Front, Confédération des Français Musulmans Répatriés d'Algérie (both coded Muslim and hyphened), or Zentralrat der deutschen Sinti und Roma (coded Sinti and Roma and hyphened). Excluded are cases where the name of an organization refers to the country of residence only in a geographical sense (e.g., Zentralrat der Juden in Deutschland, or Nederlands Centrum Buitenlanders), as well as cases where it cannot be determined whether the reference expresses a hyphened identity or is only geographical (e.g., Ligue Nationale des Musulmans de France).

Turning to the results in Table 21, we see that status identities based on the receiving states' policy categories are most frequent in France, where policies and public discourse are constructed around the individualized category of *immigré* and particularistic collective identities are regarded with suspicion within the context of the universalist, republican conception of the nation. Policies exist for first-generation *immigrés* and to some extent for second-generation *jeunes d'origine immigré*, but the possibility of durable minority formation is not acknowledged. The most important status category in France in the period under study was that of illegal immigrants, who under the label of *sans-papiers* mobilized broad public support for their demand to be legalized. In the other four countries, we find very few claims by illegal immigrants. Claims by asylum seekers were relatively rare in France, however. This results from the fact that a structurally similar type of immigrants (who are sometimes labeled as economic refugees) enters France (and other southern European countries such as Italy and Spain) through the channel of illegal immigration, whereas in northwestern Europe, where asylum rights tend to be more generous, these migrants prefer the formal channel of applying for political asylum or refugee status. A final status group worth mentioning in France are the so-called Harki, immigrants of Algerian origin who served in the French colonial army and were forced to leave the country at independence. The name Harki is derived from the village militias that the French set up against the Algerian Front de la Libération Nationale (FLN) independence movement.

In Germany, and even more so in Switzerland, status identities are much less important. These countries' refusal to acknowledge their factual status

Table 21. Collective identities in public claims making

Identities	Netherlands	Great Britain	France	Germany	Switzerland
Policy-status identities (%)	25.5	19.2	41.3	10.7	7.0
Foreigners (%)	9.7	–	–	4.1	2.0
Minorities/*allochtonen* (%)	5.4	8.9	–	0.1	2.0
Immigrants (%)	0.3	–	11.6	0.8	–
Asylum seekers (%)	8.7	8.8	1.9	5.4	2.0
Illegal immigrants/*sans-papiers* (%)	1.3	0.7	22.8	–	–
Harki (%)	–	–	4.5	–	–
Aussiedler (%)	–	–	–	0.3	–
Other (%)	–	0.7	0.6	–	1.0
Racial identities (%)	1.7	43.0	0.0	0.3	0.0
Black (%)	1.3	32.4	–	0.3	–
Asian (%)	–	9.6	–	–	–
Other (%)	0.3	1.1	–	–	–
Religious identities (%)	18.6	18.0	22.4	2.7	1.5
Muslim (%)	16.4	16.9	22.1	2.3	1.0
Hindu (%)	1.3	0.4	–	–	–
Other (%)	0.9	0.7	0.3	0.4	0.5
Ethnoreligious identities (%)	8.1	7.0	19.6	21.4	20.6
Jewish (%)	8.1	5.5	19.6	21.4	20.6
Sikh (%)	–	1.5	–	–	–

Table 21. Collective identities in public claims making (continued)

Identities	Netherlands	Great Britain	France	Germany	Switzerland
Ethnic and national identities (%)	55.7	19.1	16.7	67.2	70.4
EU countries (%)	0.3	1.9	–	0.6	3.0
Ex-Yugoslav ethnicities (%)	2.6	1.1	–	1.8	15.6
Sinti and Roma (%)	0.7	0.4	–	6.4	0.5
Other European (%)	1.0	1.6	0.3	0.4	5.5
Turkish (%)	14.4	0.4	1.0	21.4	3.0
Kurdish (%)	8.4	0.4	1.9	30.4	27.6
Iranian (%)	2.0	–	–	3.0	0.5
Indian subcontinent ethnicities and nationalities (%)	–	5.6	–	–	–
Tamil (%)	–	0.4	–	–	5.5
Tibetan (%)	–	–	–	0.5	5.5
Chinese (%)	1.3	0.4	0.3	0.2	–
Moluccan (%)	3.0	–	–	–	–
Other Asian (%)	3.0	2.2	0.3	0.8	0.5
Morocco (%)	7.7	–	1.3	–	–
Algerian (%)	0.7	0.7	1.3	0.1	0.5
Maghrebian/Arab undifferentiated (%)	0.3	–	4.1	–	–
Other African (%)	5.3	3.7	6.0	1.1	1.5
Caribbean and Latin American (%)	4.7	1.5	–	0.1	1.0
Hyphened identification with country of residence (%)	1.0	5.5	14.7	5.2	12.6
Total (%)	110.6	111.8	114.7	107.5	112.1
N	298	272	313	921	203

as immigration countries has left the immigration and integration policy domains greatly underdeveloped. As a result, there are few legal frameworks and institutional points of access that offer opportunities to mobilization along the lines of policy status. The only state-sponsored—but in terms of rights, resources, and policy access rather marginal—status identities in these countries are those of foreigner and asylum seeker, and what little mobilization along status lines we find occurs under these two identities. The results for the status group of *Aussiedler* in Germany are notable. Although they number more than two million (about as many as the immigrants of Turkish origin), we found only a few claims by this group (0.3 percent). The reason seems to lie partly in their relatively privileged position. Upon arrival, *Aussiedler* immediately receive German citizenship with all the rights attached to it. In addition, they can claim several social rights as if they had been living and paying contributions in Germany all their lives. They are also offered extensive free language courses and special assistance in finding jobs and housing (see Koopmans 1999). Meanwhile, these privileges have been reduced, and because of the adverse situation on the German labor market, many *Aussiedler* are unemployed. So far, this has not led to an increase in the number of claims by *Aussiedler* because the group has a serious collective identity problem that stands in the way of mobilization. Officially regarded as ethnoculturally German, they find it difficult to develop a distinct collective identity that can serve as a legitimate basis for making claims on the state. Most of them are culturally distinct: many speak Russian at home, they watch and read Russian media, and their youth spend their evenings dancing to the latest Russian hits. Moreover, many native Germans regard and treat them as Russians. The social reality therefore is that the *Aussiedler* are an ethnocultural minority and experience many of the same problems that other migrant communities do. However, the state does not recognize this Russian, or hybrid Russian-German, identity and continues to adhere to the myth that the *Aussiedler* are not really an immigrant group, but "returnees" who "come to live as Germans among Germans," as the official mantra puts it.

Regarding status identities, Britain and the Netherlands occupy intermediary positions between France on the one hand, and Germany and Switzerland on the other. In line with these countries' culturally pluralist policies, we find a sizable number of claims under the label of minorities and under the related Dutch policy category of *allochtonen* (persons of foreign origin). We also find a high number of claims in the Netherlands based on the foreigner identity—a much greater percentage even than in Germany and Switzerland. This is almost entirely due to one very prominent organization, the Dutch Centre for Foreigners (Nederlands Centrum Buitenlanders)—a state-subsidized organization that was set up in the guest worker era to assist, and represent the interests of, labor migrants. Its prominence is still indicative of the hybrid nature of the Dutch integration model, with its partial roots in a German-style guest worker regime on the one hand, and a civic, culturally pluralist tradition rooted in pillarization and colonialism on the other.

The results for racial identities are extremely clear-cut: racial—particularly black—identities are by far the most important type of collective identity among migrants in Britain, but they are virtually absent everywhere else. This may not be so striking for the German and Swiss cases, but it is so for France and the Netherlands, which have populations of African descent with black phenotypic features of similar size as in Britain. Moreover, many blacks in France and the Netherlands come from the same geographical area, the Caribbean, as the majority of their British counterparts, and share the same history of deportation, slavery, and racism. This example very powerfully shows how important national opportunity structures are for shaping collective identities. The prominence of race in Britain's integration regime has offered an exceptional opportunity to immigrants of African descent to achieve a presence in the public sphere that is unrivaled by their French and Dutch counterparts, and has also put them in a privileged position vis-à-vis other minorities in Britain. Race relations policies were later expanded to include migrants from the Indian subcontinent under the racial label of Asians. Although much less prominent than black, Asian collective identities also play a considerable role in claims making by British migrants.

Proceeding to collective identities on a religious basis, we again find a striking contrast, this time between Britain, France, and the Netherlands on the one hand, and Germany and Switzerland on the other. Although the latter two countries both have sizable Muslim populations that are, at least in the case of Germany, comparable to Britain, France, and the Netherlands, Muslims are almost completely absent from the German and Swiss public spheres. Contrary to the view of Islam as a transnational collective identity, we see that German and Swiss Muslims have little inclination to make claims based on their religion. This is not to say that migrants of Muslim belief are not active claim makers in Germany and Switzerland. However, as we shall shortly see, they make such claims on the basis of their ethnicity and nationality rather than their religion. We contend that this is so partly because German and Swiss assimilationist policies and public discourse offer few opportunities for such claims making. In addition, as long as migrants in these countries mirror the state's view by not seeing themselves as part of the German community, religious rights and equality are not a salient political issue for them. Once a large number of Muslims, as in Britain, France, and the Netherlands, have become citizens, they will both have improved opportunities for making claims and feel more strongly entitled to rights and treatment fully equal to those enjoyed by Christian (and sometimes also Jewish) denominations.

However, we also find an indication for intergroup differences that seems to be unrelated to the receiving state's integration policies. Compared to Muslims, we find Hindus to be much less prominent in the public sphere in the two countries that have significant populations of Hindu belief, Britain and the Netherlands. While in the Netherlands this difference can at least partly be explained by the fact that there are about nine times more Muslims than Hindus there, this explanation does not hold for Britain with its large population of Indian origin. We suspect that this difference is due to the different nature of the two religions, particularly the fact that Islam—at least in its recent manifestations around the world—is a much more public religion than Hinduism. This explains why Muslims have made more claims for religious rights than Hindus have and also why Islam is singled out as a threat to Western values by opponents of immigration and multiculturalism much more than Hinduism is. This interpretation of Islam as a more public religion, which cannot be relegated easily to the private domain, also helps to explain another important finding that goes against our emphasis on the nation-state's capacities to shape migrant identities, namely, that France turns out to be the country with the highest percentage of Muslim claims. The one important deviation that occurs, if we restrict the sample to claims where we had the full name of the organization that made the claim, also points in the direction that the Muslim identity is especially resistant against state attempts to channel migrant identities. For the full sample we found almost 10 percent claims by Asians in Britain, but this racial identification almost completely disappears (1.2 percent) among the sample based on organizational names, while the relative weight of Muslim claims increases. This suggests that the "Asian" identity for migrants from the Indian subcontinent that is officially sponsored in Britain is not taken up to a significant extent by Pakistani and Bangladeshi immigrants, whose Muslim identity is apparently more meaningful to them.

Turning now to the ethnoreligious identities, we see that there is a stark contrast in Germany and Switzerland between the invisibility of Muslims and the highly prominent position of Jews in the public sphere. As victims of the Holocaust, Jews are considered highly legitimate speakers on racism and xenophobia. The number of claims on immigration and integration issues by Jewish groups is larger than the number of Muslim claims even though there are many more Muslim than Jewish immigrants in these countries. This is another example of how diverging state integration approaches and the symbolic inclusion or exclusion of groups in political discourse can have striking consequences for these groups' collective identities and mobilization opportunities.

Next, we look at national and ethnic identities. As expected, such identifications are most prominent among migrants in Switzerland, closely followed by Germany, where more than two-thirds of all claims were made in the name of national or ethnic collectivities. Officially defined and treated as *Ausländer* (foreigners), migrants identify and behave as such and organize and make claims as Turks, Bosnians, or Iranians, rather than as immigrants, Asians, or Muslims. Ethnic and national identifications are—with less than 20 percent—least prominent in Britain and France, where historically rooted civic traditions of citizenship lead to a relatively quick erosion of identities based on migrants' countries of origin. The Netherlands (56 percent) are in between but, perhaps surprisingly, much closer to Germany and Switzerland than to Britain and France. The most important reason is that Dutch multiculturalism extends rights and incorporates migrant organizations on the basis of the nationality of origin and not on race as in Britain or immigrant status as in France.

If we look in more detail at the ethnic and national groups present in the claims making, we see that these reflect to an important extent the composition of the migrant population in the various countries. However, there are some clear under- and overrepresentations of groups that deserve our attention. Perhaps the clearest case of underrepresentation are migrants from EU countries. With their secure residence status, full labor market access, freedom of movement, and partial political rights, these migrants have almost the same legal status as natives. In addition, they are hardly subjected to discrimination and are not (any longer) perceived as culturally very different from the native population. Thus, EU migrants have little need for making claims on their host societies. The only partial exception is Switzerland, which is not an EU member, although it has adapted in many ways to EU legal regimes. Consequently, Switzerland is the only country where claims by EU migrants (particularly Italians) attain at least a modest level of visibility. A similarly low level of mobilization is found in the Netherlands and Britain for certain categories of colonial migrants, who have been socioeconomically successful and are culturally perceived as adapted and unobtrusive. In Britain, this explains the low level of mobilization of Indians

(Statham 1999), and in the Netherlands the absence of a large number of claims by people of Indonesian origin. All Indonesian claims in the Netherlands were made by Moluccans, who are a distinct group that still strives for independence of its homeland from Indonesia and who have long cherished a myth of return that has prevented their integration into Dutch society. It is less clear why the number of claims by Caribbeans (Surinamese and Antilleans), who make up about one-sixth of the total population of migrant origin, is so low in the Netherlands. This cannot be explained by these groups' having already achieved full equality, since their living conditions (unemployment, schooling, housing, and so on) are still considerably worse than those of the native Dutch, although they are clearly better than those of Turks and Moroccans (CBS 2001). Research done by Fennema and Tillie (1999) suggests that this low level of mobilization of Surinamese and Antilleans may be partly due to the fact that, compared to Moroccans and Turks, these groups have weakly developed ethnic community networks.

The group most strongly overrepresented is the Kurds, who account for about 20 percent of migrants from Turkey but who are responsible for a sizable part of claims making in the three countries with large contingents of Turkish immigrants: Germany, the Netherlands, and Switzerland. Of course, this has much to do with the Kurdish independence struggle, which went through a particularly "hot" phase during the 1990s. However, there is also quite some variation between these three countries regarding the prominence of Kurdish claims. Although as a percentage of the population the Netherlands have more Turkish immigrants than Switzerland and almost as many as Germany, the percentage of Kurdish claims is much lower in the Netherlands (8 percent versus 28 percent in Switzerland and 30 percent in Germany). Another comparison worth calling attention to is that between the two countries with large Maghrebian populations, France and the Netherlands. Although as a percentage of the population Maghrebians are twice more numerous in France, we find about 50 percent more claims on the basis of Maghrebian identities in the Netherlands. This illustrates the general tendency that identities referring to migrant homelands are strongly constrained by the French universalist regime, while in the Netherlands such identities are officially sponsored (e.g., by subsidies and consultation rights for Moroccan organizations). A final group that is clearly overrepresented are the Roma and Sinti in Germany (6 percent of all claims). The reason is the group's status as Holocaust victims and the public legitimacy and privileged treatment by the state that this entails in the German context.

Finally, we look at hyphened identifications with the country of residence. As expected, such identifications are strongest in France, where the republican tradition demands any particularist identities to be subordinated to allegiance to the French nation. The relatively high number of hyphened identities expresses the conformity of migrants' public identities with this ideal where the legitimacy of particularist claims is mitigated by the use of the adjective "French." Almost half (6.7 percent out of 14.7 percent) of the hyphened identities stemmed from groups with a French Muslim identity. Faced with the reality of a religious identification that was not going to be assimilated away, the French authorities themselves have called for the development of a French Islam, and the prevalence of French Muslim identities constitutes an adaptation by migrants to this discourse. This reading is confirmed by the fact that in the other countries hyphened Muslim identities are not very frequent: 1.5 percent in Britain, and none at all in Germany, the Netherlands, and Switzerland. The high level of hyphened identities in Switzerland is entirely due to Jewish groups. In Germany, 3.7 percent out of 5.2 percent are Roma and Sinti organizations. While it is unsurprising that we find few hyphened identifications in the exclusionary contexts of Germany and Switzerland, it is noteworthy that such identities are not very widespread in the two countries with multicultural policies either. In the Netherlands, in particular, we find even fewer hyphened identities than in Germany and Switzerland. Multicultural integration policies apparently do not produce strong identifications with the country of residence.

The pressures in France to put one's allegiance to the French nation above any particularist identities has caused a methodological problem for us that has probably led to an underestimation of the level of migrant activism in France. In the other countries, we rarely had problems determining whether we were dealing with a claim made by migrants, but this problem occurred quite frequently in France. The reasons were twofold. First, in an apparent attempt not to make any illegitimate distinctions based on ethnicity, our newspaper sources sometimes obscured that we were dealing with claims making by migrants. For instance, riots in the suburbs were sometimes attributed to youth without any further specification, although anyone familiar with the French context knows that these rioters were almost exclusively of migrant, particularly Maghrebian, origin. Where context knowledge, including follow-up articles, allowed us to attribute these events to Maghrebians or immigrants, we coded them as such, but in other cases we had to exclude them because we could not be sure whether a migrant group was behind them. The second source of identification problems in France was that organizations composed mainly of migrants sometimes do not make this explicit in their names, but instead choose a universalist label.

Again, we included such cases where context knowledge allowed us to do so. An example is the antiracist organization France plus, which is run by migrants of Maghrebian origin. This organization illustrates the power of the French universalist discourse in an exemplary way: the particularist migrant identity is symbolically reduced to an unspecified extension ("plus") of the dominant allegiance to the French Republic. In other cases, mobilization under a universalist flag took the form of truly mixed organizations, which mobilize both migrants and their French supporters. Such organizations were not included for the analysis of migrant claims in this chapter, and will be dealt with in chapter 6 on antiracist and pro-minority mobilization. The most important example is SOS racisme, which is partly rooted in the *beur* movement of Maghrebian youth, but also mobilizes many native French.

Summing up, these results provide strong and suggestive evidence for the importance of national citizenship and integration regimes in shaping migrant mobilization. These factors go a long away in explaining cross-national differences (e.g., the prevalence of status identities in France, of racial identities in Britain, and of ethnic and national identities in Germany and Switzerland) and also account for some of the intergroup differences within countries (e.g., the low mobilization levels of EU migrants everywhere, or the special position of Jews and Roma, particularly in Germany). However, in line with the conceptual model we outlined earlier, we also need to take homeland influences into account, such as the political conflict in Kurdistan. Finally, there remain intergroup differences that can be explained neither by national nor by homeland influences and that point to specific nonreducible characteristics of migrant groups. The independence dream of the Moluccans or the weak community networks of Caribbean migrants in the Netherlands are examples of such group-specific factors.

Homeland and Transnational Orientations

We now turn to how migrant claims reflect national or transnational orientations. We distinguish three types of transnational claims making. The first type might be called transplanted homeland politics. In this type, migrants make claims in the country of settlement, but these refer in all other respects to the country of origin. A typical example is claims made by exile groups or branches of homeland-based organizations,[3] directed at or against the homeland regime or targeting homeland regime representatives or institutions in the country of settlement. In the case of homeland-based interethnic or religious conflicts (e.g., between Serbians and Albanians),

such claims may also take the form of conflicts between the involved ethnic groups in the country of settlement. The next two types are more substantively transnational in the sense that they are a hybrid of homeland
and country-of-settlement orientations. The second type consists of claims
whose ultimate political aim is oriented toward the homeland, but which
mobilize organizational networks or political opportunities in the country
of settlement to these ends. A typical example is claims making by ethnic organizations originating in and addressed to the government of the
country of settlement, asking the latter to intervene with the homeland government on behalf of the group's interests (e.g., the Federation of Kurds
in the Netherlands offering a petition to the Dutch Parliament protesting
the genocide against the Kurds in Turkey). Third, the claim structure may
also be the reverse, when groups originating in the homeland mobilize
homeland-based organizational resources and opportunities to intervene on
behalf of the group's interests in the country of settlement (e.g., when Milli
Görüş sets up an Islamic center in Germany).

In Table 22 we contrast these three forms of transnational claims making with claims making by migrants and minorities that stays entirely within the political context of the country of settlement, i.e., where organizations originating in the country of settlement advance claims on authorities
in the country of settlement in order to further the interests of a constituency in the country of settlement (e.g., a letter by the National Federation of
Chinese Organizations to the Dutch government calling on it to pay more
attention to social problems within the Chinese community). The literature on transnational communities and diasporas leads us to expect sizable
numbers of transnational and homeland-directed claims in all countries.
Although this approach does not make explicit predictions about cross-
national differences, one of its arguments is that transnational tendencies
are enhanced by the receiving states' increased acceptance of cultural differences, which allows migrants to retain strong material and emotional ties to
their homelands. We might thus expect transnational claims to be more frequent in the multicultural contexts of Britain and the Netherlands. A focus
on institutional and discursive opportunities leads to different expectations.
From this perspective, homeland-oriented and transnational claims are
most likely in countries such as Switzerland and Germany where the state
offers migrants few institutional opportunities and rights, and symbolically
excludes them from the national community. Lacking strong identification
with the country of residence as well as opportunities to effectively improve
their situation, migrants will mirror the state's rejection of them by staying

strongly focused on their countries of origin. In the other three countries, the level of transnational claims should be much lower, especially in the French context, with its strong rejection of cultural particularism.

The results in Table 22 do not fit the predictions of the culturalist, transnational communities perspective. We find widely divergent levels of transnational claims making, ranging from less than 10 percent in France to more than 58 percent in Switzerland. These differences are largely in a different direction than what the culturalist perspective leads us to expect. Transnational claims making is not more frequent in countries that provide immigrants with a broad set of rights and a high degree of acceptance of their cultural difference, but in Switzerland and Germany. In line with the political opportunity perspective, the most important type of transnational claims making in these two countries is transplanted homeland politics, in which the role of the country of immigration is merely as the geographical stage on which homeland political conflicts are carried out (43 percent in Switzerland and 27 percent in Germany). Among the more genuinely transnational claims, Germany and Switzerland lean heavily toward claims that mobilize country-of-residence resources and opportunities on behalf of aims situated in the country of origin (16 percent in Germany and 12 percent in Switzerland). In Germany, for instance, the Iranian National Resistance Council on several occasions called on the German government and business community to sever contacts with the Iranian regime. In Great Britain and France, by contrast, transplanted homeland politics is the least

Table 22. Distribution of migrant claims across four types of claims making

Claims	Netherlands	Britain	France	Germany	Switzerland
Transplanted homeland politics (%)	9.1	1.8	2.6	27.3	42.9
Homeland-directed transnationalism (%)	9.1	3.3	3.9	15.6	12.3
Country of residence-directed transnationalism (%)	6.4	5.5	2.9	3.5	2.0
Purely national claims (%)	75.5	89.3	90.7	53.5	41.4
Unknown (%)	–	–	–	0.1	1.5
Total (%)	100.0	100.0	100.0	100.0	100.0
N	298	272	313	921	203

frequent of the four types of claims making (1.8 percent and 2.6 percent respectively). The two genuinely transnational types are a bit more numerous, but about 90 percent of claims in both countries remain firmly tied to the national context of the immigration country and involve neither homeland-based actors or addressees, nor homeland political issues. The Netherlands again occupies an intermediary position. About 24 percent of all migrant claims in the Netherlands had a transnational dimension and 9 percent of those were of the transplanted homeland politics type. This intermediary position is related to our earlier finding of the relatively strong role of national and ethnic identities in migrant claims making in the Netherlands.

While these results point toward an overriding role for the national citizenship and integration regimes of the country of settlement in explaining the spatial orientation of migrant claims making, we have seen earlier in our discussion of collective identities that homeland influences and specific characteristics of migrant groups may also play a role. To what extent can such factors explain the cross-national differences in homeland-directed versus country-of-settlement-directed claims making? To investigate this question, Table 23 displays for different migrant groups the percentage of their claims that were oriented toward aims in the group's country or region of origin. In order to avoid cells with too few cases for analysis, some of the analytically less interesting distinctions of Table 21 were collapsed together.

If we first concentrate on a comparison among the main identity types, we see that status identities correlate with low numbers of homeland-oriented claims and a concomitantly strong orientation on the country of settlement. This is not surprising, since status identities are by definition based on the receiving state's categorizations. In line with the political opportunity perspective, homeland-directed claims in the name of status identities occur most frequently in Germany and Switzerland. It is a highly remarkable finding that none of the claims made in the name of racial identities were oriented toward the situation of blacks in migrants' homelands or in other foreign countries. The claim that the black racial identity is a transnational phenomenon thus receives not the slightest support. Race is an identification relevant almost exclusively to the British context, where the state's policies are built around the category of race, and it is used to make claims that are exclusively oriented toward migrants' position in the country of settlement. A similar conclusion can be drawn for claims by Jewish groups, which mostly focus on the country of residence, particularly on antiracism and demands related to the Holocaust and the Second World War. By contrast, claims by Jewish groups referring to Israel or to Jewish

Table 23. Percentage of claims on homeland issues for different migrant identity groups

Identity groups	Netherlands	Great Britain	France	Germany	Switzerland
Policy-status identities (%)	5.3	0.0	3.9	13.1	7.1
Racial identities (%)	0.0	0.0	–	(0.0)	–
Religious identities (%)	10.7	12.2	7.1	32.0	(66.7)
Muslim (%)	12.2	13.0	7.3	38.1	(50.0)
Other (%)	0.0	(0.0)	(0.0)	(0.0)	(100.0)
Ethnoreligious identities (%)	7.4	10.5	3.3	0.0	9.5
Jewish (%)	7.4	6.7	3.3	0.0	9.5
Sikh (%)	–	(25.0)	–	–	–
Ethnic and national identities (%)	30.1	7.7	17.3	61.7	74.1
Ex-Yugoslav ethnicities (%)	50.0	(0.0)	–	64.7	80.7
Sinti and Roma (%)	(0.0)	(0.0)	–	0.0	(0.0)
Other European (%)	(0.0)	0.0	(0.0)	0.0	56.3
Turks and Kurds (%)	51.5	(0.0)	44.4	69.0	83.6
Indian subcontinent (%)	–	14.3	–	–	–
Moluccan (%)	55.6	–	–	–	–
Other Asian (%)	18.8	25.0	(0.0)	83.7	58.3
Maghrebian (%)	7.7	(0.0)	23.8	(100.0)	(100.0)
Other African (%)	0.0	0.0	0.0	18.2	(33.3)
Caribbean and Latin American (%)	0.0	(0.0)	–	(100.0)	(100.0)
Hyphen-identification with country of residence (%)	(33.3)	13.3	8.7	2.1	0.0
Total (%)	18.1	5.2	6.4	42.9	55.1
N	298	272	313	921	203

Note: Percentages for cells with five or fewer cases are in parentheses.

communities elsewhere were very rare. Transnational claims thus play a marginal role even in this paradigmatic case of a diaspora. The Muslim identity is associated with a higher level of transnational involvement, but with strong cross-national variation. In France, with its policy emphasis on stimulating a French Islam, Muslim claims refer rarely to transnational issues. In the Netherlands and Britain, Muslim claims referring to homeland or transnational issues are somewhat more frequent, but not very much so. In the three countries where Muslim claims play a significant role, we seem to be dealing with a strongly domesticated Muslim identity. Only in Switzerland and Germany do we find high percentages of Muslim claims with transnational orientations (e.g., conflicts between Turkish Alevites and Islamic fundamentalist groups).

With the exception of Britain, national and ethnic identities are associated with the highest level of homeland orientation, but again there is strong cross-national variation. In Britain and France, we not only find few claims in the name of ethnic and national identities, but even those that are made rarely refer to homeland issues. In the Netherlands, ethnic and national identities are more often linked to homeland issues (30 percent), but the majority of claims concern the groups' position in the Netherlands. This is a result of the specific way in which the Netherlands define "minorities"—on the basis of national origin. In the Dutch context, to make claims based on a Turkish or Surinamese collective identity does not necessarily imply a strong attachment to Turkey or Surinam, but reflects the categorizations the state uses for granting access to the policy process. Within the category of national and ethnic identities, there is quite some variation among groups. In France, the Netherlands, and Britain, there are several ethnonational groups that made no homeland-directed claims at all (other Africans, other Europeans, and Caribbeans in all three countries, as well as ex-Yugoslavs, Turks and Kurds, and Maghrebians in Britain, and other Asians in France). The same is true for Roma and Sinti in all five countries. There are also a number of ethnonational groups that have strong homeland orientations in several, though not all, countries: Turks and Kurds, ex-Yugoslavs, and other Asians (e.g., Arabs, Afghans, Lebanese), as well as the specific case of the Moluccans in the Netherlands. The explanation for these strong homeland orientations lie primarily in the violent conflicts and oppressive regimes in these groups' homelands.

Transnational connections of the latter type are central to the culturalist perspective, and the question should be asked whether the aggregate differences in the strength of homeland and transnational orientations that we find between our five countries cannot be largely explained by differences in the composition of their migrant populations. While we do not deny that homeland influences and cultural characteristics of migrant groups play a certain role, there are three important reasons why these intergroup differences are peripheral rather than central to understanding migrant claims making. The first reason can be read directly from the table. If we hold the collective identity constant and compare the countries for each group separately, we find a recurrent pattern. Apart from a very few exceptions, the highest levels of homeland orientations are found in Germany and Switzerland, with the latter country attaining the highest levels in most cases. Britain or France have the lowest levels of homeland orientations, while the Netherlands are often situated in between. The two exceptions to this rule are in themselves telling. First, hyphenated identities are least often associated with homeland-oriented claims in Germany and Switzerland. This is explained by the groups who display such hyphenated identities in these countries: Jews, who are responsible for all hyphenated identities in Switzerland, and Roma and Sinti, who make up two-thirds of hyphenated identities in Germany. Second, there is no clear pattern for Jewish claims, but the level of transnational claims is lowest (zero) in Germany. This fits with the fact that German Jews can claim a set of rights, including virtually unlimited immigration and generous state sponsorship of their religion and organizations, that is incomparable to any other immigrant group (Laurence 2001). The weak transnational orientation of German Jews is therefore an exception that proves the rule that the stronger the rights position and symbolic inclusion of migrants in the country of residence, the more will homeland attachments erode.

The second reason why we should be careful not to give too much weight to intergroup differences is that to some extent we are "sampling on the dependent variable": we see high levels of homeland orientation among Kurds, Iranians, and ex-Yugoslavs, and say these are obviously explained by homeland conflicts. However, what about the negative cases, where we have intense homeland conflicts without much repercussion in the claims making of migrants from these countries? Were not Pakistan and India several times on the brink of war recently, did not Muslims and Hindus (e.g., Ayodhya), and Sikhs and Hindus (e.g., Amritsar), clash violently in India on several occasions during the period of our study? What about the bloody civil war in Algeria, taking place almost at the doorstep of France? In the light of the intense political conflicts in these regions, it is astonishing, and testimony to the strong integrative power of these countries' citizenship regimes, that there has been so little mobilization on homeland issues by Algerians in France and by South Asian groups in Britain.

The third and analytically most important reason why we should not overestimate the role of interethnic differences—and here we refer back to Table 21—is that inclusive citizenship regimes such as those of Britain and France not only affect the degree to which certain identity groups make homeland-oriented claims, but shape the very identities of these groups. As a result, Algerians or Pakistani in these countries are often no longer visible in the public sphere as such, but appear as Muslims, general speakers for minorities or immigrants, or, in the British case, as representatives of the racial group of Asians. Similarly, most claims by migrants from the Caribbean in Britain are made under the label of blacks, and not under the flags of Jamaica or Trinidad. By bending collective identities in this way, inclusive citizenship regimes channel migrant identifications away from the national and ethnic categories of their homelands. Therefore an honest comparison between, for example, the claims making of Turks in the Netherlands and in Germany should look not only at claims made under the label of Turks, but also at claims made by nonethnic Muslim or minority organizations in which members of the Turkish community may participate. As Table 21 indicates, this is not likely to produce a very different picture for Germany, but it certainly would alter the perspective for the Netherlands, and would result in a greater difference in the level of homeland orientation between German and Dutch Turks than the one found on the basis of the national identification alone. Of course, since Turks become publicly invisible as Turks and indistinguishable from other Muslims or minorities as soon as they mobilize under a different collective identity, we cannot give exact figures for such a comparison, but the direction in which the result would go should be clear.

Another alternative for our interpretation in terms of national opportunity structures focuses on the contrast between colonial migration and guest worker migration. The lower levels of homeland orientations among migrants in France, Britain, and the Netherlands might be due to the fact that colonial migrants in these countries were already familiar with the culture and language prior to migration and in many cases could claim citizenship rights. They will thus perhaps more easily assimilate to the political culture of the country of immigration. We can test the postcolonial hypothesis by investigating whether the cross-national differences among the five countries disappear if we exclude postcolonial migrants from our sample. This is easier said than done. Once migrants take on collective identities other than those of their country or ethnicity of origin, it becomes difficult to distinguish colonial from noncolonial migrants. For instance, blacks in Britain will often, though not exclusively, come from former colonies in the

Caribbean or Africa. The same is true for Muslims in Britain and France who will often, but not always, be from former British India or French North Africa. In the Dutch case, it is somewhat easier to make an accurate distinction because national identifications are more frequent and because the category of Muslims is almost exclusively noncolonial.[4]

To allow a test of the postcolonial hypothesis, we have taken an inclusive operationalization of postcolonial migrants that includes (a) migrants identifiable by the nationality of a former colony (e.g., Surinamese in the Netherlands, or Algerians in France); (b) postcolonial status groups (e.g., Harki); (c) religious groups that are mostly postcolonial (Muslims in Britain and France, Hindus in Britain and the Netherlands); and (d) racial groups that are mostly postcolonial (blacks in Britain and the Netherlands, and Asians in Britain). The results in Table 24 do not support the postcolonial hypothesis: in all three former colonizing countries, the difference between the level of homeland orientation among postcolonial and other migrants is negligible. In other words, all migrants in these three countries, whether colonial or noncolonial, are less preoccupied with homeland politics than migrants in Switzerland and Germany.

Action Repertoires

The impact of political opportunity structures on the repertoire of collective action is a well-established finding in the social movement literature (e.g., Kitschelt 1986; Kriesi et al. 1995). The general thesis is that where institutional channels of access to the decision-making process are closed to a challenger, it will resort to unconventional, extrainstitutional action forms in order to make its demands heard. According to Kriesi et al. (1995,

Table 24. Homeland orientations among postcolonial and other migrants

Claims	Netherlands	Britain	France	Germany	Switzerland
Homeland claims for postcolonial migrants (%)	15.2	4.6	8.2	–	–
Homeland claims for other migrants (%)	18.5	6.5	5.4	42.9	55.1
Postcolonial claims of all migrant claims (%)	11.1	71.7	35.1	0	0
N	298	272	311	925	199

ch. 2), such access is determined by two characteristics of a political system. First, the degree of horizontal and vertical centralization of power determines the number of points of access to the political process. The more independent levels of access (e.g., strong local and regional authorities or a strong judiciary), the likelier it is that a collective actor will find a hearing within institutional politics. In highly centralized systems, to the contrary, it is much more difficult to penetrate the policy process. Second, access depends on informal elite strategies for dealing with societal challengers. Often rooted in the way in which elites have historically dealt with the resolution of traditional cleavages, such as those between labor and capital, center and periphery, and church and state, some countries are characterized by consensus-oriented strategies where elites try to include a wide range of actors and interests in policy making. Other countries are characterized by a higher degree of political polarization and exclusive strategies with regard to challenging minorities. Based on these two dimensions, France is a country with a closed political opportunity structure, with a high level of institutional centralization and generally exclusive elite strategies. Switzerland is the clearest case of an open political system, with a consensus-oriented political culture and multiple access points as a result of its federal structure and the availability of referenda and public initiatives. The other three countries are intermediate cases, Germany combining open institutional structures with exclusive elite strategies, and the Netherlands and Britain combining centralized institutions with consensual elite strategies (Kriesi et al. 1995, 37; Koopmans 1996b).

To some degree, such opportunity structures influence the mobilization of any collective actor, regardless of its status and aims. However, as we have argued in the introduction, we also need to take aspects of political opportunity structures into account that differ across policy fields and among societal actors. A decisive factor shaping the political opportunities of migrants is the degree to which they have obtained citizenship and thereby the right to vote. In Switzerland and Germany, where most migrants do not have voting rights (and in Switzerland, consequently, do not have the possibility to use direct-democratic channels of access), migrants' access to the policy process is structurally limited to a far greater degree than in the other three countries. Similar specifications have to be made regarding the cultural dimension of citizenship. Where, as in France, many demands for cultural rights for minorities are considered illegitimate, it will be more difficult for migrants to gain policy access in such matters than in self-declared multicultural countries such as Britain and the Netherlands.

Our hypothesis is that the action repertoires of migrants will be determined by both the general national opportunity structure and the migrant-specific opportunities derived from national conceptions of citizenship (Table 25). In none of our countries do the effects of general and specific opportunities go in exactly the same direction. The greatest contrast between the two occurs in Switzerland, where we expect the most moderate action repertoire on the basis of its general political opportunity structure, but where the conception of citizenship leads us to expect the exact opposite. The resultant expectation is that Swiss migrants will be much more inclined to use extrainstitutional forms of mobilization than other actors do in the Swiss polity. A similar, but less pronounced radicalizing effect is expected in Germany, while for the other three countries, the open citizenship regime—and in Britain and the Netherlands also a high level of tolerance for cultural difference—leads us to expect a more moderate repertoire than on the basis of the general opportunity structure alone.

The results in Table 26 are fully in line with our expectations. If we take the percentage of extrainstitutional protests (demonstrative, confrontational, and violent) as an indicator of the radicalism of the action repertoire, we find the most moderate repertoire in Britain, closely followed by the Netherlands, then France and Germany, and finally Switzerland. Considering only violent protests, the order is slightly different, with France now as the most moderate case, closely followed by the Netherlands, and then Britain, Switzerland, and Germany. These results may be influenced by the different weights of homeland-directed claims in the different countries. These will generally be more radical than claims focusing on the country of residence for two reasons. First, the political opportunity structure for such claims is usually very closed because the country of residence can (and often will) do little to implement homeland-directed claims, and

Table 25. Hypothesized effect of national opportunity structures on the action repertoire of migrants

Opportunity structures	Nether-lands	Britain	France	Germany	Switzer-land
General political opportunity structure	Inter-mediate	Inter-mediate	Radical	Inter-mediate	Moderate
Conception of citizenship	Very moderate	Moderate	Inter-mediate	Radical	Very radical
Overall	Moderate	Moderate	Radical	Radical	Radical

the homeland regime itself cannot be directly addressed. Second, the action repertoire of homeland-oriented claims is likely to strongly mirror the cultural repertoire of mobilization of the country of origin. Many of these homelands are characterized by high levels of repression and political violence, and therefore homeland-oriented claims making will often display similar radical features.

Indeed, in all five countries, homeland-oriented claims more often take extrainstitutional forms and frequently involve violence. Still, the cross-national differences are in line with the expectations about the impacts of national opportunity structures and citizenship regimes (not shown in the table). The share of extrainstitutional protests among homeland-oriented claims is highest (91 percent) in Switzerland, followed by Germany (77 percent), France (75 percent), the Netherlands (63 percent), and Britain (57 percent). Thus, even homeland-oriented migrant activism is affected by the opportunity structures of the country of residence. Migrants in Switzerland and Germany act as "foreigners" not only regarding the aims they advocate, but also in terms of the action repertoires they employ. Migrant claims that are directed at the country of residence are everywhere much more moderate than homeland-related claims. However, here too cross-national differences go in the direction of our expectations (not shown in the table). Extrainstitutional protests are least frequent in the Netherlands and Great Britain (both 20 percent), followed by Germany (29 percent), Switzerland (38 percent), and France (46 percent). The position of France indicates that the general closure of the French political system has a stronger effect on

Table 26. Action forms of migrant claims making

Actions	Nether-lands	Britain	France	Germany	Switzer-land
Public statements (%)	71.5	64.7	47.3	47.4	28.6
Judicial action (%)	1.3	12.9	4.8	1.6	1.0
Other conventional action (meetings, petitioning) (%)	0.3	0.4	2.5	2.5	3.5
Demonstrative protests (%)	13.4	5.5	19.5	16.9	46.3
Confrontational protests (%)	7.4	7.4	21.1	12.3	6.9
Violent protests (%)	6.0	9.2	4.8	19.2	13.8
All protests (%)	26.8	22.1	45.4	48.4	67.0
Total (%)	100.0	100.0	100.0	100.0	100.0
N	298	272	313	921	203

migrants' action repertoire than the more inclusive opportunities following from France's civic conception of citizenship. The radicalism of Swiss migrants is again the most remarkable finding, since it stands in sharp contrast to the moderation of the collective action of the native Swiss who, unlike migrants, can profit from the wide range of channels of access to the policy process offered by the country's decentralized and direct-democratic institutions.

The Substantive Focus of Migrant Claims on Immigration and Ethnic Relations

As a final step, we take a closer look at the kind of demands migrants make on the country of settlement. Of course, the more we go into the details of specific issues, the more national idiosyncrasies play a role, and we will discuss these where necessary. Nevertheless, it is possible to formulate a few general expectations based on the different countries' citizenship and integration regimes. We again expect important differences between Germany and Switzerland and the other three countries. Among the three main policy fields, integration politics is very weakly developed in Germany and Switzerland, and there are few legal frameworks or institutional addressees to which migrant demands can refer. Claims for equal political, social, and cultural rights can be effectively framed only if they can refer to shared understandings and legal frameworks that define migrants as a legitimate part of the national community entitled to equal treatment and not as foreigners or guests subject to a separate body of aliens legislation. Effective claims making in the policy fields of immigration politics and antiracism, by contrast, does not depend to the same extent on such rights and entitlements. In the immigration and aliens field, we are mostly dealing with claims regarding immigrants who are not citizens, and therefore we do not expect large systematic differences between our countries here. The framing of demands in the antiracism field does not need to be based on an inclusive definition of national citizenship that includes migrants, either. In Germany and Switzerland, many claims against xenophobia refer to universalist principles such as human dignity or to the need to be hospitable and tolerant and treat one's guests accordingly. Because the state is not the primary addressee of many antiracist claims, we expect differences in antiracist claims to be related to the strength of extreme-right and xenophobic parties and movements. We have seen in chapter 2 that xenophobic and extreme-right groups are most prominent in France and Germany and to a somewhat lesser degree in Switzerland.

A further general hypothesis concerns the cultural dimension of citizenship, which will have an impact on the extent to which, within the field of integration politics, migrants make demands for cultural rights or recognition of their cultural, ethnic, or racial differences. The opportunity structure for such demands is most favorable in the Netherlands and Britain. The other three countries lag far behind in the degree to which they facilitate demands based on cultural differences, and we therefore expect France to be closer to Germany and Switzerland. The consequences of France's refusal to recognize particularist identities go beyond explicitly cultural demands. The lack of recognition for cultural or ethnic differences as a policy category also implies that France has, compared to Britain and the Netherlands, a weak institutional and legal framework to combat racism and discrimination.

If we look in Table 27 at the results for the three main policy fields, we find that indeed integration issues are least important in Germany and Switzerland. As expected, France occupies an intermediary position, while in Britain and the Netherlands integration issues are by far the most important field for migrant claims. Regarding immigration and aliens' politics, the only significant cross-national difference is the high level in France, which is due to the strong mobilization of *sans-papiers* in the period of study, and may therefore to some extent be an idiosyncratic effect of the exceptionally massive and successful campaign for legalization by this group. Antiracist claims reflect to an important extent the strength of the extreme right. However, the share of antiracist claims by migrants in France is lower than one might expect, also compared to the importance of antiracism in the wider public discourse in this country (see Table 15 in chapter 2). The explanation is that antiracist claims making in France usually takes place in mixed organizations on the basis of universalist collective identities, which obscures the participation of migrants in such mobilization.

We now turn to the detailed subcategories within these three policy fields. In immigration and aliens politics, we see that France has a very high percentage of claims for rights and recognition, which is again mainly due to the *sans-papiers* campaign. Issues of entry and exit, by contrast, particularly the issue of expulsions, are very prominent in Switzerland and to a lesser degree in Germany. The weight of the expulsion issue, which puts the legitimacy of migrants' presence into question in a very direct way, is indicative of the marginal legal status and weak discursive legitimacy of immigrants in these two countries. Moving on to the integration field, the result for France regarding the share of claims for religious and other cultural rights defies our expectations. Claims for religious rights are as frequent in France as in Britain and not very much less prominent than in the Netherlands. Muslim groups are responsible for almost half of the claims for cultural and religious rights in France, and another 30 percent were

Table 27. Substantive focus of migrant claims on immigration and ethnic relations

Claims	Netherlands	Britain	France	Germany	Switzerland
Immigration, asylum, aliens politics (%)	23.6	19.8	37.5	27.2	26.3
Residence rights and recognition (%)	7.4	6.6	28.5	9.6	0.0
Entry and exit (%)	9.7	7.0	6.3	11.5	20.0
Other (%)	6.5	6.2	2.7	6.1	1.4
Minority integration politics (%)	55.1	55.0	30.3	18.7	27.5
Citizenship and political rights (%)	6.5	3.1	1.5	5.4	1.3
Social rights (%)	9.8	10.8	4.1	0.6	6.3
Religious rights (%)	15.7	12.0	12.4	2.6	3.8
Other cultural rights (%)	5.1	5.1	6.0	2.7	2.6
Discrimination and unequal treatment (%)	4.6	19.8	1.5	1.7	2.5
Crime and political extremism (%)	10.2	1.6	3.0	2.1	0.0
Other/general integration issues (%)	3.2	2.6	2.8	3.6	6.2
Antiracism (%)	16.2	19.4	25.5	53.4	40.0
Institutional racism (%)	3.7	7.4	0.7	4.0	1.3
Noninstitutional racism, xenophobia, extreme right (%)	12.5	12.0	25.1	49.4	38.8
Inter- and intra-ethnic conflicts (%)	5.1	5.8	6.4	0.6	6.3
Total (%)	100.0	100.0	100.0	100.0	100.0
N	216	258	267	470	80

demands for recognition by Harki, who are also Muslims. In Britain and in the Netherlands, Muslim groups also made most of the religious and cultural claims. By contrast, it is striking that the few cultural rights claims that were made in Germany and Switzerland were not predominantly made by Muslims. Instead, half of these claims came from Jewish and Roma and Sinti groups, which provides further evidence for the privileged legal and discursive position of these two groups due to their status as Holocaust victims.

Britain distinguishes itself by a very high number of claims against discrimination and unequal treatment (20 percent). The extensive framework of equal opportunity and antidiscrimination legislation in this country makes such claims a resonant and potentially effective way for migrant groups to advance their interests. Given that race is the category on which this legislation is based, it is not surprising that a full 70 percent of such claims were made by racial groups, primarily blacks (49 percent), but to some extent also by Asians. By far the most important objects of criticism were the police and judiciary. On a much lower level, but still significantly higher than in the other three countries, we find similar claims in the Netherlands. As expected, the absence of a legal and discursive framework of equal opportunity and antidiscrimination in France gives migrants few opportunities for demands against racial, ethnic, or cultural biases in social institutions. The level of antidiscrimination claims in France is actually even lower than in Switzerland and Germany. We find similar differences regarding claims on institutional forms of racism, which were especially salient in Britain. Both in Britain and in the Netherlands, the police was the most important object of claims of this type. In Switzerland and Germany, on the contrary, the main issue was alleged racist discourse by politicians that was seen as legitimizing the extreme right. In France, institutional racism was a nonissue, and there was not a single case of allegations of racism within the police force. One might take this as a flattering result for the French police in comparison to their colleagues in Britain and the Netherlands, but a more plausible interpretation is probably the lack of an institutional and discursive framework to effectively address discrimination and racism within state institutions. The fact that both institutional racism claims and antidiscrimination claims were even less frequent in France than in Germany and Switzerland hints strongly in this direction.

Finally, a not very large category of claims consists of interethnic and intra-ethnic conflicts that were related not directly to homeland issues but to competition between groups within the country of settlement. In Britain, they included a conflict among rival Muslim groups on the right to use a mosque, clashes between Indian and Pakistani youth, and a fight between African and Islamic fundamentalist students over the alleged stabbing of a black student by a Muslim on religious grounds. In the Netherlands, conflicts were more often about interorganizational relations. In 1992, for instance, several minority organizations, especially of a North African and Muslim background, criticized the Dutch Centre for Foreigners for not being representative and unjustifiably presenting itself as a central speaker for migrants' interests.

Conclusions

We began this chapter with the observation that while many forms of migrant claims making over the last decades could easily be integrated into the democratic process and have often served to strengthen it, other forms of migrant activism may undermine this process, or at least seriously challenge it. We identified two such types of migrant activism. Most observers agree that a strong homeland orientation among migrants is detrimental to their integration into the country of settlement, and homeland-directed activism often takes violent forms—as is confirmed by our data. More controversially, migrant claims for special cultural rights and exemptions from duties are sometimes seen to undermine social cohesion and solidarity. The question is how the receiving society can develop policies that stimulate those forms of migrant participation that contribute to the democratic process and contain those that challenge it. On the theoretical level, many recent studies have emphasized the continuing cultural and political ties that migrants maintain between the country of settlement and their places of origin. This view of migrants as transnational communities implies that their behavior and identities have become increasingly resistant to the receiving states' policies of citizenship and integration. This culturalist perspective lies at the root of two opposed political responses to migration: a reaffirmation of exclusive and assimilationist conceptions of citizenship on the one hand, and the embracing of a postnational multiculturalism on the other. We have contrasted this culturalist perspective with a political opportunity approach that emphasizes the continuing relevance of national citizenship and integration regimes in shaping migrants' claims making.

The verdict regarding the explanatory power of these two theoretical perspectives is straightforward: our data provide little support for the culturalist view of migrants as transnational communities and strong evidence for the continued relevance of national integration politics. We found strong and striking cross-national differences in migrant claims making, which remained when we controlled for differences among migrant groups. In addition, we found transnational types of claims making to be most important where the culturalist perspective expects them least, in Germany and Switzerland. Far from being a modern phenomenon spurred by increasingly open citizenship and tolerance of cultural pluralism by the receiving states, strong transnational orientations turn out to be migrants' responses to traditional, exclusionary citizenship regimes that put up high barriers to migrants' access to the political community. This leads us to draw a first practical lesson from our analysis: the political response to migrant extremism and political violence related to homeland conflicts is often to make it more difficult for individual migrants to obtain citizenship rights. Our findings show that such an exclusive policy is not the solution to homeland-directed extremism but one of the prime causes that sustain it.

Our findings also show, however, that there is no reason for the multiculturalists to give up any role for the nation-state in shaping and steering migrants' political and cultural integration. Among the three countries that have developed active integration policies and have sought to make migrants into citizens—France, Britain, and the Netherlands—we find important differences that correspond to the particular ways in which these countries approach the problems of equal rights and cultural diversity. In France, particularist identities are shunned, and we find many migrants mobilizing around universalist identities, emphasizing their status as immigrants rather than primordial ethnic affiliations, or emphatically mobilizing around hyphened identities, such as French Muslims. While facilitating mobilization around such universalist identities, France's limited cultural pluralism and the nonrecognition of particularist identities also restrict migrants' opportunities in other ways. Claims within the integration field, which often deal with migrants as minorities within the national community, were less frequent than in Britain and the Netherlands. Particularly, we found in France very few claims—even fewer than in Germany and Switzerland—against discrimination and racism within institutional contexts. We maintain that this is not because such racism is less widespread in France, but because in the republican tradition it is legally and discursively inconceivable that state institutions such as the police or the education system could be biased on racial, ethnic, or cultural grounds.

The Dutch case teaches us that too much cultural pluralism may not be the solution either, particularly if, as has been the case in the Netherlands, cultural rights are extended on the basis of migrants' ethnicity or national origin. This radically multicultural approach has certainly had some positive results, especially the fact that Dutch migrants have a very moderate action repertoire that rarely involves violence. However, in other respects the strong state sponsorship of particularist identities has consequences that are sometimes similar to those of the exclusive policies of Germany and Switzerland. Thus, we found national and ethnic identifications to be almost as important among Dutch migrants as in Germany and Switzerland, and hyphened identifications with the country of settlement were even less frequent than in these two countries. Homeland-oriented mobilization was more frequent than in France and Britain, although Dutch migrants came nowhere near the strong preoccupation with homeland politics that we found in Germany and Switzerland. Given the strong facilitation of migrant organizations and tolerance of cultural diversity in the Netherlands, the relatively weak share of migrants in public debates on migration and ethnic relations that we encountered in chapter 2 is also a disappointing result. Our conclusion is that the strong facilitation of cultural difference has insufficiently stimulated migrants to orient themselves toward and to participate in Dutch society—a reading of our results that is in line with conclusions drawn from Dutch migrants' weak levels of integration in socioeconomic domains such as the labor market and the education system (Mollenkopf 2000; Thränhardt 2000; Koopmans 2003a, 2003b).

At least regarding the aspects of migrant integration that we have investigated here, Britain seems to have found the best balance between tolerance for cultural diversity on the one hand, and adaptation of migrants to a set of common cultural standards in the public domain on the other. Britain shares with France very low levels of ethnonational identifications and homeland-oriented mobilization among migrants. Unlike France, however, migrants have been able to play a much more important role in the public discourse because their claims making is less restricted by public taboos on particularist demands and much more strongly facilitated by a regime of antidiscrimination and equal opportunity legislation. Britain has had one advantage compared to both France and the Netherlands that is hard to copy: its use of race as the basis for its integration policies. The racial category has the advantage that it is a much more superficial—in the true sense of the word—identity than ethnicity or religion. As a result, policies against racial discrimination or facilitating migrant organization along racial lines perhaps do not bear the same risks for cultural retrenchment and social segregation as policies organized along ethnocultural lines, such as in the Netherlands. The point, of course, is that the experience of Nazi occupation and the Holocaust has completely delegitimized the use of race as a category for public policies or discourse on the European continent.

However, Britain's integration regime along racial lines has clearly failed to achieve its aims regarding one important group of migrants, Muslims from the Indian subcontinent. The British authorities' attempt to incorporate this group in the racial category of Asians, and thus to simply extend the race relations regime that was originally set up for Caribbean blacks, has largely been a failure. Our data show that those officially labeled as Asians do not see themselves as such but mobilize mainly on the basis of their religious identity as Muslims. Conversely, this group also experiences discrimination from the majority society not because of its racial but because of its religious difference. Britain is not the only country where Muslim claims making defies national integration regimes and deviates from the general pattern of our findings. In France, where our political opportunity approach predicts limited mobilization along religious lines, we in fact found the highest level of Muslim mobilization of all five countries. The strong public presence of this group also explains the fact that we found a higher level of demands for religious and cultural rights in France than we expected. We suspect that the reason why our results for Muslims deviate from the general pattern is that religious identities are particularly resilient and stable. Our results show that national integration regimes can be remarkably successful in eroding migrants' identifications with the national and ethnic categories of their original homelands and in shifting their identities and interests instead toward status or racial categories defined by the country of settlement's incorporation regime. However, migrants' religious affiliation is not so easily absorbed or deflected, especially if we are dealing with a religion that makes strong claims regarding its members' public appearance and behavior such as Islam. We cannot yet determine to what extent there are perhaps qualitative differences between the claims made by Muslims in different countries that we have not been able to discover in the aggregate analysis so far. Moreover, we cannot yet draw confident conclusions about the meaning of the demands for cultural and religious rights made by Muslims. Are they of the kind that might contribute to a fragmentation of citizenship? Or do Muslims merely ask for the same rights that established Christian and Jewish denominations already enjoy? It is to these questions that we turn in the next chapter.

4

Minority Group Demands and the Challenge of Islam

Over the last decade much has been written on multiculturalism in relation to citizenship. Increasing clashes between minority and majority populations over issues, such as language rights, regional autonomy, political representation, education curriculum, land claims, immigration and naturalization policies, and national symbols, are seen by some as the central defining feature of contemporary societies and as "the greatest challenge" (Kymlicka 1995a, 1) to the liberal nation-state. Such problems are seen to arise from the increasing demands that are put forward by migrants and minorities for special group rights and recognition, exemption from duties, and support from the state for their cultural differences and identities. They are also considered to be widespread; for example, Gutmann states, "[I]t is hard to find a democratic or democratizing society these days that is not the site of some significant controversy over whether and how its public institutions should better recognize the identities of cultural and disadvantaged minorities" (1994, 3). A broad range of such group demands by migrants have appeared on the public stage, including exemptions from laws that penalize cultural practices, assistance to do things the majority can do unassisted, self-government for national minorities, external rules restricting nonmembers' liberty to protect the group members' culture, incorporation of religious legal codes within the dominant legal system, special group representation within government institutions, and symbolic recognition within the broader state community (see Levy 1997).

Within academic debates on multicultural rights, different normative evaluations have been put forward in many important contributions, (see Bauböck 1994; Miller 1995; Spinner 1994; Taylor 1992; Philips 1995; Canovan 1996; Gilbert 1998; Glazer 1997; Modood 2000; Huntington 2002). On one side, proponents of multicultural rights (e.g., Young 1998) see migrants' claims making for special group rights and recognition as a justified and liberating challenge to the unified, undifferentiated citizenship of the liberal nation-state that is underwritten with an in-built "white" cultural hegemony. On the other, detractors of multiculturalism (e.g., Schlesinger 1998) see new demands for group rights and recognition as a dangerous attack on the shared communal values and solidarity that underpin the basis of citizenship in liberal nation-states and that are necessary for social cohesion. Many scholars tread somewhere in the middle ground of this normative terrain. For example, Kymlicka and Norman argue that the depictions in such polemics have become unhelpful to understanding the problematic: "No one can rest content with the sort of rhetorical generalizations that characterised the 'culture wars' of the 1980s and early 1990s. Critics of minority (group) rights can no longer claim that minority (group) rights inherently conflict with citizenship ideals; defenders of minority (group) rights can no longer claim that concerns about civility and civic identity are simply illegitimate attempts to silence or dismiss troublesome minorities" (2000, 41).

Following on from chapter 3, where we examined the general cross-national differences in migrants' claims making, here we focus specifically on the nature of the challenge of migrants' claims making for group demands to their European societies of settlement by recourse to our comparative data set.

The Challenge of Migrants' Group Demands

Others have used the terms "multiculturalism" or "differentiated citizenship" to refer to migrants' particularist group demands. Because we use the term "multiculturalism" for a policy approach, we propose to use the term "group demands" as an umbrella term for the political field of claims by migrants for group-specific rights, recognition, and exemptions from duties with respect to the cultural requirements of citizenship in their societies of settlement. Although this category is heterogeneous, all group demands share two features: first, they are demands that go beyond the set of common civil and political rights of individual citizenship that are protected in all liberal democracies; and second, they are demands that, if realized, constitute the recognition and accommodation by the state of the distinctive identities and needs of migrant groups.[1]

Regarding the purported challenge of multicultural claims by migrants, a first point to make is that the idea of a unitary citizenship based on equal individual rights, on which liberalism rests, is an ideology and not an accurate depiction of reality for the typical liberal nation-state. On the contrary, most nation-states attribute some group rights in the form of corporatist or federal arrangements, and most nation-states give preferential treatment to specific religions over others. Thus in Britain, the historical accommodation of church and state has left the monarch both head of state and head of the Anglican Church. Religious institutions receive no direct state support, but the state privileges its own religion within its understanding of politics. Catholic and Jewish faiths have over time achieved a near parity with the Anglicans, and thereby receive substantial state funding for their faith-based denominational schools. However, the state has been more resistant to the idea of funding the schools of the newcomer religion Islam. Despite long-standing requests, it is only in the last couple of years that funding status has been granted and even then only to a few Muslim schools.[2]

Another important point is that although controversies about multiculturalism are often played out publicly through symbols, such as headscarves and minarets, the conflicts are not only about forms of cultural expression and identities; they are also conflicts about the distribution of material resources. For example, in Germany a "Church tax" is levied on individual employees, and state funds are distributed to recognized religions. If Turkish migrants were allowed to contribute to their own faith denomination, which they are not, would this not only bring symbolic recognition, but also make it difficult for the state to deny granting tax revenues to Islamic organizations, which is what it does for Christian and Jewish ones (see Laurence 2001)? This example demonstrates that many cultural demands are not just about value conflicts, but also about material stakes in society. Cultural demands that are made by migrants in policy fields such as public education or welfare, where the state has responsibilities for providing and distributing services, present challenges to a preexisting institutionalized context in which the native "white" population has defined stakes. If granted, such demands require changes in existing institutionalized practices and in many cases a redistribution of public resources that brings them into competition with those of other community groups, such as old, gay, disabled, poor, homeless, and unemployed people. Such cases of migrants' group demands are more likely to face trenchant opposition because they appear to challenge the perceived interests of the host public. Thus the state is often required to take a stand and act as an arbiter between native and migrant stakeholders.

Although some cultural demands by migrants are for parity of treatment with other religious and ethnic groups, others go further, requesting special treatment for the group relative to other members and groups in society. Some exceptional demands are easily accommodated by liberal states. Indeed, in the case of reparations for Nazi crimes in the Holocaust, the German state has itself promoted preferential treatment for the associational activities of Jews and Roma. Other demands are less easy to accommodate because they actually challenge the very essence of liberal values. For example, Muslim migrants wishing to practice polygamy, female circumcision, or sharia divorce would be committing acts that contradict most liberal states' legal and moral understandings of equality between individuals and between men and women. How common or representative of cultural demands such cases are, is, of course, an empirical question. We suspect that many migrants in Europe are likely to adhere to more secular or modern understandings of Islamic practice, and that practices of this kind would be likely to diminish over time, making them atypical rather than the norm.

Examples such as female circumcision or sharia divorce are perhaps more present in academic literature than they are representative of real cases in the social world. Most public controversies are over the position of Islam in institutional settings and issues such as single-sex Islamic schooling or arranged marriages for young girls. Should the state intervene to protect the rights of the woman or the child, or alternatively should the individual be allowed to exercise their freedom of choice and religious belief, even when translating such beliefs into action contravenes liberal norms? Taking the example of separate schooling for Muslim girls in Britain, this would be a demand for parity rather than exceptional treatment with respect to other faith groups, some of which have state-sponsored single-gender schools. However, the important difference between Catholic girl schools and Islamic girl schools is that Islamic schools put religious faith at the center of the educational process and promote a set of values that are less commensurable with liberalism than the teachings of modern institutional and secularized Catholicism. States are wary of offering an equality of group rights to Muslims if these will be used to promote values or practices that contradict the values underpinning the host society. In some cases, Muslim parents' arguments for their own faith schools make little effort to fit within the cultural pluralism of the national civic community, for example, when they express fears at the possible westernization of their children. Important here is that some Muslims see Islam as being more true than other faiths and more authoritative than the state. This is problematic for liberal democracies, which are able to offer at most only a parity of political space to migrant religions that is equivalent to that already allotted to other religious faiths, many of which have already been domesticated, rendered benign, and institutionalized by the secularizing tendencies of political accommodation.

Another point, with respect to the high resonance of issues relating to migrants' group demands in public debates, concerns the native publics of the host society. Native publics and their liberal intellectuals often come to see themselves as the defenders and upholders of the myth of a unitary national citizenship. However sincere such allegiances to liberal principles may be, it is also the case that their proponents may be wedded to a version of those concepts that is now a historical anachronism or, alternatively, based on nostalgia for the nation's past. In cases such as Rushdie in Britain or the headscarf affair in France, public discourse dynamics tend to take over, and the facts of the actual problems become distorted under a barrage of rhetoric about national values and identity. Thus the importance and nature of the multicultural challenge may be twisted and overblown in the public imagination.

Although the multicultural citizenship debates have inspired a number of studies with a more empirical focus (e.g., Joppke 1996, 1999; Rex 1996; Modood and Werbner 1997; Martiniello 1998; Kymlicka and Norman 2000), up to now the rigor of the philosophical debates has not been matched by systematic empirical evidence that would allow us to ascertain the importance and nature of migrants' cultural group demands, either with respect to other types of claims making or cross-nationally. Against this, there has recently been a trend toward edited volumes of national case studies on the position of Muslim migrants in Western societies (Vertovec and Rogers 1998; Haddad Yazbeck and Esposito 2000; Alsayyad and Castells 2002; Haddad Yazbeck and Smith 2002; and Hunter 2002). However, such contributions often fail to compare Muslims with other groups or to draw systematic cross-national conclusions.

Over the last decades, there have been a long series of dramatic episodes where Western societies have vociferously wrestled with their liberal dilemmas over multiculturalism and Islam. Headscarf affairs resonated most loudly in France, but also took place in Britain and then later in Germany and Switzerland. Similarly, the fatwa issued against Salman Rushdie and the publication of his *Satanic Verses* sparked intense debates about Islam among European intellectuals and publics alike, as have international events, such as 9/11, two Gulf Wars, the ongoing Israeli-Palestinian conflict, and the terrorist attacks on Madrid in 2004. Spectacular examples of Muslims' group demands have been cause célèbres for public debates across Europe, and academic research is littered with case study anecdotal accounts of Rushdie and the headscarf affair in France. What is less clear is the extent to which such cases are representative and what they are actually representative of. Such issues can only be resolved by empirical investigation. The fact that our sample has been collected on regular days across time, and across countries, gives us the opportunity to examine the scale of group demands compared to other forms of claims making and to undertake qualitative analyses on cross-nationally representative samples of migrants' group demands.

The Scale and Source of Migrants' Group Demands

A first empirical question is the extent of migrants' claims making for group demands in the five countries, which gives an indication of the scale of the purported challenge they present to liberal nation-states. Table 28 shows cases where the substantive focus of migrant claims making is for group demands relating to cultural or religious differences.[3] It gives figures, first, for all collective actors (first row), and then for migrants (second row), as a proportion of all claims making on immigration and ethnic relations. The third row shows migrants' claims for group-specific demands as a proportion of migrants' claims making.

Table 28. Share of claims making about group demands in immigration and ethnic relations, 1992–98

Claims making	Nether-lands	Britain	France	Germany	Switzer-land
Claims about group demands out of all claims making in immigration and ethnic relations (%)	5.5	7.7	6.6	1.2	1.2
Migrants' claims for group demands out of all claims making in immigration and ethnic relations (%)	2.0	3.4	2.1	0.4	0.4
N	2,286	1,313	2,388	6,432	1,365
Migrants' claims for group demands out of all migrants' claims making (%)	20.8	17.1	18.4	5.3	6.4
N	216	258	267	470	80

First, we see that, quantitatively, even when we include the claims by nonmigrant collective actors, the proportion of claims making on group-specific demands remains very modest: Netherlands, 5.5 percent; Britain, 7.7 percent; France, 6.6 percent; Germany, 1.2 percent; and Switzerland, 1.2 percent. Second, migrants' group-specific demands constitute a very small proportion of all claims, accounting for 2.0 percent in the Netherlands, 3.4 percent in Britain, 2.1 percent in France, and a miniscule 0.4 percent in both Germany and Switzerland. According to such figures, the dooms-day scenario of "tribal antagonisms" (Schlesinger 1998, 13) pulling socie-ties apart at the cultural seams, or Huntington's (2002) "clash of civiliza-tions" imported by immigration, appear to be strongly overstated, at least for the case of migrant populations in Europe, as does Kymlicka's vision of multicultural demands being the "greatest challenge" to the liberal state (1995a, 1).[4]

In addition, Table 28 shows a difference between those countries that substantially grant political rights to migrants, where group demands ac-count for a fifth of migrants' claims making (Netherlands, 20.8 percent; Britain, 17.1 percent; France, 18.4 percent), and those which do not (Ger-many, 5.3 percent; and Switzerland, 6.4 percent) and have roughly three times less. This finding demonstrates that nationally specific approaches to granting formal citizenship rights matter in giving migrants the confidence to feel sufficiently part of a society to make group-specific demands on it. However, another finding from Table 28 goes against the expectations that are derived from national approaches for institutional channeling and po-litical opportunities, including our own developed in this book. Following our discussion of cross-national differences in chapter 3, we would expect to find much lower levels of migrants' group-specific demands in France than in countries such as the Netherlands and Britain, which officially see them-selves as multicultural and multiracial societies and which tolerate cultural diversity as one of their constituent principles. On the contrary, our data show similar levels of group-specific demands in France, Britain, and the Netherlands. This points to a limitation of national citizenship approaches in explaining migrant behavior and shows that there is a grain of truth in the multicultural thesis that sees demands for group rights and recognition as a product of migrants' claims making that is relatively autonomous from the state's integration policies. To investigate this further, we need to know which types of migrants make group demands.

Table 29 shows the type of collective identities expressed by migrants when making group demands in the three countries where we have a suf-ficient number of cases, the Netherlands, Britain, and France.[5] The most

Table 29. Collective identities used by migrants for making group demands, 1992–98

Collective identities	Netherlands	Britain	France
Policy-status identities (%)	15.6	4.6	32.7
Foreigners (%)	8.9	–	–
Minorities/*allochthonen* (%)	4.4	4.6	–
Immigrants (%)	2.2	–	10.2
Illegal immigrants/ *sans-papiers* (%)	–	–	2.0
Harki (%)	–	–	20.4
Racial identities (%)	2.2	22.7	0.0
Black (%)	–	18.2	–
Asian (%)	–	2.3	–
Other (%)	2.2	2.3	–
Religious identities (%)	60.0	65.9	53.1
Muslim (%)	46.7	61.4	51.0
Hindu (%)	6.7	2.3	–
Rastafarian (%)	2.2	2.3	–
Other (%)	4.4	–	2.0
Ethnoreligious identities (%)	2.2	6.8	8.2
Jewish (%)	2.2	6.8	8.2
Ethnic and national identities (%)	31.1	0.0	6.1
Sinti and Roma (%)	2.2	–	–
Turkish (%)	15.6	–	–
Chinese (%)	2.2	–	–
Moluccan (%)	2.2	–	–
Morocco (%)	6.7	–	2.0
Other African (%)	2.2	–	4.1
Surinamese (%)	2.2	–	–
Hyphened identification with country of residence (%)	2.2	9.1	14.3
Total (%)	111.1	109.1	114.3
N	4 5	44	49

striking feature is that more than half of these migrant group demands were made using religious forms of identification in France (53.1 percent), six-tenths in the Netherlands (60.0 percent), and two-thirds in Britain (65.9 percent). In addition, we see that the vast majority of these group demands were made by migrants identifying themselves as Muslim or Islamic (France, 51.0 percent; Netherlands, 46.7 percent; Britain, 61.4 percent).[6] This is surprisingly high for Britain, which sponsors the Asian identity for Indian subcontinent minorities, and for France, whose policies are against recognizing specific groups of migrants. At the same time, we discover that in the European context group demands are made principally through one religious self-identification, i.e., Muslims, which contradicts the image popular within multicultural literature that claims making for group demands is a way for migrants to express their cultural differences per se, which would lead one to expect a plethora of many different migrant identities being expressed.

We find a relatively low number of group demands made by migrant faith groups other than Muslims. Although Britain and the Netherlands have significant migrant populations of Hindu faith, who face exactly the same multicultural and state/religion policies as Muslims, there is little evidence for Hindus making group demands using religious identities (Netherlands, 6.7 percent; Britain, 2.3 percent). Likewise, the Jewish ethnoreligious group actually mobilizes less in the group demands field than they do overall. Jews make 2.2 percent of group demands in the Netherlands, 6.8 percent in Britain, and 8.2 percent in France, while chapter 3 showed they account for 8.1 percent of all claims making by Dutch migrants, 5.5 percent by British, and 19.6 percent by French migrants respectively (see Table 21). This low presence of group demands in the claims making repertoires of Jews stands in sharp contrast to Muslims, for whom between four-tenths and two-thirds of all claims making was for group demands (Netherlands, 50.0 percent; Britain, 67.5 percent; and France, 41.7 percent). Thus claims making for group demands appears to be specific to migrants identifying themselves as Muslims.

With respect to the differences between Jews and Muslims, one can point to the much longer history of political accommodation of Jews within Western European societies. In addition, the vast majority of Jews practice their faith, if at all, to the same limited extent as the vast majority of nominal Christians. Such factors may explain why Jews make few group demands relative to Muslims. However, such differences do not hold for Hindus, who came in the same waves of migration, from the same regions, and who have received similar levels of political and religious accommodation as

Muslims. Although Hinduism in some of its manifestations can promote values that are equally as incommensurable to liberal democratic values as Islam, Hindu group demands are largely invisible in the public domain.

We consider that the relatively low level of Hindu group demands compared to Muslims is a result of the different infrastructures of the two religions in their societies of settlement. Islam is a more collective and public religion, centered on the mosque, whereas there are many different types of Hinduism, traceable in part to regional or caste differences, and the home is often the principal location for worship in a religion that demands few public celebrations (Hiro 1991; Rex and Tomlinson 1983; Poulter 1998). As a nonproselytizing decentralized religion that is practiced privately, Hinduism as a new minority religion has fitted more easily within the political space granted. In addition, Hindu temples have not taken on the same functions for the migrant community of service provision and negotiating at the interface with the host political authorities that the mosque has for Muslims. As a consequence Muslim self-identification appears to be particularly resilient, even leading to demands for group rights and recognition in its own name.

In sum, we find important group-specific differences and an especially high propensity of group demands by Muslims. The key finding is that regardless of the differences in national contexts for attributing group rights, it is principally only Muslims who make group demands. We argue that this finding provides strong suggestive evidence that there is something about the relationship between liberal states and their Muslim migrants that leads to group demands. On one hand, it could be that there is something specific about the political position of Muslims in their societies of settlement that leads to claims making for group demands, independent of national context. Here, we hypothesize that *it is the public nature of the Islamic religion and the demands that it makes on the way that followers conduct their public lives that makes Islam an especially resilient type of identity and that results in claims making for group demands.* On the other hand, it could be that there is something specific in the way that liberal democratic states attempt to accommodate their Muslims that leads to group demands. Here, we hypothesize that *there are specific deficits in liberal states' cultural provision for migrant and religious group needs that impact disproportionately on groups who are practicing Muslims.* In order to investigate these questions, empirically and cross-nationally, we now undertake a detailed qualitative analysis of Muslims' group demands. First, however, we need to supplement our previous discussions on the cultural dimension of these countries' configurations of citizenship by looking briefly at how they have politically accommodated religions, another important and related aspect of the relationship between states and migrants regarding cultural diversity, that has tended to be overlooked by much of the migration literature (see Statham forthcoming).[7]

The Political Accommodation of Islam

We saw in chapter 3 that the Netherlands, Britain, and France have employed different approaches to incorporating migrants, which appears to have striking impacts in shaping the general political self-identification of migrants. Liberal states make very little effort to convert migrants away from their religious beliefs, which are often held as a matter of individual conscience. Given our findings that multicultural debates in Europe tend to be about the position of Islam, we will now provide some detail on the different ways that our countries have attempted to accommodate religious differences within their political frameworks, in particular with respect to Islam.

Overall, of our three countries France grants least political space for religious differences to be expressed in public life. The French state is aggressively secular; the 1905 law separating church and state prevents the public funding and official recognition of religious communities, although it does affirm the principle of equality in the free exercise of religion for all French citizens. The French state sees displays of religious faith in the public domain as a challenge to the concept of laïcité, its own secular republican ideology for a universal undifferentiated citizenship extended to all its individual citizens. As a consequence, the interaction between the state and the visible presence of Islam, with mosques, minarets, and public calls to prayer, readily becomes a public controversy and a French-style clash of cultures. Over time the state has acceded to minimalist commitments to the basic requirements for Muslims to practice their religion, including prayer spaces and food requirements. However, the centralization and organization of Catholic, Protestant, and Jewish religious communities by the Napoleonic state was only fully replicated for the newcomer religion Islam in December 2002. Discussions had been ongoing since 1990 to establish a high authority of Islam and foundered many times on the insistence by politicians that such an institution would remain a strictly religious council and not become an institutional forum for political consultation (Laurence 2003). In the end, the French Council for the Muslim Religion was the first formalization of relations between Muslims and the state and is partially elected and partially appointed. After talks with seven Muslim federations and five large mosques, the council took on tasks of arranging chaplaincies in the army and prisons, acquiring burial sites, delivering halal meat certificates, organizing pilgrimages, and building new mosques and prayer halls. Nonetheless, this new institutional development has not quelled the political controversies between the state's upholding of the *laïcité* principle and the public visibility of Islam. In 2004, the French justice minister Perben barred a woman from a court jury for wearing a headscarf because he considered that open signs of religious commitment prevented the impartiality necessary in French courts. In the same year, and with the public support of President Chirac, the French Parliament passed a bill by 494 votes to 36 banning the Islamic headscarf and all other overt religious symbols from schools, a piece of legislation that was then passed on to the Senate.

In Britain, religious institutions receive no direct state support, and the role of religion in public institutions is relegated to a matter of private individual conscience, but the state does privilege its own Anglican religion within its understanding of politics. Thus more than twenty Anglican bishops sit in the second chamber (the House of Lords), and the Church of England, headed by the monarch, stands as the official national religion. The limit that British law sets in extending rights to migrant religions was most clearly demonstrated by the ruling in the Rushdie affair that blasphemy did not extend to Islam.[8] A key feature of the Race Relations Act is that it basically attributes rights to secular and not religious groups of minorities. Although Britain has special laws with regard to racial discrimination, there are no parallel laws that make religious discrimination a crime.[9] Furthermore, several ruling interpretations of the 1976 Race Relations legislation have steadfastly refused to extend group rights against discrimination to Muslims, although two ethnoreligious groups, Sikhs and Jews, have been legally considered ethnic groups since 1983.[10] Thus even when the Commission for Racial Equality brought a case against an engineering firm that refused to employ Muslims because it saw them as extremists in 1991, the employer was found guilty only of indirect discrimination against the racial category of Asians, and his anti-Muslim sentiments went legally unpunished (Vertovec 1996, 177; Lewis 2002, 250). In some ways reminiscent of France, British multiracialism has been far from reticent in opposing the extension of group rights to Muslims. The state has only recently allowed state funding for a few Islamic faith schools, which Anglican, Catholic, and Jewish denominations have enjoyed for many years. In addition, there has been a concerted campaign by British Muslims and Race Relations campaigners to coin the phrase "Islamophobia" as a specific form of racism.[11]

As we saw in the last chapter, Dutch elites considered that integration is most likely to be accomplished through confident subcultures, making the preservation of minority cultures an essential part of their incorporation. In the 1990s, Dutch minority policy moved away from this idealist undiluted multiculturalism and toward a more British-style focus on socioeconomic parity when the realization set in that maintaining group diversity could also mean structuring disadvantage for those groups. Nonetheless, the Dutch approach still retains important distinctive characteristics with the result that it offers a wider and deeper range of cultural opportunities for minority groups than Britain, which is important because it encouraged the preservation of a wide range of homeland, national, ethnic, and religious identities. The "pillarized" system of consociational politics has a tradition of delegating state prerogatives to religious communities. As a result, religious group rights extend much further than those granted in Britain so that, for example, religious groups have the legal right to government funding for their schools. This Dutch multiculturalism *avant la lettre* has gone a long way toward including religious minorities within its definition of the national political community, which fuses the religious and secular associational activities of groups in society. Thus the opening of Parliament is officially blessed by the leaders of the Netherlands' minority religions. We find a state-funded Islamic broadcasting network (Moslim-omroep), an Islamic school board, an Islamic pedagogic center, and more than forty Islamic schools, which are fully government funded with a regular Dutch curriculum. Just as the "old" Christian and Protestant pillars had their own state-sponsored semiautonomous institutions in education, health, welfare, and the public media, such rights could not be denied to the new cultural and religious minorities.

Among our three countries, there is sufficient variation to examine whether the different ways that states attribute rights through their political accommodation of migrants and religions have an impact in shaping Muslim claims making for group demands. Here the continuum runs from the Netherlands, which offers the strongest version of cultural pluralism by granting group rights and exemptions to a broad range of minority and religious groups, to France, whose civic universalism embodied in the principle of *laïcité* opposes all differentialism, with the object of making—to paraphrase Eugene Weber (1976)—"migrants into Frenchmen." Britain with its peculiar race relations formula comes in between, recognizing some degree of migrants' group rights through a broad state-sponsored ascriptive identity of race but not extending these privileges to minority religions. We now propose to examine the relationship between Islam and political accommodation through a detailed comparison of our samples of Muslim group demands.

The Challenge of Islam: Muslim Group Demands

Figure 6 shows the analytic dimensions of group demands that we apply in our qualitative comparison of the Netherlands, Britain, and France.

Following the discussion in the introduction, we distinguish between two types of group demands for rights: exceptional and parity. By "exceptional," we refer to those group demands for rights that are not already granted to other native cultural, minority, or religious groups. Claims for exceptional group rights demand something substantively new or a special exemption for the migrant or religious group, which, if realized, sets the group apart from all other groups. It is particularly challenging to the form of cultural pluralism sponsored by a country's policies because it demands group rights, and exemptions from duties, that go beyond those granted to other national minority and religious groups. For example, those claims relating to conflicts over Muslim women wearing the headscarf in French state institutions where religious symbolism is prohibited are examples of exceptional group rights demands. By contrast, parity demands for group rights request the same privileges and exemptions from duties that are already extended to other religious and minority groups. Here the group demand is for equality with other groups who are already granted special treatment. Such demands for parity are generally less challenging and easier to accommodate than exceptional ones, because they do not directly challenge the logic of the category system used by a country's migrant or church/state policies. They only demand that the privileges already granted to some minorities are extended to another migrant group. For example, if Turkish Muslims in Germany request state subsidies for religious and cultural organizations of the kind already granted to Jews, then this is a parity demand.

Not all group demands are for rights; there are group demands that are weaker and that simply mobilize the group's collective identity in the

Type of group demand	Exceptional, parity, or collective identity
Motivational impetus for group demand	Proactive or reactive
Level and form of protest action for group demand	Low, medium, or high level Demonstrative, confrontational, or violent in form
Overall orientation	Acculturative or dissociative

Figure 6. Analytic dimensions of Muslims' claims making for group demands.

public domain rather than engaging in the context of rights on offer from a country's multicultural policies. An example of this would be the Islamic federation in Berlin denying that it had links with the extremist group Milli Görüş, stating, "we want to transmit the Islamic religion, not politics." This is not a demand for group rights made on the host state and society, but an assertion of group identity that is made in it. Our analysis will focus principally on cases of exceptional and parity group rights demands because these are more explicitly formulated, though we shall still refer to collective identity group demands where they are relevant.

Second, we consider the nature of the relationship between the state and native public on one side, and the Muslim group on the other, which produces a group demand. We refer to this as the *motivational impetus* of a group demand. A proactive group demand is mobilized autonomously by the Muslim group independently from actions by the state and host society actors and is a more assertive form of claims making. Conversely, a reactive group demand is when it mobilizes in response to an intervention by state or native public actors, for example, when the state officially bans a form of religious expression in public places.

Third, we look at the type of action form used to mobilize a group demand. Here we use the standard social movement categorizations for protest action repertoires that range from conventional and demonstrative to confrontational and then to violent forms.

Overall, the strategic orientation of group demands may be either *acculturative* or *dissociative* in their relationship to a state's cultural pluralism. Acculturative claims making fits within the state's framework and policies for categorizing minority or religious groups, whereas dissociative claims making challenges the state's approach to minority and religious differences by making demands that go further than, or ignore, current formulations. In general, one would expect exceptional rights demands to be dissociative because they are the most demanding on the dominant host culture. They are subsequently also likely to lead to reactions by state institutions and native public discourses, which may result in conflicts. Parity rights demands also have a potential to become highly controversial and provoke strong host society and state reactions. However, parity group demands are more likely to be acculturative than exceptional demands because they try to fit into an existing framework of political accommodation.

The Netherlands: Islam Pushing for a New "Pillar"

The examples of Muslim group demands in our Dutch sample cover issues that are common to the literature on multiculturalism. Six cases refer to issues about Islamic schools, six are about attempts to set up a Dutch imam school, and the remainder cover requirements and exemptions for halal meat, provision of religious and cultural centers, imams for Muslim prisoners, broadcasting rights for Muslims, and divorce by sharia law.

Of the group demands by Muslims in the Netherlands, sixteen of the twenty-one cases in our sample are demands for parity group rights with other groups, four of the cases are claims for exceptional group rights, and only one case stands outside the context of rights demands and mobilizes a collective identity.

Concerning the action forms used to mobilize demands, there is only a single case of protest. In this instance, the Aya Sofia Association and the Mosque Neighbourhood Association Milli Görüş in Amsterdam West organized a six-thousand-strong demonstration against the refusal of the borough government to permit a large cultural center. In all other cases, Muslims used conventional action forms for claims making, including public speeches and statements. This predominant use of conventional action forms gives a first indication of the receptiveness of Dutch multicultural politics to group demands.

At first glance, our findings fit the cozy image that Dutch group-based multicultural policies produce a pacified and acculturative form of group demands by Muslims. As we have seen, the Dutch state grants minority group rights almost automatically in a way that encourages migrants to see themselves as new groups with new group demands. Indeed, the Dutch political space is so receptive to group claims that even for Muslims, a group that other countries find difficult to accommodate, it is hard to make exceptional group rights demands. This is because the Dutch state appears ever willing to acknowledge another cultural religious pillar within its national political community, using the principle that what is already granted to some groups must therefore be extended to all groups.

Another finding that points to the confidence of Muslims in the Netherlands for making group demands is that seventeen of the twenty-one cases of Muslim group demands were proactive, compared to only three that were reactive and one that was neither. Again, this seems to point to the beneficial outcomes of the Dutch-style group-based multiculturalism that creates incentives for Muslims to make this type of demand. Before getting too carried away with the benefits of Dutch multiculturalism, however, it is worth looking more closely at specific examples of these claims and the nature of the controversies that they represent.

Turning to the exceptional group rights demands, a first example is where a separate Islamic Butchers' Association is set up with the claim that Muslims are unable to follow the regular training and education of butchers because their faith prohibits them dealing with pork. Another exceptional group demand occurs when the Union of Moroccan Muslim Organizations in the Netherlands (Ummon) advocates educating imams in the Netherlands and providing education in the language and knowledge of Dutch society for foreign imams. These are good examples of Muslims in the Netherlands having the confidence to proactively demand new exceptions as a group in the belief that this will be straightforwardly accommodated by the state. Although they are examples of exceptional group rights demands, the strong group-based enforcement within Dutch multicultural policies means that overall these claims are acculturative rather than dissociative in nature, and unlikely to provoke reactions from the host society.

In contrast, it is the strength of the enforcement of the group rights principle by Dutch politics that actually causes another of our examples of exceptional group rights demands. In this case, Muslims challenge the consequences for them of the overliberal tendencies within Dutch multiculturalism. The Dutch Muslim Council and the Moroccan Women's Society come out publicly against the bill proposed by the secretary of justice to recognize and accommodate one-sided marriage dissolution according to the laws of immigrants' countries of residence. Here the dissociative basis of the Muslim demand is against the proposed policies of the Dutch state. In this example, the rosy image of the consequences of cultural pluralism Dutch-style begins to slip. Indeed, the biggest threat or challenge to the integrative capacity of the nation-state in this instance is from the overwillingness of Dutch policy makers to grant exceptional group rights rather than from the Muslims' group demands.

Looking now at some Dutch examples of Muslim demands for parity rights, it is clear that many of these would constitute demands for exceptional group rights in Britain and France. Thus the Islamic Broadcasting Foundation claims that its right to broadcast on the public channel is a good way of advancing the integration of Muslims into Dutch society. The Halal Food Foundation announces that it hopes to end the unreliable supply of ritually slaughtered meat for the Islamic consumer after being granted the right to introduce their own hallmark, a concession giving them a parity of rights with Jews. The Islamic Council of the Netherlands and researchers associated with the Islamic Chair of the University of Amsterdam make a demand that there should be between twenty-five and thirty imams employed in prisons. According to their research, this would bring Islam proportionally in line with other faith denominations. These examples demonstrate, first, the far-reaching sponsorship of group rights by the Dutch authorities, and second, that this creates a political space and set of incentives for group demands by Muslims. This legitimation of group demands by Dutch multi-cultural policies has the effect of making those Muslim group demands seem officially benign that in Britain and France would most likely provoke reactions from states and native publics.

In the cases relating to training imams, we find the following group demands: The Center for Islamic Studies advocates state sponsorship for the education of imams on a par with that provided for Christian vicars and priests on the condition that the government does not interfere in the substance of the education. In a case already referred to, the Union of Moroccan Muslim Organizations in the Netherlands (Ummon) makes a request for additional Dutch-language training and knowledge of Dutch society as part of the education for imams. The holder of an Islamic profes-sorial chair at a university comes out in favor of a Dutch imam education, as does a resident imam. Against this, the president of the Turkish–Islamic Cultural Federation strongly criticizes the proposals of the Dutch liberal member of Parliament Dijkstal to found a Dutch imam school. Here we find a range of different positions being expressed by leading organizations from different factions within the Muslim community, all in response to an agenda of group rights set by the state. These examples of claims making about imam education illustrate that Dutch state policies tend to promote controversies and competition over resources within different factions of the Muslim communities, rather than between the native population and Muslims.

Such factionalism within Muslim communities may lead to the pro-liferation of ever smaller denominations of groups who demand their own group rights from the state. Further evidence for this comes from our claims on Islamic schools. In one case, the Foundation of Islamic Primary Edu-cation (IQRA) demands that different denominations from within Islam have the right to separate schools.[12] In another, the headmaster of the Yunus Emre Islamic primary school in The Hague advocates that a new school should be founded for a more orthodox Islamic education. On the same matter, the Islamic School Board Association (ISBO), an umbrella orga-nization for twenty-nine Islamic schools in the Netherlands, publicly rules that the distinction between whether a school follows liberal or orthodox Islamic teaching is unimportant. Once more, this issue demonstrates that Dutch multiculturalism encourages Muslims to set up ever smaller denomi-national groups by establishing new organizations that they expect will re-ceive state recognition and subsidies. Also, the orthodox Islam that these smaller factions will teach is likely to reproduce the separatist tendencies that will lead to Muslim communities that are internally cohesive but inward-looking, and which hardly fit into Dutch society. Here we witness once more that Dutch liberal multiculturalism lets community group rights take precedence over the national community. Such an approach takes Dutch society in a direction that may reproduce parallel and divided rather than cohesive societies.

Britain: Islam as a Challenge to Race Relations

In our group claims by Muslims in Britain, five cases relate to the issuing of a fatwa against Salman Rushdie for publishing the *Satanic Verses*.[13] Another five relate to the perceived stigmatization and lack of respect by the native population and within the public sphere for Islamic symbols and people. Of the remainder, a significant proportion are about the relationship between the state and the Muslim community, including claims about state subsidies and recognition for Islamic schools, religious education in state schools, antidiscrimination measures for Muslims, treatment of Muslims in state prisons, the suitability of social amenities provided by authorities for Muslims, and finally the political representation of Muslims.

Of the twenty-seven group demands, nine are for exceptional group rights, nine are for parity group rights, and nine do not make rights demands but mobilize collective identities. This differs from the Dutch case where most demands are for parity rather than exceptional rights. In general, this indicates that Muslims in Britain have more difficulty fitting their demands within the framework of state-sponsored multiculturalism than their Dutch counterparts.

Regarding the motivational impetus of Muslim group demands, we find a strong tendency for proactive claims in Britain, with twenty proactive cases, five reactive, and two unclassifiable, which is similar to the Dutch. This shows that British Muslims, like their Dutch counterparts, have sufficient incentives from their country's multicultural policies to assert themselves autonomously instead of simply reacting to issues raised by the state and host society. However, in contrast to Dutch Muslims' assertiveness, which was almost entirely acculturative and for parity demands, a significant proportion of assertiveness by British Muslims is dissociative and for exceptional demands (all nine cases of exceptional demands are proactive). Dutch multicultural policies appear to stimulate a type of Muslim proactivism for group demands that is easily absorbed by state authorities in a noncontested way. In contrast, the more restrictive British definition of multicultural group rights seems to produce a different type of proactive Muslim group demand that is more confrontational.

This confrontational nature of Muslim group demands in Britain is underlined by their action forms. In seven out of twenty-seven cases, Muslims use protest to mobilize their group demands, and five of these are confrontational or violent events. In one protest, Muslim youths gas bomb a bingo hall in Luton. They are protesting against a company called "Mecca" using its brand name on public display to promote gambling. In another, Muslim tenants launch a petition against Blackburn Council requesting that their toilets be repositioned so that they no longer face Mecca. In a further two cases, Muslim parents organize boycotts by their children of state schools against what they see as the harmful effects of comparative religion lessons in the national curriculum. In the last of the confrontational/violent protests, two hundred people attend a Nation of Islam (UK) rally, a black rights group.[14]

Turning to the nine exceptional group demands, all of which are proactive, three refer to the Rushdie affair and challenge the sovereign authority of the British state. In one case, the Muslim Parliament[15] appeals to the authority of Islamic law above British law: "He (Rushdie) has committed a capital offence. An Islamic legal authority has passed a judgement. It's just like a court passing a judgement in this country. The Muslim community feels that this judgement is right and legal." In others, again by the Muslim Parliament and by the Bradford Council of Mosques, anti-Rushdie sentiments are tempered by emphasizing that campaigns against the *Satanic Verses* should remain within British law. In another, a Muslim prisoner challenges the state's strip search method, arguing that he was entitled to maintain his religious beliefs and that a decision not to provide him with modest clothing was "unlawful and unreasonable." The boycott against comparative religion classes in the national curriculum, already mentioned, was supported by the Association of Muslim Schools, who argued: "If they get bombarded with different ideologies and different thinking, the Muslim child gets so clicked on to what the teacher is saying, that he or she thinks whatever the teacher is saying is the truth." The welfare provision of state authorities is the target of criticism in the other demands. For example, the Muslim Parliament argues that the Commission for Racial Equality is inadequate for addressing discrimination against Muslims and advocates the setting up of a Muslim welfare state. In one case, however, a nonstate actor is the target. Muslims in Nottingham criticize a shop owner for displaying shoes in his window that have verses from the Koran printed on them: "It is more serious than Salman Rushdie. Rushdie wrote a book which you carry in your hand. Here the holy name goes on the feet!"

These examples show that exceptional group demands by Muslims do not fit easily in British race relations politics and are not easily accommodated by it. The demands we cite, in particular those on Rushdie, are highly incommensurable with the values of minority politics sponsored by the British state. This finding is evidence that there are aspects of Islamic religious belief that require rituals, practices, and the expression of beliefs in the public domain that British policies have difficulty accommodating and that lead to conflicts. According to our interpretation, this British Muslim assertiveness is not simply an inherent characteristic of Islamic belief systems but is an outcome shaped by the type of political opportunities produced by British-style cultural pluralism. As we discussed earlier, British Muslims achieve group rights as racial, ethnic, or national minority groups but not as a religious minority group. Hence, Muslims are included as a special group in the political community only indirectly as ethnic or racial minority groups, and not directly as Muslims, which is how they see themselves. Living in a country with which they identify as much as other ethnic minorities,[16] Pakistani and Bangladeshi Muslims feel aggrieved that their preferred form of self-identification is not legally sanctioned. They see themselves as less protected from discrimination by the state than other minority groups and as believers of a faith that the state has been unwilling to uphold on a par with other minority religions. The comparison with the Netherlands is instructive. Whereas Dutch multiculturalism creates pressure for too many types of groups to be included in society, causing competition between minorities, British race relations leaves Muslims feeling excluded as a group, and they assertively make demands on a state that they perceive as relegating them to a second-class status in the national community.

This interpretation receives further support from our examples of parity group demands, which are more acculturative, and construct a vision of how Muslims would like to position themselves within the race relations framework. A first case appears in the context of the Runnymede Trust's consultation document on Islamophobia, which calls for radical changes in the attitudes of politicians, media, and community leaders to fight discrimination against "British Muslims [sic]." Here the Muslim College criticizes the state for not extending the same antidiscrimination measures to Muslims as it does for others, arguing that "the vast majority of our community want to live in this country and want to be citizens of this country. It is our right as citizens to be able to say to the country, 'Here, we think your policies are wrong.'" In another example after the 1995 Bradford race riots, Muslim community leaders and the Muslim Parliament claim that "Pakistanis are twice as likely to be unemployed than Afro-Caribbean or

Indian people; there is no other reason for this than discrimination or de-
monisation of Muslims." In a similar vein, two editors of Muslim newspapers criticize the suitability of the Commission for Racial Equality for
Muslim racial problems; one states, "the Muslim population is doubly discriminated against firstly because of their skin colour, and secondly because
of their religion." Such claims are not confrontational expressions of cultural difference per se, but constitute reasoned arguments for more space to be
granted within British multiculturalism so that Muslims can act as full and
equal citizens in the national community. Such examples are not atypical;
in others, the UK Action Committee on Islamic Affairs calls on political
parties to court the Muslim vote or face a profound cost to social harmony,
and a local Islam society liaises with the borough council to better understand why there is less usage of leisure facilities by the Muslim community
than other sections of the population.

Although these parity demands often use the civic language and terminology of race relations and express the aim of improving the integration of
Muslims in British society, this does not mean that accommodating such
group demands would be unproblematic. The Muslims' perceived grievances are not just about higher levels of discrimination than other minority
groups in society experience, but about how to fit their religious faith community into the landscape of British civic values. This is what is meant by
"double discrimination"—as a minority and as a religious group. In Britain,
where the state relegates religious practice to a matter of private individual
conscience, it is difficult to accommodate organizations that integrate the
functions of civic association and religious faith provision in the public domain. As we discussed earlier, the public nature of religious practice and its
overreaching into associational and political activities make Islam a special
case among British minority religions.

In the last two cases of parity demands, the state's drive to provide a
universal national education comes into conflict with Muslims for whom
religion and faith is a way of life and not simply a ritual act or private belief.
In one case, a Muslim father believes that Trafford Council discriminated
against his daughter by paying fees for Catholic pupils to attend an independent Catholic school but not for his daughter to attend an independent
Islamic school. An important difference between Catholics, and for that
matter Jews and other minority religions, compared to Muslims is that in
practice their religious denominational schools are for the most part religious in name but serve a largely secular population. We outlined earlier
that the British state has been fairly consistently resistant to granting funding for Islamic schools compared to other faiths, even though there are now

a handful. The reason for this is the fear that ways of life that are founded on non-British values will be promoted by Islamic schools. Such a stance contrasts sharply to that of Dutch policy makers prior to their recent policy shift, and it defines the cleavage of race relations vis-à-vis Muslims. On the one side Muslims assert their civic credentials as British Muslims, aggrieved at what they perceive as the discrimination against them by the state and native society. And on the other, the state pretends that Muslims are part of the British community, but steadfastly refuses to grant them the group rights that they fear would foster a segregated community of religious zealots living outside of British law.

France: Islam in Response to *Laïcité*

In contrast to the Netherlands and Britain, the French sample of Muslim group claims is strongly shaped by one of the defining moments of the relationship between the French state and Islam, the headscarf controversy *(affaire du foulard)* in state schools. Fourteen of the twenty-five cases are demands that directly referred to wearing headscarves in public institutions, and four-fifths of these were made in 1993 or 1994, when this case was especially visible and resonant. The headscarf-related issues include calls for dialogue with and respect for all faiths and traditions, criticisms of the *circulaire Bayrou* in which a government minister ruled that headmasters could exclude pupils wearing the headscarf as an ostentatious sign of religion from state schools, protests against the exclusion of pupils for wearing headscarves, and calls for the establishment of private Islamic schools following these expulsions. Regarding the other issues, five refer to the comparative position of Islam relative to other monotheistic religions in French political life, a few concern the founding of Islamic universities for training imams, and the remainder concern religious education in schools and the building of mosques.

Concerning the type of group demands by French Muslims, most are for exceptional group rights (sixteen of twenty-five cases), only five are for parity group rights, and in four the group simply express their collective identity. In contrast to the Netherlands (less than a fifth) and Britain (a third), this higher proportion of exceptional group rights demands points toward cross-national differences, which reflect the different ways that the countries recognize cultural and religious groups. Whereas Dutch multiculturalism is open to all group demands, and British race relations is open to some group demands but not Muslims as "Muslims," the French republican secularism *laïcité* strongly resists all group demands, especially those that are religious. An effect of this state-enforced *laïcité* is demonstrated by the orientation of French Muslims' group demands, which are predominantly dissociative in their relationship to the state's policies.

This overall dissociative nature of group demands in France is closer to the British case than the Netherlands. However, there are also differences between Britain and France in the way that group demands originate. British Muslim group demands are mostly proactive, whereas in France there are equivalent numbers of reactive (thirteen) and proactive (twelve) demands. In general, it appears that, like the British, French Muslims make group demands that confront the state authorities' policies for cultural pluralism. However, unlike the British, a significant proportion of French Muslims' group demands are made in response to actions by the French state. This shows a more defensive stance by French Muslims than their British counterparts and gives a first indication that it is the French state's assertiveness in applying a universalist and assimilationist approach to cultural pluralism that defines the context of claims making for group demands.

Perhaps surprisingly, given this apparently hostile institutional setting, we find fewer protest events for mobilizing group demands in France than in Britain, and all three French protests have demonstrative rather than confrontational or violent action forms. Each French protest event occurred in response to the expulsion of pupils from state schools for wearing the headscarf. In Grenoble, a thousand Muslims demonstrate outside the appeal committee hearing for a student excluded from class for wearing a headscarf during gym. As one placard makes clear, the protest is against "an antireligious *laïcism* that is a threat to social peace," whereas others assert the importance of the headscarf as an identity for Muslims in France: "France is my freedom, my foulard too" and "Muslim yes, French too." The other two examples of protests are by a hundred people against the expulsion of four pupils in Goissainville (Val d'Oise), and then another of about three hundred at Garges-lès-Gonesse, organized by the son of a director of the Association islamiste de Garges. In these instances, Muslims are defending what they perceive as their group rights against the assertive actions of the state authorities who are enforcing republican principles.

Looking at examples of exceptional group demands, we see more evidence for the defensive nature of group demands by French Muslims in the face of the enforcement of republican ideology by the state authorities. Twelve of the sixteen cases are reactive, and fourteen of the sixteen cases referred to headscarves. One non-headscarf example is a proactive demand by the Centre européen de recherché et d'information sur l'islam (CERISI) for an Islamic university to train imams, to promote Islamic values, and to build a framework for Islamic associational activity. This is more akin to the types of demands that appear in Britain and the Netherlands.

The indivisible, undifferentiated universalism of French republican civic values is centered on the equality of the individual citizen and leaves very little political space for the expression of cultural group difference within politics. In addition, the strong statist secularism *laïcité* is an ideology that is antireligious, allowing virtually no space for any form of expression of religious faith within public institutional politics. Religious organizations in France are brought under the control of the state to ensure that they focus on purely religious matters and do not stray into the realms of political activity. Our headscarf cases provide important insights on the nature of these conflicts between Muslims' group demands for the public expression of Islamic identity on one side, and French institutionalized *laïcité* on the other.

In one case, Abdallah Ben Masour, general secretary of the Union des organisations islamiques de France (UOIF), declares at a gathering of three thousand to eight thousand that "*laïcité* must not be allowed to become a new religion, but a neutral space where liberty is given to everyone. A twelve-year-old child is presented by the media like an enemy of *laïcité* just because she wants to do her thing." In a similar vein, the UOIF affirms its support for the principles of *laïcité* but adds that this includes a respect for the right to difference *(droit à la différence)*. This demand occurs in response to minister of education Bayrou's declaration upholding the stance that wearing a headscarf is not to be permitted at state schools if it is used as an ostentatious religious symbol. In another instance, after the Conseil d'Etat annulled the exclusion of three girls suspended from school for wearing headscarves in Seine-Saint-Denis, Dalil Boubakeur, rector of the Muslim Institute and the Grande Mosqée de Paris, called on Muslims to live in peace and mutual respect and in dialogue with their neighbors, but also expressed his satisfaction with what he interprets as this recognition by the state of Muslim specificity and respect for some of its traditions in the law. There are several examples of this kind, where the claim reaffirms the principle of *laïcité* but in doing so requests more space for the expression of cultural difference within it, often making clear, however, that this is an expression of culture not politics. A minority of cases are more separatist in their orientation and conclusions. In another response to the Bayrou declaration and the exclusion of pupils in Lille, the president of the regional Islamic council and of the Lille-Sud Mosque declares that he is scandalized by the level of rejection that appears on the back of the concept of *laïcité*, and that now it is time to turn to private schools, as the state has left Muslims no other choice.

One would expect it to be anomalous to have a demand for exceptional group rights that is acculturative with respect to French *laïcité*. However, there is one case that is unusual but nonetheless revealing about French conflicts over Islam. Here the Union des jeunes musulmans (UJM) of Lyon publicly criticizes the state authorities who have stamped the identity card of a woman, which bore a photo of her wearing a headscarf, with the words "practicing Muslim" *(musulman très practicant)* in the distinguishing marks category. The UJM expresses its concern about the segregationist attitude of the authorities with respect to the French Muslim community *(la communauté musulmane française)* and demands equal treatment for all citizens of the country, whereby a principle for the liberty of cultural expression ought to be enforced within the framework of a well founded *laïcité*. Here the UJM use the republican principle of *laïcité* to denounce what they see as the possible stigmatization of French Muslims who may be singled out as a group by other sections of French society. They fear that being given the dubious exceptional right of being publicly demarcated as different on their identity cards may be used against them. Interestingly, the authorities dismiss this event as an individual error by a member of their staff, and reassert the indivisibility of French citizenship.

The examples that we have described show that conflicts over group rights in France are in many cases highly visible and resonant because they are located in institutional settings of interactions between the French state and Muslims. In the vast majority of cases, Muslims are responding to the actions of state authorities carried out in the name of republican *laïcité*. To explain why Islam faces such strong cultural opposition from the French state, it is important to see that the French state views Muslim associational activity as a double challenge to its authority. First, Islam is a group identity that allows the largest set of migrants to organize collectively within France, thus promoting precisely the type of sectional group political interests that are anathema to the French understanding of citizenship. Second, Islam is the faith of a significant section of the population who practice their religion and whose religious belief places certain demands and restrictions on the way that they approach the duties of the public life of the citizen. From this viewpoint, Islam allows the collective organization and promotion of a set of religious beliefs and values that challenge the politicized secularism of the state and its opposition to religious faith in the public domain.

In many of our cases, French Muslims make group demands that try to negotiate a degree of recognition for Islamic symbols and values within the understanding of belonging to the French nation. This is also evident in their demands for parity group rights, which either refute religion by advocating a secular form of Muslim civic associationalism, or alternatively argue that religious practice is outside of the political realm. For example, the president of l'Union des familles musulmanes-Islam de France (UFM) argues that the family way constitutes an opposition to Islamic extremism and that the aim of this secular association is to reconcile the rights and duties of Muslims resident in France, the Arab culture *(la culte arabe)*, and the French civil code. The claimant distinguishes here between a political Islam of extremism, which he rejects, and the potential contribution of civic associations of recognized secular minorities (of Muslims) to French political life. Expressing similar sentiments, the general secretary of the UOIF calls for an "Islam de France," arguing that it is a nonnegotiable prerequisite for engaging in French political life, that all allegiance to a foreign country must be renounced, and that the democracy, laws, and values of the republic must be respected. In another case concerning the role of Islam as a religion, the rector of the Paris Mosque expresses disappointment that the president of the republic has not invited a Muslim representative to his ceremony of good wishes *(voeux)* for the heads of the religions, alongside the archbishop of Paris, the head rabbi of France, and the president of the Protestant Federation. Nonetheless, he also uses this opportunity to make the point that the Paris Mosque was founded by a French state decree, and thereby tries to legitimate the principle that the state should take on the same relationship that it has with the other faiths by establishing a centralized Islamic religion. In our other cases, Muslims' demands for parity rights simply request the same basis for Islamic religion within France as the restricted role already granted to other faiths, namely, that they concentrate on worship not politics. Thus the aptly named Association pour le dialogue islamo-chrétien et les rencontres interreligieuses (ADIC, Association for an Islamo-Christian Dialogue and Interreligious Meeting) calls for "fraternité" (brotherhood—echoing the French state's motto *liberté, egalité, fraternité*) between the three monotheistic religions in France.

Our discussion shows that the strict separation between religion and politics that is enforced by the French state makes any publicly visible form of association by Muslims appear problematic and a challenge to the principle of *laïcité*. France, like Britain, is unwilling to accommodate political space for Muslims but is more forthright and explicit in enforcing this stance. Muslims in France have never been under any illusions that religious faith is not part of civic public life, and they are granted far fewer group rights in recognition of their status as discriminated migrants than in Britain. In both countries, conflicts arise where state authorities interact with Muslim groups. British Muslims make demands for group rights that are more assertive than their French counterparts, who mostly defend their group against the state's public enforcement of *laïcité*. However, in both countries, Muslims make efforts to define Islam within national belonging. This is especially evident in France, where there are group demands for an "Islam de France," or a secular associational Islam, or a benign apolitical religious Islam, but very little evidence for separatist demands or expressions proclaiming the political authority of Islam over the state. Nonetheless, the French state's entrenched opposition to all religion in public life, on one side, and its suspicion that Islam entails political aspirations, on the other, leads to this ongoing problematic relationship between France and her Muslims.

Conclusion

This chapter set out to address the leading question regarding the nature of the challenge of group demands to liberal democratic states by undertaking a systematic comparative analysis of migrants' claims making in Britain, France, the Netherlands, Germany, and Switzerland. To our knowledge, we have been the first to test the assumptions underpinning the multicultural citizenship debates with empirical evidence drawn from a systematically retrieved sample of this scale and type. Our approach has allowed us to conduct a qualitative analysis of country cases that at the same time can be located within the macro picture of overall claims making on immigration and ethnic relations.

Our first important findings concern the scale of claims making for group demands and the self-identifications used by migrants to make them. Viewed quantitatively, our evidence shows that the prominence of group demands within the literature on multicultural citizenship appears to be widely exaggerated, at least with respect to the European context of postwar migration. Controversies over group demands were most prominent in Britain, but even there accounted for only a 7.7 percent share of claims making over immigration and ethnic relations, and were least prominent in Germany and Switzerland, where the figure was a tiny 1.2 percent. This seems to indicate that the strong emphasis on group demands within the migration literature over the last decade has not been matched by reality. Far from the images of societies pulling themselves apart at the cultural seams (see, for example, Huntington 2002), the cultural difference of migrants in their European societies of settlement does not appear to be the main characteristic of their own claims making, nor does it appear to be on a scale that would threaten the social cohesion of societies. However, as our qualitative analysis showed, this should not be interpreted as meaning that migrants' group demands are easily accommodated and unproblematic. To be fair, the objective of much literature on multiculturalism has been normative and theoretical rather than empirically based, but we nonetheless suspect that many scholars have tended to raise the high prominence of a few cases, such as the headscarf affair, to general theories about the integrative capacity of the liberal nation-state.

A second important point is that our evidence shows that group demands are not a general phenomenon. We found cross-national differences with virtually no claims making for group demands in Germany and Switzerland, the countries that have done least to make migrants into citizens and whose policies tend to keep migrants politically and culturally apart from the host society. From this we conclude that migrants have to receive some degree of incentives from host societies before they feel that they are sufficiently politically empowered to make demands for special treatment as a group within their societies of settlement. We found roughly the same modest levels of group demands in France, which officially shuns all recognition of minority identities, and the Netherlands, which goes out of its way to recognize a whole range of migrant identities, and Britain, which sponsors racial identification but does not recognize migrants' religious identities. Contrary to previous research (Ireland 1994, 2000; Koopmans and Statham 1999a) and our general findings in chapter 3, this shows that, at least regarding claims making for group demands, there are important limitations on the degree to which nation-states have been able to shape migrants' political behavior in their own image.

On the surface, this finding seems to show that group demands are to a certain extent independent from a country's policy approach for accommodating cultural diversity. However, closer inspection of our data points to a specific exceptional case of claims making by groups using Muslim or Islamic self-identifications. Muslims made half or more of the group demands in Britain, France, and the Netherlands. This shows that European public controversies about claims for group demands are not about migrants' cultural differences per se, but arise from a specific contradiction of Islam in the liberal nation-state. We consider that one reason why Islam is less easily shaped and transformed by minority policies than other types of migrant identities is due to its fusion of civic and religious functions. This limited separation of civic and religious roles in public life becomes embedded institutionally in the infrastructure of the Muslim migrant communities, in particular through the activities of the mosque, which is the focus of community life and the community's interface with political institutions. While secular civic migrant associations would be directly confronted by minority policies and face incentives and pressures to adapt, state institutions make fewer attempts to transform the religious faith of migrants. The combination of civic and religious roles in Islam appears to make it a particularly resilient form of identification and a source for group rights demands. This resilience of Islam to political adaptation was demonstrated by comparison with another migrant religion, Hinduism. Muslim and Hindu migrants share similar characteristics: they settled in the same waves of postwar migration, they come from the same regions of origin with the same postcolonial traditions, and they have the same type of community structure based on familial ties and patron-client relationships. However, in contrast to Muslims, our data show that Hindus are largely conspicuous by their public absence. We argued that this Muslim exceptionalism was due to the more visible and public nature of the religion and the demands that it places on followers and their interactions with core public institutions.

To gain further insight into the nature of the challenge of claims making for group demands by Muslims in Western Europe, we undertook a qualitative cross-national comparison, summarized in Table 30. Our qualitative analysis of group demands by Muslims showed that the more open Dutch and the more restrictive British and French attempts to accommodate cultural difference had all encountered problems that are difficult to resolve. The proactive and acculturative nature of Islamic group demands in the Netherlands, mobilized by conventional action forms, stands in contrast to the dissociative Muslim claims making that we find in Britain and France.

Closer inspection reveals that the outcomes of Dutch multiculturalism do not support the notion that granting multicultural rights strengthens political integration in multiethnic societies. For a start, we find the Dutch state sometimes promoting group rights for Muslims that more liberal Muslim groups do not want. The secretary of justice's bill to allow one-sided marriage dissolution puts group law above national civic law by denying the individual equality of women. Here the famous Dutch tolerance seems prepared to sanction similar attitudes among the Islamic faith community— i.e., inequality of women—to the illiberal ones that it has long tolerated for decades from Protestant fundamentalists. This is only one case, but it is instructive about the impact of Dutch policies on associational activity by Muslims. The state grants so many group rights that being acculturative in the Dutch political context substantively means not being integrated into

Table 30. A summary of qualitative findings on Muslims' claims making for group demands, 1992–98

	Netherlands	Britain	France
Rights granted			
Formal citizenship	Yes	Yes	Yes
Minority group rights	Yes	Only racial and ethnic groups	No
Religious group rights	Yes	No	No
Muslim claims making			
Type of group demands	Parity	Exceptional and parity	Exceptional
Motivational impetus	Proactive	Proactive	Reactive/proactive
Relative level of protest	Low	High	Medium
Form of protest	Demonstrative	Confrontational/violent	Demonstrative
Overall orientation	Acculturative	Dissociative	Dissociative

the national community, and in some cases being separated from it. Dutch multiculturalism's toleration of Islam may lead to fewer public conflicts, but this can also be read as a lack of care for ensuring community cohesion. If the native Dutch communities are self-organized in their own pillars and their lives do not come into any institutional contact with Muslims, then why should they be bothered by Muslims' strange demands and odd-sounding customs? Precisely these problems and the fear that policies were structuring the disadvantage of minorities led to the shift in Dutch policy thinking toward a more British-style integrationist approach.

British Muslims are similarly assertive compared to their Dutch counterparts. However, their group demands are more often for exceptional rights and dissociative. We find British Muslims mobilizing assertively, sometimes violently, and often in ways that directly target the workings and principles of state authorities. On one side, the state remains unwilling to grant rights to Muslims, fearing that the associational activities of the Muslim community cannot easily be included within its secular integrationist formula, not least because they aim to promote a political role for the Islamic faith. On the other, we find incommensurable demands by Muslims that appear to make such fears well founded. To be fair, we also find a significant number of British Muslims' group demands that are made *within* the race relations framework and that would be relatively easily accommodated if Muslims were categorized as an ethnoreligion in British law. Nonetheless, we consider that it is unlikely that British multiracial politics will be able to accommodate Islam without ongoing conflicts.

Compared to the British, French Muslims are more reactive than assertive in mobilizing their demands on the state, lacking the degree of legitimacy that accrues to British Muslims indirectly as a recognized minority. The advocacy of French Muslims for religious recognition is also more defensive. For example, while British anti-Rushdie claims making demands political recognition for the Islamic religion within blasphemy laws, the religious demands in France tend to be more acculturative, such as those made by the rector of the Great Mosque of Paris, which ask for little more than accommodation for Islam within the French state's system of control for religious communities. We also found several examples of Muslims drawing on republican *laïcité* as the legitimating basis for their demands. The headscarf cases, the definitive events in our sample, showed that many claims are reactive against interventions by the state to ban the ostentatious display of religious symbols in public life. The institutional conflicts about the place of Islam in France are often brought forward by the state asserting its *laïcité*. We consider that this outcome of a more defensive than assertive political Islam arises from the harsh political context that Muslims face for expressing their group differences. Attempts to turn Muslims into Frenchmen have shaped a sort of French Islam, but at the same time, this is not a pacified Islam that is able to disappear into the private realm of individual faith. The more Muslims see themselves as French citizens, the more they will demand their rights, first as a minority and then as a religious group. In time, French Muslims could become as assertive as their British counterparts, which would most likely provoke stronger state reactions.

In short, we tested three national approaches for the accommodation of Islam and found them all to be problematic, but in different ways. The Dutch case shows that attributing group rights too easily may result in migrant groups increasingly turning inward, identifying less strongly with the majority society, and becoming tied up in internal factional community politics. The British case suggests that the political participation of Muslims with group-specific incommensurable demands can lead to seemingly irresolvable conflicts. And the French case shows that strong assimilative pressures can push such migrant groups away from identification with the political process and into a choice between a neutered or politicized Islam.

This gloomy overall conclusion arises at least in part from the fact that Islam cannot simply be confined to religious faith but advances into the realm of politics where the state's authority and civic citizenship obligations reign supreme. However, it is important to note that this phenomenon of migration bringing new religious groups into the community of liberal democracies is not without historical precedent. For example, the large-scale immigrations of Irish Catholics in the nineteenth century, and then Jews from Eastern Europe, are important forerunners of distinct religious and ethnic migrant groups that over time the British nation-state incorporated into its self-understanding of the political community. Likewise, the political crisis brought by the Dreyfus affair in France and Karl Marx's reflections on the Jewish question bring to light that continental Europe has faced similar previous dilemmas with respect to their Jewish minorities. Although accommodating Islam will be marked by conflicts, it is perhaps better to have political conflicts over being part of a national community than to have resident minorities who see themselves separate from the native civil society. One possibility is that the passage of time will bring more "domesticated" nationalized forms of Islam, whose demands are more easily included within existing frameworks and whose believers share more of the secularized core values of the native majority publics. Alternatively, failure by political institutions to specifically recognize and include Islam may lead

to grievances and turn future generations of Muslims either toward political ideologies that challenge the West, such as radical Islam, or a life of
alienation and anomie. Future outcomes will depend on the willingness of
the Muslim communities to adapt and European states to negotiate viable
forms of accommodation. For the time being, however, it seems clear that
controversies over Muslim group demands are likely to go on and on.

5

The Extreme Right: Ethnic Competition or Political Space?

In this chapter, we shift our attention to another collective actor that plays an important role within the field of immigration and ethnic relations: the extreme right. The last two decades have witnessed the rise and continued saliency of right-wing extremist parties that have xenophobic and racist positions, or at least positions that are against the rights and interests of immigrants (see Elbers and Fennema 1993; Hainsworth 1992; Ignazi 1992; Kitschelt 1995; Kriesi 1999). Parties such as the Republicans in Germany, the British National Party, the Swiss Democrats (formerly National Action) in Switzerland, the Center Democrats in the Netherlands, and above all the Front National in France are typical examples. Our central task here is to explain variations in xenophobic claims and, more generally, in the mobilization by the extreme right across our five countries.

By "xenophobic claims" we mean strategic intervention, either verbal or nonverbal, in the public domain "by groups who react to and mobilize against the presence of migrants and ethnic groups, demanding that the state enforce measures that exclude such groups from social, political and cultural rights" (Statham 1997, 14). The definition of the extreme right is less straightforward. Most attempts at defining and classifying the extreme right deal with parties. Typologies are usually based on the ideology of extreme-right parties and on the issues they address (see, for example, Backes and Moreau 1993; Betz 1993; Elbers and Fennema 1993; Griffin 1992; Hainsworth 1992; Kitschelt 1995). Perhaps the common denominator of all those actors who can be considered as belonging to the category of the extreme right is their ethnocultural stance. Thus, in line with our general framework, we stress the ethnic elements of the discourse and mobilization of the extreme right—a collective actor that conveys an ethnocultural conception of national identity, emphasizing cultural difference as a major barrier toward integration and societal cohesion, and that opposes the idea of the nation as a political and civic community (Koopmans and Statham 1999b). Of course, this approach does not exhaust the various ideological and discursive elements of this actor and does not do its full complexity justice. Yet, it focuses on the distinctive characteristic of the extreme right with respect to the political field of immigration and ethnic relations. By doing so, this allows us to link the claims made by extreme-right actors with the prevailing configurations of citizenship.

The success of extreme-right parties varies strongly across countries. While, for example, the French Front National gained the support of 15 percent of the electorate in 1997 and triumphed over the Socialist Party in the first round of the presidential elections in 2002, the British National Party has remained steadfastly at the political margins. Previous work has tended to overlook cross-national differences in favor of a focus on the conditions that have facilitated the emergence or breakthrough of extreme-right parties. In addition, it has tended to focus on parties and electoral strength, stressing two main sets of factors: demand-side and supply-side. The former refers to the conditions that have led to the creation of a social and cultural reservoir to be exploited by far-right political organizations, such as value change and structural cleavages related to the modernization process (e.g., Betz 1993; Flanagan 1987; Ignazi 1992; Minkenberg 1992). Supply-side factors include political and institutional aspects, such as the structure of the electoral system, the responses of established actors, and the dynamics of party alignment, demarcation, and competition (e.g., Betz 1993; Kitschelt 1995; Kriesi 1999; Koopmans 1996a; Schain 1987; Thränhardt 1995), that provide the extreme right with a political niche to be exploited.

With regard to explanations for the rise and mobilization of extra-parliamentary forms of the extreme right (e.g., racist and xenophobic violence perpetrated by skinheads or other groups of apparently disaffected youngsters), there is relatively little systematic research. To find a theoretical framework to explain this form of right-wing extremism, we must resort to the social movement literature. There we find two competing explanations: one focusing on grievances and ethnic competition, the other on opportunities and institutional frameworks (Koopmans 1996a). Grievance theories see the cause of extreme-right violence as discontent with respect to the main target of this collective actor, i.e., foreigners, migrants, and asylum seekers, and as a response to growing pressures stemming from new immigration and its consequences. In contrast, opportunity theories emphasize the role of political elites and institutions in shaping the mobilization of extreme-right actors.

In this chapter we shall combine political-institutional and cultural-discursive factors within a revised political opportunity approach. In addition to political-institutional variables, which must be considered when explaining collective mobilizations, we look at the impact of national configurations of citizenship as a relevant political opportunity structure for the claims making of the extreme right. Broadly stated, the main thesis is that the collective definitions of citizenship in the five countries provide different sets of discursive opportunities that determine the degree of visibility, resonance, and legitimacy of xenophobic claims and extreme-right actors. This, in turn, affects the role that political-institutional variables, such as political alignments, party competition, and the presence of a political entrepreneur channeling extreme-right demands into the political system, have on this type of claims making. We argue that the political space made available for the mobilization of the extreme right by the policy positions of mainstream parties on issues pertaining to immigration and ethnic relations is a crucial determinant. Thus, the extent and forms of claims making by extreme-right actors stem more from the competition between parties in the institutional arenas than from the competition between ethnic groups, i.e., between the majority native population and minority groups of migrant origin.

In the next section, we address in more detail existing explanations of the mobilization of the extreme right, both in its partisan and extra-parliamentary forms. Then we propose a theoretical framework for understanding the claims making of the extreme right, which attempts to combine political-institutional dynamics and configurations of citizenship. Drawing from this theoretical framework, we propose a way to conceptualize the specific opportunity structure for the extreme right as a combination of discursive opportunities (determining the degree of visibility, resonance, and legitimacy) and the political space made available to the extreme right. The remainder of the chapter tests some hypotheses drawn from our theoretical framework by using our cross-national comparative data. Specifically, we discuss the presence of the extreme right in the public domain (including its organizational forms), its action repertoires, and its contribution to claims making in the field of immigration and ethnic relations.

Two Competing Explanations of Extreme-Right Mobilization

Translated into social movement jargon, the distinction between demand-side and supply-side explanations generally reflects the *differences* between grievance and opportunity theories, two of the major competing social movement theories, or at least two major competing accounts for the radicalization of protest. *Grievance theories* stress the objective conditions that are assumed to lead to subjective grievances or discontent. This, in turn, is seen as the principal determinant of the mobilization by social movements. Collective behavior and relative deprivation theories are probably the best-known variants of this model (e.g., Gurr 1970; Kornhauser 1959; Smelser 1962; Turner and Killian 1957). Mostly, such accounts assume that social movements are based on anomie and are a collective response to individual frustrations and deprivations. On our current topic, for example, this view would consider that economic downturns impact increasingly on lower-skilled workers, who then suffer disproportionately from unemployment, bad housing, marginalization, and isolation (Heitmeyer 1992; Heitmeyer et al. 1992; Kowalsky and Schroeder 1994). Subsequently, this creates a group of socially excluded people who are considered a resource pool for potential mobilization into extreme-right and xenophobic activities. A similar approach, and arguably more convincing, is ethnic competition theory, which sees racial violence as a result of the competition between ethnic groups over scarce resources (Barth 1969; Belanger and Pinard 1989; Nagel and Olzak 1982; Olzak 1992; Olzak and Nagel 1986).

Opportunity theories, in contrast, argue that social movements do not depend on the amount of grievances but stem above all from the political opportunities that are made available to them at a given time (e.g., Kitschelt 1986; Kriesi et al. 1995; McAdam 1996, 1999; Tarrow 1998; Tilly 1978). Among the aspects of the political opportunity structure that may translate grievances into mobilization are the relative openness or closure of the institutionalized political system, the stability or instability of elite alignments that support a polity, the presence or absence of elite allies, and a state's capacity and propensity for repression (McAdam 1996). In this perspective, the structure of political opportunities constrains and shapes the extent and forms of mobilization by social movements, which channel their action repertoires into either moderate or radical forms. Regarding the extreme right, this view argues that the socially excluded will become engaged in xenophobic activities only to the extent that the institutional context provides favorable opportunities for the rise of extreme-right political behavior.

These two competing explanations make opposed predictions about the use of violence for political purposes. Grievance theories assume that the more intense the objective condition or problem, the stronger the grievances and the more radical or violent the collective response. Opportunity theories, in contrast, assume that violence increases to the extent that there are no other alternative political options available for making demands. In other words, not only protest but also violence are political resources in the hands of the powerless (Jenkins and Perrow 1977; Lipsky 1968; Piven and Cloward 1979).

Grievance-type explanations are popular among extreme-right activists and media and public accounts (Koopmans 1996a). For example, racist attacks on hostels for refugees in Germany in the early 1990s were often presented in the press as morally condemnable but understandable due to the growing number of asylum seekers.

To test the grievance position cross-nationally, we have constructed a summary indicator for the objective situation for each country. This includes three factors that are often assumed to create actual or perceived frustrations and deprivations among sectors of the native indigenous population—the "losers" of the modernization process (Kriesi 1999)—with regard to immigration and migrants, and thus lead to racist violence and/or extreme-right mobilization: the proportion of population of migrant origin, the immigration rate, and the unemployment rate. The ranking of our five countries according to this indicator is the following (from the worst to the best objective situation): Switzerland (35), Germany (27), the Netherlands (23), France (22), and Britain (18).[1]

By contrast, opportunity theories consider that mobilization by the extreme right will become violent to the extent that other channels are not available to express this type of demand. According to this, we would expect the extreme right to be more moderate where extreme-right parties are a relevant force in the political system, and conversely more radical or violent where there is no such institutional ally (see Koopmans 1996a). To test this type of explanation, we have calculated the average percentage of votes received by extreme-right parties in the five countries during the 1990s: France, 12.2 percent; Switzerland, 8.4 percent (excluding the Swiss People's Party); Netherlands, 2.5 percent; Germany, 2.1 percent; and Britain, less than 1.0 percent.[2] Thus, extreme-right parties perform very differently across our countries. In France and, to a lesser extent, in Switzerland far-right parties on average scored relatively highly in the 1990s, but in Germany, the Netherlands, and especially Britain they remained relatively marginal political actors, at least in electoral terms.[3]

Simply comparing the ranking between the five countries for the objective situation regarding immigration and for the electoral strength of extreme-right parties already casts serious doubt on the grievance explanation. For the grievance position to hold, we would have had to find a strong positive correlation between the two summary indicators. Britain does have a low score in both respects; however, we find that France has a low objective situation score but the strongest far-right party. Likewise, but in the opposite direction, Germany ranks high in grievances, but low in electoral strength. In sum, we see no systematic correlation that suggests a direct impact of the size of migrant population or immigration rate on the success of extreme-right parties.[4]

On the basis of our claims-making data, we will see whether grievance explanations perform better for the presence of the extreme right in the public domain. First, we outline a more general theoretical framework for understanding xenophobic and extreme-right claims making that is based on insights from the opportunity approach.

A Theoretical Framework for Understanding Xenophobic and Extreme-Right Claims Making

Figure 7 gives the basic features of a theoretical framework for analyzing xenophobic and extreme-right claims making. We see xenophobic and extreme-right claims making as determined by the interplay of three factors: national

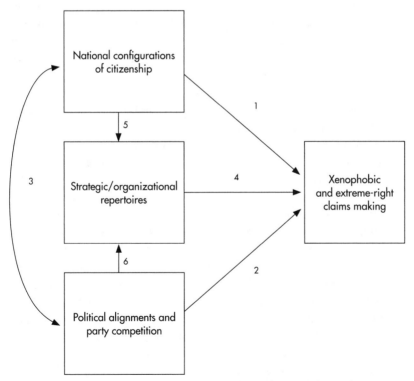

Figure 7. A theoretical framework for the analysis of xenophobic and extreme-right claims making.

configurations of citizenship, an institutionalized political system, and strategic/organizational repertoires.

First, the opportunities and constraints set by *national configurations of citizenship* influence the extent and forms of claims making by the extreme right (arrow 1). To explain the relevance of this, we briefly retrace the steps of our approach that has been outlined in more detail in previous chapters. To define the prevailing model of citizenship in a given country, we focused on two dimensions: (1) the formal criteria of inclusion in or exclusion from the national community, or the individual equality dimension; and (2) the cultural obligations imposed on outsiders to become members of that community, or the cultural difference dimension (Koopmans and Statham 2000). In the policy area of immigration and ethnic relations, these two dimensions refer to citizenship rights as a crucial factor for determining the ways in which migrants are incorporated into the receiving countries (Brubaker 1992; Castles 1995; Favell 1998; Smith and Blanc 1996). On the formal side, we distinguished between an ethnic-cultural and a civic-territorial basis for countries to grant citizenship rights, whereas on the cultural side, citizenship acquisition implied either the cultural assimilation of newcomers to the dominant (national) culture or, alternatively, some recognition that their ethnic and cultural differences were permitted in the self-understanding of the national community, thus allowing retention of migrant identities. By combining the dimensions, we obtained our four ideal-typical conceptions or models of citizenship: assimilationist, universalist, multiculturalist, and segregationist. As we have discussed at length in the introduction and chapter 1, our countries approximate these ideal types: Germany and Switzerland are closer to the assimilationist, France to the universalist, and Britain and the Netherlands to the multiculturalist positions. Just as we saw in chapter 3 how these different configurations of citizenship were important in shaping the claims making of migrants, they are also determinants of the types of opportunities that are available for the extreme right to oppose migrants and immigration.

In this view, xenophobic and extreme-right claims should be facilitated where they resonate better with the prevailing configuration of citizenship and where they are deemed more legitimate in the sense that they have greater acceptability in the public domain. For example, favoring nationals over foreigners in the job market—a typical demand of the extreme right—might be more viable in a country characterized by assimilationist approaches to the extent that such claims are likely to be more visible, more resonant, with the collective self-definition of the nation and appear more legitimate within such a political framework. In contrast, it might be more difficult to make similar demands in a state where a more republican rights-based policy style prevails, or even more so in countries that have a more pluralist approach to cultural group rights.

Second, xenophobic and extreme-right claims making are affected by features of the *institutionalized political system* and the political process. Two seem particularly relevant: the structure of political alignments, and the dynamics of party competition and demarcation strategies of established parties (arrow 2). As a number of authors have stressed (e.g., Betz 1993; Kitschelt 1995; Kriesi 1999; Koopmans 1996a; Schain 1987; Thränhardt 1995), these supply-side factors are crucial in that they enlarge or limit the political space available to emerging and outsider parties to increase their electoral strength. In addition, they are a key feature of the institutional opportunity structure for the mobilization of extreme-right actors outside the parliamentary arena.

Our main argument is that configurations of citizenship and political institutions combine to form an opportunity structure that constrains and channels the claims making in the field of immigration and ethnic relations (arrow 3). An important way in which configurations of citizenship and the dynamics of party alignment and competition are interrelated is through the incorporation of the ideological components of the prevailing configuration of citizenship or of the collective definition of national identity in the agenda and program of established parties, and more generally in the polity (Koopmans and Statham 1999b). This is likely to create a different mix of opportunities for extreme-right actors to the extent that established parties occupy the potential political space and adopt preemptive strategies toward the extreme right.

The third factor in our theoretical framework is represented by the *strategic/organizational repertoires* of the extreme right itself (arrow 4). Here we refer to the different forms that the political mobilization of this collective actor may take: either as an important political party engaged in the electoral struggle, or alternatively as extraparliamentary mobilization (i.e., a social movement). These organizational forms may be considered as two strategic options available to extreme-right actors for addressing their claims to the political authorities (Koopmans 1996a). If one option is adopted, the other becomes less viable. As we shall see, this aspect is particularly relevant for explaining the action repertoires of the extreme right because the political space for radical and violent actions expands or shrinks depending on which organizational form is prevalent.

Of course, organizational form is also influenced, at least partly, by the national configurations of citizenship and by the dynamics of political alignments and party competition. On one hand, just as the prevailing configuration of citizenship enables or constrains the extraparliamentary mobilization of the extreme right, it also determines the opportunities for the emergence of a strong far-right party (arrow 5). On the other hand, such opportunities also depend on the strategies and behaviors of other parties, especially established ones (arrow 6). We turn to the issue of what direction this is likely to take, and what predictions we can make on the basis of this theoretical framework regarding the extent and forms of the claims making by the extreme right, in the next section.

The Specific Opportunity Structure for the Claims Making of the Extreme Right

In the introduction, we argued that social movement scholars have tended to specify political opportunity structures at a too general level, without taking into account the characteristics of particular issue fields and collective actors. For example, Kriesi et al. (1995) explain cross-national variations in the extent and forms of the mobilization of new social movements through certain characteristics of the political system that grant different degrees of institutional access and yield different levels of repression. Yet, opportunity structures vary from one issue field to another as well as between collective actors. Therefore, we need to define a set of political opportunities that are specific to the field of migration and ethnic relations. We have done so throughout the book by stressing the impact of citizenship and migrant integration regimes. However, in the case of the native response to immigration by the extreme right, the *specific opportunity structure* also results from more traditional institutional factors such as the dynamics of party competition. Here we conceptualize the specific opportunity structure of the extreme right as a combination of two dimensions that depend on the three factors outlined above. The three factors determine the extent and forms of xenophobic and extreme-right claims making in two ways. First, they provide different sets of *discursive opportunities,* which can be either strong (or favorable, that is, when extreme-right actors and claims are highly visible, resonant, and legitimate) or weak (or unfavorable, that is, when extreme-right actors and claims have a lower degree of visibility, resonance, and legitimacy). Second, they can provide either a wider or narrower *political space* for the emergence of such claims. The combination of these two dimensions yields four distinct opportunity structures for the mobilization of the extreme right, shown in Figure 8.

The first type we may call *institutionalization* (or institutionalized right-wing mobilization). It results from strong discursive opportunities and a

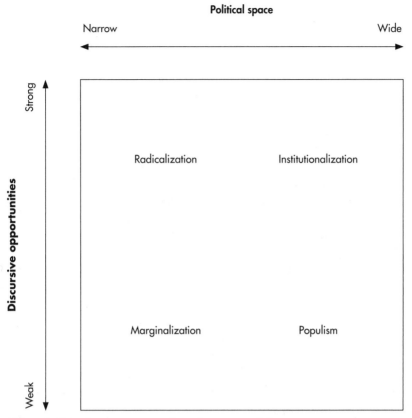

Figure 8. Specific opportunities for right-wing mobilization.

wide-open political space. In this situation, chances are higher that there will be a strong far-right party, for the established parties, especially those on the right of the political spectrum in closer competition with the extreme right, leave open a broad political space that can be exploited by the latter. The crucial aspect is perhaps the differential degree to which established political parties have occupied anti-immigrant positions within the public discourse. If this has not occurred, extreme-right parties have better chances to be electorally successful. The presence of a strong party, in turn, is likely to reduce the share of extraparliamentary mobilization and lead to moderate forms of claims making. However, given the higher degree of visibility, resonance, and legitimacy of xenophobic and extreme-right claims, the overall level of mobilization is expected to be high.

At the other extreme, we have *marginalization* (or marginalized rightwing mobilization). Here the extreme-right actor has at disposal neither favorable discursive opportunities nor a political space for emergence. As a result, we expect a low level of mobilization but at the same time a radical action repertoire; it is also unlikely that a strong party will emerge in such a situation.

The remaining two cases represent intermediate situations. The type resulting from a combination of strong discursive opportunities and a narrow political space is *radicalization* (or radicalized right-wing mobilization). As its name suggests, here we expect the extreme right to express itself primarily through extraparliamentary mobilization because the narrow political space is unfavorable to the emergence of a strong party. Furthermore, the action repertoire should be particularly radical, partly due to the absence of a strong party and partly due to the poor opportunities on the institutional side. Given the higher degree of visibility, resonance, and legitimacy, however, the overall level of mobilization should be rather high, as compared to marginalization.

Finally, if weak discursive opportunities combine with a large political space, we have a situation of *populism* (or populist right-wing mobilization). The broad political space should favor the emergence of a strong far-right party. At the same time, however, the weak discursive opportunities are expected to counter this tendency and hence to lower the level of mobilization in this respect. Furthermore, very radical and outright racist claims have little visibility, resonance, and legitimacy in this context. Therefore, we are likely to observe a more moderate type of right-wing populism mobilizing anti-immigrant sentiments.

From our theoretical framework and the related specific opportunity structure for the extreme right that we have just outlined, we now turn to empirical analyses. We aim to place our five countries within this typology and explain cross-national variations in the extent and forms of xenophobic and extreme-right claims making.

Overall Presence of the Extreme Right in the Public Domain

Concerning discursive opportunities, we expect the extreme right to be stronger in countries where an ethnic definition of the nation prevails because in such countries the position of the extreme right on immigration and ethnic relations issues will resonate with the legitimate ethnocultural conception of citizenship and national identity. Extreme-right actors also emphasize a monist view of the cultural obligations attached to citizenship, for example, when they claim that migrants should adapt to the habits and customs of the host society and that natives need not reciprocate. Conversely, in countries where the definition of the nation contains important civic-political elements and a pluralist view of cultural difference for minorities within national belonging, extreme-right claims are likely to be less visible, resonant, and legitimate in public discourses. Thus, with regard to discursive opportunities derived from citizenship configurations, we would expect the presence of the extreme right in the public domain to be higher in Germany and Switzerland (assimilationist), intermediate in France (universalist), and lower in Britain and the Netherlands (multiculturalist).

One way to determine empirically the extent to which members of the polity incorporate ethnocultural elements of the national identity is to look at their position in the migration political field.[5] Our assumption is that the higher the proportion of antiminority, racist, and xenophobic claims, the greater the incorporation of ethnocultural elements in the polity and, as a result, the narrower the political space available to the far right. Yet the political space available to extreme-right parties also depends on other factors, such as the electoral system and the specific strategies of established parties. Thus, the crucial aspect here is whether established parties, in electoral competition with extreme-right parties, cover the electoral terrain of the extreme right in public discourses. The most important aspect for our present purpose is the average position of established parties and the political space they leave to extreme-right actors in the five countries. Table 31 summarizes this information in a straightforward way. The first two rows give, respectively, the most pro-migrant and the most anti-immigrant position. The third row gives the range between these two positions, which represents the political space for the extreme right.

Germany provides the narrowest political space for extreme-right parties. The lowest average position of an established party (in this case, the Christian Socialist Party [CSU]) has an important anti-immigrant stance, as the score is quite negative compared to the other countries except Britain. Most important, the range between the most pro-migrant party (the Party of Democratic Socialism [PDS]) and the most anti-immigrant one (the Christian Social Party [CSU]) in Germany is the widest. The political space for the extreme right is also relatively narrow in Britain, where the lowest average position (the Conservative Party) is even more negative than in Germany, and the range between the most pro-migrant party (the Labour Party) and the most anti-immigrant one (the Conservatives) is nearly as large. At the other extreme, France provides the most favorable context for the emergence of the extreme right, as the lowest average position (the Rally for the Republic [RPR]) is the most positive among the five countries, and, above all, the range between the most pro-migrant party (the Communist Party) and the most anti-immigrant one (the RPR) is the smallest. The

Table 31. Summary of average discursive positions by established parties

Positions	Netherlands	Britain	France	Germany	Switzerland
Highest average position	0.68 [Groenlinks]	0.77 [Labour]	0.76 [PCF]	0.91 [PDS]	0.75 (0.75) [SSP-PSS]
Lowest average position	-0.05 [VVD]	-0.44 [Conservative]	0.38 [RPR]	-0.39 [CSU]	-0.25 (-0.07) [SVP-UDC] ([FDP-PRD])
Range between highest and lowest positions	0.73	1.21	0.38	1.30	1.00 (0.82)

Note: Includes all forms of claims. Takes into account actors having participated as first actor only. Results are expressed on a scale ranging from -1.00 to +1.00. Code -1.00 corresponds to antiminority, racist, and xenophobic claims. Code 0 corresponds to neutral, ambivalent, and technocratic claims. Code +1.00 corresponds to pro-minority, antiracist, and anti-extreme-right claims. Figures are computed on the basis of party positions shown in Table 34. Figures between parentheses for Switzerland consider the Swiss People's Party as belonging to the extreme right.

resulting political space available to the far right is particularly large. Finally, Switzerland and the Netherlands represent intermediate cases, as the range between pro-migrant (the Socialist Party and the Greens respectively) and anti-immigrant parties (the Swiss People's Party and the People's Party for Freedom and Democracy [VVD] respectively) is neither the highest nor the lowest.[6] Thus, with regard to political space, we expect the presence of the extreme right in the public domain to be highest in France, lowest in Germany and Britain, and intermediate in Switzerland (intermediate-low) and the Netherlands (intermediate-high).

If we combine the two types of explanation (discursive opportunities and political space), we arrive at the following predictions about the overall presence of the extreme right in the public domain, shown in the third row of Table 32: high in France, very low in Britain, and at an intermediate level in Germany, Switzerland, and the Netherlands.

Table 33, showing the involvement of the extreme right in acts of claims making in the five countries, allows us to see whether these predictions are correct. The table reports the percentage of claims for each country where racist or extreme-right actors were involved.[7] Furthermore, it makes a distinction within the extreme right between parties, other organizations and groups, and unknown actors (which are mostly xenophobic or violent actions with no actor reported). A first conclusion is that our findings demonstrate that grievance theories have little explanatory power with respect to the mobilization of the extreme right. If we compare the distribution referring to the totals (last row) with the ranking of the five countries according to a summary indicator of objective conditions, we observe a lack of correlation between the two measures. Thus, grievance theories fail to explain not only the electoral strength of the extreme right but also its mobilization as measured by its involvement in claims making.

Table 32. Predictions about the extent of claims making by the extreme right

	Netherlands	Britain	France	Germany	Switzerland
Discursive opportunities	Low	Low	Intermediate	High	High
Political space	Intermediate-high	Low	High	Low	Intermediate-low
Overall	Intermediate	Very low	High	Intermediate	Intermediate

Table 33. Share of claims by the extreme right in the public domain

Claim makers	Nether-lands	Britain	France	Germany	Switzer-land
Parties (%)	5.0	1.0	18.3	2.0	5.4
Other organizations and groups (%)	2.3	1.9	2.5	6.5	3.2
Unknown actors (%)	2.3	0.1	0.8	6.0	0.8
Other and unknown actors together (%)	4.6	2.0	3.3	12.5	4.0
Total (%)	9.2	3.0	21.1	14.1	8.9
N	2,484	1,345	3,231	8,341	1,676

Note: Includes all forms of claims. Claims of the extreme right may also deal with issues outside the field of immigration and ethnic relations.

Conversely, our findings largely support our hypotheses concerning the combined effect of discursive opportunities and the political space available to the extreme right. With more than 20 percent of claims overall, the extreme right has been much more active in France than in the other four countries. Indeed, its presence in the French public domain is more than twice that in Switzerland and the Netherlands, where as expected it is at an intermediate level. In addition, also at an intermediate level, though higher than in these two countries, the extreme right in Germany seems to take advantage of the strong degree of visibility, resonance, and legitimacy of its claims in that context. Finally, as expected, the extreme right seems particularly weak in Britain, where it was involved in only 3 percent of the claims.

Our findings also point to a crucial difference in the distribution of claims across the two main forms for the extreme right. According to the theoretical framework, national configurations of citizenship and the political process between parties influence the strategic/organizational repertoires of the extreme right, shaping a choice between two main organizational forms: as a political party or as extraparliamentary mobilization (including unorganized, spontaneous actions). The extreme right in Western Europe, in both its traditional and new variants, has usually been channeled into parliamentary politics, thus taking the form of a party. The extent to which this is likely to occur, however, varies strongly across countries and depends in part on the interplay of the dominant conception of the nation on the one hand, and the dynamics of party alignment, competition, and demarcation on the other. As the table shows, in Switzerland, the Netherlands, and above all France parties play the biggest role, but in Britain and especially Germany the opposite is true. In this regard, we observe a very strong correlation between the predictions deriving from the political space model and the distribution of claims by extreme-right parties. The same also holds true for the correspondence between the predictions of the discursive opportunity model and the distribution of claims by other extreme-right organizations and groups, although to a lesser extent.

If we collapse the two rows referring to other and unknown actors, we have a clearer picture of the relative shares of the partisan and the nonpartisan forms of extreme right in the five countries (fourth row).[8] The party form dominates claims making in France, while the social movement form largely prevails in Germany, the two countries that are most opposed in terms of political space. Compared to the presence of extreme-right parties, extraparliamentary mobilization is also more evident in Britain. Finally, Switzerland and the Netherlands are characterized by a rather homogeneous distribution of claims across the two forms.

While this distribution largely reflects the political space made available by the positions of established parties in the migration political field, when we look at the relative presence of the party and social movement forms of the extreme right, we should also take into account the different electoral strength of extreme-right parties in the five countries. It is likely that parties are more often present in the public domain when they have a strong institutional representation, for they have both more opportunities to address the public and more political responsibility to do so. In electoral terms, these parties are very strong in France, relatively strong in Switzerland, weak in Germany and the Netherlands, and very weak in Britain. This might further strengthen their strong involvement in claims making in France and contribute to explaining their stronger presence than expected in Switzerland.

Action Repertoires

In the introduction, we discussed two competing explanations for racist and extreme-right violence: grievance and opportunity approaches. Grievance theories assume that the more intense the objective condition or problem (for example, a sizable migrant population or increasing flows of immigrants), the stronger the grievances and the more radical or violent the collective response. Opportunity theories, in contrast, assume that violence increases to the extent that other options are lacking for articulating collective interests (for example, a strong extreme-right party). More specifically, political opportunity theorists have linked cross-national variations in the action repertoires of social movements to differences in institutional opportunity structures (e.g., Kitschelt 1986; Kriesi et al. 1995; Tarrow 1998).[9]

Our aim is to explain the action repertoires of the extreme right by reference to a specific opportunity structure formed by discursive opportunities and the available political space. Concerning the discursive side, we expect the extreme right to be more radical in assimilationist countries where it is more legitimate, and more moderate in multiculturalist countries where it is less legitimate. Universalism, in this respect, is an intermediate case. Thus, as far as public resonance and political legitimacy are concerned, we can make the following predictions about extreme-right action repertoires: radical in Germany and Switzerland, moderate in Britain and the Netherlands, and intermediate in France.

The predictions in spatial terms are partly different. As the figures in Table 33 suggest, the political space for the extreme right is relatively limited in both Germany and Britain, somewhat larger in Switzerland and the Netherlands, and relatively large in France. This translates into a more closed opportunity structure in Germany and Britain, a more open one in France, with Switzerland and the Netherlands in between. From this, we would expect the extreme-right action repertoire to be radical in Germany and Britain, moderate in France, and at an intermediate level in Switzerland (intermediate-radical) and the Netherlands (intermediate-low).

A third important aspect of the specific opportunity structure is the electoral strength of the extreme right. Here we follow Koopmans (1996a) in establishing a relationship between extreme-right radicalism and the presence of a strong extreme-right party. In this view, racist and extreme-right violence is lower where extreme-right parties are stronger, and vice versa. The use of violence is a costly strategy because of the risks of repression and moral sanctions. Therefore, when more viable alternatives exist, the amount of violence should diminish. The presence of a strong extreme-right party provides such an opportunity. If this view is correct, we should observe a negative correlation between the presence of important extreme-right parties and the levels of racist and extreme-right violence. Given the electoral strength of the extreme right in the five countries under study, we predict in this respect a radical action repertoire in Germany, Britain, and the Netherlands, a moderate one in France, and an intermediate one in Switzerland.

If we combine these hypotheses we arrive at the overall predictions shown in the fourth row of Table 34, which summarizes the discussion. The action repertoire of the extreme right is expected to be very radical in Germany, radical in Britain, moderate in France, and at an intermediate level in Switzerland and the Netherlands.

Table 35 confronts these predictions with our data. The table divides into three parts: the upper section gives the distribution of extreme-right claims

Table 34. Predictions about the action repertoire of the extreme right

	Nether-lands	Britain	France	Germany	Switzer-land
Discursive opportunities	Moderate	Moderate	Inter-mediate	Radical	Radical
Political space	Intermediate-moderate	Radical	Moderate	Radical	Intermediate-radical
Electoral strength of extreme-right parties	Radical	Radical	Moderate	Radical	Inter-mediate
Overall	Inter-mediate	Radical	Moderate	Very radical	Inter-mediate

Table 35. Action repertoire of the extreme right

Actions	Nether-lands	Britain	France	Germany	Switzer-land
Public statements (%)	45.6	42.5	72.0	12.3	62.1
Conventional political actions (%)	1.8	12.5	11.7	6.7	8.3
Meetings (%)	–	2.5	10.1	4.1	2.1
Judicial action (%)	1.8	7.5	1.3	1.7	0.7
Direct-democratic action (%)	–	–	–	–	4.1
Petitions (%)	–	2.5	0.3	0.9	1.4
Protest actions (%)	52.6	45.0	16.2	81.0	29.6
Demonstrative protests (%)	6.1	5.0	6.6	12.0	3.4
Confrontational protests (%)	22.4	5.0	2.9	12.4	4.1
Violent protests (%)	24.1	35.0	6.7	56.6	22.1
Total (%)	100	100	100	100	100
N	228	40	683	1175	145

pertaining to the field of immigration and ethnic relations, the middle section concerns other claims (for example, antiestablishment claims or claims dealing with mainstream political issues), and the lower section considers all extreme-right claims. Concerning action repertoires, we basically use the same classification as in chapter 2, which distinguishes between three main forms of action: public statements, conventional political actions (meetings, judicial action, direct-democratic action, and petitions), and protest actions (demonstrative, confrontational, and violent protests).

The results largely support our expectations. Germany clearly has the most radical extreme right, followed at a distance by Britain. At the other extreme, the French far right is the most moderate. Last, Switzerland and the Netherlands stand somewhere in between, but closer to Britain than France. This holds for the migration political field and even more so for extreme-right claims in general. Incidentally, we may note the particularly high proportion of confrontational protests in the Netherlands. This seems to be a peculiarity of political mobilization in this country. Kriesi et al.'s (1995) data point in the same direction.

Importantly, these findings show the limits of the traditional opportunity approach. For example, Kriesi et al.'s (1995) model would predict the most radical repertoire in France and the most moderate in Switzerland, whereas the largest share of violent protests occurred in Germany, and the French extreme right had the most moderate action repertoire. Clearly, Kriesi et al.'s findings cannot be generalized to all social movements, and political opportunity structure ought to be specified for each movement or each movement sector separately.

The important factors appear to be the presence of a strong extreme-right party within the established political system and the political space available. On one hand, there is a clear negative correlation between electoral strength and the proportion of protest actions: the lowest share of protests occurred in France, which is the country with the strongest extreme-right party, and the highest in Germany, which does not have a strong party. Britain and the Netherlands, which are characterized by weak far-right parties, display an important unconventional mobilization as well. Finally, Switzerland is an intermediate case, both in the electoral strength of extreme-right parties and in the share of protest actions. On the other, if we focus on violent protests, the ranking of the five countries on the indicators of political space (see Table 31) follows exactly that of the amount of xenophobic violence. Thus, the incorporation of ethnocultural elements into the programs and discourses of members of the polity reduces the opportunities for the emergence of the extreme right and at the same time tends to radicalize its action repertoire.

Finally, we see that grievance theories are of little help and offer at best only a limited explanation of racist and extreme-right violence in our five countries. The correlation between violent protests and our summary indicator of objective conditions with respect to immigration is far from perfect. True, France, which ranks very low for the objective condition, has the most moderate extreme right, but the correspondence stops there, as the distribution of violent protests in the other countries does not reflect the objective pressure coming from migration.

The Contribution of the Extreme Right to Claims Making on Immigration and Ethnic Relations

Thus far, we have considered all extreme-right claims, regardless of their thematic focus. We would now like to restrict our focus to claims addressing issues pertaining to the political field of immigration and ethnic relations in order to assess the contribution of the extreme right to this field. Do the factors that determine the claims making by the extreme right in general (i.e., its overall presence in the public domain) also account for its claims making in the more specific migration political field?

Table 36 presents the share of extreme-right claims on immigration and ethnic relations by issue field. The upper section refers to the entire field of immigration and ethnic relations and shows the presence of all types of extreme-right actors (first row) as well as excluding parties (second row). The lower section focuses on two more institutionalized issue fields: immigration, asylum, and aliens politics (third row) as well as minority integration politics (fourth row). We have excluded the less institutionalized antiracism and xenophobia issue field from this latter section of the table.

If we first look at the entire field, we can conclude that our hypotheses about the overall presence of the extreme right in the public domain (Table 32) to a large extent hold also for claims making in the more specific field of immigration and ethnic relations. France still ranks first and Britain last. The results for the other three countries are somewhat less consistent, but in general they confirm the prediction of an intermediate to low level of mobilization. Yet, the level of mobilization of the German extreme right is stronger than expected, and its presence is stronger in the migration field than overall. This is largely because in Germany a higher proportion of general, unspecific xenophobic claims are made outside institutional arenas by extraparliamentary organizations and groups.[10] This is evident if parties are excluded from these distributions. As we saw earlier (see Table 33), the level of mobilization diminishes dramatically in France if we exclude extreme-right parties, especially the Front National. At the same time, this

Table 36. Share of extreme-right actors in claims making

Issue fields	Netherlands	Britain	France	Germany	Switzerland
All political fields					
Immigration and ethnic relations politics (%)	6.8	2.7	10.2	10.4	7.0
N	2,286	1,313	2,388	6,432	1,365
Immigration and ethnic relations politics (excluding extreme-right parties) (%)	4.2	1.8	2.6	9.2	3.2
N	2,286	1,313	2,388	6,432	1,365
More institutionalized issue fields					
Immigration, asylum, and aliens politics (%)	1.0	0.6	3.2	0.6	3.9
N	1,125	486	882	2,586	787
Minority integration politics (%)	1.0	0.2	11.6	0.6	6.0
N	630	479	465	710	234

Note: Includes all forms of claims.

shows again that the strength of this party is detrimental to the mobilization of other extreme-right organizations and groups, not only overall but also when it comes to specific issues pertaining to immigration and ethnic relations. More generally, those countries, like France and to a lesser extent Switzerland, that have an important partisan extreme right leave a narrower space for the mobilization of extreme-right tendencies outside institutional arenas.

If the distribution of extreme-right claims across our five countries looks quite different depending on whether we include certain parties or not, it also varies according to which of the two more institutionalized issue fields we consider. Two findings deserve mention here. First, the mobilization of the extreme right concerning immigration, asylum, and aliens politics is higher in France and even more so in Switzerland than in the other three countries. Second, mobilization in the field of minority integration politics is particularly high in France, relatively high in Switzerland, and low in Britain, the Netherlands, and Germany.

These findings may be interpreted with respect to the varying strength of extreme-right parties in our countries. The presence of the extreme right in the two more institutionalized issue fields (immigration, asylum, and alien politics as well as minority integration politics) is stronger where far-right parties are stronger. This might be because these parties make more policy-oriented claims in comparison with other extreme-right organizations and groups. In other words, their institutional position leads them to focus on specific policy issues rather than making unspecific xenophobic claims. This is particularly true for the minority integration issue field that often represents the focal point of political debates and tends to polarize the position of parties and that of extreme-right parties in particular.

Finally, concerning the substantive focus of claims, as compared to other actors, the extreme right seems to be more concerned with keeping foreigners out than with signaling the difficulties of integrating them in the host society. The extreme right often emphasizes such issues as security, control, and law and order, which in the migration field pertain to the regulation of immigration flow (e.g., entry and border control, registration and internal control, residence rights, expulsions, illegal immigration). However, France is an exception, as in this country the extreme right much more frequently addresses issues concerning the situation of resident migrants than issues concerning the entry into or exit from the country.

This seems to be a result of the specific combination of inclusive and exclusive elements in the French conception of citizenship as it relates to immigrants. On the one hand, the inclusive nature of individual access to

French citizenship makes integration issues more salient than in Germany and Switzerland. On the other hand, the strong rejection of cultural group rights offers a legitimizing discursive frame of reference for interventions of the extreme right in this field that is absent in the multicultural contexts of Britain and the Netherlands. Indeed, the claims made by the French extreme right in the field of integration politics refer to the alleged inability to assimilate of Muslim immigrants and the rejection of the automatic acquisition of French citizenship by way of the jus soli. In the eyes of the extreme right, such unconditional attribution of citizenship conflicts with French republicanism because it creates *faux français* (false Frenchmen)—French by nationality, but not by culture. In the Dutch and British context, such an argument would be widely seen as illegitimate, but in the French context it resonates with the unitary conception of national identity and the rejection of group allegiances.

Conclusion

Prevailing conceptions of citizenship are often seen as one of the factors explaining the emergence of the new radical right (e.g., Kitschelt 1995; Kriesi 1999). In general, this aspect remains underdeveloped in existing accounts, which mostly focus on political and institutional variables. Recent work in the social movement perspective has begun to inquire into the impact of collective definitions of the nation and membership in the national community on the possibilities for extreme-right actors to mobilize existing potentials. Koopmans and Statham (1999b), for example, have attempted to explain the differential success of the extreme right in Germany and Italy with the role of ethnic and civic conceptions of nationhood. Here we followed this line of reasoning in order to account for cross-national variations in the extent and forms of claims making by the extreme right in the public domain, both within and outside immigration and ethnic relations politics.

In addition to citizenship and integration regimes, we must also consider certain aspects of the institutional political system and the political process. Thus, importing insights from spatial theories of political behavior, we have proposed a theoretical framework for understanding xenophobic and extreme-right claims making, arguing that variations are to a large extent determined by the interplay of three factors: national configurations of citizenship, the dynamics of political alignments and party competition, and the strategic/organizational repertoires of the extreme right (in particular the electoral strength of extreme-right parties). Confronting a number of hypotheses derived from this theoretical framework, we were able to show empirically how political-institutional and cultural-discursive opportunities account for differences in the extent, forms, and contents of xenophobic and extreme-right claims making.

Combining the cultural and spatial dimensions, we singled out four distinct opportunity settings for the mobilization of the extreme right: institutionalization, which favors the emergence of a strong extreme-right party, a large presence in the public domain, and a moderate action repertoire; marginalization, where the extreme right does not possess a strong party and displays a low level of mobilization, but has a radical action repertoire; radicalization, where the extreme right expresses itself primarily through a significant and radical extraparliamentary mobilization; and populism, which is more difficult to characterize because of the contradictory nature of different elements of the opportunity structure.

Based on the assessment of the prevailing configurations of citizenship, which provide different sets of discursive opportunities to extreme-right actors and their claims, and the empirical measure of the political space available to this type of actor, we are able to place the five countries of our study within this typology. France best exemplifies the case of institutionalization, Britain that of marginalization, Germany that of radicalization, and the Netherlands that of populism. Switzerland yields a hybrid situation in this respect (also illustrated by the ambivalent position of the SVP with regard to the extreme right), one that is located somewhere between the French and German cases, but closer to the latter.

Our analysis points to the importance of distinguishing between the two principal organizational forms through which extreme-right interests and identities emerge in the public domain: parties and social movements. This distinction is important not simply for descriptive reasons, but because the electoral strength of extreme-right parties becomes a factor that explains the rise of xenophobic and extreme-right violence outside institutional arenas.

Importantly, our analysis indicates that processes of social and cultural change do not impinge directly on the public articulation of collective interests and identities. Contemporary right-wing extremism is not a direct reaction to a fundamental change in culture and values that has occurred in Western Europe. It depends instead on the politicization of new cleavages or the repoliticization of existing ones. It also relates to the saliency of certain policy areas, and immigration and minority integration are certainly among the most important of such areas today. The amount and forms of claims making by the extreme right largely depends on the political space made available to them by other collective actors within this political field. In this regard, the policy positions of mainstream parties on immigration and ethnic relations is an important feature of the discursive opportunity structure for the mobilization of extreme-right and xenophobic actors. The extreme right finds more access to the public domain to the extent that established actors (i.e., mainstream parties) do not colonize their political space. In the case of extraparliamentary groups, the very presence of a strong extreme-right party is itself part of this opportunity structure.

In explaining the presence of the extreme right in the public domain, one also has to take into account such institutional factors as the electoral system and, more generally, the structure of the political system in a country. The structure of political alliances and the relationships between different strategic/organizational repertoires are also relevant. These aspects pertaining to the institutional framework and the political process of the political system are central to an explanation for the emergence of the extreme right because they are an important part of the political opportunity structure that channels and constrains extreme-right mobilization, which depends more on such opportunities than on the level of grievances in society. Put differently, objective and subjective grievances are a necessary but insufficient single condition for extreme-right emergence. In short, the political space made available through the political process, rather than the dynamics of ethnic competition, give the better explanatory account for extreme-right claims making in Western Europe.

6

Interest or Identity? Pro-Migrant and Antiracist Actors

Over the past two decades, immigration and ethnic relations have become highly politicized issues. Evidently, state actors have largely contributed to this politicization by framing the issues and implementing immigration and integration policies. However, as in any other political conflict, many other actors voice their views and politicize public issues. These political debates on migratory flows and migrant settlement are not just a conflict between different actors with opposing interests who put forward propositions for changes to state policies; they are also a conflict over different conceptions of national identities. Political actors enter the public space to support or contest dominant conceptions of citizenship. As we have already seen, migrants intervene in public debates based on their own interests that ideally stress a multicultural conception of nationhood. They claim inclusion within national community and tolerance regarding their cultural diversity. Extreme-right actors also defend a specific vision of the nation. Their ethnic-segregationist definition of national community is drastically opposed to migrants' understanding of nationhood. Exclusion and the native community's self-protection from "otherness" are recurring themes of the extreme right.

A further group of actors contributes to the politicization of migration issues. This group consists of those native actors who support migrants and oppose racism. They engage in public debates to oppose state policies, which they see as increasingly restrictive to newcomers, for example, by opposing deportations, restrictive entry requirements, and reductions of social benefits to asylum seekers, and introduce ideas and counterdiscourse regarding migrants' rights provision. They have also been particularly active in promoting political rights for minorities and extending social rights to people who are no longer temporary laborers but permanently settled immigrants. Lastly, they mobilize against all forms of discrimination that migrants suffer. One important dimension of this over the last two decades has been their intense campaigning to combat the rise of the extreme right in Europe, for which they have mobilized a counterdiscourse against the extreme right's propaganda depicting migrants as a major threat to national identities. Two types of actors support migrants: those such as unions, churches, radical-left groups, or human rights associations that are not specifically organized to protect migrants, but which at times join in public debates on behalf of migrants, and those political actors who are specifically organized to defend and advance the position of migrants. These pro-migrant and antiracist organizations are actors who have formed specific group identities and organizational structures around supporting and promoting migrants.

Compared to the other collective actors we have discussed, those who mobilize to support migrants and prevent racism are different because they enter the public domain to defend a constituency group of "others" rather than themselves. Such actions can be understood as a form of political altruism.[1] The concept of political altruism raises a number of theoretical issues, not least those outlined by Olson's (1965) study on individual interest and collective action. Among others, one important question is whether political altruism ought to be understood within the theoretical framework of an "interest" paradigm, which is mainly supported by "rational choice" scholars, or alternatively whether an "identity" approach that primarily sees collective action as an identity and solidarity process is more appropriate.

Collective identities are one of the basic components of collective actors (e.g., J. Cohen 1985; Melucci 1996; Tilly 1978; Touraine 1984). Christian, feminist, leftist, and humanist identities have been mobilized in "political altruism" protests (Passy 2001). It is due to the mobilization of such identities with the help of selective frames that political altruism removes collective action barriers and makes participation conceivable (Koopmans 2001b).

Political altruism can be conceived as *interest-oriented* protest. However, in such an interest-based perspective, pro-migrant and antiracist organizations are not mobilizing a particular vision of nationhood or specific conceptions of citizenship through their defense of migrant populations. A second analytical conception of these specialized actors supporting migrants sees them as political actors who enter the public arena to defend a specific vision of the nation. In this perspective, political altruism is conceived as *identity-oriented*. Pro-migrant and antiracist groups are seen to promote and advance a specific understanding of national identities. This understanding of nationhood diametrically opposes the definition of the national community held by the extreme right. Instead of seeing the cultural differences brought by immigration as a threat to national cohesion and identity, pro-migrant and antiracist activists define the nation as an open and universal sphere. This understanding is based on the idea of "protector universalism" (Taguieff 1997), whereby the national community has to be inclusive and manage ethnic relations on a universal and egalitarian basis. As Wieviorka points out, "the strength of antiracist action is that it inscribes itself in the public space by pleading in a universal manner, on behalf of general principles" (1998, 138).[2] Thus, in opposition to slogans of the extreme right, such as "la France aux français" (France for the French) or "Ausländer raus" (Foreigners out), which mobilize an ethnic understanding of nationhood, pro-migrant and antiracist actors advocate "open borders," "des papiers pour tous" (papers for all), or "Ausländer, lasst uns nicht mit den Deutschen allein" (foreigners don't leave us with just the Germans), which clearly promote a *civic conception of the nation*.

In the *interest-oriented* stance on political altruism, where pro-migrant and antiracist actors act specifically to defend the interests of migrants, we would expect such actors to be particularly active in countries where *the situation of migrants* is especially difficult and threatening to their interests. By contrast, mobilization by pro-migrant and antiracist actors would be less necessary in national contexts where the interests of migrants are taken into account by the state or other institutional actors. In our five countries, we have seen that none of the states promotes conditions for the inclusion of migrants within the national community that are ideal in the sense of producing a situation in which there is no discrimination. However, we have also seen that considerable variation exists between the countries. From the interest theoretical perspective, we suppose that pro-migrant and antiracist groups are likely to be particularly active in Switzerland and Germany, where an ethnic-assimilationist conception of citizenship does not facilitate the entry or the inclusion of migrants within national communities. In Britain and the Netherlands, we would expect to find weak political activity by these groups because the inclusive and pluralist conception of nationhood in both countries favors a better treatment of migrants than it does elsewhere. Lastly, France, with its paradoxical conception of citizenship, would be an intermediary case, with a weaker level of activity of pro-migrant and antiracist actors than Britain and the Netherlands, but higher compared to Switzerland and Germany.

In the identity-oriented conception of pro-migrant and antiracist mobilization, it is not the situation of migrants that is seen to condition their presence in the public domain, but a *shared understanding of citizenship* that defines specific conceptions of national belonging and "otherness." This shared understanding of nationhood shapes a structure of constraints and opportunities for identity-based political altruism, just as it does for other actors mobilizing a specific construction of national identity. In this view, pro-migrant and antiracist activism introduces and carries demands that acquire political legitimacy by resonating with and thereby contributing to the dominant conception of nationhood in the public domain. This is most likely to occur in national contexts that have defined an inclusive as well as universalist and egalitarian conception of citizenship. France represents the archetype of such a conception of nationhood. If political altruism is identity-based, we would expect an important mobilization of pro-migrant and antiracist protest in this country. Britain and the Netherlands, which like France share a civic tradition of nationhood and a strong conception of equality treatment, between groups as well as between individuals, would also be expected to provide pro-migrant and antiracist actors with significant opportunities for entering the public arena to defend migrants. Thus, similar patterns of mobilization for such actors can be expected in France, Britain, and the Netherlands. By contrast, the Swiss and German understanding of nationhood, based on an ethnic and assimilationist conception, is likely to establish high material and symbolic barriers against pro-migrant and antiracist actors organizing themselves to defend a more inclusive conception of national community.

Further backing for the identity stance comes from those who argue that "otherness" refers to national self-understandings of who is "in" and "out" of the community of citizens. Taguieff (1988, 1995) sees racism as a form of distinction between "us" and "others," where the ethnocentrism and superiority of one group ("us") dominates over "otherness." Despite its vision of the fundamental inequality between social groups, racism is not just a homogeneous expression of the hatred of others. Like his French colleague Wieviorka (1998), Taguieff identifies two main paths for expressing the hatred of "otherness." The first is "differentialist racism," which is based on a denial of common humanity and postulates the existence of an intrinsic distinction between human groups. This expression of racism aims to preserve differences and maintain ethnic group purity and is a *segregationist* view that groups should be maintained separately. A second path for racist expression is based on a conception of "otherness." "Universalist" racism defines a common humanity, but one where human groups are not equitably distributed along a universal scale. According to this *universalist* position, the superior races have to civilize the other groups or enable inferior races to disappear. While racism is based on a differentiation of social groups, antiracism is rooted in the principle of an *intrinsic equality between human groups*. For both Taguieff and Wieviorka, both forms of racism are opposed by a form of antiracism. First, antiracism can be a *universalist antiracism*, where it is seen to be based on the unity of humanity, which excludes any particularist identifications, and works on the principle of equality defined by the Enlightenment tradition. The abolition of all inequality—perceived or real—between groups, between "us" and "others," is the common norm of this antiracism. Such an expression of antiracism ought to resonate more easily with conceptions of nationhood based on a universalist or republican tradition, such as that in France. Second, antiracism may be based on a differentialist vision of "us" and "others" that acknowledges that particular collective identities do exist and they should be respected and protected. The common norm of this *differentialist antiracism* is the protection of human diversity, but on a principle of equality between groups. This vision of antiracism is closely linked to the communitarian understanding of justice and equality (see, e.g., Taylor 1992). We expect that a multicultural conception of nationhood, such as that in Britain and the Netherlands, would facilitate the political expression of differentialist antiracism. Overall antiracism, whether the universalist version or differentialist, is based on the common principle of fundamental equality between either individuals or groups.

Between Cultural and Political Struggle

Following our proposition that political altruism is an identity-based form of collective action, it is important to specify how we conceptualize the factors for claims making on behalf of migrants. We see conceptions of nationhood and constructions of citizenship as a constraining frame, as well as an opportunity for actors to take part in public debates and defend their vision of national identity. In the introduction, we outlined that opportunities and constraints are both institutional and discursive. Nationhood conceptions thus constitute a field-specific opportunity structure that facilitates or constrains the public interventions of political actors defending a particular vision of national community and "otherness." This opportunity structure offers cultural resources of political legitimacy to intervene in public debates, and resonance for political demands that are based on the dominant national self-understanding of citizenship. However, in addition to these framing processes, there are other processes that account for activism to defend migrant rights, and these are located simultaneously at the level of *institutions* and concrete *interactions* between political actors.

At the institutional level, as Figure 9 illustrates, two sets of structural factors shape the political expression of actors defending migrants. First, *citizenship institutions* that uphold "national citizenship and integration conceptions" create a constraining frame that can potentially explain the differences between collective action or political altruism from one national context to another. Political resources, legitimacy, and resonance derived from these institutions help to make sense of the formation of specific group identities and the elaboration of particular political aims by actors mobilizing for migrants (arrow 1). Thus, according to the nature of citizenship institutions, or a shared conception of nationhood, claims making for protecting and defending migrants should vary considerably from one

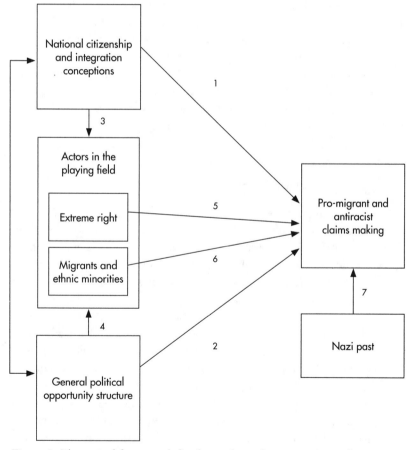

Figure 9. Theoretical framework for the analysis of pro-migrant and antiracist claims making.

nation-state to another. For example, at least to a certain extent, the French conception of nationhood could explain the strong and durable mobilization of French civil society to support the *sans-papiers* throughout the 1990s (see Siméant 1998). The exclusion of thousands of individuals from the national community by the fact that they do not have a status within the community is difficult to justify in the French Republic, where each individual has to be treated with strict equality and cannot be left aside. This conception offered material and symbolic resources for pro-migrant and antiracist groups as well as other civil society actors (human rights associations, churches, artist groups, and so on) who, for example, sustained the occupation of Saint Bernard's Church in support of the regularization of illegal migrants in 1996.

Shared understandings of nationhood and citizenship provide political actors with resources of legitimacy to enter the public space, but at the same time this also provides the resources for state actors to construct and support institutions dealing with migrant integration and discrimination. Such institutions legitimize claims making on the part of those who defend migrant rights. In other words, they expand the institutional material and discursive opportunities. For example, the broad antiracist, antidiscriminatory, and pro-minority policies supported and upheld by the Commission for Racial Equality in Britain can be expected to facilitate and shape the resultant mobilization of antiracist and pro-migrant actors (see Statham 2001a, 2001b; Koopmans and Statham 1999c). A similar process is likely to be found in the Netherlands.

Another important factor that shapes the interaction between contenders in this field are *political institutions* that constitute the general political opportunity structure of a country (see Figure 9). Political institutions are important in shaping the specific forms of political expression of protest actors. According to the degree of institutional access and the nature of informal political strategies of the state—which can be either integrative or exclusive—challengers may make use of a moderate action repertoire or, alternatively, of more radical or even violent forms of action to be heard by the state. Arrow 2 captures the strategic relation between general opportunity structures and patterns of claims making. For example, these political structures might explain why, after the violent skinhead racist attacks against asylum centers in the early 1990s, Swiss activists for migrants did not resort to violent or even confrontational claims to get their message across in the public domain.

Institutions are important in defining a frame for their actions, but antiracist and pro-migrant activists act not in a void but in an organizational field; they are confronted by other political actors who intervene in the field of immigration and ethnic relations. In other words, as we outlined in the introduction, actors who support migrants are involved in the interactive dynamics of the "playing field." They adapt and react to other collective actors' claims and actions. These interactive dynamics that take place in the public space can potentially modify the institutional frame just discussed. However, such dynamics in the playing field are by no means free of structural constraints and, in our case, are likely to be strongly shaped by citizenship institutions as well as general political institutions that, to a large extent, define how movements interact with the state. These influences are indicated by arrows 3 and 4. While citizenship and political institutions define rather stable opportunities for action, the interactive dynamics in the playing field transform action opportunities in the short term. For actors who support migrants, two main movement actors need to be considered: the extreme right and migrants. As we now discuss, the collective actions of these modify the conditions facing pro-migrant and antiracist actors and affect their action repertoires as well as the content of their claims making within the field of public contestation.

Protest actors do not just evolve in a dynamic interaction with the state, even if this interaction is a crucial one and has been central to the study of contentious politics (e.g., McAdam 1982; McAdam et al. 2001; Tarrow 1994; Tilly 1978). They are also involved in an interactive dynamic with other actors and notably countermovements. As Meyer and Staggenborg emphasize, "movement and countermovement engage in sustained interaction with one another and not just the state" (1996, 1629). For contentions where antiracist and pro-migrant actors are engaged, the extreme right constitutes an important countermovement that influences their protest. In fact, antiracist actors have often been conceptualized by social scientists as a countermobilization to xenophobic discourses and practices (e.g., Solomos and Back 1996; Taguieff 1995; Wieviorka 1998). Thus, we expect that the political activity of the extreme right as well as its action repertoire significantly influence antiracist countermobilization (arrow 5).

As Meyer and Staggenborg (1996) argue, a movement creates conditions for the mobilization of a countermovement. According to these authors, three conditions govern the mobilization of counterprotests: a countermovement becomes strong (1) when a movement shows signs of success, (2) when the interests of some populations are threatened by movement goals, and (3) when favorable opportunities are available for a countermovement's mobilization. Unlike Meyer and Staggenborg, we suggest that these conditions, particularly movement success and threats to existing interests, do not necessarily promote the rise of a countermovement. In line with our position that antiracist actors' raison d'être is not only opposing the extreme right but defending a specific conception of national community, we see these first two conditions as facilitating factors. They might increase the possibility for organization and mobilization of actors supporting migrants, but only in national contexts where these actors have political and social resources at hand to oppose the extreme right. In this respect, even though we do not conceptualize political opportunities in the same way as Meyer and Staggenborg, we nonetheless share a similar idea regarding the crucial role of political opportunities in protest emergence and development.

Extreme-right mobilization is thus likely to modify protest conditions determined by citizenship and political institutions. First, we hypothesize that a strong and successful extreme-right claims making, which evidently threatens the interests of migrants and above all their security within the host society, will stimulate antiracist mobilization. The massive mobilization by Germans in support of migrants and their rights in response to xenophobic attacks by skinheads in the early 1990s is a clear example of such interactive dynamics between extreme-right and antiracist protest.

In addition, extreme-right protest is likely to alter the action repertoire of the counterprotest. As Meyer and Staggenborg underline, "interactions between opposing movements prevent the complete institutionalisation of tactics by either side" (1996, 1651). Opposing movements adjust their tactics in response to one another (McAdam 1983). A movement using confrontational action strategies might push the countermovement into reacting with similar political tactics. In other words, the interactive spiral between movement and countermovement does not facilitate the institutionalization of movement strategies. From this we assume that antiracist actors are likely to make less use of conventional actions when the extreme right is strongly involved in public debates. Moreover, following the argument of organizational isomorphism advanced by neoinstitutionalist authors (e.g., Powell and di Maggio 1991), we hypothesize that when an extreme right is violent, it is opening the door to a radical and violent response from the countermovement. This is a situation that Germany and Britain have experienced. For example, there have been many episodes of clashes between neo-Nazis and antifascists and between the Anti-Nazi League and the British National Party on the streets of Britain.

Finally, a strong mobilization of xenophobic actors is also likely to influence the content of claims making by countermovements. Specifically, it pushes them to intervene more frequently on antiracist policy than in other political areas. The French case illustrates such dynamics. During the rise of the Front National and the repeated public interventions of Le Pen against migrants ("We have six million immigrants in France, and six million unemployed"), against ethnic minorities ("Muslims cannot be assimilated into French society"), or to reshape history ("the *Shoah* as a detail of history"), French antiracist actors were systematically on the front line to oppose such xenophobic statements and called on political authorities to ban Le Pen's party and reinforce antiracist legislation.

Protest by migrants also shapes the interactive dynamics of antiracist and pro-migrant actors by modifying the mobilization conditions defined by the institutional setting. In countries where migrants are well-organized political actors and strongly active in the national public sphere, action by native groups to support them is less necessary, and, importantly, it is often perceived as less legitimate. Actually, migrants themselves are the most qualified to mobilize against the discrimination, xenophobia, and other social problems that they experience in their everyday lives. However, and in line with our opportunity approach, political mobilization by migrants is likely to have a relatively small impact on the conditions for antiracist and pro-migrant protest because such actors also need resources of political legitimacy and resonance to organize and mobilize. Thus, in Switzerland, for example, the weak political activity of migrant groups is not likely to increase pro-migrant and antiracist protest because they themselves have few opportunities for entering the public space. By contrast, we hypothesize that migrant protest and activisim affects the substantive field of intervention by pro-migrant and antiracist actors (arrow 6). For example, in Britain and the Netherlands migrants are fairly active in public debates when defending the conditions of their residence and settlement, and much weaker when intervening on the modalities of entry into and exit from the national territory, which Hammar (1985) calls "immigration policy." In these national contexts, where according to the Dutch and British conception of nationhood native support for migrants receive incentives of political legitimacy, activists mobilizing on behalf of migrants ought to be found to especially target immigration policy, a field where migrants' own organizations are relatively weak.

A last factor that may influence protest activity by native supporters of migrants is past historical legacies, or more precisely a Nazi past. By this, we mean political events in modern history that have had a decisive impact on the sense of national identity and responsibility. For our five-country comparison, this factor is especially important for Germany. The Shoah and the Nazi experience are still strongly present in German collective memory and result in a strong national sensitivity and sense of responsibility concerning issues of racism, xenophobia, and anti-Semitism (e.g., Koopmans 1999; Laurence 2001). In Germany, the Nazi legacy is likely to strongly influence claims making by pro-migrant and antiracist actors as well as altering the structural conditions defined by citizenship and political institutions (arrow 7).

After the Second World War, Germany was intensely preoccupied with making sense of its past, and also with fighting the heavy burden of guilt with regard to racial hatred. For example, these "coping with the past [*Vergangenheitsbewältigung*]" efforts involved a specific politics for facilitating the integration of German Jews and the elaboration of policies to combat anti-Semitism and other types of racism. After the Holocaust experience Germany has been particularly attentive to xenophobia and racism. Germany has been unable to prevent the rise of the extreme-right wing and xenophobic hatred in the postwar period, but it strongly legitimizes actors fighting against racist discourses and practices. The massive reaction against racist attacks in the early 1990s cannot be understood without referring to the legacy of the Nazi past. At the same time, Switzerland was confronted with a similar wave of racist attacks, but the reaction of the Swiss population was in no way comparable to that in Germany.

This combination of institutional (conception of nationhood, political institutions, and legacies of the past) and interactive (extreme right and migrant mobilization) factors constitutes our analytical framework for accounting for political action by antiracist and pro-migrant actors. However, out of this set of factors, we argue that the conception of nationhood is the most decisive because it offers resources of political legitimacy and resonance for antiracist and pro-migrant actors to get organized and enter the public space. Without this legitimacy, barriers to collective action and entering the public sphere would be difficult to overcome. We now examine this hypothesis in the following sections by addressing the levels of activism of pro-migrant and antiracist actors, the action repertoires that they use, and by looking at the contents and language of some of their campaigns, within a cross-national comparative framework.

Political Activity of Antiracist and Pro-Migrant Actors

Antiracist and pro-migrant actions are both expressions of political altruism for supporting migrants, but have some differences. As previously mentioned, *antiracism* puts forward the idea of migrants' inclusion based on universal principles of equal treatment. Such claims can refer either to a libertarian or to a communitarian conception of equality, claiming equal treatment either between individuals or between groups. This political expression of altruism should therefore more easily resonate with conceptions of nationhood that are based on a civic definition of national community, combined either with a universalist understanding of migrants' integration or with a differentialist one. In other words, the struggle against racial discrimination, as well as against the extreme right, is likely to find greater political resources and legitimacy in France, but also in Britain and the Netherlands, which conceive migrants' integration from a more pluralist point of view. In these three political contexts, antiracism should be much stronger than in Germany and Switzerland.

The *pro-migrant* political expression of altruism differs from antiracism by mobilizing particular and plural identities of migrants. In other words, pro-migrant groups often mobilize to support one specific social category. They support specific ethnic groups (Turks, Spaniards, Asians, blacks, and so on), specific migrant categories (asylum seekers, illegal immigrants, and so on), or specific social categories within migrant populations (female refugees, illegal migrants' children, female Somali refugees, and so on). Their action is oriented toward specific categories of migrants, and thus they give them differentiated support according to their ethnic origin, migrant status, or social status. While antiracist groups do not usually explicitly stress specific migrant identities, and their group names clearly reflect the universalist conception of their support for migrants (e.g., SOS-Racisme, Rassemblement contre l'intolérance et le fascisme, Antiracist Alliance, Campaign for Racial Justice), pro-migrant organizations are clearly oriented toward the defense of specific groups. Here again, organizations' names are revealing: Aktion für Abgewiesene Asylbewerber, Comité de soutien aux parents étrangers, Comité de soutien aux requérants d'asile du Kosovo, Joint Council for the Welfare of Immigrants. Efforts to politically support specific categories of individuals or groups, which focus on particular identities based on ethnic or social categories, are likely to find more opportunities in national arenas with a pluralist conception of ethnic relations, such as Britain and the Netherlands, or alternatively in countries where an ethnic understanding of nationhood is dominant, such as Switzerland and Germany.

Thus, in Britain and the Netherlands, we would expect both antiracists and pro-migrants to be present in public debates. By contrast, the republican conception of citizenship in France constrains support for migrants based on ethnic or social categories. In this political context, antiracism, specifically "universalist antiracism," should be the main avenue to defend migrant rights. Finally, in Germany and Switzerland, when the generally weak native support for migrants reaches the public space, it finds much better opportunities for doing so by mobilizing in support of specific groups. In these two countries, we would expect pro-migrant groups to be more active than antiracist organizations.

Conceptions of nationhood shape the general political opportunities for antiracist and pro-migrant protest, but political dynamics in the playing field also affect possibilities for acting in the public space. A strong extreme right might reinforce the antiracist sector in countries offering opportunities to organize and express such types of migrant support. Such conditions are met in France, where both the conception of nationhood and a strong extreme right stimulate antiracist action in the public domain. To a lesser extent, such conditions are also met in Germany, where the historical context provides the antiracist sector with more favorable opportunities than in Switzerland.

Table 37 shows the distribution of the different types of civil society actors making claims in support of migrants and minorities in the five countries, with a special emphasis on the sector that specializes in such activities: pro-migrant and antiracist actors. To a large extent, our findings from Table 37 support our expectations derived from the interplay between institutional settings and political dynamics on the playing field, notably between antiracist and extreme-right actors. Antiracism is significantly more prominent in France (29.9 percent) compared to the other countries (ranging from Switzerland with 7.7 percent to Germany with 17.7 percent). This can be traced to France's facilitating conception of nationhood and facing a strong extreme-right challenge throughout the 1990s. By contrast, France has the smallest pro-migrant presence with only a tenth (11.2 percent) of civil society actors comprised of organizations that defend specific ethnic or social categories of migrants. Here the dominant French understanding of citizenship makes it difficult to mobilize in support of particular identities. Such pro-migrant organizations are twice as visible in Britain (21.6 percent) and the Netherlands (21.7 percent), which support more differentialist understandings of citizenship. At the same time, though less than in France, they sustain some degree of antiracist activism (Britain, 14.7 percent; Netherlands, 13.8 percent). These results give support to the hypothesis that a civic conception of nationhood combined with a pluralist management of ethnic diversity offers opportunities for both types of political altruism in support of migrants.

With respect to the German case, again the combination of political opportunities and a strong extreme right affects the presence of antiracist claims making. While German antiracism does not benefit from favorable opportunities derived from the national self-understanding of nationhood,

Table 37. Civil society actors mobilized in support of migrants and ethnic minorities

	Netherlands	Britain	France	Germany	Switzerland
Specialized actors defending migrants (%)	35.5	36.3	41.1	32.5	25.6
Pro-migrant actors (%)	21.7	21.6	11.2	14.8	17.9
Antiracist actors (%)	13.8	14.7	29.9	17.7	7.7
General solidarity organizations (%)	5.1	12.5	12.9	8.8	14.1
Professional organizations (%)	32.8	14.7	9.0	14.5	17.6
Unions and employees' organizations (%)	2.3	8.2	14.4	8.7	9.9
Churches (%)	5.5	5.3	7.8	12.4	8.0
Radical-left organizations (%)	0.9	–	0.6	9.6	–
Employers' organizations and firms (%)	3.4	5.6	0.8	2.4	3.5
Media and journalists (%)	4.7	6.6	4.0	3.5	4.2
Other civil society organizations (%)	9.8	10.7	9.4	7.7	17.3
Total (%)	100	100	100	100	100
N	470	319	658	1,651	313

Note: Analyses computed without ethnic minorities and extreme-right actors.

it does benefit from legitimacy for acting in the public space, due to the special condition of Germany's postwar preoccupation of distancing itself from its Nazi past. This provides antiracist organizations political resources to offer a counterdiscourse to the extreme-right protest sector. It explains why antiracist activism is more prominent in Germany (17.7 percent) than in Britain (14.7 percent) and the Netherlands (13.8 percent), not least because of the strong antiracist mobilization against extreme-right attacks on asylum seekers and skinhead violence in the early 1990s. Finally, the Swiss case is similar to the German, but without the legitimating factor of guilt for the Nazi past in the national identity. Thus in Switzerland antiracist actors have fewer opportunities to enter the public domain, even though extreme-right actors are fairly active and violent in Switzerland. As a result, Switzerland (7.7 percent) has the weakest antiracist sector among our five countries. Regarding pro-migrant activism, Swiss (17.9 percent) and German (14.8 percent) civil society has a higher public presence than the French (11.2 percent), which is indicative of the impact of an institutionalized national self-understanding that separates out different and specific categories of migrants.

Political Legitimacy and Action Repertoire

As this book has shown with regard to migrant and extreme-right mobilization, collective understandings of national belonging are important factors shaping the action repertoire of political actors who enter the public space to support a specific vision of the nation. Political actors benefit from broader legitimacy when the conceptions of citizenship that they promote in the public agenda resonate with the overall dominant conception of nationhood. Social movement research shows that actors' political legitimacy to a large extent defines the action repertoire at their disposal to enter the public domain (Kitschelt 1986; McAdam 1982; McAdam et al. 2001; Tarrow 1989; Tilly 1978). Legitimate actors do not need to use radical forms of action when addressing their demands to power holders. Conversely, actors without sufficient political legitimacy need to enter the public domain forcefully, which often means by using radical forms of action. Thus, protagonists acting in support of migrants who promote an inclusive conception of national identity are able to articulate their political demands relatively easily and with a moderate action repertoire in those nation-states that have a dominant self-understanding of national identity that is inclusive.

The support of the native population for migrants takes two basic forms of political expression—antiracist and pro-migrant protest—which we propose to analyze separately because they benefit differently from resources of political legitimacy derived from the dominant conception of nationhood. First, in countries that facilitate the expression of civic identities, either in the form of equal treatment between all individuals, as in France, or between groups, as is the case in Britain and the Netherlands, we would expect antiracist actors to express their demands and contentions without using radical forms of action. By contrast, in Germany and Switzerland, where nationhood is defined in ethnic and assimilationist terms that do not provide antiracist groups with much political legitimacy, the expression of their contentions is likely to be much more radical, making use mainly of protest action and even disruptive and violent forms of action. Second, regarding pro-migrant actors who mobilize around particular identities, these should be able to articulate their demands relatively easily and with a moderate action repertoire in Britain and the Netherlands, where there is a shared understanding of the national community based on a pluralist conception. Thus, in Britain and the Netherlands both antiracist and pro-migrant groups should be rather moderate. We should also find a similar pattern of mobilization for pro-migrant actors in Germany and Switzerland. Access to German and Swiss citizenship is conceived in ethnic terms, and this facilitates ethnic differences and distinctions by category between individuals and legitimates political action that mobilizes such differences. Consequently, such legitimacy should moderate the action repertoire of pro-migrant groups in both national contexts. Lastly, in France, where the republican conception of nationhood has erected high material and symbolic barriers for pro-migrant actors to support migrants by mobilizing their ethnic (or categorical) differences, the lack of legitimacy of such actors should facilitate a more radical action repertoire when addressing their political demands.

Also political institutions and extreme-right mobilization should have a decisive impact on the antiracist and pro-migrant action repertoire. As social movement scholars have emphasized, the state plays a structuring role in protest politics. Contenders mainly address their political claims to power holders who ultimately decide whether to consider or ignore such claims. Concrete interactions gradually emerge from contenders' interventions and authorities' responses. State institutional design and informal political strategies from power holders shape, at least to a certain extent, concrete interactions between "members" and "challengers" (Kriesi et al. 1995). The combination between state institutions and political practices toward contentious politics tends either to moderate or to radicalize the action repertoire that is derived from citizenship configurations. Based on these two dimensions, Switzerland appears to be the clearest case of an open political system that limits the "radicalism" of native support for migrants in both its political expressions. France, by contrast, has a very closed political opportunity structure that has the effect of radicalizing antiracist and pro-migrant protest. The other three countries are intermediate cases, combining open institutional structures with exclusive elite strategies, or vice versa.

Groups acting in support of migrants, specifically antiracist actors, enter into interactive dynamics not only with political authorities but also with the movement that they combat, the extreme right. A first consequence of the interactions between extreme-right actors and antiracist protest is radicalization of the action repertoire of antiracist protest. Unlike pro-migrant contentions, antiracism has a clear and concrete adversary in the street. This physical confrontation between the extreme right and antiracists inevitably leads to a radicalization of antiracist protest, independent of citizenship and political institutions. Thus, we would expect a more radical action repertoire from antiracist protest than from pro-migrant actors in all countries. Whereas we expect radicalization of antiracist protest in our five countries, it can be even stronger, first when the extreme right is highly active in a national context, and second when the far right is itself radical and uses violence. Following Meyer and Staggenborg's (1996) argument, in which interactions between opposing movements prevent the complete institutionalization of the action repertoire by either side, we can easily imagine that when the extreme right is strongly involved in public debates, even with very moderate forms of action, as is the case of France, antiracist groups tend to react more radically than other movements that do not have to face an opposing movement. Finally, by extending Meyer and Staggenborg's hypothesis and by drawing on neoinstitutionalism that puts forward the idea of organizational isomorphism, we can predict that when the extreme right is violent, as it was in Germany in the early 1990s, antiracist actors will be more radical.

Table 38 shows the action repertoires of antiracist and pro-migrant actors in our five countries. By examining forms of actions chosen by these actors in the 1990s, we find close links between the structural conditions defined by the conception of nationhood and concrete interactions between actors struggling in the public space. If we take the percentage of extrainstitutional protests (demonstrative, confrontational, and violent) as an indicator of the radical nature of the action repertoire, we find the most moderate repertoire among antiracist groups in Britain, France, and the Netherlands. Half, or even more, of their claims making is articulated with institutional actions (public statements and conventional action). Here we

Table 38. The action repertoire of antiracist and pro-migrant actors

	Netherlands	Britain	France	Germany	Switzerland
Antiracist actors (%)	100	100	100	100	100
Public statements and conventional actions (%)	49.3	68.8	53.4	29.5	24.0
Protest actions (%)	50.7	31.3	46.6	70.4	76.0
Demonstrative protests (%)	37.3	14.6	37.0	60.2	56.0
Confrontational protests (%)	9.0	–	4.1	4.9	12.0
Violent protests (%)	4.5	16.7	5.5	5.3	8.0
N	67	48	219	304	25
Pro-migrant actors (%)	100	100	100	100	100
Public statements and conventional actions (%)	89.2	91.6	61.0	86.4	85.1
Protest actions (%)	10.8	8.5	38.9	13.6	13.8
Demonstrative protests (%)	8.5	7.0	23.3	10.5	12.3
Confrontational protests (%)	1.5	1.4	13.3	2.7	–
Violent protests (%)	0.8	–	2.2	0.3	1.5
N	130	71	90	295	65

can see the direct impact of the conception of nationhood. Protest activism defending a civic conception of nationhood finds much stronger legitimacy in countries where the collective conception of nation is based on civic and egalitarian conceptions of national community. The opposite situation is exemplified by the cases of Germany and Switzerland. In both countries, lack of legitimacy encourages antiracist groups to use mainly protest action. Few institutionalized channels are available for antiracist claims in countries with an ethnic conception of nationhood.

Having underlined such straightforward differences between national contexts, which provide support to our hypothesis on the impact of a state's citizenship institutions on antiracist protest, we still must emphasize the differences of the action repertoire within groups of countries that share a similar conception of nationhood. As Table 38 underscores, antiracist actions in France, Britain, and the Netherlands present some clear differences. Interaction with state actors and with the extreme right explains such variations. In France, the closure of political institutions and the strength of the extreme right radicalize the action repertoire of antiracist groups. For example, comparing France and Britain, fewer opportunities exist for French antiracists to articulate their claims making through institutional channels. More generally, the closure of French political institutions tends to radicalize protest (Duyvendak 1994; Kriesi et al. 1995). French antiracist actors, as well as other protesters such as farmers, civil servants, or movements for the unemployed, have to take to the streets to be heard by French authorities. Moreover, the important presence of the Front National also radicalizes French antiracist protest. We all remember the huge public demonstrations following the first round of the presidential elections of 2002, after Le Pen had received enough votes to push the Socialist Party out of his way for the second round of voting. Other examples where French antiracist groups took to the streets en masse occurred in the early 1990s after Le Pen's bodyguards threw a young North African into the Seine and after the desecration of the Jewish cemetery of Carpentras.

While the extreme right in France is strong but moderate in its action repertoire, in Britain we find the opposite situation, which clearly impinges on antiracist protest. Whereas British antiracist protest is moderate, to a large extent, thanks to the existence of important institutionalized channels for claims making, antiracist groups nevertheless occasionally use a very radical action repertoire. With respect to political violence, British antiracist groups are by far the most disruptive in our five-country comparison. British antiracism is mainly expressed through an institutional action repertoire, but when it does make use of protest action, half of such actions are violent. This use of the most radical forms of action can be understood if we take into account that the British extreme right is not only one of the weakest in Europe, but also one of the most radical. Nevertheless, this finding has to be put into perspective, as the absolute number of cases of antiracist violence is very low.[3]

Interactive dynamics also shape the antiracist action repertoire in both ethnic-assimilationist countries. In Switzerland, where antiracist actors benefit from even weaker political legitimacy than in Germany (where the legacy of World War II and the Holocaust strengthens antiracist legitimacy), antiracists mainly use protest action, but are not as confrontational and violent as citizenship institutions would lead us to expect. The openness of Swiss policy tends to deradicalize antiracist protest movements that still encounter important barriers when articulating their political demands. Despite having the fewest political opportunities, Swiss antiracist groups mainly use demonstrative protest to combat racism and xenophobia.

As we expected, due to the existence of a concrete adversary in the street, antiracist protest is much more radical than pro-migrant contention. Looking at confrontational and violent forms of action, Table 38 clearly emphasizes this difference between the two types of protest. Considering all countries taken together, pro-migrant actors generally express their political demands with institutional forms of action and make only marginal use of political violence. This is true even for France, where few political opportunities for pro-migrant protest exist.

As for antiracist protest, the political legitimacy provided by conceptions of nationhood has a decisive impact on the action repertoire of pro-migrant organizations. In Britain and the Netherlands, groups defending migrant rights articulate their claims making mainly, or even exclusively, through institutional channels. Due to their weaker political legitimacy, German and Swiss pro-migrant protesters make less use of public statements and conventional actions than their counterparts in Britain and the Netherlands. In France, however, where the defense of migrants comes up against important barriers when articulating particular identities, we see how these groups have to address their claims making via protest action and even with confrontational public demonstrations. In this regard, France differs considerably from the other national contexts. The closed nature of French political institutions further reinforces the radicalism of pro-migrant actors.

Antiracism between Universalism and Differentialism

We now move on to explore different types of antiracism. As previously mentioned, two main conceptions of antiracism can be distinguished (Taguieff 1995; Wieviorka 1998). They are two ideal types of conceptions of "otherness" that rest on distinct ontological postulates. First, "universalist antiracism" is grounded on the principle of *unity of humanity*, which rejects particular identities and promotes the conception of an intrinsic equality between individuals. The objects of claims making by political actors promoting this conception of antiracism can be status identities (e.g., immigrants, asylum seekers, *sans-papiers*) but rarely have an ethnic, racial, or religious label (e.g., Bangladeshi, black people, Muslims).

The second version of antiracism rests on a distinct conception of "otherness" based on the principle of *tolerance toward diversity*. In this antiracist ideal, plural identities are recognized and respected as such. This promotes the right to difference and cultural relativism. The political expression of differentialist antiracism should refer to particular identities and stress the idea of tolerance toward cultural pluralism. It also promotes the idea of equal treatment, not only between individuals but also between groups. In other words, the political framework of this conception of differentialist antiracism refers to specific group identities (e.g., Asians, Africans). It also fights discrimination, but unlike the universalist version of antiracism, this movement promotes equal treatment between groups. Finally, the object of their claims making is mainly individuals who are victims of racial discrimination or specific groups whose particular ethnic, religious, or racial identities are targeted.

The hypothesis that we want to discuss here is that both antiracist versions—universalist and differentialist—are not constructed in a social and cultural vacuum, but are rooted in specific historical traditions, notably linked to social and cultural boundaries erected and grounded in the long process of nation building. More specifically, we hypothesize that political actors who need legitimacy and resonance to enter the public sphere find better opportunities to express one or the other conception of antiracism in specific countries. For example, in the three countries where antiracism has found greater political legitimacy—France, Britain, and the Netherlands—the antiracist framing repertoire should be distinct. France, which is sustained by republican ideals, should facilitate the political expression of a universal conception of antiracism. By contrast, Britain and the Netherlands, which are built on a pluralist conception of the nation, should provide political actors with better opportunities to express a differentialist repertoire of antiracism.

To test this hypothesis, we compare the content of antiracist organizations' claims making in two distinct contexts of citizenship: France and Britain. It is important here to determine whether antiracists have unspecific or status identities as the main objects of their political claims or, alternatively, whether they explicitly mention particular group identities once they enter the public sphere. We conduct a qualitative analysis of the campaigns and discourses of a selected number of antiracist organizations in both countries. Via Internet sites, we analyze the campaigns and discursive framing of six antiracist organizations (three per country) that have been the most active during the period under study in this volume (1992–1998).

Examining the Ligue contre le racisme et l'antisémitisme (LICRA), the Mouvement contre le racisme et l'amitié des peuples (MRAP), and SOS-Racisme action campaigns and their public presentation on their Web sites provide us with further empirical grounding for the universalist repertoire of French antiracism. A first indication for French universalist antiracism comes from the campaigns themselves. Most of these are organized to combat discrimination and unequal treatment. One example is the SOS-Racisme campaign on job discrimination (discrimination à l'embauche) and their efforts to collect evidence and take legal action against entrepreneurs who discriminate against people of color. Also, the MRAP national campaign against all types of discrimination, in 2003, focuses specifically on migrants' political exclusion, using the self–evidently universalist slogan: "Same ground, same right, same voice" (Même sol, même droit, même voix). To give another example, MRAP's campaign against national preference, proposed by the extreme-right municipalities to exclude migrants from social services, claims, "it's the under-citizens who are created" (ce sont des sous-citoyens qui sont créés). Similarly, MRAP and LICRA are both involved against the double-penalty procedure claiming that this is "another form of penalty complementary to the nationals" (une autre forme de peine complémentaire aux nationaux). Note once again the universalist language of the rhetoric. Finally, all three antiracist actors have organized education and sensitizing campaigns against racism based on a universalist conception of antiracism.[4] Only the SOS-Racisme campaign has put forward some ideas of plurality and tolerance toward diversity by organizing a bilingual poetry competition for young pupils. This tolerance of plural identities, however, is—as we shall see—still far from the British conception of multiracialism.

In France, specific identities are rarely mobilized publicly. Instead, we see a clear tendency to generalize and universalize group-specific violations to all other nonwhite groups. LICRA's main aim is to fight anti-Semitism, and we might expect that the Jewish community as a specific group occupies center stage in their preoccupations. Yet this is generally not the case. Racist violence against Jewish people is addressed either from the angle of individual trials (against Le Pen, skinheads, far-right media, and so on) or by fighting denial statements or books, or by publicly naming and shaming. Also, when LICRA promotes campaigns around anti-Semitism by organizing seminars for improving knowledge on history and ethnic discrimination, they address not only the history of anti-Semitism but also other ethnic forms of discrimination (e.g., the history of eugenics, the Ku Klux Klan, the Rwandan and Armenian genocides). Such a stance systematically avoids a communitarian and ethnically oriented vision of racist discrimination. Finally, LICRA's language for campaigning is highly revealing with its two seminal slogans being "Neither rights to difference, nor rights to indifference" (Ni droits à la différence, ni droits à l'indifférence) and "At birth all the men are equal. And after?" (A la naissance tous les hommes sont égaux. Et après?). According to its own self-understanding, LICRA has a "universalist vocation." Though perhaps less so than LICRA, both MRAP and SOS-Racisme self-identify with republican universalism, too. MRAP struggles "against inventing under-citizens for whom access to school, health, social goods, etc., is not granted" *(contre la fabrication de sous-citoyens pour qui l'accès à l'école, santé, biens sociaux, etc. ne leur sont pas octroyé), and SOS-Racisme borrows from French culture to bring to the fore the question of universalism, "Alexandre Dumas, a universal symbol" (Alexandre Dumas, un symbole universel).* SOS-Racisme is the only organization where we find any differentialist message, notably when the association organized debates on "multicultural France" (la France métissée) or held festivals *(blacks, blancs, beurs).* However, these are only the expressions of a plural conception of antiracism and are certainly not equivalent to the British expression of antiracism.

Campaigns organized by the Antiracist Alliance (ARA), the National Assembly Against Racism (NAAR), and the Anti-Nazi League (ANL) put forward a much more differentialist conception of antiracism. First, and unlike France where we found generalist and color-blind antiracist organizations, in Britain organizations clearly exhibit their privileged links with specific ethnic communities. ARA presents itself as "the first black-led, broad-based coalition campaigning to stem the rising tide of racism, anti-Semitism and support for the extreme right. The ARA is supported by 800 organisations including black and Jewish organisations." NAAR is also an active umbrella organization that brings together trade unions, churches, students, and refugee associations, as well as black associations. ARA not only formally incorporates ethnic minorities associations but also develops strong links with specific community associations for particular campaigns. ANL expresses a less explicitly differentialist form of antiracism with the aim of fighting the extreme right and all forms of fascism. However, even the ANL has organized debates with various organizations (unions, students' associations) and with minority societies and declares, in a way reminiscent of NAAR, that "The agenda against racism must be set by those who experience it, therefore black communities."

Antiracism appears to be very different on one side of the Channel than on the other. This impression is further reinforced when we look more closely at campaigns by British antiracist organizations. Similar to France, Britain has general campaigns against racism that are rooted in the universalist tradition of antiracism. For example, NAAR organized educational programs on asylum and immigrant rights, and ANL initiated debates to combat revisionism. In the same vein, we find national and local campaigns against racist violence, such as the "Say no to racist violence in Greenwich" campaign organized after racial violence against blacks and Asians in February 2003. Throughout parliamentary consultation on the revision of the Nationality, Asylum, and Immigration Bill (2002), NAAR organized a lobbying campaign that highlighted the racist repercussions of the new law—notably the idea of imposing a language test for applicants for British citizenship—and criticized the bill claiming that it "shores up backward-looking ideas of Englishness and fosters racism." These generalist campaigns on racism, which at first glance seem similar to French antiracist campaigns, show how their framing in the British context is different and, as the last quotation stresses, how British antiracism rejects the idea of a standardization of identities as well as the principle of assimilation to the British cultural standard.

Besides these more "universal" campaigns to combat racial discrimination, other campaigns have put the spotlight on a clear differentialist understanding of antiracism in a way that would be inconceivable in the French context. In 1997, ARA organized a conference on "Black Business and Employment." The forum addressed many "fundamental issues affecting young black people," racial discrimination, and prejudices on the basis that "highly qualified black people found it very hard to find jobs in industry and they demanded fairness and equality." Besides equal treatment on an individual basis (i.e., between individuals), ARA also addressed the issue of equality in communitarian terms (i.e., between groups). It asked for raising "awareness of various incidents and human rights injustices that the black community in Britain had to face every day." The need for group awareness in order to redress unequal treatment between groups (i.e., between "British" and "all non-white" groups) is visible also in another ARA campaign, "For the Awareness of Caribbean and Asian People" (1997), a campaign that pinpointed the specificity of discrimination faced by those communities. Both campaigns asked for equal treatment between groups and addressed the issue of taking into account a plural vision of discrimination. Likewise, a NAAR campaign against racism provides another good illustration of such differentialist antiracism. This campaign aimed to build what was called a "black alliance" of various ethnic minority groups in order "to achieve a greater quality for all our people" and for that, they added, "We have to bring together the broadest possible alliance of African, Caribbean and Asian organizations on the basis of respect for our social, political and cultural diversity." Equal treatment between groups with tolerance for diversity appears to be the British antiracist leitmotiv.

Contrary to France, British antiracist organizations can overtly point a finger at ethnic and racial identities, as we can see clearly in an ANL campaign declaration against prejudices conveyed by popular media: "They ignore the positive additions black and Asian people have made to our economy, culture and way of life. And, even though more white people—Australians, South Africans, people from the European community, Americans—come into the country each year, immigrants are almost always referred to as black or Asian." Particular identities are clearly mentioned in all three organizations' campaigns. They speak of "black people discrimination," "Caribbean and Asian awareness," "black alliance," and so on. Thus, differentialist framing structures antiracist organizations' public discourse, and ethnic differences are highlighted.

Furthermore, British antiracist organizations make use of a language that opposes racial groups. The main distinction is, not surprisingly, the opposition between "white" and "non-white" communities. ANL organized a public demonstration, "Love Music, Hate Racism," where the main slogan was "Black and White United against Nazi-British National Party." Another example is the "Black alliance" campaign organized by the NAAR, which claimed, "We see our fight against racism in Britain as part of the struggle of the non-white majority of humanity against racism and every other form of oppression." Unlike the universalist tradition of antiracism that sees unity in humanity, differentialist antiracism, as the last quotation makes clear, conceives of humanity as a conglomerate of groups, with each community facing particular problems, discrimination, and prejudices. In addition to mentioning various groups on the basis of their particular identities, British antiracist organizations also strive to raise group awareness, that is, group transformation in the Marxist understanding of "a class for itself." The ARA's campaign in 1997 raised the issue of "the lack of awareness of many members of the black community" and, in the same vein, the NAAR's campaign to unify "black organisations" against racism declared that "we uphold the principle of black unity" and asked for tolerance regarding "our social, political, and cultural diversity."

In France, antiracism is clearly grounded in universal principles, notably of unity of humanity, and a denial of particular identities in order to obtain a strict equality between individuals belonging to the same national community. Equality between groups and tolerance for plural identities would constitute a major breach of republican ideals. Apart from a universal tradition of antiracism that we found in generalized campaigns against racism and fascism, the main political expression of antiracism in Britain is rooted in a differentialist tradition of antiracism. This tradition points out not only the existence of plural identities, but also the existence of specific discrimination faced by each identity and, above all, the idea that identities have to be considered and respected in their diversity. Thus, we find two very distinct conceptions of public support for victims of racial prejudices and discrimination.

Political Altruism on Behalf of Migrants as a Specific Defense of the Nation

Our main inquiry in this chapter concerned the basis of political altruism on behalf of migrants and minorities: do antiracist and pro-migrant organizations mobilize specifically to defend the interests of migrants, or, alternatively, do they enter the public space to promote and advocate a specific conception of the nation? Our study provides strong supportive evidence for the idea that this form of political altruism is best understood as identity-oriented. Antiracist and pro-migrant activists act to defend a specific understanding of nationhood: that of an open, accessible nation, "without borders," and following the Enlightenment understanding of equality. This stance may be supported in two ways: in a liberal tradition promoting equality between *individuals,* or in a community understanding of equality between *groups.*

Dominant conceptions of nationhood were seen to play a decisive role in the mobilization of this type of collective actor, as well as shaping the forms and content of their public claims. Contrary to the hypothesis seeing political altruism primarily as just an expression of defending the specific interests of migrants, antiracist and pro-migrant actors in Switzerland and Germany were not very active. By contrast, in France, Britain, and the Netherlands, where migrants' political conditions are, without being ideal, much better than those in Germany and Switzerland, pro-migrant and antiracist actors were much more involved in public debates. In France, Britain, and the Netherlands, such actors found more favorable opportunities to mobilize in support of migrants and oppose ethnic and racial discrimination because they benefited from political legitimacy when entering the public sphere by advocating a conception of nationhood that resonated with the dominant

INTEREST OR IDENTITY?   231

understanding of citizenship. We were able to demonstrate such variations between countries in the public visibility, action repertoires, and contents of pro-migrant and antiracist actors' claims making. In addition, our analysis of campaigns and their discourses showed that framing is very different in Britain and France. In Britain, a differentialist conception of antiracism is voiced that promotes equal treatment between groups and enables actors to frame a principle of tolerance by referring to particular identities. By contrast, in France we find a universal antiracism that is based on a principle for the undifferentiated treatment between individuals.

Our study also showed that it is necessary to take into account other actors, specifically the extreme right and migrants themselves, who intervene in the playing field. The presence of the extreme right was also seen to structure political activity of the antiracist sector to a certain degree. A strong extreme right appears to increase the level of antiracist mobilization. Similarly, strong political activity on the part of migrant groups, as is the case in Britain and the Netherlands, also shapes pro-migrant and antiracist mobilization. Above all, this influences the content of antiracist and pro-migrant claims by orienting them toward fields of protest neglected by migrants. Such interactive dynamics modify the mobilization conditions of antiracist and pro-migrant actors. However, our key finding remains that the mobilization of the antiracist and pro-migrant groups strongly reflects the different national opportunity structures shaped by conceptions of citizenship and national identity.

7

Contested Citizenship: Conclusions and Future Directions

This book presents a new approach for analyzing immigration and ethnic relations politics. We proposed a conceptual framework based on citizenship by integrating approaches drawn from the previously distinct social movements and migration fields. First, we set out to demonstrate the systematic differences in approaches to citizenship in the countries by examining their institutional policy approaches for granting rights to migrants. Subsequently, we used our cross-national empirical data on political claims making to test the main theses in the literature on citizenship, immigration, and ethnic relations. Each chapter took up the challenge to answer a key research question through recourse to our own comparative evidence. Our aim was to contribute empirically grounded knowledge to a field where this has tended to lag behind theoretical speculation. At the same time, by addressing questions in immigration and ethnic relations, we hope also to have made a contribution of more general relevance to several core sociological questions—political participation, integration, social cohesion, globalization, multiculturalism—about liberal democratic societies.

In this final chapter, we first synthesize our positions in the key debates in a summary overview. Then we discuss two contemporary trends in Europe's immigration and ethnic relations politics: the renationalizing tendencies in the turn away from overt multicultural policies, and the denationalizing tendencies that potentially arise from political denationalization in the European region. Last, we indicate some possible future directions for research. Our aim in this chapter is not to integrate the conclusions of the previous chapters into something substantively new; we simply want to direct the reader backward to key substantive findings with respect to the different research questions and forward to recent developments and possible research avenues.

National Configurations of Citizenship: Convergence or Divergence?

We argued that the principal reason why postwar immigration to Western Europe has been and remains an issue for intense political conflict is that it raises fundamental questions about the nation-state: its sovereignty in controlling its borders, its attribution of citizenship, and its identity, the self-understanding that defines belonging to a national community. The strong cross-national differences that we demonstrated in the contentious politics of immigration and ethnic relations are best explained by the different configurations of citizenship that are expressed through national policies for integration and the recognition of cultural difference. One of our main objectives has been to try and specify more clearly what these configurations of citizenship consist of.

In the introduction, we outlined the political space for positions on immigration and ethnic relations by combining two dimensions of national citizenship: first, the equal individual rights dimension, the basis for individual access to citizenship, either by ethnic bonds or by civic rights attributed on the territorial principle; and second, the differential group rights dimension that ranges from a monocultural view of the national community to one that facilitates the retention of cultural differences for specific groups within national belonging. This two-dimensional political space led us to identify four ideal-typical conceptions of citizenship: segregationism, assimilationism, universalism, and multiculturalism (see Introduction, Figure 1). These ideal-types for conceptions of citizenship can be used to distinguish between the political positions of different nation-states and for different actors in the policy field within a nation-state, and to trace the policy positions of countries and actors across different time periods. In order to make the model more dynamic and less dependent on the national clichés that have been common in the citizenship debate, we integrated this view of conceptions of citizenship into a political opportunity model for explaining levels of political contention.

Earlier attempts at applying the political opportunity approach to immigration and ethnic relations (see especially Ireland 1994, 2000) have been much less explicit in specifying the nature of the institutional variables that interact with and shape migrant behavior. The same can also be said about those approaches drawn from the "new institutionalism," such as Adrian Favell's research (1998), which pointed out that these institutional variables also have a discursive dimension, as "public philosophies of integration," which is important in explaining their national path dependency. Both contributions were invaluable steps in taking cross-national comparative research forward. However, we felt that it was important to be more systematic and to identify the variables that this approach sees as shaping the perceptions and subsequent actions of collective actors more precisely. Such a step was necessary both for migration and social movement research. Social movement approaches have also had a tendency to be rather vague about the extent to which manifest political opportunities are issue-field specific and not simply derived from general features of political systems.

We specified the political institutional dimensions by referring to the sets of rights and duties of citizenship that define the relationship of migrants to the state institutions of their societies of settlement. Institutionalized into policy approaches, these were seen as defining the channels and resources that allow migrants, their supporters, and their opponents to mobilize political demands on the state. At the same time, we specified a role within this institutional framework for discursive opportunities—the legitimating discourses about citizenship and cultural notions of belonging and national identity—that determine which points of view about the relationship between migrants and the state and host society are held to be more sensible, realistic, and legitimate.

Of course, the proof of the pudding is in the eating, and it was important to demonstrate the importance of citizenship as the basis for cross-national differences in policy approaches. This was the task of chapter 2. First, we wanted to substantively flesh out what we meant by configurations of citizenship and move beyond the impressionistic differences that often figure in the literature. Second, we felt that it was important to demonstrate that the use of citizenship for political opportunity structures is not just a heuristic device but is grounded in the actual policies that states have for migrants. To show that there is more to citizenship than the narrow legalistic definitions of formal citizenship, which is how it often appears in Brubaker-derivative comparisons, it was necessary to empirically demonstrate the actual positions of our states in relation to each other by using our own explanatory framework. Third, this empirical comparison of our countries' policies along different dimensions of citizenship fulfilled a vital role for the book as a whole by providing information on the independent variable and a basis for expectations about claims making.

Chapter 1 is different from previous attempts to aggregate how states attribute rights to migrants because it defines empirical indicators for both dimensions of citizenship. This enabled us to position our countries accord-

ing to their policy positions, comparatively and at three points across a period of twenty-two years (1980–2002). To our knowledge, we are the first
to gather systematically comparable information on the cultural dimension of citizenship. Our findings were striking and conclusive. There are
clear-cut differences in the citizenship configurations of our five countries,
with Switzerland and Germany closest to the assimilationist ideal-type,
France closest to the universalist position, and Britain and especially the
Netherlands close to the multiculturalist pole. We also found that none of
our countries had remained static over the past two decades in the way that
rights are attributed to migrants. This is important because it demonstrates
that although there are significant national differences in the countries'
approaches to citizenship, there is also scope for significant change within
the given set of parameters of a national approach. We see political contention over immigration and ethnic relations as an influential factor that feeds
back and contributes to such changes within a national configuration of
citizenship.

The leading substantive question of chapter 1 was whether the countries'
configurations of citizenship were experiencing convergence or divergence.
Apart from Britain, which was already located at the civic-territorial end of
the spectrum, we found a general move away from ethnic conceptions of individual access to citizenship rights. This was particularly relevant for those
countries with a guest worker policy tradition. Germany and Switzerland
have over time retreated from the sharp ethnic basis of their citizenship
configurations and moved toward the more civic stance of France, Britain,
and the Netherlands. This provides some support for the general view that
liberal states cannot normatively sustain a situation where a large number of
permanently resident migrants and their offspring are denied formal access
to civic and political rights.

By contrast, our findings on the ways that countries define cultural obligations and minority group rights as a basis for citizenship demonstrated
an overall divergence. Here the Netherlands and Britain have moved toward
policy positions that permit a greater degree of cultural diversity and minority group rights. Germany too has moved away from its ethnic cultural
monism over the last decade, which demonstrates that granting minority
group rights is independent from and may even precede the formal acquisition of citizenship. In contrast, assimilationist Switzerland and universalist France have been relatively steadfast in refusing to grant concessions to
migrants in the cultural sphere. Consequently, the differences between cultural approaches to migrant integration are much more pronounced today
than they were in the early 1980s.

Citizenship and Contentious Politics

In chapter 2, we set out to use our political claims making data to test hypotheses drawn from theories of postnational citizenship. Postnationalists argue that migrants in liberal nation-states have achieved many civil and social, though not political, rights as full citizens. They argue that migrants have successfully made claims to such residence and welfare rights by drawing on universal rights of personhood that are formalized in international human rights conventions and institutions. Some have gone as far as stating that these universal personhood rights have largely taken over from national citizenship as the main source of rights (Jacobson 1996; Soysal 1994). In chapter 2, we laid out objections to the postnational thesis regarding the sources of rights, the benefit of supranational policies to migrants, and the extent of the erosion of national sovereignty (see especially Joppke 1997, 1999). Instead of rejecting postnationalism out of hand, however, we used our data to locate examples of postnational claims making in their relation to the broader context of claims making in immigration and ethnic relations politics. Our aim was to demonstrate empirically the relationship between nation-states and supra- and transnational politics in this contentious field.

Based on our findings, a general point to make against postnationalism is that it can give no answer to the striking national differences that are evident in the claims making in the five countries. Postnational theories see nation-states being subjected to similarly strong supranational and transnational political pressures and norms, which would lead us to predict general cross-national similarities rather than differences. On the contrary, not only did we find differences in the political claims raised by actors, and the prominence of different types of actor, but these differences could in many cases be traced to the national configurations of citizenship, as we demonstrated initially in chapter 1 but more directly in subsequent chapters. However, the most relevant findings specific to postnationalism concerned the nature and extent of claims making beyond the nation-state. Contrary to postnationalists' expectations, we found that the vast majority of collective actors making demands in the five countries did not extend organizationally beyond the territorial scope of the nation-state. Likewise, the number of claims that we found with a substantive scope of reference beyond the nation-state was somewhat higher, but again unimpressive in scale. In addition, we found remarkably little involvement by European actors and few references to European issues.

Digging deeper, our actual examples of claims making beyond the nation-state paint a very different reality than that presented by postnational theory. Postnationalists depict restrictive nation-states being forced by supranational norms and transnational interdependencies to liberalize their immigration controls and grant rights to migrants. Our evidence showed this impression to be overly one-sided. In fact, we found the European and international arena to be dominated by nation-states through their international and supranational coordinations of border controls and recognition regimes, as well as international measures to combat crime and terrorism. Such claims beyond the nation-state were found to be generally less supportive of immigration and migrant rights than national ones, which goes against the assumed benevolence of the supra- and transnational arenas relative to national ones. With respect to the European Union, lauded by some postnationalists for eroding the anti-migrant tendencies of sovereign nation-states (e.g., Sassen 1999), our data showed that the European Union is not pro-migrant relative to the nation-state, nor is it more conducive to participatory involvement by civil society actors, nor do migrants see it as an institution that is particularly worth making demands on. In the supranational field outside the European Union, however, we found some evidence that conformed more closely to the postnational image. There were examples of claims referring to international treaties and norms, often linked to the United Nations, and where NGOs, civil society actors, and migrants were able to benefit from supranational normative and institutional opportunities, at least to some extent, and certainly much more than with the European Union. Last, our search for an emergent trend of increasing supra- and transnationalism over time, much vaunted by postnationalists, pointed if anything toward a trend for renationalization and not denationalization.

Overall, our evidence provides very little support to those radical postnationalists who argue that "transnational migration is eroding the traditional basis of nation-state membership, namely citizenship" (Jacobson 1996, 8) or that "in terms of its translation into rights and privileges, it [national citizenship] is no longer a significant construction" (Soysal 1998, 208). Persistent national differences, and the limited actual level and substance of claims making beyond the nation-state, leaves postnationalism looking like a general normative theory that is a long way away from any tangible substantive reality. Moreover, postnationalism's underlying notion of the "supranational good" versus the "national bad" is a simplistic and not very useful depiction of the politics within and beyond nation-state.

In chapters 3 and 4 on migrants, and in chapters 5 and 6 on xenophobic and antiracist reactions from native populations, we wanted to pitch the explanations drawn from our national configurations of citizenship approach against competing hypotheses about migrant, racist, and antiracist political mobilization. Our citizenship approach defined the nature of the political opportunities that are available for these competing actors in their attempts through their claims making to push policy approaches in segregationist, assimilationist, universalist, or multiculturalist directions. As migrant populations are the intended beneficiaries or objects of such policies, it is our findings relating to their political behavior that are perhaps most decisive.

Migrants deserve special attention because they have been previously defined as another potential source of transnationalization and denationalizing tendencies. The "transnational communities" approach within migration studies (e.g., Portes, Guarnizo, and Landolt 1999) presents another argument for the relativization of the nation-state. Here migrants are seen to form transnational communities, or diasporas, retaining their cultural differences and strong ties with their homelands and thus undermining nation-states' attempts to assimilate migrants to national politics and culture (Kleger 1997; Shain and Sherman 1998; Schiller, Basch, and Blanc-Szanton 1997). Migrants in the image of transnational communities are seen as operating politically beyond and outside of the context of the nation. For us a leading question was to what extent migrants are the carriers of such purported transnationalizing trends or, alternatively, to what extent their transnationalism and other forms of political behavior were in fact the outcome of integration policies of the receiving states. A subsequent question concerned evaluating the type of policy approaches that had been most successful in increasing the inclusiveness of democratic rights and strengthening the bond between the liberal state and migrant populations.

Our data on migrants' claims making did include some of the type of examples that appear in the transnational communities and diaspora literature. However, our evidence pointed decisively toward the continued relevance of national approaches to integration. We found significant cross-national differences between the levels and forms of transnational claims making by migrants, and these were best explained by the type of citizenship that a country uses for politically including migrants in its national community. Thus, ethnic assimilationist Switzerland and Germany define their former guest workers as "foreigners," and this is how they see themselves, directing their energies into often violent "transplanted homeland" affairs, much more than their counterparts in the Netherlands, Britain, and France. Furthermore, these strong and striking national differences held when we controlled for differences among migrant groups. Thus, contrary to the view that transnational migrant identifications are encouraged by increasingly open citizenship regimes backed by a state-sponsored cultural pluralism, our findings demonstrated that migrants' transnationalism is in most cases a response to the exclusionary citizenship of countries that have put up high barriers for migrants' access to the political community.

Such findings point to a first conclusion regarding the impact of integration policies. Most observers consider strong homeland orientations among migrants to be detrimental to attempts to make them part of the society of settlement, especially when they are manifested as violent confrontations, such as those between Turks and Kurds in Germany. A common political response to such violent and illegal clashes between "foreigners" on domestic soil has been that access to citizenship and the national community be restricted or denied for groups who are seen as potentially dangerous and volatile components of society and a threat to social order. However, the implications of our analysis run counter to this. In our view, it is when citizenship is made accessible to migrants that migrant communities begin to see themselves as nationals and the homeland fades into becoming a tradition and heritage. Thus we found few clashes between Indians and Pakistanis in Britain, compared to those between Turks and Kurds in Germany, though no one could argue that conflicts between the two Indian subcontinent countries are more pacified than those in Turkey. Failure to grant citizenship to migrants and to provide opportunities for political inclusion actually seem to be factors that lead them to invest their political energies outside of the place where they are settled and live. On this basis we would expect Germany's Turks and Kurds to become less involved in homeland conflicts in future generations, to the extent that their resident populations take up the new opportunities to become German citizens.

It also matters *how* nation-states make migrants into citizens. France's highly restricted cultural pluralism and refusal to recognize particularist identities has led to migrants who mobilize emphasizing their allegiance to the universality of the French state, for example, as French Muslims, or, alternatively, using identities that express their status as immigrants within France. It seems that just as migrants' transnationalism is shaped by national citizenship, so is the apparent multiculturalism of migrant political behavior. This was further demonstrated by the differences between the Netherlands and Britain, the two multiculturalist countries that attribute special rights to minorities in their integration politics in an attempt to combat the institutional and societal discrimination that prevents the substantive realization of individual equality for migrants. The overt cultural pluralism of Dutch migrant politics produced somewhat mixed outcomes.

On the plus side, Dutch migrants' claims making was less violent and more moderate than elsewhere, but against this migrants were less prominent in the public domain than in Britain and France. In addition, the sponsoring of a plethora of particularist identities by Dutch policies appears to have stimulated the maintenance of homeland identities to a greater extent than in Britain and France, though not on a scale similar to Switzerland and Germany.

Such findings about the Dutch case cast some degree of skepticism on the impression given in much of the normative multiculturalism literature that the extension of group rights is an unambiguously good thing for migrants. Against this, we felt that it is more accurate to depict the relationship between acquiring differential rights and migrants' binding to a country's political community as curvilinear. In this view, the British approach for attributing group rights to broad categories of minorities on the basis of constructed ascriptive identities of race appears to have had the most success at bringing minorities into the domestic political domain.[1] Whereas the use of ethnocultural categories in Dutch policies runs the risk of cultural retrenchment and social segregation, the—in the European context idiosyncratic—British use of race molds migrants into a single special group within British politics and clearly defines the limits of differential rights and expectations on both parties to this agreement. Our point here is not normative. Before overstating the apparent benefits of British multiracialism, it is important to note that the benefits of race relations policies seem to have served middle-class elites from ethnic minorities, whereas costs appear to have been borne disproportionately by one group, Pakistani and Bangladeshi Muslims, whose trajectory for adaptation to British society has been served less well.

In chapter 4, we sought to refine the view on national differences by examining the question of multiculturalism and migrants' demands for group rights with a special focus on Muslims. This chapter also enabled us to demonstrate the qualitative detail of our claims-making data and thereby move beyond simply talking about differences between aggregated categories. Following the prominent controversies over multiculturalism, we asked whether migrants' demands for group rights were a threat to cohesion, leading to fragmentation and segmented societies or whether they contributed to the vitality of citizenship by negotiating the passage of migrants into a full membership of the community.

Our evidence shows that the prominence of group demands within academic controversies over multicultural citizenship appears to be widely exaggerated, at least with respect to Europe. Images of societies tearing themselves apart at the cultural seams or being fundamentally transformed by migrants' differentialist demands seem to be wide of the mark. Also, migrants' group demands do not appear to be a general phenomenon affecting European countries. Germany and Switzerland, the countries that have done least to make migrants into citizens and whose policies tend to keep migrants politically and culturally apart from the host society, registered virtually none. From this we conclude that migrants have to receive some incentives from host societies before they feel sufficiently politically empowered to demand special treatment as a group.

In countries that do attempt to make migrants into citizens, Britain, the Netherlands, and France, we found similar, albeit modest, levels of migrant group demands. This was a surprising finding for France, which, compared to Britain and the Netherlands, makes far fewer attempts to recognize the particular cultural identities of migrants. This demonstrates that there are important limitations on the degree to which nation-states have been able to shape migrants' political behavior in their own image, at least regarding their demands for special group rights and recognition. Closer inspection revealed that European public controversies about claims for group demands are not about migrants' cultural differences per se, but appear to arise from a specific contradiction of Islam in the liberal nation-state. In part, we took from this that religion is a particularly resilient aspect of migrant culture that is often difficult for liberal states to accommodate. States can require migrants to learn a new language, but it is harder to ask them to learn a new religion, in particular when liberal states uphold the freedom of religious practice. However, not all migrant religions have been as culturally resilient as Islam. We found virtually no group demands by the large number of migrants of Hindu faith in Britain and the Netherlands, although they have similar backgrounds, settled at similar times, and faced similar policy conditions as Muslims. Our explanation for Muslim exceptionalism was that unlike most other migrant faiths, Islam (or at least politically salient representations of it) makes important demands on the way that its followers behave in public life. This public visibility of Islam, where Muslim communities self-organize in a way that often fuses civic and religious functions, sustains the group identity of Muslims, thus apparently proving resilient to the attempts by liberal states to shape and adapt the group's identification into its incorporation approach.

Our detailed qualitative analysis of examples of Muslims' demands for exceptional and parity group rights in Britain, France, and the Netherlands demonstrated the importance of a state's tradition for the political accommodation of religion and tried to unpack the different national flavors of controversies over the relationship between Muslims and the host state and society. In each country, Muslim group demands were made in a language that addresses the state's policies for recognizing cultural difference and facilitating the public presence of religion. In France, Islam is a mouthpiece against exclusion by a state that implements policies for undifferentiated individual citizenship through its own secularist ideology of *laïcité* and that denies Muslims a *droit à la différence*. In Britain, it is a mouthpiece for challenging a race relations system that is perceived as unjust because it denies religious recognition for Pakistani and Bangladeshi Muslims, who find their racial categorization as Asians insufficient to meet their aspirations for equality. Last, in the Netherlands, Muslims aspire to be included as a new pillar in Dutch political life, following in the pillarization tradition by which Dutch society has self-organized along confessional lines.

Our chapters on the responses of the native publics to the presence of migrants showed that the extreme right, on one side, and antiracists, on the other, intervene in shaping the political relationship of migrants with their host states. Our findings once more pointed to strong national differences in institutional arrangements and legitimating discourses that can be traced back to configurations of citizenship. In chapter 5 on the extreme right, a specific opportunity structure was defined for explaining cross-national differences, and this was pitted against approaches based on ethnic competition and grievances. Our claims-making data was placed alongside variables relating to social structural features of society, such as immigration levels and unemployment rates, that could plausibly be the basis for grievance-motivated ethnic competition by majority populations against migrants. Against this, however, a more satisfactory explanation for the levels and types of extreme-right mobilization in our five countries came from a political process model that combined configurations of citizenship with dynamics of party political alignments and party competition, and the strategic repertoires of the extreme right. Thus, rather than an objective level of grievances against migrants or against immigration flows, we found that the space given by the political system for expressing perceived grievances provided a more convincing explanation for the presence of the extreme right.

Finally, chapter 6 showed that native support for immigrants cannot be understood as simply a response to exclusive state policies and societal racism and xenophobia. Pro-migrant and antiracist mobilization tended to be strongest in countries with an inclusive conception of citizenship, where migrants form a legitimate part of the national community. Another important factor was found to be the presence of the extreme right, with a strong extreme right leading to movement and countermovement dynamics, thus increasing mobilization by antiracist and pro-migrant activists. In addition, a qualitative analysis of campaigns and rhetoric showed important differences in what type of antiracist stance is emphasized. While in France we find a strong emphasis on equality and universal values, British campaigns focus more on the differential problems and rights of specific migrant groups.

The Decline of Multiculturalism: Renationalizing Migrant Politics?

There are two ways of understanding multiculturalism.[2] The first refers to the empirical reality that the metropolitan cities of Western Europe are today populated by peoples of different colors, religions, and ethnicities, and that this is a situation that has politically normalized to the extent that it no longer provokes reactions from the white ethnic majority. In this view, those xenophobes who actively militate against the presence of racial, religious, and ethnic minorities are pariahs; to paraphrase the remark of British Prime Minister Tony Blair, "racists are the only minority." The second is official multiculturalism, whereby states have policies that deliberately and explicitly recognize and protect migrants as distinct ethnic groups. In the recent past, it seemed that there was an incontrovertible political consensus supporting multicultural policies backed by the mantra that "we are all multiculturalists now" (Glazer 1997), to the extent where differentialist positions were even discussed as policy alternatives in France (Brubaker 2003). Since the beginning of the twenty-first century, however, the apparent benefit of multiculturalism, both as an idea and as a policy, no longer appears self-evident to policy makers across Europe.

A contributing factor to this change in political climate has undoubtedly been the shock wave sent through liberal states by the 9/11 terrorist attacks on the United States in 2001, and then the Madrid outrage in 2004. Post–9/11 and Madrid, the loyalty of many Muslims to their societies of settlement has been placed in question by governments and publics across Europe. In many cases, the fears and feelings of insecurity of the native populations—whether based on objective grounds or not—against the perceived threat of hostile and dangerous alien cultures on home soil, has provided a constituency of voters for the extreme right. Electoral successes in the new century by the Pim Fortuyn list in the Netherlands, Jean-Marie Le Pen in France, the People's Party in Denmark, the Freedom Party in Austria, the Vlaams Blok in Belgium, and even local gains by the previously weak British National Party in Britain, have been on a platform appealing to native anti-Islamic and anti-immigrant sentiments. These parties have mostly abandoned old-style racism in their political rhetoric for a focus on the cultural "inability to assimilate" of immigrants, and Muslims in particular. In part due to co-optation by political elites of this stance, official multicultural policies have entered a period of skepticism about their benefits and past achievements. In truth, however, with the exception of the Netherlands and Sweden, multicultural policies in the strict sense were in many countries, such as Britain, less of a reality and more of a normative rhetoric designed to present a cozy image of mutual tolerance. In Europe official multicultural policies never went close to granting group rights in the same way as those in countries such as Canada, partly because their objectives were directed at migrants and not the population as a whole. As we have seen, only the Dutch from our cases adopted an overt policy for attributing multicultural rights to minorities. Even there the shift in the 1990s from minorities' policy to integration policy moved the emphasis from special policies for migrant groups to policies for individual migrants within Dutch society (Entzinger 2003). Similar trends also occurred in Swedish policies (Soininen 1999). This civic-universalist policy shift has brought new assimilative cultural demands on resident migrants—language skills, knowledge of national culture, participation in citizenship rituals—for the acquisition of national citizenship. Here we briefly review these shifts against multicultural politics and investigate some of the factors that have brought them about. We first outline the Dutch experience, as an example of the renationalization by liberal nation-states of multicultural politics. Then we refer to some similar tendencies visible in Britain, our other country that had proceeded at least some way down the path of cultural pluralism. Our aim is to investigate to what extent this apparent public renationalization of multiculturalism is a reflection of real policy failures and/or an outcome of political discourse dynamics.

Traditionally, Dutch policy makers and social scientists have been quick to hold up their immigration and integration policies as exemplary. At the national level heated public debates occurred from time to time, but the general consensus was that the Dutch situation was better than in other countries, which were seen as plagued by ghettoization, ethnic violence, and xenophobia. Superficially, there seemed to be much to commend Dutch multiculturalism. Dutch ethnic minority organizations were often regarded with envy by their European counterparts due to their sizable budgets and easy access to policy makers, made possible through an extensive network of subsidies and advisory bodies. Also, the Netherlands have not seen the kind of large-scale outbursts of ethnic violence that have occurred at times in France and Britain. Unlike neighboring Belgium, radical right-wing parties had until recently failed to make any significant impact on Dutch elections, and widespread racial violence, such as that witnessed by Germany against asylum seekers, had not occurred. Public debates seldom contained explicit negative references to ethnic minorities. Critical discourse by public figures such as Frits Bolkestein and Paul Scheffer, though provocative and risqué in Dutch terms, would have been run-of-the-mill in most other European countries. Finally, public opinion, as recorded in the continuous Eurobarometer polls, showed the Dutch to be—or at least to declare themselves to be—the most tolerant nation in Europe.

The dramatic rise of Pim Fortuyn's party in 2002 exploded the official political myth that the Dutch multicultural policies were a success. Fortuyn's interpretation of the situation tapped into fears of ordinary Dutch people and matched their lived experiences of minority-related crime and segregation in cities. Before this brought the issue to the forefront of public debate, there was already considerable factual evidence for the failure of Dutch migrant policies to achieve their goals, not least the report by the independent WRR (Netherlands Scientific Council for Government Policy) in 1989. Too much state sponsorship for multiculturalism appeared to have led to the fragmentation of migrant communities along ever smaller ethnic and religious group lines, resulting in an institutionalization of inequality. Undoubtedly, multicultural rhetoric has benefits in stimulating tolerance within national self-understandings of membership to the political community, but there are limitations to the extent to which this can serve also as a policy for social integration.

Research on the social consequences of Dutch multiculturalism when compared to the political position of migrants in Germany is revealing in this respect. When judged by social outcomes for migrant populations, the lack of political rights for Germany's second-generation "foreigners" has not prevented them from achieving significantly higher levels of employment and experiencing less segregation in schools, less dependency on welfare, and being less often convicted of crimes than their counterparts in the multicultural Netherlands (Thränhardt 2000; Koopmans 2002).[3] Such advances for German migrants have been made in part through collective action and participation in trade unions, which has offset their formal exclusion from the most visible part of the political arena. In contrast, the Dutch case shows that political approaches based on inclusive formal citizenship but with differentialist group rights are no guarantees for migrant integration into society. On the contrary, national ideologies of multiculturalism may simply serve to reproduce and reinforce national myths about the presumed tolerance of the native majority public, leading to complacency about the reality of migrant participation in society.

The Dutch system of *verzuiling* was developed in the early twentieth century as a means to pacify conflicts between native religious and political groups with considerable success. However, it was never meant to serve as an instrument for the integration of immigrants and has proven to be inadequate for that purpose. Neither immigrants nor native Dutch people are helped by applying principles that were originally meant for a native population with a largely similar socioeconomic status, common history, and political culture to the integration of newcomers with different cultural backgrounds. This only offers new ethnic and religious groups a formal and symbolic form of equality, which in practice reinforces ethnic cleavages and reproduces segregation on a distinctly unequal basis. There is relatively little to lament in the Dutch turn away from overt multicultural policies; it is clear that they required revision to address the real situation of minorities. The inability of Dutch political elites to reexamine their attachment to multiculturalism, partly due to "political correctness," meant that they were usurped by a populist politician who knew that the public experienced the effects of differences between official myth and reality. Fortuyn made it acceptable to publicly speak the previously unutterable. The repercussions of this on Dutch politics continue after his assassination. His renationalizing antimulticultural rhetoric opened up new opportunities for racist sentiments that challenge the thinner understanding of multiculturalism as mutual tolerance.

As we have seen, Britain has sustained only a limited version of multiculturalism based on race. Although less dramatic than the Dutch case, the decline of multiculturalism as a normative policy concept is underlined by recent shifts toward having thicker civic citizenship requirements for migrants in Britain. The race riots in Bradford, Burnley, Oldham, and Leeds in the summer of 2001 were a shock for British minority politics.[4] There had not been a serious race-related disturbance for several years, and this one, unusually, involved Muslims. Prior to the riots, British policy thinking on integration had strayed very little from the race relations path. Nonetheless, the conclusions of the government-commissioned Cantle report, *Community Cohesion,* sound strongly reminiscent of debates about the failings of Dutch multiculturalism.[5] It concludes: "Whilst the physical segregation of housing estates and inner city areas came as no surprise, the team was particularly struck by the depth of polarization of our towns and cities. . . . Separate educational arrangements, community and voluntary bodies, employment, places of worship, language, social and cultural networks, means that many communities operate on the basis of a series of parallel lives. These lives often do not seem to touch at any point, let alone overlap and promote any meaningful interchanges" (9).

The policy proposals put forward by Cantle to address these problems were strongly social integrationist and, importantly from our viewpoint, advocated the introduction of a proactive "meaningful concept of citizenship" with the objective of bringing greater social cohesion. Although ignoring several others, the Labour government took up this idea of civic citizenship as a mechanism for getting migrants and minorities to define themselves within the national community. Home Secretary David Blunkett opened up a debate on national citizenship, key features of which were included in the government's "Secure Borders, Safe Havens" white paper, and subsequent Nationality, Immigration, and Asylum Bill (2002). The main thrust of the policy thinking was strongly universalist. Labour advocated induction and language classes for migrants plus a ritual ceremony for acquiring naturalization and citizenship. These were intended to foster an association and allegiance among migrants for British national values and institutions. It seems that the home secretary wanted to assert his "tough" credentials for the native public in the political debate against the perceived "political correctness" of the minority lobby, and at the same time to define clear limits for the future extensions of multicultural group rights for British Muslims. This interpretation is supported by the fact that at no place in the document did the government state what a meaningful basis of British citizenship would consist of. Here the de facto cultural pluralism of the British state militates against a single civic blueprint for Britishness and core values. For example, since English is not the only language of the United Kingdom, prospective candidates for British citizenship would be permitted to take their assimilative language classes in Welsh or in the Gaelic Scottish used by a handful of people in the Hebrides. Requiring migrants to swear allegiance to the queen, who is head of the Church of England, would demand of them a commitment that many Britons—either as republicans or as members of other faiths—are unwilling to make, but leaving the head of state out of an oath of allegiance in a constitutional monarchy would be extremely difficult.

When the British citizenship ritual made its debut in 2004, newcomers were required to swear allegiance to the queen and the United Kingdom, with God as an optional extra. Educational classes in citizenship are due to start in 2005, though the citizenship ritual has been much watered down, a pale imitation of the U.S. equivalent, largely due to the difficulty in defining core Britishness. It is hard to see how the introduction of a citizenship ritual for migrants wishing to become British could possibly contribute to alleviating the problems pointed to by the Cantle report, not least because most of the Pakistani and Bangladeshi Muslims in the northern towns are already British citizens. From the British case, we see that the normative policy rhetoric from a few years ago, which was in favor of multiculturalism, has shifted to one that advocates a thicker national citizenship, where migrants, and Muslims in particular, are expected to publicly have prior allegiance to Britain.

Multiculturalism appears to have lost its legitimacy and public saliency for policy thinking in recent years, and to have been replaced by a renationalizing orthodoxy. In part this change bears the imprint of living post–9/11, but the Dutch case shows that it was also due to an inability of the reality of overt multicultural policies to meet the expectations set by the normative rhetoric that launched them.

Globalization and the European Union: Denationalizing Migrant Politics?

A possible source of a denationalizing for immigration and ethnic relations politics would be the emergence of supra- and transnational institutions exercising power over such policies. The European Union is perhaps the most developed example of political denationalization where countries have undertaken to coordinate their activities across boundaries. It is therefore important to give some indication of such developments and their consequences.

There are severe limitations and barriers to transnational mobilization by migrants in Europe, not least of which is that activists come from different national contexts and face different country-specific problems, often from a weak resource base. Defining a common European agenda for bottom-up transnational activities is seldom a concern of most antiracist and migrant activists (Lloyd 2000; Favell and Geddes 2000; Guiraudon 1998). In addition, the European Union offers little sustenance by way of a transnational civil society. When European institutions have funded organizations, this has often led to fears of co-optation, lack of representativeness, infighting, and in some cases detachment from the grass roots. Such failures have not been because of a lack of cooperation or will by the EU institutions. In fact, most efforts would not have lived a day without the generous financial support of the European Commission. Tellingly, both the European Migrants' Forum and efforts to set up a European antiracist network failed because of internal controversies along national lines—national lines, it should be emphasized, referring to the participating migrant organizations' countries of residence, not referring to their ethnic homelands. Thus, the fledgling attempts to institutionalize some form of a migrant and minority representation in the European Union have so far yielded little transnational fruit.

The European Union's intervention into immigration policy derives from its earlier self-understanding as a functional treaty-based regime between states that was designed to build a common economic market ensuring internal free movement of goods, persons, services, and capital. These origins have limited the scope of European-level migration policy making largely to enhancing labor mobility between member states and EU citizens. By contrast, influence over the immigration of nonnationals from outside the Union has been strongly guarded by nation-states. Subsequent European policy developments have been based on interstate acts of cooperation, which have followed a security, public order, and restrictive logic (Joppke 1997; Guild and Harlow 2001; Statham 2003b). European migration policy is thus built on a paradox. On one side, the European Community and its successor, the European Union, have adopted the market globalization ethos that primary migration improves prosperity, when referring to labor mobility between member states and EU citizens. However, by direct contrast, the European Union has maintained a resilient stance against primary immigration from outside its borders, a stance that has been captured by the metaphor of "fortress Europe" in public and academic discourses. Thus, the European Union's commitment to market globalization and the freedom of labor movement stops decisively at its own geographical borders. With respect to extracommunitarian immigration and asylum, the European Union behaves collectively in the same way as a restrictive nation-state, often even pushing agreed standards down to the lowest common national denominator.

The European Union is ambivalent in that it restricts as well as promotes globalization tendencies, acting largely as an intergovernmental organization of nation-states. It is perhaps therefore hardly surprising that it often fails to conform to the transnational universalistic values at the heart of the vision of postnational membership that we discussed earlier. The European Union's weak development as a forum for political contention, not only in immigration and ethnic relations politics but also more generally, is hardly surprising given the weakness of its own representative institutions, such as the European Parliament, and the predominance of intergovernmental forms of decision making, such as the Council of Ministers. In this constellation, nation-states remain the central actors and the principal addressees of demands from civil society organizations. Only nation-state representatives both have the capacity to advance such societal interests and can be held accountable if they do not adequately do so, regardless of whether this requires state action on the national or EU level.

Although there has so far been little indication of a general shift of the locus of politics from the nation-state to the supranational EU level, the role and influence of the nation-state has nonetheless been changed by these transnational developments. Thus, faced by the increased transnationalization and mobility of capital, nation-states have lost much of their regulatory capacity in the economic sphere, which has also affected their capacities to maintain extensive nationally defined welfare programs. In the cultural sphere, too, the recent exponential increase in worldwide communication and cultural diffusion has made it virtually impossible for nation-states to maintain a distinguishable national politics of culture, information, and communication—though the French seemingly fight a rearguard battle in this respect. To understand how these changes fit with the continuing importance of the nation-state as a locus for politics, we need to distinguish between the nation-state's sovereignty and its capacity for autonomous action.

The concept of sovereignty is usually taken to mean that a nation-state has power and control over its own future: that it has, in other words, the ability to make final decisions and to make and enforce the law in a given community or territory. A loss of sovereignty implies a loss of legal and actual control over the determination of the direction of national policy. Sovereignty must be distinguished from autonomy. The idea of autonomy refers not to the capacity of nation-states to set goals, but to their ability to achieve goals and policies once they have been set, because in an interdependent world all instruments of national policy may be less effective. It is a diminution of the capacity to achieve national policies—a loss of national autonomy—which may alone be behind the anxieties about a loss of sovereignty. Held asks, "has sovereignty remained intact while the autonomy of the state has diminished, or has the modern state actually faced a loss of sovereignty?" (1996, 407).

The answer to Held's question is, we suggest, that in spite of the decline in its autonomous capacity to act, the nation-state is still the most important locus of sovereignty. The loss of regulatory capacity of nation-states as a result of processes of globalization has not been compensated at the supranational level. Thus, Streeck and Schmitter describe the process of European Union as "negative integration" through preemption of national regulatory regimes without a simultaneous supranational restoration of regulatory capacity (1996, 185). It is also important to note that such deregulation is not imposed on nation-states, but is actively promoted by them in an effort to further economic globalization (Sassen 1998, 54). This is perhaps the main paradox of our present situation: the nation-state's capacities are partly eroding, but there is nothing at present that can credibly fill the void.

It is possible that the process of European unification will in the future lead to real transfers of sovereignty, accountability, and collective identity from the national to the supranational level. So far, however, even the transfer of immigration issues to the first, more supranational pillar of the European Union does not appear to have produced many substantive changes in the exercise of power and direction of policy. In addition, the increasing heterogeneity of the European Union since its expansion to twenty-five members may turn out to work against a future scenario of supranational developments by making common ground even harder to find. Last, the dilemmas that nation-states have faced in regulating migration and integrating migrants will not dissolve in the face of the emergence of a European polity. Such a Europe, too, will have to develop rules and discursive legitimation specifying who will be granted access to the European Union, who is eligible to become a member of its political community, and how to deal with cultural diversity and demands for special group rights. These are fundamental dilemmas that any form of political regulation of migration and ethnic relations will have to deal with; they do not arise from specific deficiencies of the nation-state that will magically disappear with the arrival of some form of postnationalism.

Future Research Directions

Through cross-national research we have arrived at an understanding of the workings of immigration and ethnic relations politics in liberal nation-states that would have been impossible from separate stand-alone national case studies. The specific national languages of integration politics in different countries are in many cases reflected and reproduced in the studies of national scientific communities. Thus, the race-centrism of British academics stands in contrast to the universalist color-blindness of their French counterparts. It is only through cross-national exchanges that academic communities will lose the path-dependent myopias that have influenced their national research agendas. Cross-national insights make it possible to understand the national context more precisely and systematically. Cross-national learning processes have been underway within research on immigration politics over the last decade (see especially contributions to Cornelius, Martin, and Hollifield 1994; Martiniello and Statham 1999; Koopmans and Statham 2000). The aim of our MERCI project has been to produce a strict empirically based comparison of countries, to link policy approaches more systematically to the public dimension of conflicts, and to introduce more cross-thematic conceptualization so that clearly related topics such as ethnic relations and xenophobia are not seen as distinct fields. It is for the reader to judge to what extent such goals have been met and to what extent our evidence on the questions addressed is convincing. We now wish to acknowledge some of the limitations of our research and point toward possible further research developments.

Claims-making evidence about how migrants enter into the public sphere tells us much about the nature of their political relationship to their society of settlement and their cultural self-identification. However, it certainly does not present the entire picture of trajectories of migrant incorporation. To give a fuller assessment of the relative benefits of policy approaches for migrants and draw normative conclusions, it would be necessary to combine our findings on the political and cultural presence of migrants with indicators for their social and economic achievements relative to the native populations. As we mentioned earlier, the failure of Dutch multiculturalism to enhance the social position of migrants should warn us against taking the normative rhetoric of how societies see themselves as the true description of reality. We have tried to avoid hasty conclusions about the advantages and disadvantages of the different national approaches, which are open to the possibility of unintended consequences and perverse effects. Our results show that sometimes the normative justifications and empirical results of policies diverge and that what is well intended does not always produce results that in the end benefit the migrant populations toward whom such policies are directed. Such discrepancies will probably become more apparent still if one broadens the view to social and economic aspects of migrant incorporation. We therefore feel that an important direction for future research would be to apply the kind of theoretical framework that we have developed in this book to cross-national analyses of socioeconomic indicators on the positions of migrants in systems of education, employment, housing, and welfare. In addition, a related area for future research concerns the exceptionalism of Muslims. Our findings showed that Islam is especially problematic in Western public domains. It would be interesting to see whether this group-specific tendency is also replicated in the social and economic advancement of Muslims compared to other groups and across other liberal states.

One research approach that could be usefully combined with ours studies the networks and organizational links within and between migrant communities, determining whether these provide social capital for migrant groups that are independent from or shaped by political opportunities. Jean Tillie and Meindert Fennema have pioneered this agenda by applying Robert Putnam's thesis on social capital to migrant communities and examining the organizational links between different ethnic groups in Amsterdam (Fennema and Tillie 1999). It will be interesting to see to what extent this bottom-up approach to migrant political participation can be combined with, or competes with, the top-down political opportunities that are available at the local level. Although we have focused on national politics here, a political opportunity perspective leads us to expect local differences within countries. Again, more research on the differences of migrant trajectories between cities, both within countries and across countries, would be an addition to existing knowledge (though see Garbaye 2000; Bousetta 1996; Koopmans 2004a).

Finally, we think the method of political claims analysis could be usefully applied to uncover more general features of cross-national convergence or divergence, and of multilevel interactions between local, national, and supranational and transnational policy arenas. Members from our research team are already using the claims-making approach in projects funded within the European Union's Framework Five program to investigate patterns of Europeanization of political claims making across different policy domains in seven European countries (Koopmans and Statham 2000; http://europub.wz-berlin.de/), as well as a six-country comparison of the field of unemployment politics (Giugni and Statham 2002; http://ics.leeds.ac.uk/eurpolcom/unempol/).

The Coding of Political Claims Making

The Structure of Political Claims

We have defined an instance of claims making (shorthand: a claim) as a unit of strategic action in the public sphere. It consists of *the purposive and public articulation of political demands, calls to action, proposals, criticisms, or physical attacks, which, actually or potentially, affect the interests or integrity of the claimants and/or other collective actors.* Unlike the narrow definition of contentious politics that underlies studies of protest events, our definition includes political claims regardless of the form in which they are made (statement, violence, repression, decision, demonstration, court ruling, and so on) and regardless of the nature of the actor (governments, social movements, NGOs, individuals, anonymous actors, and so on). Note also that political decisions and policy implementation are defined as special forms of claims making, ones that have direct effects on the objects of the claim.

Inspired by Roberto Franzosi's (2004) idea to use the structure of linguistic grammar to code contentious events, we have broken down the structure of claims into seven elements:[1]

1. Location of the claim in time and space (*when* and *where* is the claim made?)
2. Claimant: the actor making the claim (*who* makes the claim?)
3. Form of the claim (*how* is the claim inserted in the public sphere?)
4. The addressee of the claim (*to whom* is the claim directed?)
5. The substantive issue of the claim (*what* is the claim about?)

6. Object actor: who is or would be affected by the claim (*for/against whom?*)
7. The justification for the claim (*why?*)

The ideal-typical claim has all these elements (leaving out the *when* and *where,* which are self-evident).

In grammatical terms, we may write such claims as a *subject-action-addressee-action-object-justification clause* sequence (see Table 39): the claimant, or subject actor, undertakes some sort of action in the public sphere to get another actor, the addressee, to do or leave something affecting the interests of a third actor, the object, and provides a justification for why this should be done. Many claims are not as differentiated as this type, and we may lack information about several aspects, either because the claimant did not include them or because the newspaper did not report them. The only information we always need for coding is information on the *form* (some sort of act in the public sphere has to be identifiable) and the *issue, object actor,* or *frame* that allows us to determine whether a public action relates to our topical field (i.e., it must deal with issues of immigration or ethnic relations), and whether it qualifies as a political claim according to the criterion that it must actually or potentially affect somebody's interests. This latter criterion implies that we have not coded factual statements like "According to the Ministry of the Interior, the number of asylum seekers increased by 50 percent compared to last year" because this does not entail a claim that affects somebody's interests. By contrast, the statement "The Interior Minister declared that something must be done to stop the increase in numbers of asylum seekers, which have increased 50 percent compared to last year" would be coded as a claim because if realized it would affect the interests of asylum seekers.

Examples of claims with a more simple structure are shown in Table 40. The first row illustrates a common form of "incompleteness" of claims: very frequently, no justification is given for a claim. The second row illustrates a form of direct action that contains no discursive elements but where we can derive the issue at stake on the basis of the physical object, whose integrity is directly threatened by the action. In addition, the example illustrates that sometimes claimants are unknown or anonymous. The third example is common for state actors, who do not have to make claims on others to do something but can directly make binding claims. As in the second example, the aim of the action may not be specified in a discursive statement but can be derived from the action itself. The final example is not untypical for statements by professionals and scientists, who often make no explicit

Table 39. Examples of claims with complete structure

Who (claimant)	How (form)	At whom (addressee)	What (issue)	For/against whom (object actor)	Why (frame)
A group of asylum seekers . . .	engage in a hunger strike	demanding the government . . .	not to deport to their country of origin	themselves (the group of asylum seekers) . . .	because this would be in violation of the Geneva Convention.
Amnesty International . . .	issues a press statement . . .	calling on the French parliament . . .	not to ratify the proposed law to ban the wearing of headscarves in French schools . . .	by Muslim pupils	because this law infringes on basic human rights.

Table 40. Examples of claims with incomplete structure

Who (claimant)	How (form)	At whom (addressee)	What (issue)	For/against whom (object actor)	Why (frame)
The German interior minister . . .	calls on . . .	the Italian government . . .	to step up its border control efforts to prevent the entry of	illegal immigrants.	
[unknown] . . .	sets fire to . . .			an asylum seeker center.	
The Bavarian authorities . . .	deport			a group of Kurdish refugees.	
The Dutch Central Bureau of Statistics . . .	publishes a report stating that . . .				the Dutch economy loses rather than gains from immigration.

demands but present frames referring to the consequences of certain policy actions. Even though no concrete demand is made in such cases, we still consider them political claims because the framing of an issue in a certain way rather than in another has implications for policy decisions that do affect other people's interests (in the example case, the conclusion that the frame suggests would be to restrict the entry of immigrants).

While inspired by the idea of linguistic grammar, the way we code claims does not usually literally coincide with the grammatical structure of the media text. In the case of "John hits Peter," such coincidence is given: John is subject actor/nominative case, Peter is object actor/accusative case. However, in "John gives the book to Peter," the book is in accusative case, but we would still code Peter as the object actor because he benefits from John's action. In trying to identify who is subject actor, addressee, and object actor, it is helpful to use the following sentence as a model and to translate the text in a similar form: "John asks Jim to give the book to Peter." John is subject actor, Jim is addressee, Peter is object actor, "to give the book" is the issue, and "asks" is the form. Examples with similar structures: "George Bush (John) demanded that (asks) the Taliban government (Jim) extradite (to give the book to) Osama Bin Laden (Peter)"; "Schröder (John) assured (asks) Bush (Jim) of his full support for military action against (to give the book to) the Afghan regime (Peter)"; "Chirac (John) criticized (asks) Blair (Jim) for blocking the decision-making process (to give the book to) in the European Union (Peter)."

Units of Analysis and Their Delineation

The units of analysis are instances of claims making. Our definition of claims making implies two important delimitations that require some elaboration: (1) instances of claims making must be the result of purposive strategic action of the claimant, and (2) they must be political in nature.

To qualify as an instance of claims making, the text must include a reference to an ongoing or concluded physical or verbal action in the public sphere, i.e., simple attributions of attitudes or opinions to actors by the media or by other actors do not count as claims making. Example: "The Greens, who want to extend recognition to people persecuted by nonstate organizations . . ." This does not qualify as claims making by the Greens. By contrast, the sentence "The Greens, who *said* they wanted to extend recognition to people persecuted by nonstate organizations . . ." would qualify as an instance of claims making because it contains a reference to actual verbal action. Verbs indicating action include: said, stated, demanded, criticized, decided, demonstrated, published, voted, wrote, arrested.

Nouns directly referring to such action include: statement, letter, speech, report, blockade, deportation, decision. The occurrence in the newspaper report of such verbs or nouns is a precondition for the coding of a claim. Reports that only refer to "states of mind" or motivations were not coded (e.g., references such as "want," "are in favor of," "oppose," "are reluctant to," "are divided over").

Claims must be political in the sense that they relate to collective social problems and solutions to them and not to purely individual strategies of coping with problems. For example, if a parent complains about her child's treatment in school, this is not an instance of claims making unless the case refers to a problem of wider collective social relevance (e.g., if the complaint relates to the child being forbidden to wear the Islamic headscarf in class). Other examples are court debates and rulings in asylum cases. These were only coded if the parties involved referred to arguments that went beyond the individual case.

Statements or actions by different actors are considered to be part of one single instance of claims making if they take place at the same location in time (the same day) and place (the same locality) and if the actors can be assumed to act in concert (i.e., they can be considered as strategic allies). For such cases, our coding scheme allows the coding of up to three different claimants. Examples:

- Two substantively identical statements by the same actor on two different days, or on one day in two different localities, are two separate claims.
- Statements by different speakers during a parliamentary debate or a conference are considered part of one instance of claims making as long as they are substantively and strategically compatible. Thus, different speakers may be taken together if they all express a similar point of view. However, if the speakers take positions that are substantially different enough to reject the zero hypothesis that they are "acting in concert," the statements were coded as separate claims.
- If an identifiable part of a peaceful demonstration breaks away from a march and turns violent, the assumption of acting in concert is no longer warranted and a separate claim is coded.

It is important to emphasize that an instance of claims making is *not* identical with individual statements or individual demands. One instance of claims making (e.g., an interview given by the claimant) may consist of many different statements, which may address several different issues. These are all seen as part of one and the same instance of strategic action. Therefore, our coding scheme allows the coding of up to three different addressees, up to three different issues, and up to two different frames.

Sampling Rules

1. Claims were coded from the Monday, Wednesday, and Friday issues of the source newspapers for the period 1992–1998.[2]
2. Sports, business, and other separate topical sections were disregarded, as were the separate regional and local sections in the Swiss and German newspapers. Claims reported in these sections were only coded if there was a reference to them in the national news section of the paper. In this case, only that particular claim or claims were coded. Any others that were encountered in the separate sections were disregarded.
3. The coding focused on current events that had occurred within a time frame of two weeks or less before the publication of the coded newspaper issue and excluded retrospective coverage of claims that lay further back in time.
4. Rule used for the coding of France, the Netherlands, and Switzerland for the whole period, and for Germany up to 1996: a claim must either be made in the country of coding or be addressed to an actor or institution in the country of coding.
5. Extension of rule 4 for the coding of the United Kingdom for the whole period and Germany from 1997 onward: claims are also included if they are made by or addressed to a supranational actor of which the country of coding is a member (e.g., the UN, the European Union, the International Organisation for Migration), on the condition that the claim is substantively (also) relevant for the country of coding (e.g., a statement by the UNHCR criticizing the Belgian government is not included in the British or German data, but an EU decision on common asylum rules is included because it affects all member states, including Germany and the United Kingdom). For reasons of comparability across countries, most analyses in the book are based on the part of the data circumscribed by rule 4. We use the British and German data according to the more encompassing rule 5 only in chapter 2, where we are especially concerned with the role of supranational institutions and contexts. These analyses show that rule 5 does not lead to the inclusion of a great number of claims in addition to those that are already captured under rule 4.
6. One and the same claim was coded only once, the first time it was encountered. Repetitions of the coverage of the claim in follow-up

articles were not separately coded, but that information could be used to complete the information on the original claim.

The Representativeness of Our Sources for the Wider Print-Media Landscape

To investigate to what extent our primary sources are representative for the wider print-media landscape, we have compared a range of newspapers in Germany and Great Britain. In Germany, we coded, in addition to our primary source, the *Frankfurter Rundschau* (FR), two years of the right-wing tabloid *Bild Zeitung* (BZ), one year of the German edition of the Turkish daily *Hürriyet*, as well as four-month samples from three different local dailies. In Britain, we have a cross-section of six national newspapers for the year 1995: the *Times*, the *Daily Express*, the *Daily Mirror*, the *Sun*, and the *Daily Mail*, in addition to our primary source, the *Guardian*.

The comparisons of these alternative sources to our main sources reveal important differences in the *rate* of coverage of relevant claims, especially between national quality papers and the much more limited and concise coverage in tabloid and regional papers. However, such differences in coverage rates coincide with strikingly similar *distributions* of acts on important variables. The comparison of the German left-liberal newspaper *Frankfurter Rundschau* and the right-wing tabloid *Bild Zeitung* is a case in point. The number of reported claims in the domain of immigration and ethnic relations turns out to be 4.6 times higher in the FR than in the BZ for the period from July 1991 to June 1993 for which we have gathered data for the BZ. However, distributions across different issues (asylum, integration, antiracism, and so on) do not differ strongly between the two papers. For instance, our conclusion in chapter 2 that minority integration politics is a marginal policy field in Germany holds regardless of whether we take the FR or the BZ as our source, which report respectively 5.6 percent and 4.0 percent claims that belong to this policy field. The representation of different actors in the coverage is also fairly similar. Government actors are the most important claimant category in both newspapers, responsible for 20.5 percent of claims in the FR and 24.5 percent in the BZ. Migrants appear as claimants in the FR in 5.7 percent of the cases, against 4.5 percent in the BZ, while their opponents, the extreme right, are responsible for 15.5 percent of the claims in the FR, against 19.5 percent in the BZ. Although these differences are in the expected direction given the ideological orientation of the two papers (somewhat less attention for migrant claimants in the BZ, and more for the extreme right and for established government actors), they are rather small, especially when compared to the cross-country differences that are central to our argument.

We can see this clearly if we compare the German results to the British newspapers. In Britain, too, our primary source turns out to be the richest source of information in terms of the rate of coverage (376 claims for 1995, compared to 183 claims in the *Times,* and as few as 95 in the least inclusive of the tabloid papers, the *Daily Mirror*). Among the six British newspapers, the range of variation regarding the share of claims on minority integration politics in the year 1995 runs from 16.0 percent (the *Guardian*) to 33.4 percent (the *Sun*). While this is a substantial range of variation, it comes nowhere near the much lower percentages that we find in the German newspapers. The same is true for the shares of different actors in claims making. In the tabloid *Sun,* minorities appear as claimants about equally as often as in the *Guardian* (23.3 percent and 21.1 percent respectively), and extreme-right claimants are marginal in both newspapers (1.7 percent in the *Guardian,* 2.3 percent in the *Sun*). Thus, our comparative conclusions about the relative marginality of the minority integration issue in Germany, the much higher share of migrant actors in the British public discourse, or the much greater prominence of extreme-right claims in Germany would not have been any different if we had used different newspapers as our primary sources.

A first reason for the similarities between newspaper sources in the same country is that all print media share common standards of what is considered newsworthy, so-called news values (see, e.g., Galtung and Ruge 1965; Schulz 1997; McCarthy, McPhail, and Smith 1996; Hocke 1998; Oliver and Maney 2000). These news values (e.g., which actors are considered prominent and which issues relevant) are strongly affected by the institutional and discursive opportunity structures in a country on a given issue (see similarly Ferree et al. 2002 for the abortion issue). Second, the intermedia similarities that we find are a result of our coding strategy, which focuses on the coverage of claims by other actors and systematically ignores the newspaper's own statements and journalist's and editor's own framing of events. How this affects our data becomes clear if we compare editorials (which we coded separately for the German FR and BZ) to covered claims. Considering, for instance, the position on asylum politics taken by the two newspapers in their editorials, we find that they advocate strongly opposed points of view, with an average valence of +0.63 (i.e., strongly supportive of asylum seeker rights) for the FR, and −0.56 (i.e., strongly in favor of restrictions in asylum seeker rights) for the BZ. These different editorial positions do influence the selection of claims that are covered, but only to a moderate degree, as suggested by the average valences of covered claims: +0.08 for the FR, and −0.21 for the BZ. Whereas the ideological distance in the editorials amounted to 1.19 (0.63 + 0.56), in the coverage it was four times smaller (0.29).

We further find that national newspapers report *more* events of regional scope than regional newspapers, which tend to report much about their own region, but virtually nothing about what happens in other regions and localities. For the period from July to October 1991 for which we coded three East German regional newspapers, we compared the inclusiveness of these three papers to the FR. Of all events registered by the four newspapers, 53 percent were mentioned in the FR, against a coverage rate of between 21 percent and 31 percent for the regional newspapers. The coverage of the three regional newspapers was very strongly focused on their own region (between 83 percent and 91 percent of covered events). Even though the regions that are served by the three regional papers directly border on each other, the FR—which is situated far away in the western part of Germany—easily beats the regional papers even where the coverage rate of events in immediately bordering regions is concerned. Qualitative differences between the types of claims and claimants that were covered in the regional papers compared to our primary source were even smaller than for the comparison between BZ and FR.

Variables and Categories

Our most important variables—actors (as claimants, addressees, or object actors), aims, and frames—were not coded with reference to predefined, closed category systems, but on the basis of open-ended code lists that could be extended by the coders each time a new actor, aim, or frame appeared. Basically, this first coding step does not make an attempt to classify claims into quantifiable categories, but instead is designed to retain as much as possible of the original qualitative content of claims. For Germany, for instance, we have almost seven hundred distinguishable actors and more than five hundred individual aims. These raw codes for actors and aims have been recoded and grouped in summary codes for comparative analysis at a later stage by the principal researchers themselves. Although defining aggregate summary variables for comparative analysis at a later stage is time-consuming, and to some extent constitutes a second coding, we think that it is necessary to proceed in this way. First, it is difficult to predefine category systems at a high level of aggregation when this requires exactly the kind of detailed knowledge about the subject matter that one is trying to learn in the first place. Second, if one codes straightaway at a high level of aggregation, possibilities for alternative ways of categorization are lost forever. This restricts the use of the data set to those research questions that were already explicit at the start of the project, and makes it difficult to shift attention to other questions over the course of the same study. Third, in cross-national comparative studies it is sometimes difficult to identify functionally equivalent demands in the first instance of coding because they are expressed in different types of national language and symbols—for example, in Britain demands against discrimination are often made in a language referring to racism and minorities, whereas in Germany they refer to tolerance, solidarity, and hostility in relation to foreigners. Fourth, the use of aggregated category systems places important theoretical decisions in the proper classification of claims in the hands of coders instead of the researcher (for a similar approach, see Shapiro and Markoff 1998, 73).

The resulting data set has considerable advantages. In particular, it provides an easily accessible hierarchy of aggregated data that enables researchers to answer questions at different levels. Findings at the macrolevel of international comparison can be traced back to the most detailed level of specific claims by individual actors in relation to specific events. It therefore becomes possible to focus on specific areas of interest for more qualitative analyses or to find exemplary illustrations of general patterns.

Intercoder Reliability

Because of the two-step coding strategy that we used, the final decision on the coding of the variables that were used for the analysis was in the hands of the principal researchers themselves. Consistency among ourselves was ensured by including many examples in the common codebook as well as by regular discussions of problematic cases by e-mail and at meetings. The issue of intercoder reliability therefore does not concern the coding of variables but does concern the selection of articles for coding and the identification of claims within articles (in an earlier protest event study, we concluded that these steps were crucial to the coding process from the point of view of reliability; see Kriesi et al. 1995, 269–71). The selection of articles is the most important of these. Because we retained all the original articles, it was always possible for the principal researchers to check the identification of claims within those articles that had been selected. In some cases this indeed led to corrections. However, relevant articles that had been overlooked by the coders were lost forever from our view.

In the United Kingdom the primary coding used in this study was done by only one coder, and intercoder reliability is therefore not an issue. In Germany as many as nine different coders were involved at various stages of the project. Reliability was routinely checked in all countries after the coders had completed their training, but because of the large number of coders an additional formal reliability test was conducted in Germany about halfway through the coding. Six coders were involved in this test, which involved the scanning of two newspaper issues for relevant articles and the identification of claims within those articles. The results indicated a satisfactory level of reliability for both steps: for article selection, Cronbach's alpha was 0.95, while the respective value for claim identification within selected articles was 0.92.

Further Information

For detailed information on the variables and categories that were used for the comparative analysis, the reader can consult our common codebook, which is available online at http://ics.leeds.ac.uk/eurpolcom/research_ projects_merci.cfm. The detailed country-level raw codes are available from the authors on request (contact Koopmans for Germany and the Netherlands, Statham for the United Kingdom, and Giugni or Passy for France and Switzerland).

Notes

Introduction

1. Given the lack of complete and comparable data on immigrants and their descendants who have been naturalized or who have obtained citizenship by way of jus soli acquisition, there are no precise comparative statistics on the size of the first- and second-generation immigrant populations available. According to the data of Eurostat and Sopemi, our five countries hosted 75 percent of the foreign resident population in Western Europe (European Union plus Norway and Switzerland) in 1999. However, with France, the United Kingdom, and the Netherlands, our countries include three of the European countries with the easiest nationality acquisition and therefore large numbers of first- and second-generation immigrants who are citizens. Therefore, the share of these countries in the total immigrant population in Western Europe will be substantially higher than their share in the population of foreign residents. In absolute numbers, the Italian foreign population is larger than that in the Netherlands. However, few immigrants have naturalized in Italy so far, whereas more than half of the Dutch immigrants have done so. Including this latter group, the Netherlands clearly surpasses Italy. Including undocumented migrants—for which reliable figures are lacking—it may be that Italy has more immigrants than Switzerland, which in terms of the official number of foreigners still has a small edge over Italy.

2. There are a few examples, though, which come close to this extreme, e.g., Israel and Japan.

3. Even Brubaker (1999) now seems to share this view, and in doing so departs radically from his earlier position.

4. In its most extreme form, ethnic segregationism slides into apartheid, which

267

insists on strict separation of cultural groups while structurally privileging one cultural group over others.

5. The ultimate end of the extreme right may well be segregationism or even simply throwing immigrants out of the country. However, that is not the kind of discourse with which one can win elections in France. The insistence on cultural assimilation as a precondition to citizenship is much more resonant.

6. This definition is close to Charles Tilly's definition of contentious gatherings (1995, 63). However, our definition includes a much broader range of discursive forms and is not limited to the physical mobilization of people in a public place. Tilly's notion of the public sphere, in other words, is much narrower in that he largely ignores the media in their various forms—even though he uses them as his main source—and focuses heavily on material public places as the locus of contentious interaction.

7. Empirical evidence in favor of this assumption is provided by comparisons of data from our newspaper sources on extreme-right violence to data gathered by the police in Germany. These analyses reveal that the timing of events, as well as the targets of violence, is very similar in both data sets, even though the police data contain about twelve times as many events (see Koopmans and Rucht 2002, 248; Koopmans 2001a, 128).

8. A further important qualification we have to make is that our data represent only claims making as it is made visible in the print media and cannot be generalized to the audiovisual media, which might give us a different picture of claims-making patterns. Television news is even more selective than the print media, and this medium will obviously tend to privilege claims that can easily and recognizably be visualized and/or condensed in short sound bites. While a comparison between media types would be interesting, it is also very resource-intensive and difficult in terms of designing common measurement instruments that are comparable across media types. For our purpose of cross-national comparison, between-media-type differences are less interesting than within-media-type differences among countries.

1. Configurations of Citizenship in Five European Countries

1. While we refer in the text to the academic sources that were used, it was impossible to do so (also in order to keep the text readable) for the multitude of legal texts, media sources, and Internet Web sites that we consulted. Where we had to rely on media and Internet sources, we never relied on one single source and have included only information that was confirmed by several sources. In addition to these sources, we consulted a number of experts on the various countries, whom we asked to comment on a draft version of this chapter. We thank Gianni D'Amato, Thomas Faist, Virginie Guiraudon, Betty de Hart, and Jonathan Laurence for their

valuable comments. With the help of these colleagues, we were able to add relevant information and to correct a number of errors. Needless to say, the responsibility for any remaining flaws is entirely ours.

2. For reasons of comparability, we present here only information regarding the standard naturalization criteria. In each of the countries there may be shorter waiting times for specific groups of foreigners, e.g., spouses of nationals.

3. The old German legislation specified two different waiting times: ten years for naturalization at the discretion of the authorities, and fifteen years for naturalization "as-of-right," for which a reduced catalog of criteria applied. Since this distinction between two different legal bases is not made in most other countries, we refer here to the minimum waiting time in the old system.

4. Additional reasons for refusing naturalization are condemnation for serious criminal offences and being a threat to national security. Since these criteria apply—with some rather minor variations—in all five countries, we do not consider them here as a source of variation in citizenship regimes.

5. From 1993 to 1998, there was a brief interruption of this tradition. As part of the so-called Pasqua Law of the Chirac government, automatic attribution at majority was abolished and an option rule similar to that in the Netherlands was introduced. However, in 1998 the Socialist government reinstated the original regulation.

6. In the year 2000, 44 percent of all naturalized persons in Germany retained their original nationality (*Migration und Bevölkerung,* January 2002). In the Netherlands, this figure was as high as 76 percent, and among Turks and Moroccans even a full 100 percent (figures for the years 1998–2001 from Centraal Bureau voor de Statistiek). Thus, the actual implementation of the law is not much different from the situation between 1992 and 1997, when double nationality was formally accepted in the Netherlands. This law, however, ultimately failed to pass the Senate *(eerste Kamer).*

7. Here, as for all other indicators, information referring to the situation before reunification in 1990 applies only to West Germany. For obvious reasons, East Germany granted no special access to citizenship to ethnic Germans from its Socialist "brother countries."

8. This should not be confused with regulations for former citizens who have lost the nationality and reapply for it. These persons generally need to fulfill less strict requirements to reacquire the nationality. Because this aspect does not differentiate much among our countries, we have ignored it here.

9. In this book we refer to Britain rather than the United Kingdom, which is taken to cover England, Wales, and Scotland. Northern Ireland has specific legislation within our field of inquiry, especially with regard to religious discrimination, which is different from that applied in the remainder of the United Kingdom and

was designed in response to the religious conflicts that dominate politics in that region. Our focus is therefore on mainland Britain.

10. It is unlikely that the decline after 1996 is caused by the reinstatement of the requirement to give up one's original nationality because in actual practice it is rarely implemented. The decline in naturalizations has been most pronounced for Turks, but all Turkish applicants between 1998 and 2001 were able to retain their Turkish nationality. More likely, the reservoir of potential applicants who fulfill the criteria and are interested in the Dutch nationality is simply shrinking as a result of the huge numbers of naturalizations over the course of the 1990s.

11. Our results are similar to the index values for naturalization rules computed by scholars at the Vienna Institute for Advanced Studies (Cinar 1994; Cinar, Hofinger, and Waldrauch 1995; Waldrauch and Hofinger 1997). Their index values relating to naturalization also show Switzerland as the most restrictive case, followed by Germany, and then the three other countries relatively close to each other (Waldrauch and Hofinger 1997, 278).

12. Of course, this is not completely true, especially in France, where the automatic attribution of nationality was highly controversial during much of our reference period, and was even briefly abolished in the mid-1990s. However, this intermezzo falls outside of our reference years.

13. Waldrauch and Hofinger (1997; see also Cinar, Hofinger, and Waldrauch 1995) have made an effort to build an index for the legal rights of foreign nationals, which includes our five countries. They consider a much broader range of indicators, including residence and settlement rights, labor market access, and family reunification (political rights, however, are not included by them). Their results are quite similar to our simpler measure. The rank order in their study from most restrictive to most liberal is United Kingdom, Switzerland, Germany, France, and finally the Netherlands. This is the same as the rank order we find (see Table 3), with the exception of the position of the United Kingdom, which is positioned similar to France in our data (Waldrauch and Hofinger 1997, 278). This deviation for the United Kingdom is due, as Waldrauch and Hofinger note, to the large degree of discretion of the British authorities in the context of Britain's tradition of case law. We will see that this also plays a role in relation to expulsions. Waldrauch and Hofinger conclude that "[t]herefore, the UK, being the methodological 'problem child' in the sample, might be judged by the LOI-index as being more rigid than it really is."

14. Because it exists in a similar form everywhere, we do not deal with the rule that a residence permit may be withdrawn when it has been obtained by fraud or incorrect information.

15. In some countries (e.g., the Netherlands), the conditions discussed here are specified as part of the conditions for permit renewal or cancellation. The lack

of a valid permit is then mentioned in the law as one of the grounds for expulsion. Conversely, in other countries (e.g., Germany), expulsion grounds may be explicitly listed as such in the law, and the condition that no expulsion ground applies is added to the requirements for permit renewal or continuation. Because both juridical formulations amount to the same thing, we do not make this distinction here.

16. For an overview, see Commissione per le politiche di integrazione degli immigrati 1999.

17. Some antidiscrimination provisions also exist in German labor legislation *(Betriebsverfassungsgesetz)*. However, these are much more limited in scope than the provisions in the French Labor Code. For instance, the German law protects only against discrimination of those who are already employed, not against discrimination in access to employment (Niessen and Chopin 2002, report on Germany).

18. See http://www.justice.gouv.fr/publicat/gnationae.htm: "le préfet ou le consulat vous convoquera pour évaluer votre assimilation aux mœurs et aux usages de la France et votre connaissance du français. Il fait également procéder à une enquête sur votre conduite et votre loyalisme."

19. Only the cantons of Geneva and Neuenburg have implemented a strict separation of church and state comparable with France. In many other cantons, the Protestant and Catholic churches—and in some also the Jewish community—are officially recognized by the cantonal authorities, who may even levy church taxes as in Germany.

20. Jews do have separate graveyards in both countries, but these are privately funded. Obviously, Jews can also be buried in public graveyards, but not in a separate section.

21. We considered two other indicators but did not use them in the end because they revealed little variation among our countries. The first concerns classes in immigrant languages and culture. These can be found in all five countries although the Netherlands abolished them in 2004. A relevant difference is that in France, the United Kingdom, and Switzerland such classes are not funded by the state but by the countries of origin or the immigrant community. In the Netherlands and in some German *Länder,* the state covers all the costs. The second indicator we did not use is the right of policewomen to wear the headscarf. This has recently been allowed in the United Kingdom, but in none of the other countries. Including or excluding these two indicators has only a marginal impact on the resulting summary scores for cultural rights in public institutions because they go in the same direction as the other five indicators.

22. Bavaria and North-Rhine-Westphalia offer a surrogate form of religious education. In Bavaria, Turkish pupils can follow classes organized in cooperation with the Turkish authorities, which include Islamic religious instruction. The classes in North-Rhine-Westphalia are likewise geared toward Turkish pupils, but

are organized by the regular education authorities and offer information about Islam, rather than religious instruction.

2. Beyond the Nation-State?

1. Hammar (1985) has coined the term "denizens" to capture the particular status of these permanently resident noncitizens.

2. Here and in all subsequent cross-national tables throughout the book, we will not substantively interpret the differences in the total numbers of cases among the countries. As we know from other comparative project contexts where we used newspapers as a source (Kriesi et al. 1995; Koopmans and Statham 2002), there are important differences between countries in the style of newspaper reporting. German newspapers, in particular, are very fact-oriented and report basic information on many events without elaborating most of them in detail. British newspapers provide the clearest contrast. While a typical German newspaper article may contain dozens of claims, British articles tend to be centered around one or a few claims but develop those in more detail. As a result, we find far fewer events reported in British than in German newspapers, without this implying that there are any real differences in the intensity of public controversy. Of course, it is possible—even probable—that the total numbers of cases found in our sources also reflect real differences in the weight of immigration and ethnic relations in the public debate. It is, however, impossible to disentangle this from the effect of newspaper style. We therefore compare only the percentage shares of claims across countries and ignore differences in absolute numbers.

3. The difference between discrimination claims and antiracist claims is that the latter refer to overt abuse or violence, whereas discrimination claims refer to hidden or structural sources of inequality. Our use of the term "racism" here is thus more narrowly circumscribed to abuse and violence in the public domain than it often is in common parlance. In our coding, it is not the language used in the claim that is decisive, but whether the claim refers to a structural context of inequality, in which case it belongs to integration politics, or whether it relates to a real or perceived instance of abuse or violence, in which case it belongs to racism and xenophobia. For example, claims against "institutional racism" of the police in Britain could arise in relation to either of these contexts.

4. There are a few transnational newspapers catering to business elites, such as the *Financial Times*. While these might be relevant for public debates on economic issues, they hardly play a role for debates on immigration and ethnic relations.

5. Claims with a supranational scope of reference are the only nonnational type where the percentage shares are generally lower in Table 16 than in Table 14. This is due to the decision to code national branches of international NGOs such as Amnesty International as supranational actors, even if they act entirely within a national context.

6. Of course, multileveling of claims can also occur within the nation-state context if claims simultaneously have national, regional, and local dimensions. In our coding, we have not systematically distinguished these different scopes within the national context. For the present discussion, however, it is irrelevant to what extent multilevel claims making occurs within the national context.

3. Migrants between Transnationalism and National Citizenship

This chapter draws significantly from Koopmans and Statham 2003.

1. Strictly speaking, the Moluccan and Cuban examples do not completely fit the definition because these groups are largely concentrated in just one receiving state, the Netherlands and the United States respectively.

2. Of course, the issue is even more complex because migrants may additionally identify along gender, class, caste, or occupational lines, which we ignore here for the sake of brevity and simplicity.

3. We count exile organizations (e.g., the National Resistance Council of Iran) and branches of homeland organizations (e.g., the PKK, Milli Görüş, or the Algerian FIS) as homeland-based organizations, even if they are sometimes banned in the homeland.

4. There are small groups of Muslims who are of Surinamese and Indonesian descent, but more than 90 percent of Dutch Muslims come from Morocco, Turkey, and other Asian and African countries.

4. Minority Group Demands and the Challenge of Islam

This chapter builds on the insights developed in earlier research (Statham and Koopmans 2005a, 2005b; Statham et al. 2005), and the authors are grateful for discussions with and comments by Jonathan Laurence throughout this research.

1. This definition bears similarities to that for "minority rights" used by Kymlicka and Norman (2000, 2), with the important difference that they require a state's recognition and political accommodation of identities and needs of migrant groups to be "intentional." Against this, group-specific state provisions can often simply be an extension (even reluctant) of existing arrangements almost by default to new migrant groups. Our definition is less normative than Kymlicka and Norman's and does not require (good) "intention" by the state.

2. In England and Wales, about 7,000 of the 25,000 schools are faith schools that receive state support. In 2002, there were 4,716 Church of England, 2,110 Roman Catholic, 27 Methodist, 32 Jewish, 4 Muslim, 2 Sikh, 1 Seventh Day Adventist, and 1 Greek Orthodox faith schools. It is only in the last couple of years that this funding status has been granted to Muslims.

3. According to the definition in our coding, claims become categorized as group demands only when they request group-specific provisions or exemptions

relating to cultural or religious difference. For example, this means that not all demands by Muslim groups in the education domain are necessarily group demands. Unless the claim is for a special provision for Muslims within the education system that is based on cultural or religious difference—e.g., for Islamic faith religious lessons—then the demand is just for greater participation in education and is coded as a type of demand for rights of social equality.

4. From a policy perspective, Joppke and Morawska (2003) also argue that academic debates have overstated the scale of multiculturalism with respect to migrants in Western Europe.

5. Collective identities are measured in the same way as in chapter 3.

6. After this important dominance of Muslim identifications, we see that at a secondary level there is evidence for overall national differences along the lines discussed in chapter 3. These will not be repeated. Another group-specific exception that deserves mention, however, is the Harki, who make a fifth (20.4 percent) of group demands in France. The Harki are Muslims, although—apparently unlike other Muslim groups—this is not the primary identity they choose to use to make group demands. This exceptional behavior is best explained by national context. The French state extends special recognition to this group of migrants who are descendants of soldiers who fought for *la patrie* in her colonial war against Algeria and immigrated to the Motherland after the war ended in defeat. Groups like the aptly named Justice pour les Harkis (Justice for the Harkis) use what they perceive as a special recognized group status as a legitimating resource to make demands that set them apart from other migrant groups.

7. More detailed country-specific information on the positions of Muslims and Islam can be found in Laurence 2003 for France; Rath et al. 1999 for the Netherlands; and Statham 2003a for Britain.

8. A case of blasphemy against Christianity had been successfully prosecuted as recently as 1979, against a poem asserting that Christ was a homosexual. The failure of the blasphemy cases against Rushdie was therefore not due to the secularization rendering blasphemy law archaic.

9. Such laws with respect to religious discrimination are in force only in Northern Ireland in an attempt to combat the conflicts along confessional lines between Protestants and Catholics there.

10. In *Mandla v. Dowell-Lee* (1983), a head teacher's refusal to allow a Sikh boy to wear a turban in school was successfully challenged under the Race Relations Act, and it was established that Sikhs and by extension Jews were ethnic groups. Note the parallel to the Muslim headscarf here.

11. This framing is interesting because it tries to include Islam as a category within the Race Relations framework by conflating the secular status of racial minority with that of a religious faith group. See, for example, the reports by the

Runnymede Trust on Islamophobia (1997) and the Parekh report on "the future of multi-ethnic Britain" (2000).

12. In the Dutch case, this is not an exceptional group rights demand because it is a right that is already extended, for example, to the Reformed and Calvinist denominations of Dutch Protestants.

13. This is the case even though our sample starts in 1992, a few years after the fatwa was issued against Rushdie (1989), which underlines the resonance of this case for Britain.

14. This case is the only group demand in our British sample that is not by Muslims of Indian subcontinent origin. Although scholars of religion often do not include Louis Farrakhan's Nation of Islam movement as a form of Islamic belief (e.g., Robinson 1997), our selection criteria is on how groups label themselves and are visible in the public domain, which necessitates inclusion. The Nation of Islam movement has been imported from the United States to Britain and finds support among some sections of the African Caribbean community.

15. The name of this organization, the Muslim Parliament, is somewhat misleading because it is neither a broad-based nor a representative organization of Muslims in Britain. It is entirely nominated and self-selected and exists as a forum for expression of more radical forms of Islam and for ideas that suggest secession, or at least isolation, from British society (Rex 2002).

16. Asked whether they thought of themselves as British, 66 percent of Pakistani and 60 percent of Bangladeshi minorities (predominantly Muslim) answered in the affirmative, compared to 62 percent of Indian (predominantly Hindu) and 64 percent of Caribbean minorities (Modood et al. 1997, 329).

5. The Extreme Right

This chapter draws on Giugni, Koopmans, Passy, and Statham 2005.

1. The immigration rate is calculated as the average number of nonnational immigrants per one thousand inhabitants for the 1992–98 period. The unemployment rate is also averaged over the 1992–98 period. The summary indicator of objective conditions is the rounded sum of the other three indicators. See European System of Social Indicators (immigration rate and unemployment rate); British Office for National Statistics (immigration rate for Britain); and UK Labour Force Survey (unemployment rate for Britain).

2. Average percentage of votes over three legislatures in the 1990s (France: 1989, 1993, and 1997; Switzerland: 1991, 1995, 1999; Germany: 1990, 1994, 1998; Netherlands: 1989, 1994, 1998).

3. The stunning success of the populist list headed by charismatic Pim Fortuyn in the Dutch elections in June 2002 apparently goes against the traditionally low scores of extreme-right parties in this country. This suggests that in the Netherlands

the marginalization of these parties has not lasted and that, in this situation, there are opportunities for the emergence of parties that have a populist appeal, even if the prevailing configuration of citizenship tends to delegitimize such parties and therefore is not favorable to them. However, one of the main arguments of this chapter is that the emergence of the extreme right largely depends on the political space made available to it by the policy positions of mainstream parties. Thus, the recent success of the populist right in the Netherlands might be due to the political space left open by other parties in the competition among them. In addition, in this specific case, its success was probably enhanced by the fact that the party leader was killed just nine days before the elections, which might have produced a martyr effect and hence boosted the vote for this party. At the same time, however, its success was short-lived, as internal struggles undermined its capacity to offer a coherent policy program, and today its appeal has largely waned.

4. Correlations between the four measures of objective conditions (the three basic measures and the summary indicator, not rounded) and the percentage of votes by extreme-right parties in the five countries (assuming the percentage in Britain to equal 1) are the following: 0.29 (share of population of migrant origin), −0.02 (immigration rate), 0.24 (unemployment rate), and 0.29 (summary indicator).

5. To do so, we first computed the average discursive positions of all political parties on issues pertaining to immigration and ethnic relations on a scale going from −1 (for all claims whose realization implies a deterioration in the rights or position of migrants and claims that express, verbally or physically, a negative attitude with regard to migrants or a positive attitude with regard to xenophobic and extreme-right groups or aims) to 1 (for all claims whose realization implies an improvement in the rights or position of migrants and claims that express, verbally or physically, a positive attitude with regard to migrants or a negative attitude with regard to xenophobic and extreme-right groups or aims). This provides us with a general indicator of the position of claims with regard to the rights, position, and evaluation of immigrants and ethnic minorities (and of those who mobilize against them). Both verbal and nonverbal claims are taken into account to determine their position. Neutral or ambivalent claims are coded 0.

6. In the case of Switzerland, we also give positions by considering the Swiss People's Party (SVP) as an extreme-right party (shown between parentheses in the table). The SVP was originally a center-right agrarian party but has recently moved to the right, especially in the German-speaking part of the country, and has often taken a particularly tough position against immigrants and asylum seekers. In this case, the most anti-immigrant party in Switzerland is the Free Democratic Party (FDP).

7. It is important to point out that the distributions shown in this table are based on the assumption that the amount of claims by actors other than the ex-

treme right outside the field of immigration and ethnic relations is the same, since they have been coded only for extreme-right actors.

8. In doing so, we assume that most unknown actors are other organizations and groups rather than parties. Given that parties are usually reported as actors by newspapers, this assumption seems plausible.

9. Again, Kriesi et al.'s approach would predict a radical action repertoire of the extreme right in France, an intermediate-radical one in Germany, an intermediate-moderate one in the Netherlands, and a moderate one in Switzerland (1995, 44), to which we may add an intermediate-moderate repertoire in Britain (due to the combination of closed formal institutional structures and an inclusive prevailing strategy of the authorities). In this perspective, the closed opportunities available to social movements in France, in terms of institutionalized access to the political system and in terms of propensity of the authorities toward repression, contrast with the openness existing in Switzerland. Germany, Britain, and the Netherlands in this respect are intermediate cases. As a result of these differences in the general opportunity structures, the claims making of the extreme right should be quite radical in France, moderate in Switzerland, and somewhere in between in the other three countries.

10. Often the extreme right marks its presence in the field of immigration and ethnic relations by pronouncing general anti-immigrant statements or acting violently against migrants. As we can see in the table, this kind of behavior varies greatly from one country to another. Unspecific xenophobic claims are very frequent in the Netherlands (62.8 percent of all claims by the extreme right), in Britain (62.9 percent), and especially in Germany (84.5 percent), while they are less often used in Switzerland (35.4 percent) and especially France (19.7 percent). As a result, the share of extreme-right claims dealing with antiracism and xenophobia also varies across countries (97.0 percent in Germany; 89.1 percent in the Netherlands; 88.6 percent in Britain; 66.4 percent in France; and 53.1 percent in Switzerland), which explains the difference between the distributions concerning the whole political field and those taking into account only the two more institutionalized issues fields.

6. Interest or Identity?

1. For a discussion of political altruism and the application of the concept to several different national and case studies of social movements, see the contributions to Giugni and Passy 2001.

2. "La force de l'action antiraciste est de s'inscrire dans l'espace public en plaidant de manière universelle, au nom de principes généraux."

3. We coded only eight incidents of antiracist violence in a period of seven years.

4. The MRAP campaign is titled "Caravanne de la citoyenneté."

7. Contested Citizenship

1. De Zwart (2002) calls such policy categories "avoidant," because they are meant to inhibit the official recognition of a potentially endless number of ethnic and cultural categories while retaining the possibility to implement antidiscrimination and equal opportunity policies on an encompassing basis.

2. Joppke and Morawska (2003, 8) make a similar distinction between de facto multiculturalism and official multiculturalism.

3. Mollenkopf (2000) arrives at similar conclusions when comparing the socioeconomic situation of immigrants living in Amsterdam and in New York City.

4. For more detail on this, see Statham 2003a.

5. The Cantle report, "Community Cohesion: A Report of the Independent Review Team," by the Community Cohesion Unit, January 1, 2003, can be downloaded in full at http://www.homeoffice.gov.uk/docs2/comm_cohesion.html. Also see "Secure Borders, Safe Havens: Integration with Diversity in Modern Britain," presented to Parliament by the secretary of state for the Home Department, February 2002, Cm5387; and Guild and Harlow 2001.

Appendix

1. Unfortunately, object actors and frames were not consistently coded across all countries and years. We have therefore not used these variables in the comparative analyses in this book. For an analysis using the frame variable for the German case, see Koopmans 2001b; and for the British, Statham 2001a, 2001b.

2. For Germany and Britain we have data for the full decade 1990–99, but resource constraints did not allow us to achieve this aim for the other three countries. The full French and Swiss data cover 1990–98, the full Dutch data cover 1992–99.

References

Alsayyad, N., and M. Castells, eds. 2002. *Muslim Europe or Euro-Islam: Politics, Culture, and Citizenship in the Age of Globalization.* Oxford, UK: Lexington.

Ålund, Alexsandra, and Carl-Ulrik Schierup. 1991. *Paradoxes of Multiculturalism: Essays on Swedish Society.* Aldershot, UK: Avebury.

Backes, Uwe, and Patrick Moreau. 1993. *Die extreme Rechte in Deutschland.* Munich: Akademische Verlag.

Barth, Fredrik. 1969. *Ethnic Groups and Boundaries.* Boston: Little, Brown.

Basch, L., N. Glick Schiller, and C. Szanton Blanc. 1994. *Nations Unbound: Transnationalized Projects and the Deterritorialized Nation-State.* New York: Gordon and Breach.

Bauböck, R. 1994. "Changing the Boundaries of Citizenship." In *From Aliens to Citizens: Redefining the Status of Migrants in Europe,* ed. R. Bauböck, 199–232. Aldershot, UK: Avebury.

———. 1995. *Transnational Citizenship: Membership and Rights in International Migration.* Aldershot, UK: Edward Elgar.

———. 1996. "Cultural Minority Rights for Immigrants." *International Migration Review* 30, no. 1: 203–50.

Beauftragte der Bundesregierung für Ausländerfragen. 2001. *Mehrsprachigkeit an deutschen Schulen im Länderüberblick.* Berlin: Innenministerium.

Belanger, Sarah, and Maurice Pinard. 1989. "Ethnic Movements and the Competition Model: Some Missing Links." *American Sociological Review* 56: 446–57.

Betz, Hans-Georg. 1993. "The New Politics of Resentment: Radical Right-Wing Populist Parties in Western Europe." *Comparative Politics* 25: 413–27.

Bousetta, Hassan. 1996. "Citizenship and Political Participation in France and the Netherlands: Reflections on Two Local Cases." *New Community* 23, no. 3: 215–31.

Brubaker, Rogers. 1992. *Citizenship and Nationhood in France and Germany.* Cambridge, MA: Harvard University Press.

———. 1999. "The Manichean Myth: Rethinking the Distinction between 'Civic' and 'Ethnic' Nationalism." In *Nation and National Identity: The European Experience in Perspective,* ed. Hanspeter Kriesi et al., 55–71. Zurich: Ruegger, 1999.

———. 2003. "The Return of Assimilation? Changing Perspectives on Immigration and Its Sequels in France, Germany, and the United States." In *Toward Assimilation and Citizenship: Immigrants in Liberal Nation-States,* ed. Christian Joppke and Ewa Morawska, 39–58. New York: Palgrave Macmillan.

Calhoun, Craig. 1997. *Nationalism: Concepts in Social Thought.* Minneapolis: University of Minnesota Press.

Canovan, Margaret. 1996. *Nationhood and Political Theory.* Cheltenham, UK: Edward Elgar.

Castles, Stephen. 1995. "How Nation-States Respond to Immigration and Ethnic Diversity." *New Community* 21: 293–308.

———. 2000. *Ethnicity and Globalization.* London: Sage.

Castles, Stephen, and Mark Miller. 1993. *The Age of Migration: International Population Movements in the Modern World.* London: Macmillan.

CBS (Centraal Bureau voor de Statistiek). 2001. *Allochtonen in Nederland.* Voorburg/Heerlen: CBS.

Cinar, Dilek. 1994. *From Aliens to Citizens: A Comparative Analysis of Rules of Transition.* Vienna: Institute for Advanced Studies.

Cinar, Dilek, Christoph Hofinger, and Harald Waldrauch. 1995. *Integrationsindex: Zur rechtlichen Integration von AusländerInnen in ausgewählten europäischen Ländern.* Vienna: Institute for Advanced Studies.

Cohen, Jean L. 1985. "'Strategy or Identity': New Theoretical Paradigms and Contemporary Social Movements." *Social Research* 59: 663–717.

———. 1999. "Changing Paradigms of Citizenship and the Exclusiveness of the Demos." *International Sociology* 14, no. 3: 245–68.

Cohen, R. 1997. *Global Diasporas: An Introduction.* London: UCL Press.

Commissione per le politiche di integrazione degli immigrati. 1999. *Partecipazione e rappresentanza politica degli immigrati.* Rome: Dipartimento per gli affari sociali.

Cornelius, Wayne, Philip Martin, and James Hollifield, eds. 1994. *Controlling Immigration: A Global Perspective.* Stanford, CA: Stanford University Press.

Davy, Ulrike, ed. 2001. *Die Integration von Einwanderern: Rechtliche Regelungen im europäischen Vergleich.* Frankfurt: Campus.

Davy, Ulrike, and Dilek Cinar. 2001. "Ausgewählte Europäische Rechtsordnungen: Vereinigtes Königreich." In *Die Integration von Einwanderern: Rechtliche Regelungen im europäischen Vergleich*, ed. Davy, 795–924. Frankfurt: Campus.

De Zwart, Frank. 2002. "Administrative Categories and Ethnic Diversity: The Dilemma of Recognition." Unpublished manuscript, Leiden University.

Donati, Paolo. 1992. "Political Discourse and Collective Action." In *Studying Collective Actors*, ed. Ron Eyerman and Mario Diani, 136–67. London: Sage.

Duyvendak, Jan Willem. 1994. *Le poids du politique*. Paris: L'Harmattan.

Duyvené de Wit, Thom, and Ruud Koopmans. 2001. "Die politisch-kulturelle Integration ethnischer Minderheiten in den Niederlanden und Deutschland." *Forschungsjournal Neue Soziale Bewegungen* 14, no. 1: 10–25.

Elbers, Frank, and Meindert Fennema. 1993. *Racistische partijen in West-Europa*. Leiden: Stichting Burgerschapskunde.

Entzinger, Han. 2000. "The Dynamics of Integration Policies: A Multidimensional Model." In *Challenging Immigration and Ethnic Relations Politics: Comparative European Perspectives*, ed. Ruud Koopmans and Paul Statham, 97–118. New York: Oxford University Press.

———. 2003. "The Rise and Fall of Multiculturalism: The Case of the Netherlands." In *Toward Assimilation and Citizenship: Immigrants in Liberal Nation-States*, ed. Christian Joppke and Ewa Morawska, 59–86. New York: Palgrave Macmillan.

Faist, Thomas. 1995. "Boundaries of Welfare States: Immigrants and Social Rights on the National and Supranational Level." In *Migration and European Integration: The Dynamics of Inclusion and Exclusion*, ed. R. Miles and D. Thränhardt. London: Pinter.

———. 1997. "Immigration, Citizenship, and Nationalism: Internal Internationalization in Germany and Europe." In *European Citizenship and Social Exclusion*, ed. Maurice Roche and Rik van Berkel. Aldershot, UK: Ashgate.

Favell, Adrian. 1998. *Philosophies of Integration: Immigration and the Idea of Citizenship in France and Britain*. Houndmills, Basingstoke, UK: Macmillan.

Favell, Adrian, and A. Geddes. 2000. "Immigration and European Integration: New Opportunities for Transnational Mobilization?" In *Challenging Immigration and Ethnic Relations Politics: Comparative European Perspective*, ed. Ruud Koopmans and Paul Statham, 407–28. Oxford: Oxford University Press.

Fennema, Meindert. 2000. "Legal Repression of Extreme-Right Parties and Racial Discrimination." In *Challenging Immigration and Ethnic Relations Politics: Comparative European Perspectives*, ed. Ruud Koopmans and Paul Statham, 119–44. Oxford: Oxford University Press.

Fennema, Meindert, and Jean Tillie. 1999. "Political Participation and Political

Trust in Amsterdam: Civic Communities and Ethnic Networks." *Journal of Ethnic and Migration Studies* 25, no. 4: 703–26.

Ferree, Myra Marx, William A. Gamson, Jürgen Gerhards, and Dieter Rucht. 2002. *Shaping Abortion Discourse: Democracy and the Public Sphere in Germany and the United States.* Cambridge: Cambridge University Press.

Flanagan, Scott C. 1987. "Value Change in Industrial Society." *American Political Science Review* 81: 1303–19.

Franzosi, Roberto. 2004. *From Words to Numbers: A Journey in the Methodology of Social Science.* Cambridge: Cambridge University Press.

Freeman, G. P. 1995. "Modes of Immigration Politics in Liberal Democratic States." *International Migration Review* 29, no. 4: 881–902.

Freeman, G. P., and N. Oegelman. 1998. "Homeland Citizenship Policies and the Status of Third Country Nationals in the European Union." *Journal of Ethnic and Migration Studies* 24, no. 4: 769–88.

Galtung, Johan, and Marie Homboe Ruge. 1965. "The Structure of Foreign News: The Presentation of the Congo, Cuba, and Cyprus Crises in Four Norwegian Newspapers." *Journal of Peace Research* 2: 64–91.

Gamson, W. A. 1975. *The Strategy of Social Protest.* Homewood, IL: Dorsey Press.

———. 1988. *The Strategy of Social Protest, 2nd ed.* Homewood, IL: Dorsey Press.

———. 1992. "Media Images and the Social Construction of Reality." *Annual Review of Sociology* 18: 373–93.

Gamson, W. A., and Andre Modigliani. 1989. "Media Discourse and Public Opinion on Nuclear Power: A Constructionist Approach." *American Journal of Sociology* 95: 1–38.

Garbaye, Romain. 2000. "Ethnic Minorities, Cities, and Institutions: A Comparison of the Modes of Management of Ethnic Diversity of a French and a British City." In *Challenging Immigration and Ethnic Relations Politics: Comparative European Perspectives,* ed. Ruud Koopmans and Paul Statham, 283–311. Oxford: Oxford University Press.

Gessenharter, Wolfgang, and Helmut Fröchling, eds. 1998. *Rechtsextremismus und Neue Rechte in Deutschland: Neuvermessung eines politisch-ideologischen Raumes?* Opladen, Germany: Leske + Budrich.

Gilbert, P. 1998. *Philosophy of Nationalism.* Boulder, CO: Westview Press.

Gitlin, Todd. 1980. *The Whole World Is Watching: Mass Media in the Making and Unmaking of the New Left.* Berkeley and Los Angeles: University of California Press.

Giugni, Marco, Ruud Koopmans, Florence Passy, and Paul Statham. 2005. "Institutional and Discursive Opportunities for Extreme-Right Mobilization in Five Countries." *Mobilization: International Journal of Research and Theory about Social Movements, Protest, and Collective Behavior* 10, no. 1 (December): 145–62.

Giugni, Marco, and Florence Passy, eds. 2001. *Political Altruism?* Boulder, CO: Rowman and Littlefield.

Giugni, Marco, and Paul Statham. 2002. "The Contentious Politics of Unemployment in Europe: Political Claim-making, Policy Deliberation, and Exclusion from the Labor Market; A Research Outline." European Political Communication Working Paper Series. Issue 2/02: 36. Leeds: ISSN 1477-1365. At http://ics.leeds.ac.uk/eurpolcom/exhibits/paper2.pdf.

Glazer, Nathan. 1997. *We Are All Multiculturalists Now.* Cambridge, MA: Harvard University Press.

Greenfeld, Liah. 1992. *Nationalism: Five Roads to Modernity.* Cambridge, MA: Harvard University Press.

Griffin, Roger. 1992. "Fascism." In *The Blackwell Dictionary of Twentieth-Century Social Thought.* Oxford: Blackwell.

Groenendijk, Kees, and Elspeth Guild. 2001. "Converging Criteria: Creating an Area of Security of Residence for Europe's Third Country Nationals." *European Journal of Migration and Law* 3: 37–59.

Groenendijk, Kees, Elspeth Guild, and Robin Barzilay. 2000. *The Legal Status of Third Country Nationals Who Are Long-Term Residents in a Member State of the European Union.* Strasbourg: Council of Europe.

Guarnizo, L. E., and M. P. Smith. 1998. "The Locations of Transnationalism." In *Transnationalism from Below,* ed. M. P. Smith and L. E. Guarnizo, 3–34. New Brunswick, NJ: Transaction.

Guild, Elspeth, and Carol Harlow, eds. 2001. *Implementing Amsterdam: Immigration and Asylum Rights in EC Law.* Oxford: Hart.

Guiraudon, Virginie. 1998. "Citizenship Rights for Non-Citizens: France, Germany, and the Netherlands." In *Challenge to the Nation-State: Immigration in Western Europe and the United States,* ed. Christian Joppke. Oxford: Oxford University Press.

———. 2000. *Les politiques d'immigration en Europe.* Paris: L'Harmattan/ Logiques Politiques.

Gurr, Ted R. 1970. *Why Men Rebel.* Princeton, NJ: Princeton University Press.

Gutmann, A., ed. 1994. *Multiculturalism.* Princeton, NJ: Princeton University Press.

Haddad Yazbeck, Yvonne, and J. L. Esposito, eds. 2000. *Muslims on the Americanization Path?* Oxford: Oxford University Press.

Haddad Yazbeck, Yvonne, and J. I. Smith, eds. 2002. *Muslim Minorities in the West: Visible and Invisible.* Oxford: Altamira Press.

Hailbronner, Kay. 1995. "Third-Country Nationals and EC Law." In *A Citizens' Europe: In Search of a New Order,* ed. Allen Rosas and Esco Antola. London: Sage.

Hailbronner, Kay, and Günter Renner. 1998. *Staatsangehörigkeitsrecht.* Munich: Beck.

Hainsworth, Paul. 1992. "Introduction: The Cutting Edge; The Extreme Right in Post-War Western Europe and the USA." In *The Extreme Right in Europe and the USA,* ed. Paul Hainsworth. New York: St. Martin's Press.

Hammar, Tomas, ed. 1985. *European Immigration Policy.* Cambridge: Cambridge University Press.

Heijs, Eric. 1995. *Van Vreemdeling tot Nederlander: De verlening van het Nederlanderschap aan vreemdelingen, 1813–1992.* Amsterdam: Het Spinhuis.

Heitmeyer, Wilhelm. 1992. *Rechtsextremistische Orientierungen bei Jugendlichen.* Munich: Juventa.

Heitmeyer, Wilhelm, et al. 1992. *Die Bielefelder Rechtsextremismus-Studie.* Munich: Juventa.

Held, David. 1996. "The Decline of the Nation State." In *Becoming National: A Reader,* ed. Geoff Eley and Reonald Grigor Suny. Oxford: Oxford University Press.

Held, David, Anthony McGrew, David Goldblatt, and Jonathan Perraton. 1999. *Global Transformations: Politics, Economics, and Culture.* Stanford, CA: Stanford University Press.

Hiro, Dilip. 1991. *Black British, White British.* London: Grafton Books.

Hobsbawm, E. J. 1990. *Nation and Nationalism since 1780: Programme, myth, reality.* Cambridge, UK: Cambridge University Press.

Hocke, Peter. 1998. "Determining the Selection Bias in Local and National Newspaper Reports on Protest Events." In *Acts of Dissent: New Developments in the Study of Protest,* ed. Dieter Rucht, Ruud Koopmans, and Friedhelm Neidhardt, 131–63. Berlin: Edition Sigma.

Hollifield, James F. 1992. *Immigrants, Markets, and States: The Political Economy of Postwar Europe.* Cambridge, MA: Harvard University Press.

Hunter, S. T., ed. 2002. *Islam, Europe's Second Religion: The New Social, Cultural, and Political Landscape.* Westport, CT: Praeger.

Huntington, S. P. 2002. *The Clash of Civilizations and the Remaking of World Order.* London: Free Press.

Ignazi, Piero. 1992. "The Silent Counter-Revolution: Hypotheses on the Emergence of Right-Wing Parties in Europe." *European Journal of Political Research* 22: 1–30.

Imig, Doug, and Sidney Tarrow, eds. 2001. *Contentious Europeans: Protest and Politics in an Emerging Polity.* Lanham, MD: Rowman & Littlefield.

Ireland, Patrick. 1994. *The Policy Challenge of Ethnic Diversity: Immigrant Politics in France and Switzerland.* Cambridge, MA: Harvard University Press.

———. 2000. "Reaping What They Sow: Institutions and Immigrant Political Particpation in Western Europe." In *Challenging Immigration and Ethnic Relations Politics: Comparative European Perspectives,* ed. R. Koopmans and P. Statham, 233–82. Oxford: Oxford University Press.

Jacobson, D. 1996. *Rights across Borders: Immigration and the Decline of Citizenship.* Baltimore, MD: Johns Hopkins University Press.

Jenkins, Craig, and Charles Perrow. 1977. "The Insurgency of the Powerless: Farm Workers Movements (1946–1972)." *American Sociological Review* 42: 249–68.

Jenkins, Brian, and Spyros A. Sofos, eds. 1996. *Nation and Identity in Contemporary Europe.* London: Routledge.

Joppke, Christian. 1996. "Multiculturalism and Immigration: A Comparison of the United States, Germany, and Great Britain." *Theory and Society* 25: 449–500.

———. 1997. "Asylum and State Sovereignty: A Comparison of the United States, Germany, and Britain." *Comparative Political Studies* 30, no. 3: 259–98.

———, ed. 1998. *Challenge to the Nation-State: Immigration in Western Europe and the United States.* Oxford: Oxford University Press.

———. 1999. *Immigration and the Nation-State: The United States, Germany, and Great Britain.* New York: Oxford University Press.

Joppke, Christian, and Steven Lukes, eds. 1999. *Multicultural Questions.* Oxford: Oxford University Press.

Joppke, Christian, and Eva Morawska. 2003. "Integrating Immigrants in Liberal Nation-States: Policies and Practices." In *Toward Assimilation and Citizenship: Immigrants in Liberal Nation-States,* ed. Christian Joppke and Ewa Morawska. London: Palgrave Macmillan.

Kitschelt, Herbert. 1986. "Political Opportunity Structures and Political Protest: Anti-Nuclear Movements in Four Democracies." *British Journal of Political Science* 16: 57–85.

———. 1995. In collaboration with Anthony J. McGann. *The Radical Right in Western Europe.* Ann Arbor: University of Michigan Press.

Kleger, Heinz, ed. 1997. *Transnationale Staatsbürgerschaft.* Frankfurt am Main: Campus.

Kleger, Heinz, and Gianni D'Amato. 1995. "Staatsbürgerschaft und Einbürgerung— oder: Wer ist ein Bürger? Ein Vergleich zwischen Deutschland, Frankreich, und der Schweiz." *Journal für Sozialforschung* 35, no. 3/4: 259–98.

Koopmans, Ruud. 1996a. "Explaining the Rise of Racist and Extreme Right Violence in Western Europe: Grievances or Opportunities?" *European Journal of Political Research* 30: 185–216.

———. 1996b. "New Social Movements and Changes in Political Participation in Western Europe." *West European Politics* 19, no. 1: 28–50.

———. 1999. "Germany and Its Immigrants: An Ambivalent Relationship." *Journal of Ethnic and Migration Studies* 25, no. 4: 627–47.

———. 2001a. "Alter Rechtsextremismus und neue Fremdenfeindlichkeit. Mobilisierung am rechten Rand im Wandel." In *Protest in der Bundesrepublik. Strukturen, und Entwicklungen,* ed. Dieter Rucht, 103–42. Frankfurt: Campus.

———. 2001b. "Better Off by Doing Good: Why Antiracism Must Mean

Different Things to Different Groups." In *Political Altruism?*, ed. Marco Giugni and Florence Passy, 111–31. Boulder, CO: Rowman and Littlefield.

———. 2003a. "Good Intentions Sometimes Make Bad Policy: A Comparison of Dutch and German Integration Policies." In *The Challenge of Diversity: European Social Democracy Facing Migration, Integration, and Multiculturalism*, ed. René Cuperus, Karl A. Duffek, and Johannes Kandel, 163–68. Innsbruck, Austria: StudienVerlag.

———. 2003b. "Het Nederlandse integratiebeleid in internationaal vergelijkend perspectief: Etnische segregatie onder de multicultureel oppervlakte." In *Politiek in de multiculturele samenleving*, ed. Huib Pellikaan and Margo Trappenburg, 64–100. Meppel, Netherlands: Boom.

———. 2004a. "Migrant Mobilization and Political Opportunities: Variation among German Cities and Regions in Cross-National Perspective." *Journal of Ethnic and Migration Studies* 30: 449–70.

———. 2004b. "Movements and Media: Selection Processes and Evolutionary Dynamics in the Public Sphere." *Theory and Society* 33, no. 3–4.

———. 2004c. "Protest in Time and Space: The Evolution of Waves of Contention." In *The Blackwell Companion to Social Movements*, ed. David A. Snow, Sarah A. Soule, and Hanspeter Kriesi, 19–46. Malden, MA: Blackwell.

Koopmans, Ruud, and Hanspeter Kriesi. 1997. "Citoyenneté, identité nationale, et mobilisation de l'extrême droite: Une comparaison entre la France, l'Allemagne, les Pays-Bas et la Suisse." In *Sociologie des nationalismes*, ed. Pierre Birnbaum. Paris: Presses Universitaires de France.

Koopmans, Ruud, and Susan Olzak. 2004. "Discursive Opportunities and the Evolution of Right-Wing Violence in Germany." *American Journal of Sociology* 110.

Koopmans, Ruud, and Dieter Rucht. 2002. "Protest Event Analysis." In *Methods of Social Movement Research*, ed. Bert Klandermans and Suzanne Staggenborg, 231–59. Minneapolis: University of Minnesota Press.

Koopmans, Ruud, and Paul Statham. 1999a. "Challenging the Liberal Nation-State? Postnationalism, Multiculturalism, and the Collective Claims Making of Migrants and Ethnic Minorities in Britain and Germany." *American Journal of Sociology* 105, no. 3: 652–96.

———. 1999b. "Ethnic and Civic Conceptions of Nationhood and the Differential Success of the Extreme Right in Germany and Italy." In *How Social Movements Matter*, ed. Marco Giugni, Doug McAdam, and Charles Tilly. Minneapolis: University of Minnesota Press.

———. 1999c. "Political Claims-Making against Racism and Discrimination in Britain and Germany." In *Comparative Perspectives on Racism*, ed. Jessika ter Wal and Maykel Verkuyten, 139–70. Aldershot, UK: Ashgate.

———. 2000. "Migration and Ethnic Relations as a Field of Political Contention:

An Opportunity Structure Approach." In *Challenging Immigration and Ethnic Relations Politics,* ed. Ruud Koopmans and Paul Statham. Oxford: Oxford University Press.

———. 2002. *The Transformation of Political Mobilisation and Communication in European Public Spheres: A Research Outline.* Project acronym: Europub.com. At http://europub.wz-berlin.de.

———. 2003. "How National Citizenship Shapes Transnationalism: A Comparative Analysis of Migrant and Minority Claims-Making in Germany, Great Britain, and the Netherlands." In *Toward Assimilation and Citizenship: Immigrants in Liberal Nation-States,* ed. Christian Joppke and Ewa Morawska, 195–238. London: Palgrave.

Kornhauser, William. 1959. *The Politics of Mass Society.* Glencoe, IL: Free Press.

Kowalsky, Wolfgang, and Wolfgang Schroeder. 1994. *Rechtsextremismus.* Opladen, Germany: Westdeutscherverlag.

Kriesi, Hanspeter. 1999. "Movements of the Left, Movements of the Right: Putting the Mobilization of Two New Types of Social Movements into Political Context." In *Continuity and Change in Contemporary Capitalism,* ed. Herbert Kitschelt, Peter Lange, and Gary Marks. Cambridge: Cambridge University Press.

Kriesi, Hanspeter, Ruud Koopmans, Jan Willem Duyvendak, and Marco Giugni. 1995. *New Social Movements in Western Europe: A Comparative Analysis.* Minneapolis: University of Minnesota Press.

Kymlicka, Will. 1995a. *Multicultural Citizenship: A Liberal Theory of Minority Rights.* Oxford: Clarendon Press.

———. 1995b. "The Politics of Multiculturalism: Multicultural Citizenship." In *Multicultural Citizenship: A Liberal Theory of Minority Rights,* ed. Will Kymlicka, 10–33. Oxford: Clarendon Press.

Kymlicka, Will, and W. Norman, eds. 2000. *Citizenship in Diverse Societies.* Oxford: Oxford University Press.

Lakeman, Pieter. 1999. *Binnen zonder kloppen: Nederlandse immigratiepolitiek en de economische Gevolgen.* Amsterdam: Meulenhoff.

Laurence, Jonathan. 2001. "(Re)constructing Community in Berlin: Turks, Jews, and German Responsibility." *German Politics and Society* 19, no. 2: 22–59.

———. 2003. "The New French Minority Politics." In *US-France-Analysis Brief.* Washington, DC: Brookings Institution. February.

Layton-Henry, Zig. 1990. *The Political Rights of Migrant Workers in Western Europe.* London: Sage.

Lederer, Harald W. 1997. *Migration und Integration in Zahlen.* Bamberg: Europäisches Forum für Migrationsstudien. CD-ROM.

Levy, J. T. 1997. "Classifying Cultural Rights." In *Ethnicity and Group Rights,* ed.

Will Kymlicka and I. Shapiro. NOMOS 39. New York: New York University Press.

Lewis, Philip. 2002. *Islamic Britain: Religion, Politics, and Identity among British Muslims*. London: I. B. Tauris.

Lie, John. 1995. "From International Migration to Transnational Diaspora." *Contemporary Sociology* 24: 303–6.

Lipsky, Michael. 1968. "Protest as a Political Resource." *American Political Science Review* 62: 1144–58.

Lloyd, Cathie. 2000. "Anti-racist Responses to European Integration." In *Challenging Immigration and Ethnic Relations Politics: Comparative European Perspectives*, ed. Ruud Koopmans and Paul Statham, 389–406. Oxford/New York: Oxford University Press.

Mahning, Hans, and Andreas Wimmer. 2000. "Country-Specific or Convergent? A Typology of Immigrant Policies in Western Europe." *Journal of International Migration and Integration* 1, no. 2: 177–204.

Marienstras, R. 1989. "On the Nation of Diaspora." In *Minority Peoples in the Age of Nation-States*, ed. G. Chaliand, 119–25. London: Pluto.

Marshall, Thomas H. 1950. *Citizenship and Social Class and Other Essays*. Cambridge: Cambridge University Press.

Martiniello, Marco, ed. 1998. *Multicultural Policies and the State: A Comparison of Two European Societies*. Utrecht: ERCOMER.

Martiniello, Marco, and Paul Statham, eds. 1999. "Ethnic Mobilisation and Political Participation in Europe." Special issue. *Journal of Ethnic and Migration Studies* 25, no. 4: 211.

McAdam, Doug. 1982. *Political Process and the Development of Black Insurgency, 1930–1970*. Chicago: University of Chicago Press.

———. 1983. "Tactical Innovation and the Pace of Insurgency." *American Sociological Review* 48: 735–54.

———. 1996. "Conceptual Origins, Current Problems, Future Directions." In *Comparative Perspectives on Social Movements*, ed. Doug McAdam, John D. McCarthy, and Mayer N. Zald. Cambridge: Cambridge University Press.

———. 1999. *Political Process and the Development of Black Insurgency, 1930–1970*. 2nd ed. Chicago: University of Chicago Press.

McAdam, Doug, Sidney Tarrow, and Charles Tilly. 2001. *Dynamics of Contention*. Cambridge: Cambridge University Press.

McCarthy, J. D., C. McPhail, and J. Smith. 1996. "Images of Protest: Estimating Selection Bias in Media Coverage in Washington Demonstrations, 1982, 1991." *American Sociological Review* 61: 478–99.

McCarthy, J. D., and Mayer N. Zald. 1977. "Resource Mobilisation and Social Movements: A Partial Theory." *American Journal of Sociology* 82: 1212–41.

Meehan, Elizabeth. 1993. *Citizenship and the European Community*. London: Sage.

Melucci, Alberto. 1990. *Nomads of the Present: Social Movements and Individual Needs in Contemporary Society.* Philadelphia: Temple University Press.

———. 1996. *Challenging Codes: Collective Action in the Information Age.* Cambridge: Cambridge University Press.

Meyer, David S., and Suzanne Staggenborg. 1996. "Movements, Countermovements, and the Structure of Political Opportunity." *American Journal of Sociology* 101: 1628–60.

Miles, Robert. 1982. *Racism and Migrant Labour.* London: Routledge and Kegan Paul.

Miles, Robert, and Dietrich Thränhardt, eds. 1995. *Migration and European Integration: The Dynamics of Inclusion and Exclusion.* London: Pinter.

Miller, D. 1995. *On Nationality.* Oxford: Oxford University Press.

Minkenberg, Michael. 1992. "The New Right in Germany: The Transformation of Conservatism and the Extreme Right." *European Journal of Political Research* 22: 55–81.

Modood, T. 1992. *Not Easy Being British: Colour, Culture, and Citizenship.* London: Runnymede Trust and Trentham Books.

———. 2000. "Anti-essentialism, Multiculturalism, and the Recognition of 'Religious' Groups." In *Citizenship in Diverse Societies,* ed. Will Kymlicka and Wayne Norman. Oxford: Oxford University Press.

Modood, T., R. Berthoud, J. Lakey, J. Nazroo, P. Smith, S. Virdee, and S. Beishun. 1997. *Ethnic Minorities in Britain: Diversity and Disadvantage—The Fourth National Survey of Ethnic Minorities.* London: Policy Studies Institute.

Modood, T., and Pnina Werbner, eds. 1997. *The Politics of Multiculturalism in the New Europe: Racism, Identity, and Community.* London: Zed Books.

Mollenkopf, J. 2000. "Assimilating Immigrants in Amsterdam: A Perspective from New York." *Netherlands Journal of Social Sciences* 36, no. 2: 126–45.

Morawska, Ewa. 2003. "Immigrant Transnationalism and Assimilation: A Variety of Combinations and the Analytic Strategy It Suggests." In *Toward Assimilation and Citizenship: Immigrants in Liberal Nation-States,* ed. Christian Joppke and Ewa Morawska, 133–76. New York: Palgrave Macmillan.

Nagel, Joane, and Susan Olzak. 1982. "Ethnic Mobilization in New and Old States: An Extension of the Competition Model." *Social Problems* 30: 127–43.

Neidhardt, Friedhelm, and Dieter Rucht. 2001. "Protestgeschichte der Bundesrepublik Deutschland, 1950–1994: Ereignisse, Themen, Akteure." In *Protest in der Bundesrepublik: Strukturen und Entwicklungen,* ed. Dieter Rucht, 27–70. Frankfurt am Main: Campus.

Niessen, Jan, and Isabelle Chopin, eds. 2002. *Anti-discrimination Legislation in EU Member States* (Germany, France, United Kingdom, and the Netherlands). Vienna: European Monitoring Centre on Racism and Xenophobia.

Oliver, Pamela E., and Gregory Maney. 2000. "Political Processes and Local

Newspaper Coverage of Protest Events: From Selection Bias to Triadic Interactions." *American Journal of Sociology* 106: 463–505.

Olson, Mancur. 1965. *The Logic of Collective Action*. Cambridge, MA: Harvard University Press.

Olzak, Susan. 1992. *Dynamics of Ethnic Competition and Conflict*. Stanford, CA: Stanford University Press.

Olzak, Susan, and Joane Nagel, eds. 1986. *Competitive Ethnic Relations*. Orlando, FL: Academic Press.

Overbeek, Henk. 1995. "Towards a New International Migration Regime: Globalization, Migration, and the Internationalization of the State." In *Migration and European Integration: The Dynamics of Inclusion and Exclusion,* ed. R. Miles and D. Tränhard. London: Pinter.

Parekh, Bhiku. 1998. "Integrating Minorities." In *Race Relations in Britain: A Developing Agenda,* ed. T. Blackstone, B. Parekh, and P. Sanders. London: Routledge.

———, ed. 2000. *The Future of Multi-ethnic Britain: The Parekh Report.* London: Runnymede Trust/Profile Books.

———. 2002. *Rethinking Multiculturalism: Cultural Diversity, and Political Theory.* Cambridge, MA: Harvard University Press.

Passy, Florence. 2001. "Political Altruism and the Solidarity Movement: An Introduction." In *Political Altruism?* ed. Marco Giugni and Florence Passy, 3–25. Boulder, CO: Rowman and Littlefield.

Philips, A. 1995. *The Politics of Presence: Issues in Democracy and Group Representation.* Oxford: Oxford University Press.

Piven, Frances Fox, and Richard A. Cloward. 1979. *Poor People's Movements.* New York: Vintage Books.

Portes, A. 1997. "Globalization from Below: The Rise of Transnational Communities." *Working Papers and Transnational Communities,* WPTC-98-01. At http://www.transcomm.ox.ac.uk.

Portes, A., L. E. Guarnizo, and P. Landolt. 1999. "The Study of Transnationalism: Pitfalls and Promise of an Emergent Research Field." *Ethnic and Racial Studies* 22, no. 2: 217–37.

Poulter, Sebastian. 1998. *Ethnicity, Law, and Human Rights: The English Experience.* Oxford: Clarendon Press.

Powell, Walter W., and Paul J. DiMaggio, eds. 1991. *The New Institutionalism in Organizational Analysis.* Chicago: University of Chicago Press.

Rath, Jan. 1991. "Minorisering: De Sociale Constructie van Ethnische Minderheden." PhD thesis, University of Utrecht, Netherlands.

Rath, Ian, Rinus Penninx, Kees Groenendijk, and Astrid Meijer. 1996. *Nederland en zijn Islam: Een ontzuilende samenleving reageert op het ontstaan van een geloofsgemeenschap.* Amsterdam: Het Spinhuis.

———. 1999. "The Politics of Recognizing Religious Diversity in Europe: Social Reactions to the Institutionalization of Islam in the Netherlands, Belgium, and Great Britain." *Netherlands Journal of Social Sciences* 35, no. 1: 53–68.

Rémond, René. 1982. *Les droites en France.* Paris: Aubier.

Rex, John. 1996. *Ethnic Minorities in the Modern Nation State.* Houndmills, Basingstoke, UK: Macmillan.

———. 2002. "Islam in the United Kingdom." In *Islam, Europe's Second Religion: The New Social, Cultural, and Political Landscape,* ed. Shireen T. Hunter, 51–76. Westport, CT: Praeger.

Rex, John, and Sally Tomlinson. 1983. *Colonial Immigrants in a British City.* London: Routledge and Kegan.

Robinson, Danielle. 1997. *Simple Guide to Islam.* Kent, UK: Global Books.

Roche, Maurice, and Rik van Berkel, eds. 1997. *European Citizenship and Social Exclusion.* Aldershot, UK: Ashgate.

Rokkan, Stein. 1970. *Citizens, Elections, Parties.* Oslo: Universitetsforlaget.

Rosas, Allan, and Esko Antola, eds. 1995. *A Citizens' Europe: In Search of a New Order.* London: Sage.

Rucht, Dieter, Ruud Koopmans, and Friedhelm Neidhardt, eds. 1999. *Acts of Dissent: New Developments in the Study of Protest.* Lanham, MD: Rowman and Littlefield.

Rucht, Dieter, and Friedhelm Neidhardt. 2001a. "Kollektive Aktion und soziale Bewegungen." In *Lehrbuch Soziologie,* ed. Hans Joas, 533–56. Frankfurt am Main: Campus.

———. 2001b. "Protestgeschichte der Bundesrepublik Deutschland, 1950–1994: Ereignisse, Themen, Akteure." In *Protest in der Bundesrepublik: Strukturen und Entwicklungen,* ed. Dieter Rucht, 27–70. Frankfurt am Main: Campus.

Runnymede Trust. 1997. *Islamophobia: A Challenge for Us All.* London: Runnymede Trust.

Safran, William. 1997. "Citizenship and Nationality in Democratic Systems: Approaches to Defining and Acquiring Membership in the Political Community." *International Political Science Review* 18, no. 3: 313–35.

Sassen, Saskia. 1998. "The De Facto Transnationalizing of Immigration Policy." In *Challenge to the Nation-State: Immigration in Western Europe and the United States,* ed. Christian Joppke, 49–85. Oxford: Oxford University Press.

———. 1999. *Guests and Aliens.* New York: New Press.

Schain, Martin. 1987. "The National Front in France and the Construction of Political Legitimacy." *West European Politics* 10: 229–52.

Schiller, Nina Glick, Linda Basch, and Cristina Blanc-Szanton. 1997. "Transnationalismus: Ein neuer analytischer Rahmen zum Verständnis von Migration." *Journal für Sozialforschung* 35, no. 3/4.

Schlesinger, Arthur D. 1998. *The Disuniting of America: Reflections on a Multi-cultural Society*. Rev. ed. New York: Norton.

Schulz, Winfried. 1997. *Politische Kommunikation: Theoretische Ansätze und Ergebnisse empirischer Forschung zur Rolle der Massenmedien in der Politik*. Opladen, Germany: Westdeutscher Verlag.

Shain, Yossi, and Martin Sherman. 1998. "Dynamics of Disintegration: Diaspora, Secession, and the Paradox of Nation-States." *Nations and Nationalism* 4, no. 3: 321–46.

Shapiro, Gilbert, and John Markoff. 1998. *Revolutionary Demands: A Content analysis of the Cahiers de Doléances of 1789*. Stanford, CA: Stanford University Press.

Shapiro, Ian, and Will Kymlicka, eds. 1997. *Ethnicity and Group Rights*. New York: New York University Press.

Siméant, Johanna. 1998. *La cause des sans-papiers*. Paris: Presses de Sciences Po.

Slominski, Peter. 2001. "Ausgewählte Europäische Rechtsordnungen: Schweiz." In *Die Integration von Einwanderern: Rechtliche Regelungen im europäischen Vergleich*, ed. Ulrike Davy, 709–94. Vienna: Europäisches Zentrum; Frankfurt: Campus.

Smelser, Neil J. 1962. *Theory of Collective Behavior*. New York: Free Press.

Smith, David M., and Maurice Blanc. 1996. "Citizenship, Nationality, and Ethnic Minorities in Three European Nations." *International Journal of Urban and Regional Research* 20, no. 1: 66–82.

Smith, Peter Michael. 2001. *Transnational Urbanism: Locating Globalization*. Oxford, England: Blackwell.

Snow, David A., and Robert D. Benford. 1992. "Master Frames and Cycles of Protest." In *Frontiers in Social Movement Theory*, ed. Aldon D. Morris and Carol McClurg Mueller, 133–55. New Haven, CT: Yale University Press.

Snow, David A., E. Burke Rocheford Jr., Steven K. Worden, and Robert D. Benford. 1986. "Frame Alignment Processes, Micromobilization, and Movement Participation." *American Sociological Review* 51: 464–81.

Soininen, Maritta. 1999. "The 'Swedish Model' as an Institutional Framework for Immigrant Membership Rights." *Journal of Ethnic and Migration Studies* 25, no. 4: 685–702.

Solomos, John, and Les Back. 1996. *Racism and Society*. London: Macmillan.

Soysal, Yasemin Nuhoglu. 1994. *Limits of Citizenship*. Chicago: University of Chicago Press.

———. 1997. "Changing Parameters of Citizenship and Claims-Making: Organized Islam in European Public Spheres." *Theory and Society* 26: 509–27.

———. 1998. "Toward a Postnational Model of Membership." In *The Citizenship Debates: A Reader*, ed. Gershon Shafir. Minneapolis: University of Minnesota Press.

Spinner, J. 1994. *The Boundaries of Citizenship: Race, Ethnicity, and Nationality in the Liberal State.* Baltimore, MD: Johns Hopkins University Press.

Statham, Paul. 1997. "Migration Policy, Public Reactions, and Collective Action around Ethnic Difference: Lessons from the Southern European Case of Italy." Paper for the Conference of the European Sociological Association, Essex, UK, August 27–30. Later published as "The Political Construction of Immigration Politics in Italy: Opportunities, Mobilisation, and Outcomes." *Wissenschaftszentrum* FS III, 98–102 (1998): 1–60.

———. 1999. "Political Mobilisation by Minorities in Britain: A Negative Feedback of Race Relations?" *Journal of Ethnic and Migration Studies* 25, no. 4: 597–626.

———. 2001a. "Political Opportunities for Altruism? The Role of State Policies in Influencing Claims-Making by British Antiracist and Pro-migrant Movements." In *Political Altruism?* ed. Marco Giugni and Florence Passy, 133–58. Boulder, CO: Rowman and Littlefield.

———. 2001b. "Zwischen oeffentlicher Sichtbarkeit und politischem Einfluss: Mobilisierung gegen Rassismus und fuer Migranten in Grossbritannien." *Neue Soziale Bewegungen Forschungsjournal* Jg. 14, heft 1/01: 72–86.

———. 2003a. "New Conflicts about Integration and Cultural Diversity in Britain: The Muslim Challenge to Race Relations." In *The Challenge of Diversity: European Social Democracy Facing Migration, Integration, and Multiculturalism,* ed. R. Cuperus, K. Duffek, and J. Kandel, 126–49. Vienna: Studien Verlag.

———. 2003b. "Understanding the Anti-asylum Rhetoric: Restrictive Politics or Racist Publics?" *Political Quarterly* 74, no. 1: 163–77.

———. 2004. "Muslim Controversies in Europe." *Harvard International Review* 26, no. 3 (Fall 2004).

———. Forthcoming. "The Need to Take Religion Seriously for Understanding Multicultural Controversies: Institution Channeling versus Cultural Identification." In *Dialogues in Migration Policy,* ed. Marco Giugni and Florence Passy. Lanham, MD: Lexington Books.

Statham, Paul, and Ruud Koopmans. 2005a. "Multiculturalism and the Challenge of Muslim Group Demands in Britain, the Netherlands, and Germany." In *Comparative European Research in Migration, Diversity, and Identities,* ed. C. Husband and A. Garrido. Spain: University of Duesto Press/Humanitarian Net.

———. 2005b. "Multiculturalism et conflits culturels: Le défi posé par les revendications des groupes musulmans en Grande-Bretagne et aux Pays-Bas." In *Les minorités ethniques et l'Union européenne: Politiques, mobilisations, identités,* ed. Lionel Arnaud, 139–63. Paris: Éditions La Découverte.

Statham, Paul, Ruud Koopmans, Marco Giugni, and Florence Passy. 2005. "Resilient or Adaptable Islam? Multiculturalism, Religion, and Migrants' Claim-Making for Group Demands in Britain, the Netherlands, and France." *Ethnicities* 5, no. 4 (December).

Steenbergen, Bart van, ed. 1994. *The Condition of Citizenship.* London: Sage.

Streeck, Wolfgang, and Phillippe C. Schmitter. 1996. "Organized Interests in the European Union." In *The Impact of the European Integration: Political, Sociological, and Economic Cleavages,* ed. George A. Kourvetaris and Andreas Mosconas. Westport, CT: Praeger.

Taguieff, Pierre-André. 1988. *La force du préjugé.* Paris: La Découverte.

———. 1995. *Les fins de l'antiracisme.* Paris: Michalons.

———. 1997. *Le racisme.* Paris: Flammarion.

Tarrow, Sidney. 1989. *Democracy and Disorder.* Oxford: Clarendon Press.

———. 1994. *Power in Movement: Social Movements, Collective Action, and Politics.* Cambridge: Cambridge University Press.

———. 1998. *Power in Movement.* 2nd ed. Cambridge: Cambridge University Press.

Taylor, C. 1992. "The Politics of Recognition." In *Multiculturalism and the "Politics of Recognition,"* ed. A. Gutmann, 25–73. Princeton, NJ: Princeton University Press.

———. 1994. *Multiculturalism.* Princeton, NJ: Princeton University Press.

———. 1995. "The Political Uses of Xenophobia in England and Germany." *Party Politics* 1: 323–45.

———. 2000. "Conflict, Consensus, and Policy Outcomes: Immigration and Integration in Germany and the Netherlands." In *Challenging Immigration and Ethnic Relations Politics,* ed. Ruud Koopmans and Paul Statham, 162–86. Oxford: Oxford University Press.

Taylor, C., and Robert Miles. 1995. "Introduction: European Integration, Migration, and Processes of Inclusion and Exclusion." In *Migration and European Integration: The Dynamics of Inclusion and Exclusion,* ed. R. Miles and D. Thränhardt. London: Printer.

Thränhardt, Dietrich. 1995. "The Political Uses of Xenophobia in England and Germany." *Party Politics* 1: 323–45.

———. 2000. "Conflict, Consensus, and Policy Outcomes: Immigration and Integration in Germany and the Netherlands." In *Challenging Immigration and Ethnic Relations Politics: Comparative European Perspectives,* ed. Ruud Koopmans and Paul Statham, 162–86. Oxford: Oxford University Press.

Tilly, Charles. 1978. *From Mobilization to Revolution.* Reading, MA: Addison-Wesley.

———. 1995. *Popular Contention in Great Britain, 1758–1834.* Cambridge, MA: Havard University Press.

Tölölyan, K. 1996. "The Nation-State and Its Others." In *Becoming National: A Reader,* ed. G. Eley and R. S. Grigor. Oxford: Oxford University Press.

Touraine, Alain. 1984. *Le retour de l'acteur.* Paris: Fayard.

Turner, Ralph H., and Lewis M. Killian. 1957. *Collective Behavior.* Englewood Cliffs, NJ: Prentice-Hall.

Van Hear, Nicholas. 1998. *New Diasporas: The Mass Exodus, Dispersal, and Regrouping of Migrant Communities.* Seattle: University of Washington Press.

Vermeulen, Hans, ed. 1997. *Immigrantenbeleid voor de multiculturele samenleving Integratie-, taal- en religiebeleid in vijf West-Europese landen.* Amsterdam: Institute for Migration and Ethnic Studies (IMES).

Vertovec, S. 1996. "Muslims, the State, and the Public Sphere in Britain." In *International Congress Proceedings,* 167–86. Available from British Library document supply center.

———. 2000. "Religion and Diaspora." Working Papers on Transnational Communities WPTC-01-01. At http://www.transcomm.ox.ac.uk.

Vertovec, S., and A. Rogers, eds. 1998. *Muslim European Youth: Reproducing Ethnicity, Religion, Culture.* Aldershot, UK: Ashgate.

Waldrauch, Harald, and Christoph Hofinger. 1997. "An Index to Measure the Legal Obstacles to the Integration of Migrants." *New Community* 23, no. 2: 271–85.

Walzer, Michael. 1983. *Spheres of Justice.* New York: Basic Books.

Weber, Eugen. 1976. *Peasants into Frenchmen.* Stanford, CA: Stanford University Press.

Wiener, Antje. 1997. "Making Sense of the New Geography of Citizenship: Fragmented Citizenship in the European Union." *Theory and Society* 26: 529–60.

Wieviorka, Michel. 1998. *Le racisme, une introduction.* Paris: La Découverte.

WRR. 1989. *Allochtonenbeleid.* The Hague: Sdu.

Young, Marion Iris. 1998. "Polity and Group Difference: A Critique of the Ideal of Universal Citizenship." In *The Citizenship Debates: A Reader,* ed. Gershon Shafir, 263–90. Minneapolis: University of Minnesota Press.

Zürn, Michael. 1998. *Regieren jenseits des Nationalstaates.* Frankfurt am Main: Suhrkamp.

Index

action repertoires: antiracist and pro-migrant actors, 219–24; counter-movement dynamics, 213–14; effects of political space on extreme-right repertoires, 187–88, 189–90, 194, 204; impact of political opportunity structures on, 134–38, 183, 195–99, 202, 203, 211, 212, 215, 219–24, 242, 277n9; interactive dynamics in field, 231; protest repertoires, 160, 161, 165

affirmative action: in labor market, 52, 66, 70, 71, 108; in public and private sectors, 68–69

Afghanistan/Afghans, 110, 131

Africa/Africans: African organizations in Britain, 229; as collective identity category, 119, 130, 131, 153; immigrants of African descent in Europe, 121; source of migration to Britain, 44, 134

Aktion für Abgewiesene Asylbewerber (Germany), 216

Albanians, 126

Alevites, 131

Algemene wet gelijke behandeling (1994) (Netherlands), 47

Algeria/Algerians: civil war, 113, 132; as collective identity category, 119; homeland organizations of, 273n3; mobilization of, 132, 133; post-colonial migration to France, 134

Aliens Act (2000) (Netherlands), 43

American Jewish Committee, 100

Amicales (Maghreb countries), 12, 112

Amnesty International, 85, 86, 94, 103

Amritsar (India), 132

Amsterdam, 55, 161, 162, 252, 278n3

Amsterdam Treaty, 104

Anglican Church of England: Anglican Christians, 62, 148; citizenship rituals and, 247; faith schools, 273n2; position as state church in Britain, 59, 60, 71, 157

antidiscrimination legislation, 278n1; access to citizenship rights for migrants and, 32; affirmative action and, 71; antiracist and pro-migrant

mobilization and, 211; ban on regis-
tering ethnic background in France,
47, 68; in civil law, 47–48, 49; in
criminal law, 45, 47; establishment
of state offices to deal with discrimination, 48; indicators of antidiscrimination rights, 45, 49, 50; in labor
legislation, 47–48, 271n17; migrant
claims making and, 91, 111, 141;
in Northern Ireland, 269–70n9;
provisions against racial hatred, 45,
47, 49
antifascist groups, 213
Anti-Nazi League (UK), 213, 227–29
Antiracist Alliance (UK), 216, 227–29
antiracist mobilization, 205–31; distinction between antiracist and
discrimination claims, 272n3; European Union and, 248; extreme-right
mobilization and, 22, 80, 84; national configurations of citizenship
and, 17, 78, 238, 242–43; scope of
claims making by, 102, 103; theoretical explanations for, 29–30. *See
also* pro-migrant mobilization
apartheid, 267–68n4
Appenzell Ausserrhoden (Switzerland),
44
Arabs, 131
ARD (Germany), 62
Armenians, 110
Asian/Asians: antidiscrimination campaigns in Britain, 228–29; as collective identity category, 131; Muslim
identity and, 122, 145, 242; public
broadcasting for, 62; racial category,
118, 121, 130, 133, 134, 141, 153,
154, 157
assimilation: cultural assimilation as
selection criterion for immigration

and granting of citizenship rights,
108–9, 142; extreme-right focus on
migrants' cultural inability to assimilate, 84, 202, 243–44; migrant-
sending countries' encouragement
of assimilation to host society, 112;
requirements for naturalization of
foreigners, 52–53, 247; segregating
effects of strong emphasis on, 88, 107
assimilationism: antiracist and pro-
migrant mobilization in assimilationist countries, 207, 208, 220;
approach of French state to cultural
pluralism, 169, 178, 268n5; citizenship regime type, 8, 10, 51, 53, 72,
121, 186, 191, 233, 235; cultural
rights and, 69, 71, 72, 235, 238;
extreme-right ethnocultural model
of, 14; extreme-right mobilization in
assimilationist countries, 196; poly-
ethnic rights for Muslims and, 57
Association islamiste de Garges (France),
169
Association of Muslim Schools (UK),
165
Association pour le dialogue islamo-
chrétien et les rencontres interreligieuses (ADIC) (France), 172
asylum seekers: asylum reforms in
Germany, 93; immigrant category,
87, 118, 120, 216; residence permits
for, in Britain, 42; segregationist
policy approaches and, 11; violence
against, 219, 245
attacks of 9/11, 2, 107, 150, 243, 248
attacks on Madrid (2004), 150, 243
Ausländerbeiräte (Germany), 65
Aussiedler, 37, 118, 120, 269n7
Australia, 1
Ayodhya (India), 132

People's Party (Denmark), 243
People's Party for Freedom and Democracy (VVD) (Netherlands), 192, 193
Persian Gulf states, 76
pillarization *(verzuiling)*, 62, 71, 72, 121, 158, 242
police: access to positions within for non-nationals, 49; data on extreme-right violence, 268n7; institutional racism within, 93, 141, 143; representation on immigration and integration advisory councils, 63; rights of Muslim policewomen to wear headscarf, 271n21
political altruism, 29–30, 206–10, 215–17, 230, 277n1
political claims analysis, 23–24. *See also* claims making
political discourse analysis, 23–24
political legitimacy: action repertoires and, 219–20, 223, 224; national understandings of citizenship and nationhood and, 208, 210, 211, 214, 215, 216, 225, 230–31, 275–76n3; political opportunity structures and, 78, 83, 209; in public discourse, 19, 20, 26, 90, 91, 93, 139; of racial categories in public discourse, 21
political opportunity structures: action repertoires and, 134–39, 219–21, 223–24, 277n9; antiracist and pro-migrant mobilization and, 209–15, 217, 230–31; collective identities and, 115, 121; extreme-right mobilization and, 181, 182, 183–84, 185–98, 202–4; issue-specific, 83; mobilization on immigration and ethnic relations and, 78, 80–81, 145; social capital and, 252–53;

theoretical perspectives, 16–23, 142–43, 152, 233–34
political representation rights: antiracist and pro-migrant promotion of for migrants, 206; cross-national variation in, 52, 63–66, 67, 70, 245; expulsion and, 42; minority group demands for, 146, 164
political violence: antiracist campaigns against, 226–27, 228; ethnic violence, 244–45, 246; expulsion on grounds of, 42; extreme-right violence, 183–84, 193, 213, 268n7; homeland-directed mobilization and, 2, 143, 238–39; against immigrants and minorities, 3, 84; inter-ethnic and intra-ethnic conflict and, 142; radical action repertoires, 136, 137, 187, 195–99, 211, 221, 222, 223–24, 240, 277n9
poly-ethnic rights, 51, 57
populism, 189, 190, 203, 246, 275–76n3
postcolonial migration/migrants, 1, 5, 13, 15, 44, 121, 175; citizenship rights and, 38, 113; homeland orientation and, 133; mobilization by, 123–24
postnational citizenship/postnationalism: empirical evidence against, 84–87, 90–91, 93–96, 99–101, 103–6, 236–37; multiculturalism and, 142; theoretical perspective, 28, 74–75, 76–77, 249
pro-migrant mobilization, 83–84, 102, 103, 205–31. *See also* antiracist mobilization
protest: expulsion and, 42; group demands and, 159, 160, 161, 165, 168, 169, 176; homeland-directed mobilization and, 136–37; on immigra-

Swiss People's Party (SVP), 192, 193, 203, 276n6

Taguieff, Pierre-André, 208, 209, 224–25
Tamils, 110, 112, 118
Terre des Hommes, 103
terrorism, international, 101, 237
third-country nationals/non-EU immigrants, 113
Tibet/Tibetans, 110, 112, 118
Tillie, Jean, 124, 252
Tilly, Charles, 268n6
Trafford Council (UK), 167
transnational communities/transnationalism: collective identities and, 113–14, 115; empirical evidence for, 142–43, 238–39; homeland-directed mobilization and, 127–29, 131–34; theories of, 28, 107, 108, 109–11
Turkish Ministry of Religious Affairs, 11, 112
Turks-Islamitische Culturele Federatie (Netherlands), 117, 163
Turks/Turkey: as collective identity category, 119, 130, 153, 216; conflict with Kurds in Germany, 101, 239; double nationality and, 269n6; extreme-right violence against, 3, 100; group demands and, 148; guest worker programs in Germany and, 5; homeland orientations of, 97, 131; Islamic education in Germany for, 11, 113, 271–72n22; Mehmet affair in Germany, 42; Muslim collective identity and, 133; Muslims in the Netherlands, 273n4; political claims making by, 124; public broadcasting for, 61,

63; representative councils for, 66; right-wing Grey Wolves group, 12

UK Action Committee on Islamic Affairs, 167
UN Children's Convention, 93
UN Educational, Scientific, and Cultural Organization (UNESCO), 85
unemployment, 15, 253, 275n1
Union des familles musulmanes-Islam de France (UFM), 172
Union des jeunes musulmans (UJM) (France), 171
Union des organizations islamiques de France (UOIF), 170, 172
Union of Moroccan Muslim Organizations in the Netherlands (Ummon), 162, 163
United Nations (UN), 103, 105; Swiss membership of, 94, 99
United Nations High Commissioner for Refugees (UNHCR), 84, 86, 98
United States, 1, 7, 116, 273n1
universalism: antiracist and pro-migrant definition of nationhood and, 207, 216–17; antiracist mobilization and, 138, 225–31, 243; as citizenship model, 10, 51, 186, 233; collective identities in France and, 124, 125–26, 139, 143; extreme-right mobilization in France and, 191, 196; in France, 17, 68, 69, 72, 156, 235, 251; Muslim group demands in France and, 158, 169, 170; as policy approach, 15, 238, 244, 247; postnational citizenship and, 249; racism and, 208–9
Uri (Switzerland), 35

RUUD KOOPMANS holds the chair in social conflict and change at the Free University in Amsterdam. His books include *Democracy from Below, New Social Movements in Western Europe* (Minnesota, 1995), and (coedited with Paul Statham) *Challenging Immigration and Ethnic Relations Politics.*

PAUL STATHAM is professor of social movements and public sphere and research at the University of Leeds.

MARCO GIUGNI teaches political science at the University of Geneva. He is coeditor of *How Social Movements Matter* (Minnesota, 1999) and *New Social Movements in Western Europe* (Minnesota, 1995).

FLORENCE PASSY is assistant professor in political science at the University of Lausanne.